Dahomean Narrative

Dahomean Narrative

A CROSS-CULTURAL ANALYSIS

Melville J. and Frances S. Herskovits

Foreword by Jane I. Guyer and David L. Easterbrook

Northwestern University Press

Evanston, Illinois

Northwestern University Press
Evanston, Illinois 60208-4210

Copyright © 1958 by Northwestern University Press. First paperback printing 1998.
All rights reserved.

Printed in the United States of America

ISBN 0-8101-1650-2

Library of Congress Cataloging-in-Publication Data

Dahomean narrative : a cross-cultural analysis / [collected by] Melville J. and Frances
S. Herskovits ; foreword by Jane I. Guyer and David L. Easterbrook.
    p. cm.
    Originally published 1958, in series: Northwestern University Africa studies ; no.
1, with new foreword.
    ISBN 0-8101-1650-2 (alk. paper)
    1. Tales—Benin. 2. Oral tradition—Benin. 3. Mythology, African. I. Herskovits,
Melville J. (Melville Jean), 1895–1963. II. Herskovits, Frances S. (Frances Shapiro),
1897– .
GR351.4.D35 1998
398.2'096683—dc21   97-51165
                                                                            CIP

Contents

v

II   Divination

III Hunter Stories

Dramatis personæ, 216

IV   Enfant Terrible Tales: twins, orphans and the abnormally born

Dramatis personæ, 256

VII   Tales of Women: love, intrigue, and betrayal

VIII   Explanatory and Moralizing Tales

Dahomean Narrative

Foreword to the 1998 Edition
Jane I. Guyer and David L. Easterbrook

Melville and Frances Herskovits were great collectors. Their intellectual and personal legacy from their research in West Africa, Brazil, Surinam, Trinidad, Haiti, and the United States comprises hundreds of material items, thousands of photographs, several films, and untold hours of musical recordings. Their interests included "costume, dance, folk medicine, folk religion, folk sculpture, folktales, foodways, funerary practices, games, jokes, hairbraiding, magic, music, musical instrument making, naming, proverbs, riddles, song, ritual arts, techniques of planting and harvesting, traditional architecture and ways of speaking."[1] All were part of a lifetime project, which they variously described as "scientific" and "humanistic," of providing evidence for the continuity of African culture from the Old World to the New, from the states and societies of West Africa to the plantations, peasant villages, and urban communities of the Americas. For them, tangible evidence was the foundation of the search for the truth of that continuity, or at least the grounds for combating what they saw as the false assumptions of the day that "Negroes" had no past at all beyond slavery, no cultural inheritance except that which was forged in response to domination.

While many people know the published work of the Herskovitses, few know of the existence of the collection on which they based their arguments. It functioned as the scholar's notebook: as a body of material to be understood comprehensively in order to shape an argument, as items to be mobilized to illustrate a point. Most of the collection is now kept in storage and archival sections

of major museums and libraries. None has been publicized or
published except their first book, *Suriname Folk-Lore*, in 1936;
Dahomean Narrative, their collection of the oral literature of
Dahomey, was written in 1931, but not in a formal fashion with a
scholarly introduction until 1958.

The occasion of the jubilee for the Program of African Studies
at Northwestern University, founded by Melville Herskovits in
1948, will be celebrated this year with an exhibit of their collection: objects, photographs, films, and recordings. As the key
themes of scholarship change, and as the communities depicted in
the research begin to take up the preservation, study, and creative
reworking of their own recorded traditions, collections take on a
completely new value and valence than they had for their original
architects. A verbal image is worked into a song; a filmed sequence
inspires choreography; a photograph holds a clue to family history;
an object testifies to technology; and the entire work provides grist
for the critique through which scholarship examines and reshapes
itself. We want to make this remarkable collection available to its
new constituencies.

In the same spirit we celebrate the connection between the
Program of African Studies and Northwestern University Press,
who provide us new access to *Dahomean Narrative*, an important
component of the larger collection and one which otherwise fits
awkwardly into an exhibit format. But beyond simply represent-
ing all of the genres the Herskovitses covered, there is another reason to include this work in our anniversary activities: it is one of
a very few works of which Melville and Frances are coauthors. In
an era when scholars' wives were often their husbands' secretaries
and general managers, Melville Herskovits always made it clear—
even in works that bore his name alone on the title page—that
Frances had been a full collaborator in every sense and at all stages.
The preface to his seminal work, *The Myth of the Negro Past*, pos-
itively extols her contribution. In another era she might have followed scholarly directions of her own as well. In recognition of her
contributions, we have subtitled the exhibit *The Legacy of Melville
J. and Frances S. Herskovits* and are particularly pleased to reissue
this book, their major, explicitly joint work.

The title for the exhibit—*Living Tradition in Africa and the*

Americas—also comes from this book and, of course, reflects the fundamental argument about survivals and connections that the Herskovitses pursued in all their work on the Atlantic world. But the passage in which they use the concept of a "living tradition" also conveys particularly acutely some of the questions and tensions in their own work which are certainly carried forward in subsequent scholarship. They waited twenty-seven years to put these materials out, and over that period a shift in perspective—or perhaps the particular vision of Frances, or debates with students— moved the interpretive emphasis from documenting continuities of cultural traits assumed to be brought forward from the past and inherited through the generations, to appreciating the constant contextual reworking of ideas and images through the imaginations of creative artists; from recording to participating; from applying what was seen then as a scientific approach to culture to adopting a humanistic approach. The introduction to this book ends emphatically in this latter mood even though it begins with the classic scientific description of method: "In the tradition of humanistic scholarship, it is an invitation to discover for world literature and thought vast resources which will inform and delight us. As spoken forms, the stories should preferably be read aloud" (122).

The idea of "living tradition" serves as a bridge not only across the Atlantic and the centuries but across these two different but valid approaches to cultural understanding and appreciation. Traditions can be studied as whole repertoires for their components, coherence, persistence, and processes of transmission and application to new situations. They can also be understood as resources for inspiration and guidance in the practice of living and creating. The Herskovitses used both approaches, but at the time they were writing, the combination of "living" and "tradition" still conveyed something of a tension between a focus on tradition as an inherited framework and as a resource for creating a future. So it is striking that they combined the two ideas in the context of an aspiration for the themes of their future work rather than in a commentary on the solid achievement of work already completed —even as they published materials from a distant era of their careers and collected within a classic folklore framework. One

senses that they saw new potential in these stories that had been
only dimly perceived at the time and turned to their own collection with new eyes and ears. In the introduction to *Dahomean
Narrative* they write:

> There are also the questions which remain largely for future study . . .
> the prosody of peoples who speak in languages in which tone is sig-
> nificant. . . . The entire question of imagery . . . the important use of
> the proverb for thematic statement in versification. We have another
> glimpse of the promise that lies in such a line of investigation when
> we ask ourselves whether the role a living tradition assigns to individ-
> ual self-expression has significant bearing on the dynamic potential of
> a group, politically and socially. Can it furnish us with firm leads to
> the group's receptivity to new forms, to its areas of resilience, to its tra-
> dition-bound resistances? We treat a number of these questions here.
> But, in the idiom of the Dahomeans, merely to name them means that
> "the road is open" (5–6).

The shift of emphasis from the study of "retentions" to the
study of living traditions is due to several compelling logics, the
most important of which were shifts within American anthropology in the 1920s and 1930s, and the sheer force with which the particular peoples to whom the Herskovitses devoted their work
demonstrated and proclaimed that their legacy—within Africa
and outside the continent—was a constant creative "work in
progress." The stories recorded in Dahomey, and indeed the whole
Dahomean corpus of work, opened up new vistas because they
clearly showed that African cultures were not simply sources and
storehouses of the cultural traits whose distributions and manifestations could be traced in the New World. They too were changing and growing in a twentieth-century world. Melville was not
simply collecting African stories in order to match them with comparable themes, characters, and moral messages in the diaspora, but
also documenting the performative and creative process at a particular moment, for a particular audience, within Africa. Frances,
in particular, with her continuing literary interests, was moved
enough by the Dahomey experience to make works accessible to a
different audience in a different way by publishing her own poetic

versions in English in the *New Republic*. Dahomey therefore figures as a transformative moment in the development of their approach to cultural study. The collection of these narratives realized an older tradition of scholarship and also opened new possibilities.

Melville Herskovits started his anthropological career as a student of the great figure of early twentieth-century American anthropology, Franz Boas. In the theoretical sense, Herskovits's work is a faithful application of the early Boasian tradition, using ideas developed primarily to study the vast expanses of the American continent and the complexity of Native American cultures. Cultures were seen as compositions of elements, which could be studied in two ways: in terms of a geographical distribution of discrete traits that bears testimony to the history of migrations, animosities, and exchange; or in terms of their place within the practices of particular local societies that bear testimony to the constant weaving of consonances and patterns. Over the period of Herskovits's work, theoretical interest in the discipline moved quite clearly from traits and their distribution to patterns and configurations; Boas himself was beginning to write of patterns by the early years of this century, and two of his most eminent students—Ruth Benedict and Alfred Kroeber—wrote influential books using the concepts of pattern and configuration. Nevertheless, the idea of pattern was an inductive one in this tradition of scholarship, and the method was based on detailed initial descriptions. The nature of the pattern was not derived from a social or cultural theory of key or generative elements that defined its shape at any one moment or lay at the heart of its reproduction over time. Since exhaustive basic documentation of cultural elements was a prerequisite of interpretation, until the 1940s the Boasian tradition of anthropology remained very closely linked to folklore. All students were taught to collect cultural elements and trace their distributions over time and space.

Herskovits's work was in one sense a simple extension of the Boasian method of collection—tracing and mapping from the world created by indigenous peoples on the American continent over several thousand years—an extension to a world that spanned the Atlantic Ocean, created through the confrontation of cultures over the few brutal centuries of the slave trade. Hence the focus on collection, and hence the rather simple theory of culture that Herskovits was initially operating with compared to the ideas extant among his contemporaries in Native American studies. There was baseline documentation work to be done. Although there were certainly written sources on the folklore of the Africa-descended populations of the New World by the 1920s, they had received nothing remotely like the scholarly attention devoted to Native America. It was Boas who urged that African and "Negro" cultures deserved the same study. He could not fund his projected institute for the study of Africa, but he found a collaborator in the remarkable person of Elsie Clews Parsons, a devoted anthropological scholar of independent wealth. She collected folktales, riddles, and proverbs among African-American communities, first in Rhode Island and Massachusetts in 1916–17, then throughout the South, including the Sea Islands of South Carolina, and in the Caribbean where she did her last major work in Haiti in 1927.[2] Of her work on "Negro folklore," Herskovits wrote that it comprised "the bulk of the available materials in this field" and that she "had simply turned the field around" by insisting on rigorous and comprehensive collection rather than selective concentration on familiar categories such as "animal tales."[3]

Elsie Clews Parsons's great contribution to Herskovits's work was not only the continuing interest and advice of a senior scholar—about where to go, what to search for, where to find corresponding material, and so on—but also her financial support of his field trips and publications. He was not, of course, her only beneficiary. She used her fortune to underwrite many of Boas's students' work, from Nova Scotia to Mexico, so much so that Boas wrote when she died in 1941, during her presidency of the American Anthropological Association, "I wonder how many people really know how much anthropology owes to her." She did, however, exert particularly important influences on Herskovits's work in the formative stages of his career. He was her obvious successor in the study of the folklore of Africa-descended populations. Both Herskovitses corresponded regularly with Parsons between 1927 and 1941 about all kinds of intellectual and logistical issues.

One striking characteristic of their correspondence is that

Parsons clearly considered Frances to be as active a collaborator in the collection and publication of the stories as Melville, who indicates as much in the forewords to the works published under his own name. For example, a rather uncharacteristically long letter from Parsons on 18 October 1928,[4] just before the Herskovitses' first field trip to Surinam (which she also financed), is addressed to *Mrs.* Herskovits, and is full of advice about what "you literary people" might profitably read in preparation for research aimed at contextual and historical interpretations. Frances's education never included research training, but she came from a highly cultured background and spoke several European languages. Her replies to Parsons clearly indicate the logistical and intellectual resources she brought to their joint enterprise from its very inception. The different but complementary interests in narrative of Frances Herskovits and Elsie Clews Parsons must have provided a constant incentive for careful attention to this art form. Certainly Parsons's letters constantly refer to her expectations that they contribute to the corpus that she had founded.

Parsons and Boas together suggested that Herskovits's first field research focus on Surinam. Parsons's work in Haiti had shown a complex syncretism among various European and African cultural sources. It was thought that if African cultures had survived in the New World in a less mixed form, they would be found in Surinam, where slave-descended populations had escaped into the forest and lived in communities fairly isolated from European domination and cultural influence. The "Africanisms" they found among the slave-descended peoples in Surinam during their first field trip of 1928 were so incontrovertible that the Herskovitses, still thinking in the distributional mode, immediately started to identify the particular places in West Africa to which they could trace ancestral roots. Using names of places and people, they identified the Guinea Coast—between what was then the Gold Coast and Nigeria—as the most likely source of the Surinam survivals. Again Elsie Clews Parsons was willing to make a substantial contribution to the cost of their trip, which would be matched by Columbia University, supplemented by Northwestern, and also backed by the Rockefeller Foundation and the American Council of Learned Societies for their recording.

The Herskovitses did not immediately decide on Dahomey as their next field site. First they considered a broader study, but Boas urged them not to cover the whole country, but concentrate on one place (letter to Herskovits 12 May 1930).[5] Dahomey, it was thought, would be closer to traditional African cultures than the more economically and politically dynamic British colonies, and it had hardly been systematically studied, especially in works written in English. In the end they did devote part of the field trip to Nigeria and Ghana, but spend the longest time—from 1 April to mid-July 1931—in Dahomey. As in Surinam, they both collected, covering an enormous amount of ground partly because both were able to work. Herskovits's major work from the trip, the two-volume *Dahomey: An Ancient West African Kingdom,* published in 1938, includes a specification of Frances's own contribution: "All the information pertaining to the woman's side of the culture was gathered by her, and much of the data on religion and art. Her work in the field is to no small degree responsible for the amount and quality of the data collected."[6] *Dahomean Narrative,* published twenty years later at a time when Herskovits was deeply involved in advising the U.S. government on policies toward newly independent African countries, bears her imprint to an even greater degree.

Most of the numerous publications based on that field trip were focused on tradition. The first major work published was *An Outline of Dahomean Religious Belief* (1933),[7] which may well reflect Boas's request that the Surinam work "concentrate . . . on religion and medicine, if at all possible" (letter to Parsons 11 October 1928).[8] The memoir was accompanied by a series of articles on diverse topics: general ethnology (1932), population (1932), art (1933), the history of the slave trade (1933), the institution of the best friend (1934), and woman marriage (1937).[9] Frances's publications focused on songs and poetry. None reached a wider audience than those published in the *New Republic* in 1935. In her introduction to these songs she notes, "The songs given here are from interlinear translations of native texts. . . . The resemblance of Dahomean songs both in feeling and idiom to American spirituals is significant as pointing to their common lineage."[10]

The sheer variety of topics the two researchers covered in such a short period of field research is testimony to their extraordinary energy. It also reflects the clear mandate of the folkloristic method of the time, as developed by Boas and Parsons, among others. Researchers knew what they were after: complete collections in as close to the original textual form as possible. Recording was at a premium. On the one hand, by later standards within anthropology, this method can hardly do justice to context and to the process of creativity. On the other, the materials collected are comprehensive enough to show clear evidence for creative recomposition and for syncretism of elements from different cultural sources. There are different versions of tales, additions of foreign elements to older texts, and clear reorientations of meaning that relate to historical change. The "non-traditional," the "acculturated," is not screened out. The tracing of correspondences from Old to New Worlds becomes richer and more complex as the evidence mounts for continual cultural elaboration on both sides of the Atlantic. So what was lost in depth of field experience was compensated at this stage of diaspora research by the advantages of breadth. A large and evolving multisite research agenda could be planned and realized when the methods so closely approximated basic documentation.

The Herskovitses picked up their correspondence with Parsons as soon as they returned. In 1933 Herskovits succeeded in getting a grant for the transcriber of his Surinam songs to now work on the six hundred songs they had recorded in West Africa. He asked Parsons what to do with a few songs he had recorded in Haiti: incorporate them into his own work, or have them included in a collection of hers? Their discussions of Haiti also resulted in a request for her advice in 1933: "What do you think of Haiti as a place for us to work? In view of the close correspondences that seem to obtain between Haitian culture . . . and that of Dahomey, it seemed the logical next point of attack" (letter to Parsons 29 July 1933).[11] Her reply was encouraging: "In any of the other West African islands I think you would be disappointed in African survivals" (letter to Herskovits 8 August 1933).[12] Indeed, in the fall of 1934, after a twelve-week research trip in Haiti, he wrote to Parsons, "The African survivals were so numerous, and so obvious, that they almost recorded themselves," but then admitted a new interest that would eventually take them much further afield: "But the thing that continued to fascinate us in all phases of the culture . . . was the manner in which African and French traditions have been integrated in a single system" (letter to Parsons 8 October 1934).[13] This fascination heralded a new phase of their work, focused in the Americas.

Various pressures resulted in the long delay in publication of the collection of Dahomean tales. Herskovits's theoretical interests started to shift to acculturation, and they again picked up their work in the Caribbean, Brazil, and the United States, where the search for Africanisms was less of a dominant concern. As early as 1929 Frances had written of a visit to a Sanctified Church in the Black community within walking distance of their home in Evanston where what she found "was practically a Paramaribo 'winti' dance. The same dancing, the same trembling of the body, the hand-clapping. . . . It was astonishing" (letter to Parsons 9 December 1929).[14] So the Americas took their time from Africa. The Herskovitses may also have had trouble financing transcription. The funding from the American Council of Learned Societies, which had supported work on the West Africa songs, was discontinued in 1936 due to policy change; Parsons provided them the finances to finish it. Only in 1941 do we find mention of Herskovits's intention to "get at the Dahomean tales" (letter to Parsons 11 March 1941).[15] But by then his central argument had already been finalized in the publication that same year of the book for which he remains best known, *The Myth of the Negro Past*.[16] By this stage his enthusiasm for finding correspondences— in effect, for being the kind of folklorist that Parsons had encouraged him to be—was on the wane. He continues: "I shrink from the job of doing correspondences . . . do you think it would be worthwhile to publish them as raw data with an introduction pointing out the major theoretical points that arise out of considering them?" She was not keen on this plan. His last letter before her death in December of that year reports, "The Dahomean tales are being typed, and I will be thinking about what you said . . . " (letter to Parsons 10 April 1941).[17]

We have no clear explanation as to why it took seventeen more years to publish *Dahomean Narrative* in the form which

Herskovits had proposed. It was clearly reworked by Frances and published by the press of the university at which he had gained national and international stature. But it was not a legacy project. The long introduction reflects a career of thought about culture and creativity, and prefigures ideas about continual innovation that he brought to his second phase of work on Africa, from the time of the transition to independence. And it was a popular book. The first printing in 1958 was followed by a second one in 1966 and a third in 1970. It is the only one of the major Dahomean publications that was even considered for translation into French, although the project was abandoned in 1959. Widely and favorably reviewed in sources as diverse as the *Chicago Tribune,* the *New York Times, Africa,* and the *Journal of American Folklore,* the book received no comment more direct about the value of the work than that from an external reviewer commenting on the manuscript for Northwestern University Press in 1957. In a letter dated 28 October 1957, an eminent folklorist at a major university states, "May I say, to begin with, that I found this manuscript pleasurable reading; and give you, right off the bat, my conclusion, which is this: if you decide against publishing the book, I hope that we shall get a chance to do so."[18]

The long delay between the fieldwork in 1931 and the publication in 1958 was not without costs. The academic reviews of the book were both appreciative of the contribution it made to the corpus of published West African narrative and also critical on technical grounds. By the 1950s the anthropological study of myth had been revolutionized by Claude Lévi-Strauss, who focused on the internal structure that makes mythical narratives persuasively meaningful to their audience, that is, the order in the world that is implicit in the classifications of things and people, their oppositions, and their transformations from one into another. Historian Jan Vansina had begun to use myths in another way, as a source for teasing out the history of nonliterate cultures as told in their own terms and from their own landmarks. Both of these scholarly purposes ideally depended on collection by particular methods: structural analysis needed local terminologies; historical analysis demanded multiple versions of the same story as told by people from different vantage points. The Herskovitses' methods preceded these innovations. They based their approach on the folklore studies of their time, focusing on the variety of the repertoire and the diffusion of elements from one cultural repertoire to another. More recently, scholars turn back to narratives such as these with yet another purpose, and one which the Herskovitses did anticipate in their introduction if not in their methods, namely, to try to understand the creativity, not of the basic story, but of the situational performance. Again their method is missing certain elements that one needs, particularly attention to improvisation in a particular social context and the audience's engagement with the artist. But even as generations of scholars have questioned the Herskovitses' theory of myth in the introduction or their methods of work, all have praised the sheer extent and variety of their collection, the intrinsic vividness and vigor of the stories, and the elegance of their expression. As one reviewer wrote, "it is the stories themselves . . . which hold our attention most closely."[19]

In today's new phase of cultural study, scholars, artists, and wider communities return to "raw material" with a new sense of potential inspiration. The maker of the object, the performer of the dance, and the singer of songs communicates directly, and new audiences step up to meet them with their own diverse interests and perceptions. In bringing out a new edition of these materials, Northwestern University Press, the Program of African Studies at Northwestern University, and the Herskovits Library not only commemorate the Herskovitses' work from the past but also invite new audiences to make use of it in original ways that are relevant to the present and future.

Notes

[1] Baron, Robert. "Africa in the Americas: Melville J. Herskovits's Folkloristic and Anthropological Scholarship—1923–41." Ph.D. diss., University of Pennsylvania. (Ann Arbor: University of Michigan Microfilms, 1994), 5.

[2] Zumwalt, Rosemary Levy. *Wealth and Rebellion: Elsie Clews Parsons, Anthropologist and Folklorist.* (Urbana and Chicago: University of Illinois Press, 1992), 186.

[3] Ibid., 333.

[4] Herskovits, Melville J. Papers. Northwestern University Archives.

[5] Ibid.

[6] Herskovits, Melville J. *Dahomey: An Ancient West African Kingdom.* (New York: J. J. Augustin, 1938), xi.

[7] Herskovits, Melville J. and Frances S. *An Outline of Dahomean Religious Belief.* (Menasha, Wis.: American Anthropological Association, 1933).

[8] Herskovits, Melville J. Papers. Northwestern University Archives.

[9] Herskovits, Melville J. "Some Aspects of Dahomean Ethnology." *Africa* 5 (1932): 266–96; Herskovits, Melville J. "Population Statistics in the Kingdom of Dahomey." *Human Biology* 4 (1932): 252–61; Herskovits, Melville J. and Frances S. "The Art of Dahomey: I, Brass-casting and Appliqué Cloths; II, Wood Carving." *The American Magazine of Art* 27 (1934): 67–76, 124–31; Herskovits, Melville J. and Frances S. "A Footnote to the History of Negro Slaving." *Opportunity* 11 (1933): 178–81; Herskovits, Melville J. "The Best Friend in Dahomey." *Negro Anthology Made by Nancy Cunand*, 1931–33 (London: Published by Nancy Cunand at Wishart and Company, 1934), 627–32; Herskovits, Melville J. "A Note on 'Woman Marriage' in Dahomey." *Africa* 10 (1937): 335–41.

[10] Herskovits, Frances S. "Dahomean Songs for the Dead." *The New Republic* 84 (4 September 1935): 95. Other publications of Dahomean songs presented by Frances S. Herskovits are "Dahomean Songs," *Poetry* 45 (November 1934) 75–77, and "To Destiny," "Warrior's Songs," "Poems from Dahomey," *Theatre Arts Monthly* 19 (May 1935): 340.

[11] Herskovits, Melville J. Papers. Northwestern University Archives.

[12] Ibid.

[13] Ibid.

[14] Ibid.

[15] Ibid.

[16] Herskovits, Melville J. *The Myth of the Negro Past.* (Boston: Beacon Press, 1990 [1941]).

[17] Herskovits, Melville J. Papers. Northwestern University Archives.

[18] Northwestern University Press. Records. Northwestern University Archives.

[19] *Africa Weekly*, 10 April 1959.

Preface

The narratives in this collection have taught us much about how the Dahomean sees his world and himself, and how his imagination plays on the realities of everyday life. In the shared experience of enjoying the myths and tales told us, we came to know individual Dahomeans, without their solid traditional defenses against those in authority, or the stranger. They reacted to our evident interest, and often delight, with initial wariness and even with troubled astonishment that a white outsider should get a point of satirical allusion. But in time this changed.

Many of these narratives left no doubt at the time of their telling that we were hearing a mature and subtle art form. This feeling has been strengthened while working on the texts we brought back from the field. We hope we are in some degree meeting our commitment to the Africans in many parts of Sub-Saharan Africa with whom we discussed their oral literary traditions, to extend the knowledge of African literary resources and to dispel the notions that Africans tell only simple animal stories. If our analysis serves to draw the attention of humanists to the important need to range more widely among the cultures of mankind in assessing creative achievement based on the symbolisms of language, we shall feel well repaid.

An explanation is perhaps called for of our repeated allusions to what "the Dahomeans" say. We do not intend by these to suggest unanimity in all of Dahomey on the particular points that these references touch. This use, in effect, is a form of shorthand to explain that we are not giving our own views, but those of some or many Dahomeans. Yet, in this procedure we are also following a manner of speaking that is characteristically Dahomean, which we learned from those with whom we had the closest contact. For we were continually hearing "*the Dahomean*" cited and referred to in all contexts.

We should have liked to name here the individual narrators. Over the years, however, we have held to our pledge to those who have worked with us in the field not to identify them by name. For similar reasons, we have commented with little elaboration on the "historical" tales, being mindful of political issues that may not too long remain dormant.

No special orthography has been used in this book. Fõn is a tonal language, but in these texts we have not indicated tones. Those interested in the scientific orthography are referred to *Dahomey* (especially Volume II, which has the Index) by Melville J. Herskovits. The narratives themselves, as grouped, follow largely the canons of Dahomean classification. Each section is preceded by a list of characters, given in the order of their appearance to make easier their identification when they are met in the text. The names of minor characters, whose roles are explained in the tales, and the praise-names of the *vodun* are, however, not given.

We are indebted to many sources for financial assistance in gathering these narratives, and for further support during the many years we have been working on them. Our field trip in 1931 was made possible by funds given by Dr. Elsie Clews Parsons, who aided so many of her junior colleagues to get into the field. Her grant was matched by Columbia University, at the instance of Professor Franz Boas, from funds made available at that time to the University by the Rockefeller Foundation for the purpose of stimulating financial aid to research from other sources. The apparatus and the cylinders we used for recording songs were provided by a special grant from the American Council of Learned Societies. In this connection, we wish especially to acknowledge our appreciation to Dr. Waldo Leland and the late Dr. Donald Goodchild, who showed such deep understanding of the significance and research needs of this study, which at that time was completely outside the currents of American scholarly interests.

Over the years, allocations of research funds to the project by the Graduate School of Northwestern University made available assistance for typing and retyping the manuscript. The University's Program of African Studies, supported by the Carnegie Corporation of New York and by the Ford Foundation, has provided for its publication, and in 1957 also made possible one of our survey tours in Sub-Saharan Africa, which added first-hand experience with comparable materials from other societies. Mr. J. M. Barker, Director of Northwestern University Press, and his staff have given us unstinted and enthusiastic assistance. To all these, we express our deep appreciation.

Our greatest indebtedness, however, is to the men of Dahomey (and the women, though they told us no stories), who in their own idiom are those whose "hearts have great understanding"—the creative singer-poets, the story-tellers and philosophers.

MELVILLE J. HERSKOVITS
FRANCES S. HERSKOVITS

Evanston, Illinois
March 23, 1958

Introductory

> . . . *Life is like a palm tree*
> *The fronds go this way and that*

> . . . *Humor governs the world well*

> . . . *The Proverb is the horse of*
> *conversation*

DAHOMEAN PROVERBS

DAHOMEAN NARRATIVE FORMS

1 *Some general considerations*

The student of the spoken arts of nonliterate peoples is confronted with many problems that need never concern those who deal with written literature. The critics who work with written forms from historic cultures control in good measure the essential clues to social connotation, and the referents of idiom, analogy, and allusion. Yet even within our own tradition, we need only recall the discussions that followed on the publication of James Joyce's *Finnegans Wake* to see how many questions can be posed by improvisation on established usage. And we need but mention *Ulysses* to bring to mind the questions that the restructuring of traditional categories can similarly raise—raise, that is, before the reader can grasp the clues that lay bare the expressive superstructure.

Where languages differ in their conventions of expressing time and space, of gender and number, of mode and aspect, then comprehension on the most elementary level becomes of primary concern. In addition, the point of a narrative (to say nothing of the structure that, in consonance with its own tradition, bases point on action) too easily eludes the student unfamiliar with the symbols and the implicit values of the society in which it is told. This is why, perhaps, in discussions of unwritten prose and verse forms there has been so little awareness of style, of nuance, of subtlety —in effect, such blurring of critical insight. It is, perhaps, also why

3

there has been such broad generalizing on so narrow a base of documentation: narrowed, certainly, by failing to take account of the creative process, however variable in degree, as a functioning reality in societies without written languages.

We shall discuss later some of the generalizations of students of myth and literature which have had, and continue to have, wide currency and influence, and see how their theories apply to the body of narratives which we present here—the myths, the myth chronicles, the tales, and the associated shorter forms. But in turning to the living narrative tradition of a people such as the Dahomeans, who are outside the historic literate cultures, we are putting aside the prolonged and passionately debated theogonic and etiological questions about their sacred lore—the myths, strictly speaking—and the equally debated question of the origin of the secular forms, with or without added mythic themes. We take as a given that all of Africa participates in an Old World Culture, which also includes Europe and Asia, and that this vast area has many cultural features in common, among which, most richly and ubiquitously shared, is its oral literature. By following this assumption, we are free to pay attention to far more searching problems than the insoluble one of which narratives, or proverbs, or riddles in this great interchange among peoples originated where, or how, and in what direction they traveled.

Fundamental to this approach is the rejection of terms such as "primitive" and "savage"; as "civilized" and "barbarian" or "backward"; as "greater" or "lesser" tradition. Instead we shall pose questions that are not culture-bound, such as: What functioning role does the culture assign to its spoken arts? What is its attitude toward improvisation? Is it permissive, encouraging and rewarding it; or is it indifferent or even hostile toward its exercise? Does it have named criteria which distinguish the excellence of artistry from merely competent repetitions? What in the structure of the narrative form is dictated by the fact that it is spoken, and is thus more akin to drama than are written forms? How closely and in what situations does the teller's participant audience hold him to fixed versions? Are there cultural imperatives that give an individual stamp in each culture to widely diffused themes?

What role do the spoken art forms have in social criticism? Can we find an explanation for the absence of tragic themes? [1]

In terms of a direct focus on the spoken arts of a single culture, what had been treated heretofore as problems unique to folklore stand revealed as the common problems of literary analysis—questions of content, of values, of style. More specifically these are problems of plot and its resolution; of characterization, and the cultural matrix within which both are shaped; of the unities of time and place and action, and the devices to heighten emotion and create suspense. Freed from the stereotype of the uncreative "primitive," we can move to problems of variation in style as expressed in the separate categories of narrative, and as handled by the more valued story-tellers. For just as in African art styles we are able to identify regional types (and with the evidence from more recent study, regional "schools" and even individual artists), so with the spoken arts, a broad new field of humanistic enquiry lies before us, which while recognizing the special problems in analyzing unwritten forms, accepts the underlying unities in world literature.

There are also the questions which remain largely for future study, concerning the prosody of peoples who speak languages in which tone is significant, in which the most subtle variation in meaning can be effected by tonal modulation. From the texts we collected, we know that instead of a syllabic rhyming scheme, there are in these languages tonal clusters that structure repetitive patterns in verse. The entire question of imagery, in prose as well as verse, which the Dahomeans call *mlamla*, has never had systematic attention; nor has there been recognition of the important use of the proverb for thematic statement in versification.

We have another glimpse of the promise that lies in such a line of investigation when we ask ourselves whether the role a living tradition assigns to individual self-expression has significant bearing on the dynamic potential of a group, politically and socially. Can it furnish us with firm leads to the group's receptivity to new

[1] For one of the few studies of unwritten narrative where problems of this kind are considered, in this case for Polynesia, cf. K. Luomala, *Voices on the Wind* (Honolulu, 1955, *passim.*).

forms, to its areas of resilience, to its tradition-bound resistances?
We treat a number of these questions here. But, in the idiom of the
Dahomeans, merely to name them means that "the road is open."

2   *Methodology*

The narratives in this collection were recorded in 1931 in Dahomey, West Africa. They were taken down in the centers of
Abomey, the capital of the preconquest kingdom; in Allada, the
traditional point of origin of the Aladahonu dynasty that ruled for
nearly three hundred years (before French controls were imposed) and in Whydah, the coastal city famous for its role in the
slave trade, and long the chief port of the kingdom. Excepting only
two of the twenty-six narrators, one an adolescent and the other
in his middle twenties, the tellers were well beyond middle age.
Some of them were either priests of cults or cult members of rank
in the hierarchy of Dahomean worship. Various others were heads
of families, or political chiefs. They were all men, for no woman
could be found at the time of this research who could qualify as a
French-speaking interpreter for women story-tellers.

Our method of recording was to take the text directly on the
typewriter as our interpreters translated the narrator's flow of the
story, given in Fõn, the language of Dahomey. Except for native
terms, or some locution phrased in Negro-French, which was set
down as given in order not to interrupt the flow of translation,
we wrote in English. In time these locutions became familiar, but
the original renderings of the tales are, nevertheless, interspersed
with these phrases in French and in Fõn. These repetitions by the
interpreter—when the story-teller was not French-speaking himself, as six of the twenty-six were—fell into patterned traditional
behavior. For, as seen by the narrator, the interpreter was acting
as "linguist" for the anthropologist, on the same cultural terms as
the chief's "linguist" did for the chief in his dealings with functionaries and petitioners. We have kept as close to literal translation as is possible, preserving certain stylistic and idiomatic expressions which are not common to English usage, when we felt these
were significant.

The use of the typewriter brought out interesting reactions. At first, both teller and translator, watching the play of the machine with fascination, spoke on and on; some of the fullest tales were recorded under the influence of the novelty of having what was said taken on the typewriter. Later, when they were accustomed to the sound of the keys, they would on occasion attempt to confound the *yovo*, the whites—that is, ourselves—by talking rapidly and by including the elaborations of the actual story-telling session to test our typing skill. Were it not that this field-work followed on the collecting of comparable tales from Negroes of Dutch Guiana, and that reading for the comparative analysis of the Guiana tales had given familiarity with the range of motifs that are welded into African narrative forms, the method would not have proved as rewarding as it did.[1]

We recorded the songs to the stories after the whole tale had been told, for no electronic apparatus was available at that time, and singing had to be done into the horn of a small machine that recorded the songs on cylinders. To have attempted to record songs in their proper places would have meant a serious interruption of narrative continuity. Instead, we noted the initial phrases of each song, and the full Fŏn text was taken down with word for word interlinear translations when the song itself was recorded at the end of a session. At that time, too, or later, when the script was read over, it was discussed with the interpreters. Where myths validating belief were involved, these discussions formed a basis for future conversations.

With the demonstration by Boas[2] that the mythology and tales

[1] The Guiana narratives have been published in our work *Suriname Folklore* (New York, 1936). More than 1500 tales were read in gathering the comparative data, employed to indicate the sources and relationships of motifs and stories in that collection. The Bibliography appended to the volume (pp. 761–766 comprises a complete list, as far as could be found, of titles dealing with African and New World Negro folklore, or in which stories were included, that had appeared to the time of its publication. Since not many studies of the tales of these peoples, especially as regards Africa, have been published since that time, this Bibliography will be found adequate for any further comparative work in this field until new collections are added to the resources now available. No attempt has been made in this volume to repeat the comparative analysis of our earlier one.

[2] F. Boas, *Tsimshian Mythology* (31st Annual Report, Bureau of American Ethnology, pp. 27–1037), Washington, 1909–19.

of a people constitute "the autobiography of the tribe," as he put it, it has become a truism among serious students of both sacred and secular lore that lacking a knowledge of the cultural matrix, the interpretation of narrative must rest on the surface of expression, since attempts to derive meaning inevitably follow standards set by the culture of the student rather than of the people being studied.

From this point of view, our task has been facilitated by the fact that the culture of Dahomey has already been described and analyzed.[1] We know the patterns of family life, economic structure, educational techniques; of aesthetic values, religious concepts, and ritual. Of special importance for this study is the substantial knowledge we have of the political development of Dahomey, which we arrived at by the technique of ethnohistory, whereby oral tradition and ethnographic facts, as we observed and recorded them first-hand in the field, were checked against documentation from written sources dating back to the earliest contact of literate Europe with Dahomey, roughly about 1600, and continuing through the conquest of the kingdom by the French in 1894. With the ethnographic and historic background known, we will here touch only on those facets of the culture or history which throw into special relief certain customary usages emphasized in the narratives, or clarify the meaning of certain historical allusions.

Another methodological point may be mentioned. In gathering the narratives, we made no attempt to seek out men of reputation as story-tellers. Tales were rather told by those with whom we discussed various aspects of the culture as a whole. The reasons for this lay in part in the nature of the culture itself, and in part in the expediencies of field-work. Research among the Negroes of Dutch Guiana, where Dahomean influences have been second only to those of Ashanti, had taught us to respect the proverb: "A man does not tell another more than half of what he knows."

In its broadest implications this proverb stood us in good stead in the ancestral land of Dahomey as it had in Guiana, in other parts of Africa, and among the descendants of Africans in the Caribbean and South America. There were occasions when some particularly

[1] M. J. Herskovits, *Dahomey, an Ancient West African Kingdom*, New York, 1938.

delicate matter of cult detail or social organization was being discussed—more especially when the supernatural founding ancestor of a clan was touched upon—that demanded an easing of tensions aroused by steady questioning. For the West African is never more circumspect than when discussing clan origins—though he is expansive on points of what he calls "family history." At such times, a mutually agreeable digression was a story-telling interval.

Nor was it necessary for such interludes to focus on humorous tales. Indeed, after these tense sessions, the elders found relaxation in telling about the royal ancestors and the greatness of the kingdom they ruled. Certainly, in Abomey, stories of the days when Dahomey was powerful and feared were heard more than any others, until their telling had to be diplomatically curbed in the interest of a wider sampling.[1] With men of lesser rank and age than priests, chiefs, and family heads, being on guard against women was a relished theme, and after our story-tellers came to know us well myths and tales were told about the adventures of the trickster-deity Legba, with his vast appetite for mischief and sexual philandering.

By these means, and also by the use of story-telling sessions as a warming-up period with a new informant, or while beginning work in a new locale, or when we felt the need to call on some device to check materials by indirection, a minimum of conscious selection and an appreciable degree of representativeness was achieved as regards the type of tale, regional differences, and the manner of telling.

Familiarity with the total setting in which the tale is told was gained by attendance at story-telling sessions held in the compounds at night. Here could be noted the dynamics of voice change, the play of expression on the face of the story-teller, the

---

[1] The tale of how Dahomey received its name, found incorporated in No. 96, was heard more than twenty times in Abomey alone. It is a story of respectable antiquity, a fact that will be found relevant when we discuss certain theories of "primitive" mythology; this is attested by the fact that it has been cited by most writers who have been concerned with Dahomey and have reported on their experiences there, from Dalzel (A. Dalzel, *The History of Dahomey*, London, 1793, pp. 1–2), through Burton (Sir Richard Burton, *A Mission to Gelele, King of Dahomey*, London, 1893, Vol. I, p. 105), to Le Herissé (A. Le Herissé, *L'ancien royaume du Dahomey*, Paris, 1911, p. 288).

use of gesture to vivify narration, the songs, the dance steps—in brief, all the elements that give the tale stylistic unity and amplitude. Only a hidden mechanism that would simultaneously film and record a story-telling session could fully convey the artistry of the teller of tales in this setting, and give a sense of the interplay between narrator and audience that is so important an aspect of the spoken narrative tradition.

Two types of tales are not represented here. The first includes the amorous stories that are dramatized by the adolescent boys of a compound or of a village quarter, when they meet at night in the crude structure which they themselves have built, to exchange mutual confidences and describe explorations into sexual practices. This occurs during that period in their maturation when the nubile girls are removed from play activities with them, and they are not yet of an age to indulge in adult sexual practices. Our ethnographic information is that these are woven on the simple plot of sex-play and surprise.[1]

The second group of tales are those told at gatherings of the women's social clubs, the *gbe*. The two narratives of this type found in this collection, Nos. 56 and 108, both touch on the theme of how co-wives, exasperated by a braggart husband, devise a plan to expose him to ridicule. Again our ethnographic data [2] supplement this information. Thus it was told us how, during the reign of King Glele (1858–1889), the husbands had found the songs and tales of their wives so distasteful that a group of them petitioned the King to suppress the women's associations. The influence of certain of the wives with ministers of state, and the King himself, was such, however, that these men suffered public reprimand for this suggestion.

An incident during our field-work throws light on the continuity of attitude toward these tales among the men. We were anxious to discover whether the stress on women's shortcomings, in so many of the tales told by men, is matched by parallel themes that dramatize grievances of women against men. We accordingly set about to win the confidence of a woman who was an office-holder

[1] Cf. *Dahomey*, Vol. I, pp. 277–279.
[2] *Ibid.*, Vol. I, pp. 254–255.

in several of these social clubs. After months of preparation, she agreed to recount some of their stories, using her brother, who was a member of our household, as interpreter. At the last moment, however, her husband, hearing of the proposal, forbade her to tell them to us, under threat, indeed, of breaking their union which, as a free relationship,[1] could have been dissolved at will.

The time that has elapsed between the gathering of the tales in this collection and their appearance in print has proved to be not without some gains.[2] Subsequent field experiences in the historically related Negro cultures of the New World (in Haiti, Trinidad and Brazil) and first-hand study in other parts of the African continent have enriched our understanding of the role of the spoken arts in all these cultures. The opportunity to revisit Dahomey more than twenty years after these narratives were collected has given us a very real sense of the continuities in Dahomean life, of which oral literature is so effective a vehicle. We were able again to meet some of the tellers of the tales we present here and to learn how they had taken their places in the higher age-levels of Dahomean society. One, whose favorite tale was No. 110, had become head of the ancestral cult of the royal family. Another, who contributed the Legba myth, No. 11, was *dokpwegan*, head of the young men of his community and burial chief. And a third, who had died in the interim, had as the years progressed become the narrator most sought after at the wakes that are so important in the rites of death.

There is also the wider humanistic interest in a collection such as this. We have referred to the phrasing of new questions in terms of fresh insights that are to be gained from a broadening cross-cultural base of humanistic scholarship. Much exploratory activity has occurred during the time that has elapsed between the collection and the presentation of our materials. As a result, these myths

---

[1] Cf. *Dahomey*, Vol. I, pp. 317 ff.

[2] The only collection of Dahomean narratives published since 1931 is that in P. Barreau, *Contes et Légendes du Dahomey* (Namur, n.d.), though just when and under what circumstances they were gathered we are not told. More important are the 73 myths and tales given by B. Maupoil (*La Géomancie à l'ancienne Côte des Esclaves*, Paris, 1943, pp. 733 ff.), in connection with his discussion of the divining cult.

and tales have direct relevance for questions that are being so
much discussed, as, for example, the theories about myth as these
bear on our own literature.

In 1931, moreover, there would not have been the many men
and women who, coming out of an oral tradition, are asking themselves the same questions as to the role of tradition in the creative
process, as are being asked in London and Paris and New York;
men and women with university training, who are no longer over-
whelmed by the strictures which designate their cultures as "primitive," or "savage," or "archetypal." Throughout the continent,
more and more Africans are turning to their own traditions and
their own way of life for what they write, and thereby giving us
new insights into the meaning of their oral literature.

We may cite, as one instance, a paragraph from the Preface to a
book of animal tales, written by two distinguished African educa-
tors, Léopold Sédar Senghor and Abdoulaye Sadji, for the children in the elementary schools of French West Africa to be used
in learning French:

Notre manuel se compose de récits déjà entendus par l'enfant dans sa
langue maternelle et déjà vécus de lui. . . . Nous n'avons pas voulu
procéder par pièces detachées, selon la tradition des livres de contes.
Présenter à l'enfant noir des récits isolés, sans aucun lien qui les rattache
les uns aux autres, serait tuer la vie et le mouvement dont son imagination anime ces récits. Il n'y a pas, pour lui, *des histoires de bêtes*, mais
l'histoire des bêtes. Il faillait donc trouver ce lien, et nous l'avons fait
en groupant les récits autour d'un même personnage, *Leuk-le-Lièvre*.
Ce n'est pas par hasard que nous avons choisi ce personnage. . . . Il
représente l'intelligence qui triomphe partout et toujours dans les situations les plus difficiles. Mais il fallait, pour renforcer l'intérêt des
récits, faire de l'ensemble un vaste drame. D'où, en face de Leuk-le-
Lièvre, son antagoniste, Bouki-le-Hyène, stupide et méchant, dont le
rusé lièvre fait l'éternal trompé.[1]

As we read this sequence of tales for children, incidentally, we
come upon themes that recur in the stories in this Dahomean collection, even in some of the most sacred myths.

New impulses to use the narratives of the African spoken tradi-

[1] L. Senghor and A. Sadji, *La Belle Histoire de Leuk-le-Lièvre*, Paris, 1953, p. 4.

tion have also been set in motion by the critical acclaim given the books by Amos Tutuola,[1] a Nigerian, who recounts the adventures of human protagonists in encounters with supernatural beings. We doubt if the West African of today is disturbed because the literary critics are unaware that Tutuola is drawing closely on the traditional repertory of his culture for these stories, doing what is suggested in the Senghor and Sadji volume, weaving into a sequence the adventures of what we have designated in this volume as the "Infant Terrible" stories.[2] It will be instructive for one who reads the narratives in this volume to go to Tutuola's books with the motifs and orientations of the tales given here in mind. He will find them all. Tutuola's initial theme of "The Palm-Wine Drinkard and his Dead Palm-Wine Tapster in the Deads' Town" is developed out of a basic West African motif, found in our collection in No. 68 or No. 69, of a journey to the land of the dead. Simbi, the Yoruba girl from a wealthy family (of his "Simbi and the Satyr of the Dark Jungle," who wished "to go abroad from where I will experience the difficulties of the 'Poverty' and of the 'Punishment'") finds her counterpart in the King of Adja who, in the divination tale, No. 39, wished to know what poverty was.

3 *The problem of classification*

Classification and definition have posed problems from the outset of the study of unwritten narrative. Consensus has long been sought on fixing the difference between tale, myth, and legend; the very nature of the more inclusive term "folklore" has been debated for decades. Myth, for example, is treated as the statement of an untruth; as either a rationalization or a validation of belief; as a derivation of ritual; as an expression of theology; or as a manifestation of the unconscious desires of a group.[3]

While stress on the structural aspects of the narrative of nonlit-

[1] Amos, Tutuola, *The Palm-Wine Drinkard*, London, 1952; *My Life in the Bush of Ghosts*, London, 1954; *Simbi and the Satyr of the Dark Jungle*, London, 1955.
[2] V. S. Pritchett, "Nightmare," *New Statesman and Nation*, Vol. 47, no. 5, p. 291.
[3] These points will be fully discussed below, pp. 81 ff.

erate peoples in terms of novelistic qualities threw new light on numerous problems of organization and function, the definition of the word "novelistic" in this context has remained obscure. In the literary tradition of Europe and America, the distinctions between the novel, the short story, the play are clear, and the critic or student can use this terminological shorthand without fear of being misunderstood. For other societies, however, these categories must be spelled out.

When Benedict states, "In Zuni, tales fall into no clearly distinguishable categories," and "the divisions used in this volume are for convenience of reference only, and have little to do with the literary problems of the narrator," [1] we will, if wise, not read more of organization into her categories than her statement allows. Above all, we must not be trapped by those who would generalize from this particular society to all "primitive" peoples, seduced perhaps by the stereotype of the "primitive" as lacking the power of analysis or generalization; as seeing all of life as a single stream whose components are indistinguishable in terms of broader categories.

The Dahomeans offer a striking example of how each society must be studied in terms of its own particular orientations. For example, the Dahomean has a flair for verbalization and explicit statement. He moralizes, then phrases his own rationale for evading an uncongenial situation. He is a believer in Destiny, yet constantly parries with its agents to "clear the path" that he may find the means to a desirable goal. He is aware of both the manifest and latent ancestral forces that play upon his life, and of himself as one unit in the continuum which, as he himself sees it, includes those who preceded him, himself, and the generations to come. From this point of view he is one of a family, of an aggregate of families, of a clan. But he is also consciously, astutely, and often aggressively aware of himself as an individual, with a wish to obtain an abundance of the good things of life and a degree of prestige that will reach into posterity. What is important is that the Dahomean names his abstractions, that he has words to define the categories he distinguishes.

In his classification of narrative, he identifies two broad cate-

[1] R. Benedict, *Zuni Mythology* (Columbia Contributions to Anthropology, xxi), New York, 1935, p. xxx.

gories, the *hwenoho*, literally "time-old-story," which he trans-
lates variously as history, as tradition, as traditional history, or as
ancient lore; and the *heho*, the tale. It is a distinction that the
youngest story-teller recognizes. It has bearing on culturally defined attitudes toward traditional lore and improvisation, on the
one hand, and on priorities in narration, as governed by seniority
rights, professional specialization and sexual differentiation of
roles, on the other.

Illustrations from field experience throw light on the way in
which Dahomeans recognize and respond to the categories they
have established. An elder, a family head from one of the pros-
perous agricultural villages to the east of Abomey, came one market day to return a call we had made to his village. We were in
the midst of taking down a story from a member of our household,
who stepped aside at the approach of the senior visitor. The con-
versation opened on the subject of story-telling, and we invited our
guest to tell us a story.

"What you ask for is a tale [*heho*]," he said. "Men of my age do
not tell these. We are concerned with the happenings of 'history'
[*hwenoho*]."

On another occasion, a priest of the Thunder cult, while being
questioned about a point in a myth he was telling, replied, "This
isn't a tale. It is 'history.' "

The head of an important craft-guild was discussing the origin
of his clan with us. When we asked about the clan of his senior
wife, he said, "What I told you is the 'history' of my family. I do
not know the history of those who belong to other clans. But even
if I did know some of it, I would have no right to talk about it."

We asked, "Will your wife tell us?"

"No," he replied, "a woman does not talk about such things.
Everything that concerns the *tohwiyo* [the founder of the clan]
is for men."

In each instance, the term employed for history was *hwenoho*.
When, however, discussing a narrative dealing with the exploits of
Legba, the trickster deity, the homelier phrase, "this means old-
time-story," was given in translation; though if the point of the
myth was a discussion of Legba's role in the cult of divination by
the system of Fa, then the translation was interchangeably "his-

tory," or "tradition," or "traditional history." For the French-speaking interpreters this distinction was so important that they would tell us repeatedly that "history" was to be understood as "true history" and not as a synonym for "tale." "It is not *histoire* in the sense of *conte*," they would emphasize.

The clearest statement about the two categories was given us by a story-teller in Abomey, whose explanation may be said not only to show how they are culturally defined, but to clarify their functional significance. "We in Dahomey," he explained, "say that tales [*heho*] tell of things which never existed and are inventions of people. History [*hwenoho*] is the true story, and the life of Daho-mey is based on history. But one learns from the tale what one can." [1]

Our discussion will respect the Dahomean classification, noting, however, how this is flexible enough to permit recognition of the special situation which alters cases. We shall do this, even while going beyond the dual division of narrative which they have formulated. For it is of the essence of scholarly investigation that while one holds as closely as possible to the lines drawn by the data, one also uses these as a frame within which more refined levels of classification are to be reached. In the case of the narratives, it is possible, in these terms, while accepting the categories of the Dahomeans, to distinguish within each category types of stories that, from the point of view of the materials of which they treat and the points they make, constitute valid subclasses.

Yet, whether in terms of the indigenous classes or these analytical subgroupings, we must not hold to our categories with too great rigidity. Narratives overlap even in the two major divisions, and Dahomeans themselves are hard put to it to give a categorical answer if asked to designate the type to which certain tales belong. This applies especially where the *heho* is of the type we would describe as a fable, or as a parable. Indeed, a parable has been named by one informant as falling into the proverb group.

[1] In this collection, Nos. 3, 5, 7, and 13, among others, may be indicated as examples of this use of "history" in their openings.

4 The *hwenoho*

In the class of narratives called *hwenoho*, the following subgroupings can be distinguished:

1) *Myths*, comprising chiefly stories of the deities, and of the peopling of the earth. Tales No. 1–21 in our collection are representative of this type, grouped by the Dahomeans as the "history" of the *vodun*.

2) *Clan myth-chronicles*, which recount the origin of the great "families," or clans (including that of the Aladahonu rulers), and their adventures through time. In their fullest form, these include explanations of ritual behavior, food taboos, and the positive sanctions that make up the ancestral code. Stories No. 92–96, 98–99, 102 and 148–150 are episodes from these; more excerpts from myth-chronicles will be found in *Dahomey*, Vol. I, pp. 167–191, where the social organization of the Dahomean people is discussed.

3) *Verse-sequences*, usually sung as recitatives, and composed mainly by professional verse-makers for the purpose of memorizing genealogies, and events that have been incorporated into ritual or law.

The *hwenoho*, strictly defined, is narrated with little attempt at dramatization. The interpolations which punctuate the narrative flow are those of ordinary speech and are not heightened by audience participation as in a story-telling session. In the instance of the sacred myths, they are narrated by such specialists as diviners and priests of the cult-groups. Clan myth-chronicles are told by clan elders. Many clan myths, particularly those about the *tohwiyo*, the founding ancestor, are rarely given in full, since certain portions of the narrative are held secret from all but the elders immediately concerned with clan ancestral rites. Verse sequences, in this category, are related to the family *hwenoho*.

The audience to which family *hwenoho* are recited is generally restricted to clan members; usually only the adult males who attend the councils at which they are told. But, as was pointed out to us on several occasions, a lad from seven to twelve, sitting quietly against a wall in a corner, can learn a great deal. Yet however much he may have heard and understood, and could later recall, he would not presume, at least in the hearing of his seniors, to impart any of it to his age-mates, as he could with a tale (*heho*). Again, whereas the *heho* are only told at night, the *hwenoho* are recounted at family councils, often held during daylight hours.

The Dahomean believes, and will say with conviction, that each narrative "history" is fixed and unique, both in form and content. We tried the experiment of reading to a cult head two different versions of the myth giving the quarrel of the two brothers, *Sogbo*, the Thunder, and *Sagbata*, the Earth (No. 14, as given by the chief priest of the Earth cult, and No. 3, by a priest of the Thunder pantheon). The unhesitating reply was that the gods do not reveal the same things to everyone, and that each narrator was telling "true history" according to the way the *vodun* have given it to him. In other words, belief in a single correct version does not exist. One is true for all those affiliated with the Earth pantheon, and the other for those who worship the Thunder deities. Nonetheless, since in general outline a knowledge of the cosmogonic myths is widespread, the variants, though differing in the role assigned each protagonist or in the phrasing of the issues involved, are yet so clearly structured that they incorporate the same progressions of incidents, the same actors, and the same final resolution. In other words, the sacred myths show variation based on "sectarian" or regional emphasis, and this in turn has frequently a political explanation.

What is not as readily anticipated is the patterned structuring of the clan myth-chronicles, even to the recurrence of certain incidents describing what are purported to be the experiences of the individual ancestors of each clan. In Allada, we witnessed an interesting reaction to this of a young interpreter, a man of twenty-five or six, who had come to know at greater length the "history" of his family than would ordinarily be known by a man of his age. This was accounted for by the fact that, at the time of this field-work, negotiations were going on between the clan elders in Abomey, where the ancestral house of worship was located, and the extended family in Allada which was seeking to split off from the Abomey group and establish its own ancestral house.[1] He was translating for us the clan myth-chronicles of family heads who, each in turn, told his clan "history." The consternation, disbelief, and later perplexity he registered when he heard incidents given as the experiences of the ancestors of the several narrators, which he had heard told as the special experiences of his own ancestors, are difficult to convey.

Two points are of relevance here to clarify the use of the term "myth-chronicle." The first involves the debated topic of what component of an oral tradition is valid history; the second is directed to the question of why only excerpts of these narratives are included in a discussion of the spoken arts. The first, which directly impinges on the second and which will be elaborated in more generalizing terms later, is concerned with the continuously functioning role of traditional history in Dahomean culture, with special attention to its genealogical and political aspects. The second has to do with the role of these narratives in the life of the Dahomeans as a reservoir of thematic source materials for topical improvisation in prose and verse.

As to the first, we have bound the word "chronicle" to "myth" so as to allow for the accounts of the supernatural male founder and his associated totemic helpers. Moreover, the Dahomean is never loath in any recital of events to make some allusion to the time of Dada Segbo, a mythic king who was said to reign in the early days of mankind, or to Metonofi, another king, sometimes declared as coexistent with Dada Segbo, but more generally envisaged as antedating him, or as the king who rules the Underworld, or as an invisible being who in very early times was ruler and arbiter of the destiny of living things in all the Universe. We need here say only that it is quite commonly not so much a cosmogonic referent as a metaphorical device used in both the *hwenoho* and the *heho* to establish a setting of ancient times, just as is the complementary stylistic device to name the action as having taken place during an epoch of mankind's history when animals lived and talked like men.

The unembellished enumerations of genealogies, successions, and

[1] Cf. *Dahomey*, Vol. I, pp. 143–144, for a fuller account of this situation.

place names are of no concern to us in a discussion of the spoken arts, except where these are broken by digressions which tell of the trials and triumphs of ancestral generations, usually on a theme of hunger, or rivalry, or the encounter with superhuman antagonists. Such digressions call on traditional story-telling skills and may, in fact, be told at night when sessions to tell tales are held.

It must not be inferred that only the ancestral successes are kept alive. The Dahomean is no sentimentalist. Nor has he institution-alized "national" and clan disasters into a system of "oath-taking," such as the dread *ntam kese* of the Ghana Ashanti, which could be invoked only at a great ritual and economic price.[1] The family elders in Dahomey know and repeat the incidents of ad-versity and disaster. However, certain of these are recited only on fixed occasions, before a special group of senior male kindred. They may not be repeated casually, and never by members of other clans, without reprisals from the ancestors concerned.

What of the functioning role of traditional "history" in Daho-mean culture? This is best expressed in a proverb we heard cited at every turn: "History governs the life of Dahomey." *History* as here used is a word better translated as *tradition*, but we must bear in mind that in the Dahomean view it is tradition based on actual experience. Nor is it difficult to see how in a culture as complex as that of Dahomey, in a nonliterate tradition, the insti-tutionalized ancestral cult found in the myth-chronicles (the family *hwenoho*) the mechanism for validating economic and political claims.

That the myth-chronicles did, in fact, serve such ends is docu-mented, as tradition tells, by the action taken by the Aladahonu dynasty to exercise control over them. It is recounted that first in the reign of Agadja (1708–1729), and again in the reign of Glele (1858–1889), the king, as it was euphemistically phrased, "invited" all the clans to send to Abomey the clan elders of each who were the responsible repositories of family "history." This, we were told, was because "Agadja said that in Dahomey every man must know his origin." The king addressed these men, continues the account, telling them that since the memory of man was faulty, he had assembled the best singers of the land to put their "his-

[1] Cf. R. S. Rattray, *Religion and Art in Ashanti*, London, 1927, pp. 205–211.

tories" into song, so that their past would continue to be known by their descendants. Each was asked to recite the clan "history" to a singer who, with the help of the officials of the king, put it into words to be sung. "That is why we Dahomeans say, 'Agadja invented song.'"

Glele, it is told, reassembled these custodians of tradition for the same purpose. That the procedure of Agadja had to be repeated by Glele has its political explanations; yet despite both attempts to standardize clan tradition so as to bring it into line with dynastic specifications, there is no lack of suggestion that the individual clans have kept their own counsel about the unauthorized versions. If we compare narratives 95 and 96, of the "Historical Tales," each giving a traditional version of Hwegbadja's coming to the plateau of Abomey,[1] one as told by a son of Behanzin, the king who died in exile in Martinique, the other as given in Allada by a member of the de Souza family, the famous "Chacha," we see that a variant which disparages the exploits of the royal line was being told three centuries later.

The Verse sequences, then, serve principally as mnemonic devices to preserve certain traditional accounts. The use of an authorized version of clan-origin claims, as devised and put into song by minstrels provided by the king in the reigns of Agadja and Glele, an expedient of what may be called censorship, was built on a traditional mode of commemoration. Its most renowned practitioner was the king's professional minstrel-rhapsodist, whose title was *ahanjito*. He is known throughout the writings on Dahomey as the king's Remembrancer. It was his daily task to chant the names and praise-names of the king's predecessors, before the king's awakening. His rendition had to be letter-perfect, since an omission or an error would have cost him his life. And while less than perfection in the recitation of genealogies among those of lesser rank did not bring such severe penalty, names are everywhere and at all times symbols of importance in Dahomey—as important for the Dahomean as for those who would understand the play of imagery in Dahomean expression.

[1] Historical accounts indicate that the Aladahonu reached Abomey under Dako (*ca.* 1625) and consolidated their power there under Hwegbadja (1650–1680). Cf. *Dahomey*, Vol. I, pp. 13–16.

Whether the clan *hwenoho* is narrated, chanted, or sung, it is structurally patterned to include mythic elements of origin, and traditional events as remembered through time. These name and recount the experiences of successive ancestral generations, and give the prescriptions and interdictions that have grown out of these experiences, as attributed to a specific ancestor. We have noted that certain of the episodes are common to more than one clan. Our hypothesis is that this is to be explained by several factors: a relatively common historic experience, association with other clans through marriage, the incorporation of ingenious and appealing exploits attributed to another clan into a new mythological system, and above all the play of the imagination on the traditional thematic resources of Dahomean narrative.

What is of significance for us here is that these *hwenoho* are in the fullest sense living spoken documents, important psychologically as affording a sense of time depth in cultural experience. But they are even more important in day-to-day intertribal and intratribal economic, social and political dealings, where they are productive of a whole superstructure of claims and counter-claims, and constitute a record of infringements of prerogatives and rights that only await an opportune moment for redress.[1]

It should be clear that we are here raising no ghost of euhemerism when we ascribe to portions of these clan histories the status of Chronicles. As for the elaborations, we give the Dahomean evaluation, since, in context, what for them is an historical account is, ethnographically, history.

5   The *heho*

The subclasses of the tale, the *heho*, that we distinguish, and the numbers of the narratives of our collection in each subclass, may next be given:

1. Divination Stories (Nos. 22–40)
2. Hunter Stories (Nos. 41–59)

[1] In the newly emergent self-governing areas, such claims can be expected to come to the surface.

3. *Enfant Terrible* Stories
   a) Twins (*hohovi*) (Nos. 63–67)
   b) Orphans (*nochiovi*) (Nos. 68–70)
   c) Children-born-to-die (*abiku*) (Nos. 71–72)
   d) Abnormally born (*tohosu*) (Nos. 54, 73–74)
4. Yo Stories (Nos. 75–91)
5. Tales of Women: Love, Intrigue, and Betrayal (Nos. 103–109)
6. Explanatory and Moralizing Tales (Nos. 110–144)
7. Transformation Tales, and Other Miscellaneous Types (Nos. 145–155).

The tales falling within the category of *heho* contrast with the *hwenoho* in that they permit the teller greater latitude in interpretation, in joining incidents from several stories, and in elaborating a single incident to comment on a currently apt parallel. In short, manipulation is limited only by the ingenuity of the narrator. Yet here, too, tradition sets bounds within which certain themes may be juxtaposed or joined to describe stated or implicit values, and limits the roles of the characters that may be called on. For example, the literary gallery of protagonists, whether superhuman, human, or animal, comprises identifiable personality types that are culturally standardized, a fact of which the narrator is fully cognizant. The Dahomean thinks of them in just such terms, so that each becomes a symbol, in the strict sense of the word, a "vehicle for the conception of objects."[1] "This is about Hunter," the teller will begin; or he will say, "This is an orphan story"; or "This is another about Yo," naming the mythical character who stands for all that is gross in appetite, but differs from the sexually unsatisfied trickster-deity Legba. Again, he will say, "Hyena lives alone," and just by speaking that phrase he has set the stage for evil deeds, for his audience can be counted on to know the character of Hyena. They will wait and see if this is to be a narrative made up of well-known incidents, with their familiar resolutions, or if some sly allusion will be made in the telling to some current abuse; but they will not speculate about the kind of acts Hyena will perform.

[1] Susanne K. Langer, *Philosophy in a New Key*, Cambridge, Mass., 1942, pp. 60–61.

Each of the protagonists thus evokes a great number of motifs that can be called on as the narrator desires. Part of the suspense that the accomplished story-teller creates for his listeners comes from anticipating the situational dilemmas on which he will focus for the characters he has named, and the motifs from the repertory of traditional themes which he will use to resolve these dilemmas. The point we are making was sharpened in our thinking when we were doing some comparative work on the lore of the neighboring Yoruba, and asked our informant, a university student, "Do your stories have titles?" "Yes," he said, "they are at the end." For where motifs are known, and character symbols relatively fixed, a title at the opening of a tale would be a give-away of the plot, and would dissipate suspense. Consequently, the opening sets the stage by naming the characters, and the tasks before them; but the end, whether as moral or explanation, describes the tale.

A few illustrations will clarify the nature of character symbol in Dahomean story telling. If Hunter is not involved in a contest with a supernaturally endowed human being, whose powers exceed his own by cultural definition, he triumphs over giant, or sorcerer. His traditional helpers for such feats are the "little people" of the forest, the *azizã*. Orphan, again by cultural formula, must be avenged on those who have mistreated him. The dead mother is joined by the ancestors to make this resolution unequivocal. Yo, the glutton, may win or lose. The story will be humorous, and his punishment never crushing; his victories never ones that bring prestige. Hyena, as we have said, symbolizes sordid self-gratification; he will always play a shabby role.

Since personality traits are also ascribed to the gods, this factor of character symbol enters into myths (*hwenoho*) as well. Character symbol is, however, only one of several elements in the structure of a narrative, and the teller may focus on plot instead, as the occasion suggests. Thus, for example, in No. 133, "Testing Loyalties," or in No. 48, where the precept not to reveal the origin of an individual is violated, the stress is on plot. Of stories Nos. 128 to 131, the tellers said, "This tells how the youngest is more cunning"; but here we have, in reality, only a motif, an expression of the widespread West African belief that, since a child inherits his traits from his parents, and parents as they grow older gain in experience, the last-born must be the most astute. This motif, we find, weaves through many tales, where it may be the dominant incident and therefore the core of the plot structure, as in No. 128, or may be a complementary or subordinate theme, as in No. 124, and in Nos. 129, 130, or 131. This same theme, moreover, is used to outline the character of Legba, the youngest son of Mawu, the sky-deity; or Bade, the youngest child of Sogbo, the head of the Thunder pantheon; or of Aflekete, who holds a comparable place in the pantheon of the Sea. But in the instance of the gods, it seldom needs explicit stating, for it is accepted as a sort of least common denominator in their behavior, something a Dahomean audience takes for granted.

Moralizing or explanatory elements of the Just So Story type can also be used to give a tale its individual value. The Dahomean points to such tales as the prime educational instruments at his command to teach his children fact and meaning of the world about them. Yet any arbitrary classification of tales on this basis is similarly precluded, for certain of the explanatory tales of one teller—to say nothing of the same teller on two different occasions—will when told by another have morals appended to them, or the explanatory element may be omitted in the telling and a moralizing one added. This can be seen in the tales of divination, where the diviner, the *bokonon*, adds his own formula in praise of his profession, or to warn against ignoring the advice of a diviner, or of failing to consult him, or of deceiving him. Where two, or several stories are combined into one narrative, morals or explanations are omitted or added, at the will and the artistic bent of the narrator. But this one principle is always observed: all moralizing is omitted from tales told at funeral rites. This is both an important and interesting reflection of the philosophical view of death. For the Dahomeans hold that only a fool would moralize to the dead.

We can say, then, that the narrative form, whether as "history" or tale, responds to the demands of symbolic characterization, plot, motif, and function, but that no one of these can be validly presented as a unitary category, nor are any two of them mutually exclusive. Our classification has consequently been drawn both to avoid over-simplification, and to have the necessary flexibility for a sense of relationship and overlapping of the subgroupings in the major classes enumerated by the Dahomeans. In organizing our materials in terms of our classification, the problem of comparative and cross-cultural analysis had to be borne in mind. We have, therefore, used standardized titling wherever possible, to facilitate effective reference to published source materials from related cultures.

We begin our consideration of the *heho* subcategories with the *Divination Stories*. These enter into both of our two major classes, the *hwenoho* and the *heho*. There is the tradition that all stories have come from Fa, the personified system of divination. This is expressed in the saying (in No. 24), ". . . everything that happens on earth has happened in the sky before. So Fa and Legba can advise human beings, because they themselves have discovered how to meet every possible situation in the sky."

Any tale can therefore be called on to serve as a parable in the reading of the configuration of lines made by the diviner on his divining board, according to the way the palm kernels have fallen.[1] It is the mark of the experienced diviner that he uses the more uncommon tale, such as No. 39, and yet will as often intersperse his reading of Destiny with others of the simplicity of tales that are the favorites of children, like Nos. 35 and 36, until the symbols bearing on the consultant's problem are evoked.[2]

It will be apparent that the divination stories, as grouped here, include several that might well be classified as *hwenoho*. The first two stories in this group are clearly myths, the third is a myth-chronicle, the fourth, a myth, is a parable that touches on the rivalry between diviners and cult priests. No cult initiate, however, would acknowledge this tale to be "history," just as many other tales in the section on divination stories which mention the names of the deities, though imputing no slur on the foresight and perspicacity of the *vodun* as against the powers of Fa, are nevertheless

---

[1] Cf. *Dahomey*, Vol. II, pp. 201-222 for the Fa system of divination.

[2] For a specific case of how a tale was used in divination, cf. *Dahomey*, Vol. II, pp. 212-13. A detailed analysis of the use of tales and myths by the Dahomean diviners is to be found in the work by Maupoil cited above (n. 2, p. 11), where the interpretation of each combination of throws of the seeds is illustrated by relevant narratives. For the same pattern among the Yoruba, see W. R. Bascom, "The Relationship of Yoruba Folklore to Divining," *Journal of American Folklore*, Vol. 56, No. 220, 1943, pp. 127-131.

considered imaginative tales, what we might call legends, rather than traditional and "true." It cannot be said that diviners draw on any distinct group of tales, except in a very specialized sense, where, as in No. 133, the diviner is an individual in relation to those about him, or where , as in No. 32, the theme contrasts the fate of a man or animal who divined and sacrificed to the proper deity before embarking on an undertaking with that of the one who failed to do so.

There is symbolically an interesting tradition about the vast numbers of myths and tales that are told. It is said that each distinctive tale represents a year of human existence on earth, and only after all the stories that can be used for Fa divination are exhausted will the world come to an end. This fact of the number of tales the adult hears from the lips of his diviner gives us valuable insights into the manner in which the role of divination serves as a sensitive instrument for continuous intellectual stimulation and provides a dynamic factor in creative expression. For both during consultation, and later as the individual ponders the parables cited by the diviner, he focuses his mature attention and his imaginative faculties on the meaning of the tales and their relevance for his own needs. We see, therefore, that the practice of divination, which includes many popularly used, but lesser-known forms as well as the Fa system, gives currency, intellectual function, and continuity to lore.

In terms of values, it is also interesting to observe that the concept of Fa involves insights gained from experience—in the tradition cited, of experience gained in the world of the gods. Fate, therefore, is not fixed and immutable, before which the individual must remain passive, accepting favors and blows as inevitable. It rather sets problems which are amenable to solution, if proper procedures are followed. This value of achieving through knowledge, of manifest solutions in terms of experience, with the complementary motif of winning by astute manipulation, we will find as a leit-motif throughout Dahomean narrative.

Our next subgroup concerns *Hunter*, a leading protagonist. He is envisaged as having at his command much knowledge of magic and magic cures, because he has especially close rapport with the *azizā*, his spiritual helpers. Armed with magic that makes him invisible (as in Nos. 47 and 49), he can travel at will in the forests and brave encounters with the dangerous animals and supernatural spirits.

Narrators of Hunter tales show great skill in manipulating characters in a series of situations focusing on plot. In No. 47, one motif after another is found: animals changed into young girls, riches locked away that can be come by only with the knowledge of a password, woman worming the secret from Hunter, venturing to the forbidden hiding place, forgetting the password, and so on. The introduction of the forest-dwelling Yehwe monsters serves merely to heighten suspense, and makes the plot more complex. It plays no role in the development of the original theme, except to point the moral, by indirection, that if Hunter's wife had been imprudent enough to venture there, she would have been killed. The incident, however, of Hunter killing the young Yehwe mother and her offspring deserves special comment. To the Dahomean this conveys two things. First, it emphasizes Hunter's great powers, and consequently the magical protection he receives. The narrator, as a matter of fact, interrupted his story at this point to exclaim, "That man is strong, yes?" It keys the listeners to expect dramatic encounters, for nothing could be held improbable in the life of Hunter.

The second point it makes is the inexorable nature of a man's calling. Hunter's task is to kill animals, and this he does. This motif occurs frequently. We see it again in No. 48; Hunter kills lion and buffalo, and to serpent he says, "I must shoot you, too, because I eat only meat." So it is with the killing of the young Yehwe mother, and with the need to exact his kill (as in No. 55). The more common motif, nevertheless, is to spare the pregnant Yehwe (Nos. 65 and 67). In other words, the emotion of pity, of gratitude, is present, as well as the rationalization for its suppression.

But hunting for game is not the sole preoccupation of Hunter. In No. 47 he tells his wife, "A man does not only go hunting for animals. One goes hunting for all sorts of things," and in the final incident of the story he avenges the old serpent and is rewarded with rich gifts of money and wives and cloths. Or he gains for himself a new wife (Nos. 48, 49, 50, 53, 54 and 57), though indiscretion robs him of his reward.

Hunter also traditionally extends the frontiers of his world. He achieves this territorially by pushing the areas of settlement into uninhabited bush country, or by concluding pacts of friendship with the inhabitants of distant settlements. He brings back knowledge of herbs and cures and becomes a healer. He is a scout in time of war. In No. 92 we are told that Agasu, a royal totem, was a hunter. He and two companions were fugitives from Allada. "But it is Agasu who came to rank first, because he had the gun, and he found the road." Many of the clan myth-chronicles, in their recital of migrations, allude to the separation of one household unit or a core of units from the original group, under the leadership of a hunter kinsman who, as one who had ranged over distant and dangerous parts, commanded both practical knowledge of terrain and the supernatural skills essential to reach a place of safety and promise.

Sometimes the reason for this move is economic, as when the ancestral land has suffered successive seasons of drought. At times, and not uncommonly, the reasons are political, as when, at the accession of a new king or chief, the disaffected group finds it expedient to flee and seek refuge with another ruler, or carve a homestead deep in the uninhabited forest. Thus, as character-symbol, Hunter, adds to his own calling of braving dangers of the great animals of the bush and the supernatural powers that would thwart him, that of colonizer, of healer, of military scout and of culture hero.

Significantly, in terms of the value system of the Dahomeans, we know of no tale that tells of Hunter made captive while spying on a rival kingdom, or of being repudiated by his own followers for having promised them too much. Defeat for him can only be countenanced at the hands of other forces within the framework of the Dahomean world—such as the *tohosu*, the small ancestral creatures who are the most powerful of the group of beings with which the Enfant Terrible tales are concerned.

The *Enfant Terrible Stories* have to do with the acts of certain individual human beings who, because they are able to perform feats of superior physical strength, or possess superior knowledge of magic, engage in prodigious exploits, enriching themselves and their kinsmen, or impoverishing some enemy to avenge wrongs done them. These individuals obtain their powers from supernatural agents, to whom they are said to "belong" by virtue of the circumstances surrounding their birth.

Twins (*hohovi*) are under the protection of the forest spirits. This category not only includes any children of multiple birth, but the child born after twins who is known as the *dosu* and whose powers exceed those of twins themselves, and the child born with breech presentation, *agosu*, most feared of the twin category.

Orphan (*nochiovi*, literally "mother-dead-child") derives his strength from the ancestral dead, with his dead mother acting as his guardian. These stories have as their essential theme the Cinderella motif, or the broader Good Child and Bad motif, with transformations brought about through the agency of the dead. At times Orphan may also be a hunter; and often twins are hunters and orphans as well. In the latter instance, both the magic of the forest spirits and the powers of the dead are brought to bear on the fortunes of Orphan.

The *abiku*, "children-born-to-die," are the weakest of this group. The logic of their existence has no justification in terms of human ends. They do not come as punishment for transgression of ancestral interdictions, or of the moral code of the gods. To the Dahomean, their existence expresses the vastness of the Universe, of which the world of man is but a small part, so that motivations which concern other elements of the Universe may be involved, and human well-being frustrated. In this instance it is the distress caused human parents whose children are still-born or short-lived. The *abiku* tale, then, is not one of daring, but of suffering caused by this spirit who, for the pleasure of an adventure on earth among men, enters the womb of a human mother (under a pact with a forest spirit, also known as *abiku*), to return at a fixed time. But Hunter, who, as mentioned, may also be of the twin category, by his ability to perceive what can be known only to those who have supernaturally given "sight," or by the use of magic, may defeat the power of the *abiku* child, and cause it to assume normal form.

Strongest of this group in magic endowment are the *tohosu*, the abnormally born and aborted children. Among the things that distinguish a *tohosu* from a normal child are hermaphroditism and gross physical anomalies. Abnormal traits include macrocephaly, and the appearance of teeth and abundance of hair at birth. The *tohosu* are held able to speak at birth, and to turn at will into men of any age, in order to pit their strength against giants, sorcerers and kings. The power to do this is believed to emanate from an ancestral group of spirits belonging to the water.

The *tohosu* are traced back to the time of Akaba, in a myth-chronicle (No. 73). As in the tale of the coming of the *vodun* from Adja (No. 20) and the coming of the Fa system of divination in the reign of Agadja (No. 24), this focuses attention on the political struggles that marked succession within the Alada-honu dynasty, and, as in No. 24, the intractability of the autochthonous inhabitants. Unlike the *abiku*, whose behavior is not believed to flow from any human violations of the traditional moral code, the powers attributed to the *tohosu* can be viewed as a resolution of guilt; the price the Dahomean pays for ridding himself of the forces that he sees threatening his group.[1]

Abnormal children are exposed at the water's edge shortly after birth, and only exceptionally is a child born with minor abnormal characteristics, who comes to be known as a "partial *tohosu*," permitted to live. But once destroyed, these children are held to join the category of spirits known as "kings of the water" and are regarded as among the most powerful of ancestral forces. They are exacting, and not easily placated, but capable of demonstrating spectacular powers in battle on behalf of the kingdom.

Neither in the tales about *tohosu*, nor the myth-chronicles, where political incidents are given, nor in general discussion, have we heard scepticism expressed about the reality of such powers. On the contrary, the defeat of the native kingdom was in 1931 explained to us as the result of the anger of the *tohosu* toward a royal house that had failed for generations to undertake the costly and spiritually dangerous duty of reopening a training center for the ancestral cult. It is worth noting that in 1953 such a cult center had been established, and initiatory rites were under way.

In any contests between the abnormally born and twins, the

---

[1] In general terms, the institutionalized practice of putting to death the human agent that threatens the stability of a society is common to many West African peoples, as is also the subsequent deification of such beings, or their identification with already existing deities.

former prevail. By cultural definition, the dead are more powerful than the living, however the latter may be endowed. Thus though Orphan, ill-treated by the father's junior wife, goes through many trials, he overcomes them triumphantly with the help of the dead mother. A contest between Orphan and the abnormally born would, however, be unthinkable heterodoxy, since two branches of ancestral power should not be pitted one against the other.

As we have seen, the powers of the forest may be fused in an individual who as a hunter is also a twin. If, in addition, he is an orphan, he will enjoy the still more powerful guardianship of the dead mother. Ordinarily, however, the abnormally born are a group apart, joined in a tale with others only as antagonists. Again, since the forest beings cannot prevail against the ancestral water spirits and because the dead may not be in conflict with other dead, the *tohosu* contests bring about a change in focus from character emphasis to plot. The motifs of these stories are not the material for parables. The differences between *tohosu* protagonists point no special moral. Challenges that are made and accepted involve much more the excitement of contests than the tensions of conflict. In the interweaving of twins and abnormally born in situations of mutual challenge, incidents describing the most improbable feats are the thing of the moment.

When commenting on why the *Yo Stories* are so much enjoyed, our principal interpreter cited a proverb. "In Dahomey, we say, 'Humor governs the world well.' " And Yo is the protagonist of the humorous tale. This role was assigned to him by Dada Segbo, the king who, as we have seen, ruled in the beginning of time. Yo is a living essence, but invisible. "You never see him, but they say it's an animal." He has magic charms to change himself or others into animal or insect form. In No. 87 he changes himself into a spider,[1] and in No. 91 he tosses a child into the air to punish him and turns him into a butterfly.

Yo symbolizes the impulsive, gross, and gluttonous being who undertakes all ventures because he is not one to stop and reflect. The result, as phrased in No. 79, is that "Yo spoiled many things

---

[1] Interesting in this transformation is the parallel to Anansi (Spider), the trickster of the Akan, who also earns the right to give his name to stories; *i.e. Anansesem.*

discovered by our forefathers." But even when he does succeed in accomplishing what had seemed impossible, the social usefulness of his feat is questionable, as in No. 75, where it is said, "Yo has no family, so he is no man to send for a wife," especially since the woman he brings back to Dada Segbo with the expenditure of one cowrie is a woman who ". . . knows only to kill." Nonetheless, he is not without a sense of guilt, for when, as in No. 80, they accuse Lizard of a theft he did not commit, and Lizard, who cannot deny the accusation because Yo had cut out his tongue, is flogged, Yo is uneasy. He says, "I am going away from here. Why does he look at me so?"

But when it is a matter of getting things to eat, all means are fair. Neither the food in the compound of the Thunder god, nor even that which belongs to Death, is overlooked. It is of course a time of famine when incidents of this kind take place, a season of no rains, as the tales tell. The walls in the village of Hevioso, the god of Thunder, that Yo assaults, are made of coveted foods and, as in No. 84, the children instead of rolling oranges in play, roll cakes. Of Nochiovi, in No. 85, Yo asks, "Where do you always find food? During a famine, when even chiefs have nothing to eat, you people eat." And Orphan replies, ". . . I who have no father or mother. Mawu shows me a way."

Yet though a creature of greed and gluttony, Yo is not to be compared to Hyena. Yo is laughed at, but he is not despised. The theme of his tales is insatiable appetite, but running parallel to it, as we have seen, is the theme of hunger anxiety, one that strikes a direct response in the Dahomean listener. For here, as elsewhere in aboriginal West Africa, the season of food scarcity was never far away, and bad harvests within the memory of children. When there is great hunger, Yo's actions are anticipated. The necessary counter-measures call for the astuteness of Goat, as in Nos. 89 and 90. The structure of the Yo tales does not differ from any of the other subgroupings of *hebo* stories. The very mention of Yo, however, sets the key for a tale of humorous adventure.

When we examine the *Tales of Women*, in our next subcategory, we find that, like the explanatory and moralizing tales which follow in our classification, they present themes which strike deep at the conflicts and the search for fulfillment in human living. Certain of their motifs emphasize symbolic characterization, in that the protagonist dominates the action in terms of a culturally defined role. But in the tales which have human protagonists without supernatural endowment, the stress is on plot and moral. For example, one theme concerns revealing a secret, suggestive of the Lohengrin motif. This may be by intentional treachery, through indiscretion, or in anger, as where an individual is taunted about his origin or descent. Another is that of friendship. The best or "first" friend plays an institutionalized role in Dahomean life, with important ceremonial duties on the death of the friend, and at all succeeding ancestral rites where he is singled out for special offerings.[1] The tales that tell of the loyalty of the best friend bring great emotional satisfaction. This does not prevent the theme of hypocracy, intrigue and betrayal in friendship from entering frequently, even in those friendships that had been sealed by a compact under oath, as in Nos. 44 and 45.

Still another common theme has to do with jealousy, a matter of considerable theoretical significance, as we shall see in our discusson of myth.[2] Fraternal rivalry, jealousy between parent and child, and jealousy between co-wives are recurrent motifs. This is seen in such myth-chronicles of the *Exploits of the Aladahonu Dynasty* (as Nos. 93 and 94), where the wives of the King of Adja tax the mother of Adjahuto with having conceived by a leopard; or in No. 20, where Agadja's wives quarrel about favors to Tegbesu. It occurs in many tales where a woman conspires against the child of a co-wife (as in 107), imputes her good name (in No. 92), or challenges her right to keep her identity secret (Nos. 48 and 49). But if there is jealousy between co-wives, there is also cooperation. Thus, in No. 106, we find them joining in a scheme to discipline a boastful common husband by ridicule; and while some wives are enemies, there are others, as in No. 107, who are on the side of a younger wife who is being victimized.

A very popular theme touches on the faithlessness of women. They betray their husbands' secrets and are not loath to move

---

[1] Cf. *Dahomey*, various items under "Best Friend" in Index; and also M. J. Herskovits, "The Best Friend in Dahomey," in *Negro Anthology* (Nancy Cunard, ed.) London, 1934, pp. 627–632.

[2] See below, pp. 85 ff.

on to a more advantageous mating. A woman joins her husband's household only to fulfill some design of her own patrilineal family, usually to put the husband to death in revenge for something he had done against a member of her group. The latter theme incorporates motifs of the William Tell and the Flight Up the Tree types. But there is also the love theme, telling of women so passionately devoted that the gods and Death are moved to pity (Nos. 103 and 104). In No. 60 we are also told of faithful wives who repel the advances of other men, even those of royal blood. And then, returning to the theme of women who reveal secrets, we find No. 65, where the man brings home an unknown woman who turns out to be evil, with its moral that a woman whose relatives a man does not know should not be told secrets. This is matched by No. 53, the Chosen Suitor theme, in which a young woman who rejects all those who woo her is won by an animal disguised as a man, with its moral of punishment for one who flouts family wishes.

Finally, uniting character types and situation, often as comedies of manners, are the *Explanatory and Moralizing Tales*, usually with anthropomorphized birds and animals as their characters. They may incorporate in their narrative men (No. 110) and gods as well. Included in this group is a very substantial number of stories wherein the point rests on extravagant farce (Nos. 111, 112, 131, 140, 141), usually on a theme of audacious flaunting of prohibitions. In all these, the everyday world is described and explained, and the trials and insights of the characters are those of the human beings who inhabit it. But in the exuberance of the farce there is a conscious relish for verbalizing inhibitions and dramatizing the forbidden, a point, as we shall see, that is supremely exemplified in the role and actions of Legba, the trickster-deity.

6 The narrative form

Myth (*hwenoho*). The long stories about Legba are particularly useful for a closer analysis of narrative. But before we turn to the stories, we must give attention to the role Legba plays in

Dahomean life. As had been shown,[1] he is a figure of the greatest importance both in the generalized form in which he participates in the worship of the *vodun* pantheons, and more particularly as guardian of entrances to villages, to markets, to shrines, compounds, and houses, until he is brought into the closest association of all—with a man's personal destiny (his Fa). It has been conjectured that the Christian missions, by identifying Legba with the Devil, have helped to make him an especially popular figure of Dahomean lore. Intensive study of the Dahomean world-view, however, leads us to conclude that this identification has served rather to emphasize his popularity than to initiate a new attitude toward him.

We have discussed above the Dahomean use of certain protagonists as symbols of particular personality types, and thus as cues to anticipated behavior. In these terms Legba, the arch individualist, may be thought of as the personification of the being who loves mischief, knows no inhibitions, recognizes no taboos, dares to challenge injustices, even on the part of the Creator, and to expose them. He is a moralist only when it suits his whim. His favors can be had at a price, but only if he is disposed to grant them. Yet, as we shall see when we examine the narratives in which he figures, in his ill-favored, often misshapen manifestation, he has a weakness for man as against the *vodun*.

For once he has extracted what satisfaction he can out of some scheme of mischief he has devised, he devotes himself to finding solutions for reestablishing equilibrium, as illustrated in Nos. 4 and 10.

In the broader world-view of the Dahomeans, he is the personification of philosophical accident, of the "way out," in a world ruled by destiny. Here, however, we are analyzing his role as protagonist of a group of myths, and seeing how the narrators describe and develop his character according to their own implicit values and the conventions of their craft.

The opening story of our collection tells us Legba is the seventh and youngest child of Mawu, the Creator. ". . . As you are spoiled, and have never known punishment," Mawu tells him, "I cannot turn you over to your brothers." There is no kingdom left

[1] Cf. *Dahomey*, "Index," *s.v.* "Legba"; especially Vol. II, pp. 222–230.

to assign to him, and he cannot be made subject to such elements as Earth, Sky, Sea, Atmosphere, the Forests and their wild life, or Energy ("force"). He is to know no restraints. "Your work shall be to visit all the kingdoms ruled over by your brothers, and to give me an account of what happens." Legba thus becomes what is described as Mawu's "linguist," the counterpart of the spokesman of the West African chief. He is the interpreter for *vodun* and men before Mawu, for he alone commands all known tongues.

From the point of view of style, we see with what economy Legba's character and his potential role in the Universe have been sketched. An undisciplined being is made intermediary between men and gods, and between gods and the Creator. The questions arise: Will he act irresponsibly, and create incessant turmoil? Can he exercise moral judgment? Does he know the emotion of pity?

Tale No. 4 carries the denotation of the character of Legba a step further. It tells us how, in the feud between Hevioso and their eldest brother Sagbata, Legba instigated the scheme to withhold rain from the earth, but how, on visiting the earth, and presumably seeing what suffering this has caused, he decides to put an end to the drought. "All this time Mawu was kept in ignorance of the quarrel between the brothers, Sagbata and Hevioso, and to this day knowledge of their quarrel has been withheld from her." As a result of Legba's manoeuvres, however, Mawu finally decrees that the fall of rain should be regulated from the earth, and Legba sees his brothers reconciled, "so that today man lives without fear of another such severe drought. . . ."

Story No. 9 shows us Legba's relation to man. It opens on the theme of a contest among the *vodun*, the children of Mawu, to determine who is to become their chief. This theme we come on in many tales, as when the birds or animals name the head of their group—tales in which the smallest and weakest and, from this point of view, the least likely candidate prevails because he knows how to use his wits. And so in this tale: "Long ago, Legba was the last of the gods," is the opening. But Legba wins.

A second theme introduces Legba, who has much knowledge, as maker of magic charms. "He was the first to make them." He fashions a serpent, gives it life and, as is characteristic in the operation of magic, commands it to do specific things—in this in-

stance, to "bite the sellers and the buyers" on the way to market.
Once they have been bitten, Legba offers his victims a cure and,
with his gifts from them, buys for himself food and drink. We infer
that he engages in the practice of magic because of need. It is the
theme of scarcity, of hunger, implied rather than stated. And, in
point of fact, to this day certain members of the official hierarchy
of the cult centers, both for the gods and the ancestors, would not
eat, or would eat less well, if they did not engage in divining,
healing, and the practice of magic, in addition to their cult duties.

Now comes Awe, a man who has the curiosity as well as the
courage to ask Legba, as he points to the serpent, "What is that
which bites people?" Legba answers "It is magic," and makes it for
him. And the two join in making magic to injure and magic to cure,
until "magic charms spread everywhere." A fourth theme brings
Mawu into the narrative again. She is angry at the spread of magic,
and punishes Legba by making him invisible. He can no longer go
about on earth in human form. "Now Legba is forever a *vodun*.
Awe is a man." So Awe becomes chief of magic. "Awe went
everywhere and asked who wanted to make charms [*gbo*]. Then
he gave them *gbo* and disappeared."

After the fourth point has been enunciated, it is made clear that
magic was given also to sorcerers, "those who do evil." To express
more explicitly the fact that Awe was engaged in anti-social acts,
as well as beneficial ones, we find the observation that he gave
"charms to pregnant women that the child should not come," and
". . . they had to give him many things before he was satisfied.
Then only would he give medicine. . . ." Awe became so renowned that kings came to him; but he also did harm to little
children. Here again we see the use of antithesis, whereby the skill
that brought rulers to patronize him is contrasted with the petti-
ness that caused him to deform children. In sum, magic spread,
and both good and evil medicines were thus brought to mankind.

Awe, however, is not content with amassing wealth. The same
curiosity that gave him the courage to question Legba sends him
on a new quest. "I am going to see what is Nature. Now there is
enough magic." The task he sets himself is to measure the length
of day and night. He discovers that they are equal. Presumably he

continued his experimentation, though this is implied rather than stated explicitly. His next venture is to reach the sky.

Mawu says to him, "What are you looking for here?"

Awe replies, "My knowledge is great. I now seek to measure my knowledge with that of Mawu."

Mawu and Awe thereupon engage in a contest of skills. The basic theme here is that no one but Mawu can create life.

Mawu tells him, "Your knowledge is not enough."

But the outcome of this contest appears inconclusive, for the final theme of the myth tells of Awe returning to earth, with Death following him, on Mawu's orders. Awe attacks Death, and only when Mawu threatens to take fire from man is a truce between Death and Awe established. " 'If you, Awe, attack Death, then whoever had prepared his food will find that food raw again.' . . . So Awe let Death go, in order that, among men, one could put food to cook, and it would cook quickly, and people could eat." The account ends with the cryptic statement, "Awe and Death are the two friends of the world."

Awe, then, is Legba's surrogate among men. He showed the curiosity to find out things and the courage to test his findings, to challenge the Creator and to attack Death. As a kind of culture-hero, he is neither on the side of good nor of evil, but experiments with both. His aim is not power for its own sake, but knowledge and more knowledge. Even so, he finally renounces a possible victory over Death in order to benefit mankind. The decision, however, which in effect is one that has determined the role and powers of man in relation to the Creator, suggests no simple moral of teaching man his place in the Universe.

The core of the next myth (No. 10) is an explanation of the role of Legba among gods and men; more particularly, it tells why his costume and the choreography of his ritual dancing are what they are.[1] It should be noted that the Legba dancers wear wide palm-fringe tunics, which reach from waist to mid-thigh, over

[1] This tale was told us by a French-speaking Dahomean, and is to be compared in terms of its style with the one we have just discussed, which was recounted in Fõn, by a cult-head, and translated into French for us with short pauses in the telling.

tight pantalettes. Hidden inside the tunic, and brought out at certain points in the dance is a realistically carved penis, anywhere from ten to eighteen inches in length, made of dark polished wood. The strands of the tunic in which it is hidden are said to represent the pubic hair. At a dance, a cult-member possessed by Legba may approach any woman among the bystanders and, if the woman does not run away, will pantomime the act of coitus with her. We have seen a quite young girl, as Legba, impersonating him expertly in this dance which leaves little to the imagination. The choreography was taught her by senior Legba cult members during her initiation.

The myth is set at "the beginning of time." The *vodun*, Minona, Aovi, and Legba, form a funeral band to earn cowries, the currency of the day. Metonofi, who among other identifications is sometimes equated with the Creator and sometimes with Death, is king of the land. In this tale, as we shall see, two independent themes are joined. It is interesting to observe with what economy the initial statement sketches for us the three principal characters, and sets the stage for the action to follow.

The theme of the impotence of the King of Adja is introduced immediately after the opening. From the myth-chronicles (Nos. 92, 93) we learn that because of the impotence of this king, the co-wives of Adjahuto's mother taunted him with being fathered by a leopard. This is given as the reason for Adjahuto's flight to Allada, and the founding of the Aladahonu dynasty. Fa, Destiny, as "Legba's master," and Legba are present in response to the search for remedies to restore the king's potency. Legba, in his familiar role of mischief-maker, distributes the wrong powders, so that the virile become impotent.

But here the development of this motif is checked. The audience is left in suspense. Instead, the thread of the burial band is picked up. Legba and his siblings sit down at the crossroads to divide their gains. There is wrangling, and three women, innocent passers-by, are in turn consulted. When they offer unacceptable solutions, they are killed, and Legba has intercourse with the corpse of each. Again Legba is in character. He does what no one else may do.

Three is a symbolic number. Having, as one of a group of three, witnessed and participated in three outrages, Legba decides to re-

solve the dispute by indirection, after the Dahomean pattern. He
goes off into the bush, turns a wooden dog, which he pulls out of
Fa's bag of magic, into a living one, and instructs him in a solution,
having him say, "In my group, when three divide something, and
one is left over, it is for the ancestors."

The dog is blessed by the three for this resolution of their dilemma. Na [1] says, "You will lead all the *vodun* that I command.
You will always be in the lead." Legba tells him that he will lead
all men.

The narrative now returns to the impotent men of Adja. They
have brought charges before the king against Legba, who has in
the meantime fled to "the house of Ayo, his mother-in-law." This
is to say, he has taken refuge in the Yoruba kingdom of Oyo. And
here he violates another important taboo, for during the absence
of her husband, he lies with his mother-in-law. He is arrested, and
is to be tried before the king. Three charges are lodged against
him. The first has to do with the killing of the three women, but
Legba demonstrates that he served as peacemaker by bringing the
wooden dog to life, in order, as he says, to "save other deaths." As
a result, Metonofi makes Legba guardian of men and women, and
of all the gods. "So Legba came into the houses."

The next episode deals with the second complaint, that of lying
with his mother-in-law. Legba defends himself against this charge
by asserting he lay where his wife customarily lay beside him.
"Metonofi said, since he had already made Legba guardian of all, he
could not revoke this. But because Legba always created scandals,
he was not to live in houses, but his place would always be in front
of the house." This, then, explains why the shrines sacred to Legba
are always found at the entrance to a village compound, a house,
a shrine, but never inside.

After two days, the third complaint is brought before the king
for judgment. Legba is now charged with making all the men of
the kingdom impotent. He is ordered to produce the powder he
had given these men. But when he returns with his evidence, he has
made the white powder, which gave potency, red by mixing it with
the blood of a pigeon; and has changed the color of the red powder,
which had caused them to be impotent, by adding white clay to it.

[1] That is, Minona.

When the men testify they were given the red powder, Legba is told to swallow a dose, and to return in two days to demonstrate its effect on him.

The next scene, two days later, takes us again to the compound of the king. A small shelter has been built in the courtyard, and in it is the king's daughter, wife of the King of Adja. "The men were told to enter one by one . . ." None is successful. ". . . But there were some who said it was not good to try it this way. With everyone waiting anxiously, they could not be expected to accomplish what was desired of them."

Legba mocks the waiting multitude: "He, Legba, would have intercourse with the king's daughter in public, if they wished it."

Then follows the description of Legba's entrance into the small house, to the sound of the drums he had made and caused to be played. He has immediate success. "There was blood all over the house." He emerges naked, penis erect, ". . . and when he reached anyone, he went through the motions he had made when he was with the girl." He does all this to the sound of his drums; and this, it will be observed, is his ritual dance. Among the rewards Metonofi confers upon him is the right ". . . to sleep with any woman he chooses, without distinction." He is also made the intermediary "between this world and the next."

The final episode appends a happy ending. The men are given the "good powder," and their potency is restored. Legba receives a new name, and gives a new name to the king's daughter. The explanatory ending is in a sense extraneous. It is a restatement of the relation between Legba and the dog, the animal sacred to him, whose role has been made clear in the body of the myth.

The theme of Legba's sexuality is continued in No. 11. While Legba is away, Fa takes his wife, who is still a virgin. In a few phrases the passage of time and much promiscuity by the wife is implied. "One day Legba asked his wife, 'Why do you behave so badly?' and, Nunde replied, 'Your penis is not enough for me. That is the reason I look everywhere.'" The action now shifts. All the people of the country are assembled, and Legba is lying with his wife before them. Drums are beaten and Legba sings to the assembled countrymen, explaining that he has done what he did in order to shame his wife. "Fa is my friend," he says, "and we are gods of the same quarter. . . ." This, it may be noted, is an interesting minor detail that creates a sense of human identification with Legba's grievance, for the motif brought out is the treachery of a friend and a neighbor. The result is that Legba orders Fa never to leave his own house. ". . . And we, the others, will walk about everywhere. If we find something good, we will share it with you." So Fa remains at home, but as a precaution Legba takes his wife with him wherever he goes. And Legba says, "If I find a woman, I will lie with her, no matter whose she may be."

There are two explanatory endings to this myth. "It is because of this that to this day, when someone starts the drum for Legba, he comes and dances joyously. He does all he wishes. . . . It is also because of this that Legba comes first, before Fa."

No. 22 gives yet another reason for Legba's role and behavior in the world of men. We are introduced to Gbadu, who is referred to as the power behind Fa, and as Fa himself; also as a child of Mawu, the Creator, born after the twins of the Sea pantheon. Hermaphroditic, Gbadu in this tale figures as a woman. She lives in a palm tree in the sky, and Legba ministers to her. In time, she has a family of her own of two daughters, only one of whom is named, and six sons.

Gbadu is troubled because she has no defined task, and Legba offers to teach her "the alphabet of Mawu" that he alone knows. Later he makes representations to Mawu that Gbadu should be sent among men, because ". . . there was a great war on earth, a great war in the sea, and a great war in the sky. . . . The water of the sea did not know its place; and the rain did not know how to fall. This was because all those who had been given kingdoms did not understand the language of their parents." Mawu, however, refuses to allow Gbadu to live on earth, but orders that ". . . an understanding of my language be given some men on earth. In that way men will know the future, and will know how to behave."

Then comes an explanation of the transfer to Gbadu of the keys to the future, the Fa system of divination, and of the manner of divining. This is followed by a description of the role of the children of Gbadu, who are here conceived as the teachers of the cult of Fa on earth. "Little by little people began to understand the new system, and since Aovi[1] is very severe, the cult came to be respected."

Thus far the stress is on theology, and the narrative an exposition of origins and functions, without any stylistic attempt at dramatic treatment. But at this point what appears to be an independent tale is woven into the story, and we again have a familiar Legba theme. The opening motif is, "Meanwhile, when Legba was in the sky, he slept with Gbadu, and when he came to earth he did the same with Minona." Gbadu, it will be recalled, is Legba's sister, while Minona is her daughter. That this became a well-established practice with them is indicated by the brief statement, "That continued so." As the next incident, we have the visit of Legba and Gbadu to the cult of Fa on earth. "As was their habit, they shared the sleeping-mat together, but late that night he rose stealthily, disguised himself, and went to Minona." Gbadu discovers this, and brings charges against Legba before Mawu.

Accused of having sex relations with mother and daughter, he denies this. "Mawu ordered him to undress. As he stood naked, Mawu saw how his penis was erect." Since he had lied to Mawu, and deceived his sister, Mawu orders that he never be appeased. Here an interesting passage gives us another insight into the character of Legba. "To show his indifference to this punishment, Legba at once began to play with Gbadu"—inadmissible behavior before a parent—and, when reproached, pointed out that, since his organ was always to remain erect, Mawu herself had decreed such conduct for him. The ending is explanatory: "That is why when Legba dances it is like this, and he tries to take any woman who is at hand."

It is perhaps the trait of not being cowed by those in power, more than any other, that endears Legba to the Dahomean, whose political patterns are so firmly founded on the exercise of authority and obedience to its decrees. In his defiance, he does not ask for pity. He will not openly show the hurt of punishment. He is no Job to cry out in agony. He turns the perversities of his own nature into a reproach against Mawu herself.

We have here the key to the absence of the tragic theme in

[1] Aovi is the personification of mishap.

Dahomean narrative. The Dahomean world-view dictates the mask of insensitiveness in the face of trials. To reveal one's suffering to a hostile force, superhuman or human, is to invite more recrimination. For example, to turn to the everyday world, parents do not attend any of the funeral rites for their children. The proverb says, "The young should be alive to bury the old." Mother and father, therefore, do not mourn; they show no open grief. To die young is to die by some mischievous or evil will. Their grief would only encourage a repetition of another untimely death. It follows, then, from beliefs such as these that the tragic theme cannot be articulated. We have seen grief and despair expressed in the dance. And because songs are danced to, the words to songs come as close to phrasing tragic overtones as we have encountered in Dahomey. But, as far as our experience goes, we have never heard such songs introduced into narrative.

Another Legba myth in our collection, No. 12, though it combines several well known motifs, contrives in its initial lines to add depth to the characterization of Legba. In the opening statement, we learn that Legba, presumably in the beginning of time, was a man of good will. His deeds were good, but it was Mawu who received the recognition for all the good that was done. When, acting under instructions from Mawu, Legba did men harm, and the people cried out to Mawu, Mawu told them, "It was Legba who did that." Legba protests against this to Mawu, but is told that ". . . in a country it be necessary for the master to be known as good."

This same implicit logic, interestingly enough, governed the practice of the Dahomean kings, whose judiciary officials passed heavy sentences on those brought before them, so that on appeal, the royal master could prove himself merciful by reducing the penalty.

Since Legba will not accept injustice without protest, not even injustice at the hands of his parent, the Creator, he uses his wits to humiliate Mawu before the multitude. And here again, we have the explanatory ending, telling how Mawu, in her chagrin, leaves the earth.

Two points are worth keeping in mind in relation to the thematic materials of the Legba cycle of myths. The first has to do with the complexity of Legba's character; the second with the absence of the motif of self-pity. In these stories we see the experience of deprivation and humiliation transmuted into affirmation on the theme of "The last shall be first." In our discussion of No. 22, we have pointed out the cultural explanation for the absence of self-pity and, in its most intensive form, of the tragic theme. Legba, that is, alone of all the children of Mawu, has no domain of his own. He is a wanderer from one kingdom of the gods to another, and from these to the world of men, and to the kingdom of Death. He is deformed and ill-favored. Yet by his astuteness, imagination, and wit, he has succeeded in creating for himself a role of the most universally worshipped; of the first to be propitiated; of the one who can take all women. The satisfactions his tales bring the Dahomean are self-evident; they arise out of identifications that transcend Dahomey.

Tale (*heho*). Let us now turn to some examples of secular narrative. We first consider No. 103, which introduces us to a *genre*, the love story, that deserves better representation in African collections. We call attention to it here not only because it is technically flawless, and, as a favorite of the Dahomeans, is often heard, but particularly because in a culture where the value of conformity is so explicitly recognized, this love story not only dares overlook disobedience, but instead rewards it.

The introductory statement sketches the eight long years of seclusion in the cult center that, beginning with their twentieth year, was the rule for novitiates in earlier days. The conventional unities are observed. The place is the cult-house; the action occurs during one day; the theme is love and the courage to defy the *vodun* and Death in its name, until both are moved to pity. The protagonist of the story, a young woman, has tempted a novitiate to violate the law of the *vodun*. We see the young man lying dead after the consummation of the sexual act. When the priest enters and orders the girl bound, she says, "Do not trouble to bind me. I am here." She remains seated beside her dead lover, and busies herself brushing away the flies.

The next incident is one we find in many contexts. As in No. 133, the theme is the moral challenge to find a loyalty that is willing to make the supreme sacrifice. The fellow cult-members of the dead young man, who would be expected to have the hardihood to face the test, recoil when they approach the heat of the flames. So does the mother who bore him: "If I do not die, I shall bear another son." So do his father, his brother, his best friend.

Now it is the turn of the young woman who caused his death. We see suspense built up. Oil is poured on the fire, as with un-hurried care the girl prepares herself to enter the flames. The arti-cles for a journey, which are those also used in burial rites—pipe, tobacco, chewing stick for cleaning the teeth, for herself and her lover—are collected by her, as she dances around the great fire, singing her affirmation of love. If she did not join her lover on the blazing pyre, she could not live with her own soul.

The scene of rejoicing when the two emerge alive from the flames, and the swelling of the multitude as the decree is pro-nounced to reduce the initiatory period, is theatre of the first order. With the repetition that as a result of the disobedience of the no-vitiate Hunjo, the period of seclusion, was shortened, there is a keying down of the dramatic intensity of the closing scene. The explanation of the character and powers of Metonofi ends this tale on a note that again mirrors one of the deepest-set values in Daho-mean culture, the conviction that no rule is so rigid that a way to adapt it to the exigencies of life cannot be found.

No. 131 is a moralizing tale. Here again we see stressed the value that unquestioning obedience, even to a father, is not an end to be blindly pursued. A stylistic convention, observed in this story, is that when an unsavory role is to be played, it is given to a pro-tagonist from another land, seldom one's own countryman—a not uncommon device in other societies. In this story a Mahi violates, and instructs his sons to violate, three of the strongest social pro-hibitions. The kind of death he will have, the point of the tale, is of great importance. For the place of a man in the ancestral world depends on the manner of his send-off from the world of the liv-ing. Above all, he must be provided with the things that give status in the world of the living, in order to establish his position in the land of the dead.

The kingdom of the dead is not envisaged as a place of rewards and punishments. It is where one joins the clan ancestors and where, as the most recently come and thus the youngest, one's place is the lowliest in this austere company. The work to be done is the tireless, inflexibly just guardianship of the existing and future generations of the family.

The evil deaths of this Mahi, three in number, are retribution for the three taboos he had violated. His oldest son tells what these deaths were: "First he died the soul's death. The second time he died a fiery death. The third time he died a watery death." To convey something of the directness of the language, we give the deaths he died in Fōn: "*Eku seku, eku zoku, eku toku.*" The story ends with the question: "Do you not agree that he died three deaths, for the three wrongs he did?"

No. 123 is an animal tale of the Uncle Remus type. We find here the same motifs as in the tales of human beings; in this case, the principal theme is the challenge of the youngest child. In terms of our analysis of Dahomean narrative, our interest in this tale lies chiefly in the manner of its telling, which dictates much of its structure. Interpolations, such as the exclamation of the horse Samezo, who has been ridden great distances without rest in order to prove his suitability for escape, represent for the Dahomean listener high artistry. He gasped the boy's name, we are told, ". . . but he did not die," as had the other two horses, from lesser exertion. This patterned elegance in story-telling is likewise seen in the next interpolation, a humorous one, which also introduces a note of suspense, as the explanation is given of the three gestures monkeys make when they see a human being: "Do I resemble your father? . . . Do I resemble your mother? . . . Do I resemble you?" It is not difficult to visualize the skilled narrator's treatment of this episode, and the laughter it calls forth.

Suspense is built up at the height of the contest between Mama Lolwè and Monkey, when Monkey hits on a plan to overcome his adversary. Here a series of consequences flow from his irritation with the inadequacy of his helpers. The wasp is clasped so tightly about his middle that his waist became thin, "just as he is today." Vulture earns blacksmith Monkey's displeasure, and is punished by being touched with a hot iron on the head, thus remaining forever bald. In anger Monkey pulls Goat's testicles, and lengthens them unalterably for all generations. He takes away Bat's two hind legs, giving Bat his present form.

In the incidents of forging the hoe and punishing assistants for ineptitude, we have elements obviously brought in from other tales, elements that can be omitted without altering the flow of action or the point of the story. But their inclusion shows the virtuosity of the accomplished story-teller, who pulls out incidents from his thematic repertory and interweaves them for purposes of comic relief, or suspense, with the basic motifs that carry his tale forward. The motif of tenderness toward his son, who speaks the invocation to urge on the bellows, changes for an instant the action of murderous pursuit and of punishments for failure in a critical situation. With the explanatory note on which the tale ends ("That is why Monkey has red buttocks, a large chest, and a flat belly") we are back to one of the conventional resolutions.

Stylistic Devices. We have had occasion, in the preceding pages, to comment on the economy of detail which marks the tales we have analyzed. It is immediately apparent in the unadorned directness with which (as in No. 117) the characters are announced: "There is a bird that steals chicks. And there is a hen." The stage is set, without further explanation, for the action involving hawk and chicken.

This principle of economy characterizes the developmental action as well. Thus in No. 84 Yo attempts to reach the country of Hevioso in the sky by concealing himself in a bundle which he asks Vulture (Aklasu), the messenger of the gods, to take to his (Yo's) sister in Hevioso's country. A strong wind causes Vulture to drop the bundle, and the following colloquy ensues:

Yo asked him, "Did you give the bundle to my sister?"

"I'm sorry, but the wind was too strong. The bundle was blown away while I was flying."

Yo said, "That's nothing. You are my friend, and I believe you. Tomorrow I will give you another bundle."

Aklasu said to him, "Good. But tell me, Yo, why are you so bruised everywhere?" Yo said, "I had a quarrel with a friend."

Here the whole picture of trickery and a plan gone wrong are laid out before us, but Vulture's question is the only place in the entire tale where the fact that in the fall Yo was injured is made explicit.

A further instance of economy in detail is found in No. 87,

where Yo bargains with Death, using Pig as his dupe. In the initial
episode, we are told specifically how, when Death came to the
house to strike Yo dead, Pig was made to receive the blow, and
thus was killed. The trick is repeated with Antelope, Rabbit's friend.
But it is made known to us by indirection. Yo goes to his field for
yams. "On his way he saw Antelope. He said the same thing to
her" that he had said to Pig. Rabbit now seeks out Antelope at
home, but does not find her. Her children tell him she is at Yo's
house. "So Rabbit went there, and asked for Antelope. Yo said she
was not there, but as he left, he saw Antelope's head. Yo had
thrown it on the ground." We now know the fate of Antelope. Or,
again (No. 69), with the story almost completed, a new character,
a hunter, is introduced. His only function is to witness and thus
make known the death of one of the principal characters, an incident essential to the point of the story.

Economy in narration does not, however, preclude exposition
when this is felt necessary. In No. 6 the action begins with the
second paragraph, but the opening statements serve to provide the
necessary cosmogonic setting for what follows: "There are some
who say the world is a machine. Somebody made it, but if there
was one Mawu or many, history does not tell us. . . ." On the
other hand, an element is not introduced before it is needed, as in
the instance of the hunter just cited. The point of No. 109, which
concerns the importance of guessing the name of a particular style
of hairdress, does not enter until the contest situation is firmly
established and the plot to win is delineated. "Now, this man tied
his hair like that to earn money. . . . It was also agreed that if
someone learned the name of this tying, the man would be killed."
Again (in No. 107) the name of one of the characters is given only
after the outline of the action is well understood, and at the point
where it is needed to carry on the development that leads to the
denouement.

Style and Linguistic Structure. The principal stylistic distinction
of narrative inheres in the structure of the language itself, and
focuses particularly on the verb. Action expressed in our speech
by one verb, in Fõn calls for multiple verbs, each of which describes a segment of what we conceive of as a single act. That is,
for "bring me," the Dahomean says, "take come give me." Verbs
also predicate quality and condition, and express relationships.

Again, where in English verbs express rest at a place, Fõn equivalents express motion towards or away from a place. We may say, then, that narrative flows through a sentence structure that is dominated by an imagery of motion; an imagery that raises questions of degree of empathy aroused by such statements of condition as "hunger is killing me" for "I am hungry," or "fear catches me" for "I am afraid."

The language also responds with economy, yet with nuanced elaboration, to descriptive needs, through its use of onomatopoeic words that qualify a basic verb of motion. We give below some examples from Ewe, a variant of Fõn, of words that modify the verb "to walk." [1]

> *zo bafobafo,* the walk of a small man, whose body is briskly moved when he walks.
>
> *zo behebehe,* the slouch of a weak man.
>
> *zo biabia,* the walk of a long-legged man, who strides out.
>
> *zo bohoboho,* the heavy walk of a fat man.
>
> *zo dzedze,* a free, breezy style of walking.
>
> *zo dziadzia,* energetic walking.
>
> *zo dabodabo,* to waddle (like a duck).
>
> *zo gblulugblulu,* to walk looking to the front, like a buffalo.
>
> *zo kodzokodzo,* to walk with the body bent forwards, stooping.
>
> *zo kpookpoo,* to walk quietly.
>
> *zo piapia,* to go with small feet.
>
> *zo takataka,* to walk without care.
>
> *zo tyatyratyatyra,* powerful but stiff walking.
>
> *zo tyendetyende,* to walk, moving one's belly, and with slightly-bent hips.
>
> *zo tyatya,* to walk quickly.

It is evident here that there is no poverty of descriptive detail, but only that usage governs its expression through special symbols. We observe also that whereas there is expansive use of verb forms, the modifying imagery is compressed into a reduplicated onomatopoeic figure.

We may also mention the stylistic importance for narration of the absence of the passive voice; of the use the narrator makes of the word *ka,* meaning "until," as he reduplicates it and dramatizes

[1] D. Westermann, *A Study of the Ewe Language,* London, 1930, pp. 107–109. The examples we give represent a selection from the thirty-seven forms listed.

intensity or duration; of the reworking of proverb into metaphor, as in No. 152.

One usage that is as common to discursive speech as to narrative is the interpolated exclamation from the listener, or listeners. So important is it for narrative tempo that in the absence of an audience, or where the interjection is too long delayed, the narrator himself pauses to exclaim "Good." While this pause serves stylistic ends in narration—to introduce a transition, as a memory aid, or to heighten suspense, among others—it is but part of the traditional complex of patterned responses from the listener, demanded by the canons of taste. A Dahomean views the silent European listener as either boorish, or incapable of participating adequately because of a lack of feeling or understanding.

Manipulation of tense is the instrument for handling incidents on differing time levels. In No. 26 there is a one-sentence lapse into the narrative present. "So he became king. . . . Everybody called out 'Dada!' *So as he is there living like a king, his younger brother sets out to look for him.* He looked for three years. The third year he found him." This device is also used in Nos. 43 and 54.

A variant of this is the use of the present tense in a flash-back to a preceding episode to produce a sense of an approaching climax. Thus in No. 51, when Hunter, attacked by the Yehwe monsters, is about to throw to the ground the last of the three magic gourds that are his only defense against them, and thus give his mother time to unchain the dogs who will save him, the desperateness of the situation is dramatized by the aside, *"His mother is still asleep, yes?"*

Change in time is not always expressed by the abrupt alternation of tenses. Thus, as in No. 132, the use of "then" at the beginning of a sentence indicates an earlier time level than the rest of the narrative, while "now," as used in No. 130, denotes a unitary time sequence; or, as in No. 19, the alternation between narrative past and present. Another device for registering a transition is the introduction of a proverb, as in No. 112. Here the saying, "To have a big fish, one must give something to the stream first," carries the progression from one episode to the next.

A number of other patterned usages may be mentioned. The play on words, which we have retained in No. 131, a case we have discussed earlier is also found in No. 147, where the word for pig, *ahā*, a tabooed food to the twin who is protagonist, is incorporated into the name, *Halan*, given him when he is turned into a water spirit because he had unknowingly eaten food cooked with pork. Names which characterize an individual, or mark some incident at birth or later in life, are found often in these narratives. The convention of naming the larger or more important before the smaller or lesser, as in No. 87 (". . . they dug ten or eight lengths of bamboo more . . ."), or in No. 97, where the stronger term comes before the weaker, as when the king sends a man ". . . to search and enquire . . . ," a progression which goes *diminuendo* instead of *crescendo*, is frequently encountered. The poem to Destiny [1] illustrates this: "If I have no wife, then I am poor . . . ," begins the enumeration of what makes poverty, moving successively to "children," "possessions," a torn cloth. We find imagery sharpened, also, by personification, as where, in No. 105, Death "called his first servant, Headache, and he ordered Migraine to measure his eyebrows. . . . He next called Diarrhea and he called Measles, Influenza, and Yellow Fever and said, 'Go bring my hammock.' They brought the hammock, and Death himself went to the dead body."

Time and setting are often evoked by allusion and suggestion. As mentioned, the metaphorical use of the reign of Dada Segbo or Metonofi in the opening lines of a story establishes a setting of ancient times, or serves to cloak an historic or contemporary protagonist. A parallel device, used interchangeably, is the allusion to a state of being when animals lived and talked like men. Again, to provide background for the action of a story, a market, the King's compound, the high bush, Death's Kingdom, a cult center require only naming. The one instance in our entire collection where the physical surroundings are described is found in No. 151. In this, the story of a visit to the world of the dead, the sights and sounds of the country which Bokofio must traverse is of dramatic interest. Even here, however, description is held to a minimum.

The standard ending for the *heho* category is: "The words I told, which you now have heard, tomorrow you will hear a bird

[1] See below, p. 66.

tell them to you." But a story-teller often plays with his ending, as in No. 122, ". . . and that is why one never asks Monkey 'where is Nana Lolwè?' If you did, he would point to his chest, and you would die." And the variant (No. 126): "Tomorrow morning you will hear the same story told you by a bird, but you had better not listen. If you hear it told by a bird, you will die."

7   *Riddle, proverb, and verse*

Associated with the narratives, as integral parts of them, yet distinct and with their own franchise in the life of the people, are riddles, proverbs, verses, and invocations, often in verse, that are chanted or sung. They serve to carry forward action, to provide an interlude of suspense, to give point to a resolution, and to bring the audience into close participant relationship with the teller.

Riddles (adjo). The riddle embodies some of the devices of the longer types. It is expressed with economy. Its appeal lies not only in the hidden meaning of the solution, but more especially in its *double entendre,* the play on words that is so important an element of Dahomean everyday communication.[1]

There is a tradition that the recounting of one form of the riddle, the conundrum, which can run to considerable length and is attributed to professional story-tellers, provided a profitable if dangerous means of livelihood. Wagers were laid at the courts of kings on the outcome of the guessing contest, and the stakes were high. In No. 109, in which this motif occurs, the stake was the life of the one who had posed the conundrum as against half of the kingdom and the king's daughter. According to lore, the gift of riddling and, by inference, the intellectual gifts that were needed for successful riddle-solving were so valued that a death sentence could be commuted as a reward, as is the case in No. 154. That the stakes named in tales involving the use of conundrums, or in the lore about those who originated them, are phrased hyperbolically is self-evi-

[1] For a discussion of form and degree of variation in the riddles of a related society, see W. R. Bascom, "Literary Style in Yoruba Riddles," *Jour. of American Folklore,* Vol. 62 (1949), pp. 1–16.

dent. But the professional *ahanjito* (the singer, story-teller and riddler) who wandered through the land, and had sanctioned immunity against harm to his person and license to satirize without recrimination, was as well-known a figure in Dahomey as was his prototype in much of the rest of West Africa.

A period of riddling prefaces all story-telling sessions. For the adults it is a warming-up time, a keying to attention, that keeps them occupied until late-comers arrive. For the children it has the special function of memory training, and is so recognized by the adults. To be present at one of these children's story-telling sessions, presided over by one of their age mates, and listen to the answers to the riddles coming with lightening-like rapidity is like hearing a drill in the multiplication table. Of the *double entendre* the children get nothing, though at certain points they will laugh in imitation of their elders. But their innocence of the subtleties became apparent when we questioned adolescents about the meaning of riddles and when we checked our impressions several times with two young boys, one fourteen and one sixteen, whom we knew well as members of our household. It is this *double entendre* that gives the riddle its importance in the rites for the dead. For the dead, who are being sent away from the world of the living, must savor all that gave them pleasure when alive; so at wakes the old men show their mastery in introducing riddles with the broadest innuendo, the greatest subtlety, and the sharpest suggestiveness.

Stylistically, the riddle is characterized by exaggeration, and by reference to the grotesque, the seemingly incongruous and the forbidden. The phrasing may be metrical, as in the conundrums, in couplet form, or in the style of everyday speech. The common phrasing is in declarative form. We shall illustrate only by a few examples, being concerned here with its cultural role in the complex of the spoken arts, rather than with its structural form.

My father eats with his anus, and he defecates through his mouth. ANSWER: A gun.

A tall man does not go inside a *vodun* house. ANSWER: Bamboo.

One throws a thing across the hedge, and it falls in one heap. ANSWER: A frog.

It struggles to climb the hedge fast. ANSWER: Rain.

A thing is naked going out, but returning, the body is covered with cloths. ANSWER: Corn.

A thing leaves the house bent and returns home straight. ANSWER: A water jar.

A large hat in the midst of weeds. ANSWER: A latrine.

One thing falls in the water with a loud voice, another falls in the water with a soft voice. ANSWER: A bottle of oil; a Dahomean reed carrying-basket.

Hole within hole, hair all round, pleasure comes from inside. ANSWER: A flute being played by a bearded man.

In a number of these examples, the double meaning, especially the sexual references, are obvious. In the second riddle above, however, while the imagery of putting a tall man in the little *vodun* shrine is sexual, it also has other connotations, since bamboo is associated with the dead and not with the gods. A variant of this riddle is, "A thing that gives little fruit is not picked with a bamboo," the answer here being "pepper pods." The reference to the latrine, a white man's conceit, in itself provokes laughter. The imagery in the riddle need not be sexual; it may be blasphemous, or it may touch upon doing something forbidden, such as watching the king eat, or accosting one of his wives, or touching his person or, greatest enormity of all, his head, wherein magic strength lies. The aim is to exaggerate, to shock, to challenge.

Proverbs (*alo*). In the proverb form, which includes epigram, aphorism, precept, maxim and other synonymous types, we find the quintessence of the terse statement, the poetic image. We gain from it insight into behavior, derive from it a commentary on happenings that reveal the system of values under which the culture functions. Indeed, in this last sense it makes one of its greatest humanistic contributions, for the total corpus of the proverbs of Africans, as with proverb-users in other societies, is in a very real sense their grammar of values.

Since the proverb, as found in West African and African-derived societies, has been systematically treated elsewhere,[1] it is only nec-

[1] Cf. M. Travélé, *Proverbes et Contes Bambara* (Paris, 1923); M. J. Herskovits and Sie Tagbwe, "Kru Proverbs," *Jour. of Amer. Folklore*, Vol. 43 (1930), pp. 225–293; G. Herzog and C. S. Blooah, *Jabo Proverbs from Liberia* (London, 1936).

essary here to recall that it enters into all forms of interaction. Comment on behavior, whether in commendation or criticism, and whether in the household, in the market-place, or in the law court, is interspersed with the proverb. It is a mark of elegance in speech to be able to use skilfully the apt aphorism; and proverbs are cited in arguments before the courts, much as lawyers cite precedents. Of significance for us in this discussion of the oral tradition is the fact that the proverb phrases the philosophy and poetry of the Dahomeans.

For example, the song of praise to the gods, and to the living and the dead, draws on the common store of proverbs for theme, imagery, and moral. Proverbs are also used in the drum salutations, the "drum language" so-called, in the conventional praise formulae of king and chief, and in devising new names. But it is not just an equation of proverb and praise. The songs of allusion, so full of social and political satire, or of lament, equally rely on proverbs to sharpen the irony of the one, the poignancy of the other. Only one limiting principle governs their use. The young may not presume to press a point with their seniors by using proverbs.

A few examples of proverbs frequently heard will illustrate their general form:

A snake bit me; I see a worm, I am afraid.

The big do not eat out of the hand of the small.

Who makes the gunpowder, wins the battles.

If you want a large fish, you must give something to the stream.

Mawu says, "I have sent sickness into the world, but I have also sent cures."

War lies in wait on a narrow path.

Verse (hă). The third form of Dahomean non-narrative expression we have named is verse-making, the grouping of words in tonal, rhythmic, and repetitive patterns in songs and chants. These songs and chants or invocations are structured to conform to fixed or flexible models, depending on the conventions that govern each type. The term for song and poem, significantly, is the same, *hā;* and one who originates a song is said to give it birth— *ahājito,* "song-give-birth-person." Our focus here is on songs where interest and appreciation are chiefly centered on the content of the words. Songs in this category tend to employ or rework traditional melodies to suit important words, and they call on proverbs for themes. In addition, there are dramatizations of certain portions of ritual which follow a fixed spoken sequence, using proverb and metaphor. One such example is the visit of the "impure" woman to the deity of the market at night, while seeking to be released from the taboos imposed on her by reason of the disclosure, through divination, that the child born to her was fathered by the mythological founder of her husband's clan, and not her human husband.[1] Another instance is the introduction of an interlude of farce—the dispute of false friends—in the tense succession of ceremonial acts in the rites for the dead.[2]

It is not strange that a culture as specialized as that of Dahomey has professional verse-makers. These are chiefly the originators of new songs in praise of the ancestors of important families, or of songs that celebrate the deeds of men of position, such as chiefs. Verse-makers are classed as *nolodoto* (literally, "good-memory-say-person"), and *ayisumo* ("heart-much-understand"). Since new songs are patterned after old, and proverbs are used to weave any number of variations on any theme, the person of good memory is valued for his usefulness and for his facility. In other words, he is an artificer, in contradistinction to the creative maker of verse, who, to use the Dahomean idiom, has a heart that understands much.

Not all new songs, however, are composed by professionals. It can be said confidently that the greater part are not. To understand this, and its implication for the encouragement and exercise of the creative process, we must examine the occasions that call for improvisation in song.

During the various cycles of sacred and commemorative rites, there are many ceremonies that call for new songs. For example, the deities of the Earth pantheon, Sagbata, have the special pre-

[1] Cf. *Dahomey,* Vol. I, pp. 235–238.
[2] *Ibid.,* Vol. I, pp. 273–274.

rogative of improvisation, whereas all other gods are worshipped with traditional songs. The new songs may comment on the hard times that have come since the country was "broken" (that is, conquered) by strangers; or they may mock a convert who had not fared well at the hands of Destiny; or they may relate, by allusion, how the King of the Earth deities, Dada Zodji, who punishes by giving smallpox to a serious offender against the moral code, had scourged an evil-doer. Such songs "come into the heads" of initiates in a state of possession, and are interpreted as the voice of the deity himself.

The gods of other pantheons also, on occasion, have their specially composed topical songs, even though they are of the traditionally non-improvising group, but this occurs only exceptionally. A song of this sort will be sung when a deity who is worshipped at a regional shrine has performed, let us say, a spectacular cure that other gods could not achieve; or that the same deity has been unable to achieve at other shrines of his own. This calls for new praise-names, phrased as these are in song or spoken as recitative. And when one Dahomean, realistically commenting on these names, said, "We call it *mlamla,* 'praise,' but most of the time it is flattery," he was alluding to the imagery that goes into shaping them.

In this context, it is important to call attention to the distinction that is to be drawn between the improvisation which is called for in the worship of the gods, and the set formulae which are employed to actuate magic. The *gbo* (the magic cure, the spell, the amulet) works by fixed formula. "But the *vodun* enjoy all the things human beings enjoy. They like praise," said a priest of the Sky Pantheon.

The royal ancestors, as human rulers of the Earth, have the same prerogative of improvisation as the Earth gods, but here it is not at the whim and inspiration of the deities. When ancestral rites are held, it is essential to the prestige of the head of the royal clan and the sons of the royal sons that new songs be sung. A professional singer is called in to compose the new songs for such rites, and they will be sung either by members of the family or by the composer-singer himself. These composers are paid to praise the royal dead, and to hurl defiance at the enemies of the living royal descendants.

The number of verses will vary with the theme chosen, and especially with the patron's reputation for generosity.

Yet another form of composition in verse, which is put to music, serves the utilitarian purpose of committing to memory a sequence of events. Here the emphasis is not on elegance of style—the metaphor may be evocative or not—since what is important is the simple statement and refrain that punctuate the listing of deeds, or events, or names that need to be remembered. The king's "remembrancer" who, as we have stated, chanted at daybreak the genealogy of the living monarch, called upon this mechanism; and the records of the wars were kept the same way, as were the genealogies of the clans. We were impressed how often, when we were getting ethnographic information, our informants stopped to sing a long recitative when a chronological series of names or events was needed. One such genealogical recitative that we took down, that of the royal abnormally born, is a song based on the response-and-call pattern of West African music. The leader names directly, or under a praise name, each of these beings, called *tohosu*, in chronological order. The chorus responds after each name with an elliptical allusion to an old man who went to bed hungry, this being the sharpest image of poverty, neglect, and misery that the Dahomean can evoke; concluding,

> *And he said to the woman Bodo Buiye*
> *You see, sleep denies me;*
> *Come, crush some peppers, even if coarsely,*
> *And this old man will eat.*

Naming ceremonies also provide opportunities for creative expression.[1] A wife receives a new name from her husband when she comes to live in his compound. A man of imagination makes of this name an elaborate tribute to his father, who helped him with

---

[1] The importance of names has been independently demonstrated by da Cruz, who lists over two hundred of them, each the abbreviation of a proverb which, in terms of his classification, has a moral or religious meaning; or expresses praise or flattery; or commemorates a time or condition of adversity, quarrels or provocation at the birth of the bearer; or explains some deception; or recalls some success. Clement da Cruz, "Petit Récueil des Pseudonymes (Population Fon, région d'Abomey)," *Etudes Dahoméennes*, XV (1956), pp. 5–34.

the marriage fees; or to his ancestors, who had helped him to prosper so that he could add to the number of his wives; or to the family of his new wife, who may count men of position; or to the bride herself, for her beauty or other qualities. And though she will henceforth be called only by a single word, or at most a phrase from this tribute, it is a matter of prestige that this naming be well phrased, with many allusions in proverb form, and rich imagery. The man of no expressive gifts will, if he has the means, call in a professional to help him, though if he is a person neither of substance nor pretensions he will call his new wife by a name that refers to her village, or to the quarter of the city from which she came.

Any special achievement, or any ritual that celebrates new status calls for the pronouncement of new praise names, and for important occasions these are rhapsodies in verse, declaimed and sung. The translation of this custom into the present scene in Dahomey has been achieved with no difficulty. We witnessed two instances of this when sons of chiefs returned from military service in France, and the ancestors were felicitated in their new names for having seen to the safe return of the young men from the "war."

An important opportunity for improvisation, especially for the young men and women of Abomey, is the monthly dance held in the principal market of the city, when the people of a given quarter satirize those of another in songs which serve to accompany a social dance, known as *avogan*. Since each quarter gets its turn, this is an effective device to develop new talent. Much prestige goes to those who live in the same quarter as the composers whose songs bite deepest into the shortcomings of their rivals, and thereby become the popular "hits" of the city at large. And such composers are thereafter treated with great tact. "You walk softly with a man like that," friends confided to us about one member of our own household, who was an acknowledged master of the satirical song.

New verses may originate while humble, everyday tasks are being performed. A woman, for example, who is provoked by a co-wife, sings to the rhythm of her pestle while pounding millet. Her lines name no names, but by indirection and metaphor, she

weaves a song of reproach, protest, or threat. Or when the cooperative work groups of young men, known as *dokpwe*, are
called together, many songs are sung commenting on the generosity of their last host, or on his scant hospitality, and recounting
current gossip about people in high places and low. Those who
can find new words to an old melody, or know how to reword
felicitously, or pointedly, the lines of well known songs to suit a
special incident will enjoy much popularity.

In the days of the kings, during the annual rites dedicated to the
worship of the king's head, his subjects were not only encouraged
but exhorted to invent songs and parables mocking their ruler, and
even naming the injustices they had suffered. The short interlude
of license to criticize was set aside ritually so that any repressed ill-
will for abuse at the hands of the king's agents might find release,
and thereby cease to oppress the king's subjects and "infect their
souls." For repressed grievances were felt to have the power to
harm the king's soul, as well, and bring evil on the kingdom.[1] It is
evident from the songs of this genre still sung that uncensored
self-expression was, nevertheless, held in check by the stylistic
device of indirection, and the use of the proverb.

A concluding instance of original composition serving in an institutionalized context, being, like so much in Dahomey, neither
sporadic nor at the whim of chance inspiration, concerns the annual meeting of the hunters to choose their *degã*, the chief of the
hunt, for the ensuing year. To the Dahomean, it is a rite of con-
testing for office. This time it is narrative improvisation, with or
without song sequences. Each candidate recounts to his fellow
hunters of a village or a region the adventures that come to any
great hunter. The rite is held under a sacred tree, at whose base
stands a large pottery jar filled with millet beer. Each hunter, as
he is summoned by the incumbent *degã*, comes forward and, dipping his hand in the jar, declares that he will speak the truth before
drinking from his cupped hand. He then proceeds to tell his experiences of the past year in the bush—the animals that charged

[1] Some of the psychological implications of customs of this kind, which are found
elsewhere in West Africa and among New World Negroes, have been considered in M. J. Herskovits, "Freudian Mechanisms in Primitive Negro Psychology," *Essays Presented to C. G. Seligman*, London, 1934, pp. 75–84.

him as he stalked them; the magic he called on to save him; his encounters with the helpful little people of the forest, the *azizā*, or with the giants, sorcerers, or thirty-horned monsters that breathe fire, the *yehwe*, under whatever guises they may have appeared; and the trees or animals turned human who addressed him. When each ends his recital, he makes way for the next, and the one who has most vividly described the happenings that demonstrate the greatest control over supernatural dangers is chosen as chief for the year ahead.

Imagery. At this point, we may examine some of the imagery that, though present in all forms of Dahomean oral literature, has its most striking examples in verse. Thus, in an ancestral cult song, hope for the future prominence of the clan is expressed in these terms:

> *Obscurity knows Nature will light the lamps.*

A man invoking his important ancestors, sings:

> *This river and that river,*
> *It is the Sea who is their king.*

A funeral song laments a succession of deaths in the family and, obliquely, the fate of Dahomey:

> *Sadness came to us, and you laughed,*
> *Your day will come;*
> *Sadness came to the trees, and the lianas laughed,*
> *The day of the lianas will come;*
> *The water had grief, and the fish laughed,*
> *The day of the fish will come.*

A worshipper of the serpent-deity, Dã, sings:

> *He who seeks a favor*
> *Uses a low voice;*
> *Dã says, "You who come entreating,*
> *Give me a low voice."*

A secular song, counselling prudence, ends with a well-known proverb:

> *When I am on the river,*
> *I whisper and say,*
> *"Flow softly."*
> *And for that my two feet*
> *Know the earth of the farther bank.*
> *One who is in a boat at sea*
> *Does not quarrel with the boatman.*[1]

A man lamenting his fate cries out to Destiny to make him invisible to misfortune:

> *Life has been evil,*
> *Take black clay and paint my soul!*

Here, a famous singer is addressed:

Ayobo, my song commiserates the hunter who comes on no game;
A hunter's wife does not whistle into the horn of his prey.

Ayobo, my song commiserates the man who trips;
A flat shard cannot hold water.

In this invocation to the Thunder god, Sogbo, we again see how the imagery of a proverb in general use, found in the third line, is seen to reinforce the theme of the poem:

> *Is it true our Warrior God*
> *Holds man in his grip of fire?*
>
> *War lies in wait on a narrow path,*
> *And seizes us like this,*
> *Holding us fast,*
> *Holding us.*

A series of single images taken from the larger forms may be given to show the range of Dahomean poetic expression in wisdom and cynicism:

[1] See also the variant of this verse in No. 86.

There is no enjoying beyond death.
That which your senses taste of the world goes with you.
The sun does not go in hiding in the season of drought.
The serpent does not measure its shadow against the rainbow.
You do not bridle a horse with thread.
The great sun lights the entire Universe.
Oh, small, small fire, who takes the great and devours them.
When a woman takes up a hoe, man will find no place to cultivate.

Or, in allusion to the God of Thunder, whose sacred animal is the ram,

> *Ram pounding the earth with hooves of fire.*

We give below the words to two songs from our collection that even in translation give something of the artistry of Dahomean verse. These songs are traditional cult songs, said to be of great antiquity. The first is an ancestral song; the second an invocation to Destiny, Fa.

> *The Giver of Life*
> *Placed the sun in great space,*
> *And said: No hand*
> *Shall be the length to reach it;*
> *Though clouds disappear,*
> *And we become a mountain*
> *Immovable and high,*
> *It will not be that the hand obeys not.*
>
> *The Giver of Life*
> *Placed the sun in the heavens,*
> *And said: No eye*
> *Shall have the cunning to see within,*
> *Though clouds disappear,*
> *And we become a mountain*
> *Invisible and high,*
> *It will not be that the eye obeys not.*[1]

*   *   *

[1] This translation was published in *Poetry*, Vol. 45 (1934), p. 75, under the title, "To the Envious."

I accept you, O my Destiny,
And I say to you, say,
Let poverty be a stranger in my household;
For if I have no wife, then I am poor;
If no children are born to me, then I am poor;
If I lack possessions, then I am poor;
If my cloth is torn, then I am poor.
O vodun, who creates life and its mysteries,
Let poverty be a stranger
In my household.

The next two are secular songs. The first is said to have been composed by King Behanzin while he was a prisoner in Whydah waiting to be sent into exile. At the time of this field work, this song was heard in Abomey, in Allada and in Whydah on many secular occasions, and was also often sung by the cooperative work groups (*dokpwe*).

What will he do to me,
The stranger?
He can do nothing.

In life, the fish-trap that finds no fish
Is brought back to the house;
The elephant will come back
To his father's house.

They are in the land
And they trouble me;
The townspeople insult me.
But if they greet me, I do not care,
If they do not greet me, I do not care.

In life, the fish-trap that finds no fish
Is brought back to the house;
The elephant will come back
To his father's house.

The final song, which satirizes the ways of foreign rule, was one of the most popular in Abomey at the time of this study. The burden of the song has to do with the judging of a thief at the "residence," before the court presided over by a colonial official. Thieving, a serious crime, was punishable by death or enslavement under the rule of the kings, so that for the official first to send word to the chief who had the thief in custody that it was not a court day, and then, when the chief presented himself on the day named, to order him to return that afternoon with his prisoner, contravenes basic patterns of Dahomean procedure.

> *The white man says,*
> *"Day after tomorrow."*
> *Eight hundred eighty-five,*
> *Or is it eight hundred eighty-nine?*
>
> *If this is not theft,*
> *There is no thieving;*
> *But the white man says,*
> *"In the afternoon."*

Relationship of Verbal to Musical Forms. In considering the narrative, we saw how the structure of the language imposed the pattern of emphasis on motion. We have seen, moreover, that whereas the verb was used expansively, qualifying elaborations on an act were often suggested by indirection, or compressed into a reduplicated onomatopoeic figure. The effect is of descriptive images filled in with a few rapid brush strokes, to leave uncluttered the foreground for dramatizing the thematic progressions.

Versification is governed by its reciprocal relationship with the musical form it accompanies. In a tonal language, where modulation means semantic change, it follows that new words to a traditional melody must become servant to the melodic line, whereas where the words are the important component of a song the melody of it will follow the spoken line. But since songs accompany a rhythmic pattern that is associated with each type of dance, whether religious or secular, both words and melody are structured within such rhythmic patterns. Rhythmic configurations may therefore be said to be structurally dominant for each verse type. If we consider that each deity has at the least a slow and a fast rhythm of its own, and that the dance of a commoner follows a faster beat than that of a chief, that songs of praise have their special rhythms, as do work songs or songs to war dances, then it is clear that the rhythmic patterns to which verse responds are complex indeed. But even here, response to structural demands, whether tonal or rhythmic, finds its exceptions in the ingenuity of the singer, and he adjusts his song to their requirements by per- missively traditionalized means such as adding an interpolated phrase, or use of partial duplication or elision.

Though the melodic form of the individual song is governed by the master-rhythm of its type, and the verses of the song must, in turn, conform to both the rhythmic and melodic requirements of the music to which it is set, no subordination of one of these to the others is actually experienced by composers of verse or melody. How intimately rhythm, melody, and verse are related is to be seen in the fact that, when recording songs, singers, when asked for the words, consistently sang rather than spoke them, while the proper rhythm was softly indicated, often by snapping the nail of the first finger against that of the thumb.

A device common to improvisation is the use of a refrain to gain time to think of the next thematic statement. In the traditional song, the refrain is but a repetition of a metaphor or a key image of a preceding line. Its use falls into the pattern of punctuating speech and narrative by interpolations from the listener. But the singer who improvises finds more sensitive use for this device. He may introduce with it a humorous, or malicious, or intimate per- sonal aside.

A song composed by a member of our household in praise of the loyalty of his best friend will serve to illustrate this. He had been called up for military.service to fill a quota when a fellow- member of his compound migrated to Nigeria to evade the call. He was the oldest son, and because his father was an elderly man there was tension and anxiety over the future course of family affairs. The song explains this, but it also carries from time to time the refrain:

> *Things that follow, I, a singer,*
> *In song will tell you;*
> *If I had been a rich man in this city,*
> *Then many friends would I have had.*

The same device is seen in this introduction to a woman's work-song:

> *This song is difficult;*
> *When one begins, one must reflect . . .*
>
> *O* belele, *O* belele
> *If you are away on a journey,*
> *You must return.*
>
> *O Eagle, gone on a journey,*
> *You can rest there.*

The song comments obliquely on a powerful, predatory being, as against the predictable, domestic ways of the small bird. The aside makes impersonal words intimate, emotionally charged with meaning for both singer and listener, bringing the performer and his audience into association with the implicit meaning of the words.

That this stylistic device is not confined to Dahomey, but is rather part of a West African pattern, is attested by our experience among the Yoruba, Hausa, and Ashanti. We recall in particular one incident in a morning's performance of Hausa singing teams, arranged by the courtesy of the Emir of Kano. One young man, who sang to the accompaniment of a pressure drum, introduced the refrain that though he knew he would be acclaimed a great singer after his death, he would like to reap some of the rewards of his talents during his lifetime. He received the reward of much laughter—and a gift from the Emir and his visitors.

Indirection, allusion, metaphor, and the terse aphorism are all called on in verse making. But the Dahomean also uses the simple form, the direct statement. The following invocation was sung at a very modest ancestral ceremony:

> *When one has need of something*
> *Let him ask it of his* vodun.
> *Long life, Grandfather!*
> *We kneel before you*
> *To ask for long life.*

The song continues with appeals for new wives; for children to be born to these wives; for strength to work the fields; a harvest to reward labor.

8   *Narrative and the changing culture*

The relation between a literature and the culture of which it is a part is reciprocal, and the artist is the medium through which these influences flow. The world of the story-teller is largely defined by his culture, and in composing his tale, whatever its form or length, he draws on the world he knows, whether as reality or fantasy (or one in which tradition has fused both), for setting, plot, characterization, and the sanctions that give these meaning.[1] Yet by this very act he reinforces the existing body of custom, bringing to it the validating force of emotional response.

We have already shown [2] how the culture of Dahomey defines for the narrator the limits within which he may juxtapose certain themes or call on certain characters to enact stated roles. Here we have the frame within which the teller of tales works, the frame which gives to the body of Dahomean narrative its distinctive features, and allows it to be regarded as an identifiable body of spoken art-forms. We must, however, also approach these materials from the other side, to see how the experience of the narrator is reflected in what he tells. Boas, many years ago, demonstrated this aspect of the relationship between a tale and its cultural setting. "In the tales of a people" he stated, "those incidents of everyday life that are of importance to them will appear either incidentally or as the basis of a plot. Most of the references to the mode of life of the people will be an accurate reflection of their habits. The development of the plot of the story, furthermore, will, on the whole, exhibit clearly what is considered right and what wrong." [3]

We will not be concerned here with the Dahomean incidents of

---

[1] Cf. the valuable insights into this process given by D. Eggan, "The Personal Use of Myth in Dreams," *Jour. of Amer. Folklore*, Vol. 68 (1955), pp. 445-450.

[2] *Supra*, pp. 23 ff.

[3] F. Boas, *op. cit.*, p. 393.

everyday life that are to be found in the narratives of our collection, accepting it as a demonstrated fact that the teller of a tale must draw on his cultural background to create a viable story. But how does he respond to changes in the life about him? And, obversely, with what degree of accommodation do the listeners accept the clues to a changing social setting?

Let us, for example, consider the representation in these narratives of money. In pre-European days, this took the form of cowry shells, which have been almost completely replaced, except for certain ritual uses, by the French franc. With the tradition of expressing values in pecuniary terms well established, the reinterpretation of cowries in terms of francs was no more difficult for the Dahomeans in their narratives than it was in their daily life. This is shown in Nos. 61 and 62, variants of the same tale, which describe a contest between *tohosu* and twins. In the first of these versions, meat is sold for cowries, and in the second, for francs; but in structure, character, plot, and point the tales differ only within the limits of variation set by the fact that no two tellers of tales will recount the same story in exactly the same way. Again, in No. 25, a story which in all other respects quite accurately mirrors the traditional life of Dahomey, the value of *nana* beads, and the amount given to one of the characters to buy a chicken, is in francs, quite without changing either the flavor or the moral of the tale. In No. 36, this change in the token of value is only a part of a more extensive series of reinterpretations. In telling how Rabbit cheated Death out of the money he owed him, not only are all amounts given in francs, but the teller quite ignores the fact that slavery has been suppressed in Dahomey, and substitutes the French Resident for the local chief as the official who settles the case.

We see similar mechanisms of cultural substitution at work when, in No. 64, we are told how one of the twins, a principal character, who had become wealthy through selling in the market, cleared himself of the charge of having stolen the inheritance his father had left to all his children by producing before his judge, here the king, the book in which he had "marked down everything." This is a particularly striking instance of the incorporation of a new cultural element in a traditional setting, since it will be remembered that the Dahomeans aboriginally had never developed writing. Again, in No. 27, the mythical king, Dada Segbo, in one episode of this long narrative takes "six flintlocks and one modern French gun . . ." in attempting to splinter the calabash on the head of a young woman he wishes to marry. In No. 16, Death, with European imagery, carries a scythe, but the scythe is certainly not an indigenous implement; in No. 60, the tale begins with the supernatural figures, the Nesuhwe, "in very ancient times" playing a card game; in No. 53, the man "who is not a man" before he goes to market borrows not only a cloth but also trousers.

In No. 57, which tells why women do not travel in the bush alone, the point of this story turns on the fact that in earlier days one had to go from Whydah to Abomey on foot, since, "at that time there was no train." The moral gives an even more striking instance of amalgamation of the new with the old: "It was for this reason that in olden times, it was forbidden for a woman to go from Abomey to Whydah without taking the train." And when the question was asked, "In olden times, a train?" the answer was, "No, without being accompanied by a man." Finally, in No. 155, we not only have a story in which the principal characters have the French names of "Jean" and "Joseph," but in which the latter, who "had a little education," writes down the password he hears the thieves pronounce and subsequently puts the eighty sacks of treasure taken by him in a bank vault, while Jean, who cannot write, forgets the password he has entrusted to his memory, is trapped inside, and is killed!

9   *The system of values as revealed in narrative forms*

We observe that the reality of economic change and the awareness of the role of literacy are incorporated into narrative without restructuring of plot or motif or basic values. The reaction of the audience, as we experienced it, to Dada Segbo's using modern French guns, was amusement. The Dahomean is not concerned with verisimilitude, or the dimension of actuality in his narrative renderings, providing only that the cultural imperatives set by the value system are observed.

We must therefore ask what insight the narratives give us into these cultural imperatives, which make up the system of values. It is essential to recognize, before proceeding with our analysis, that these narratives represent a give-and-take that has been going on for many centuries, both within Dahomean society and through the contacts of its members with neighboring peoples. Many are the counterparts of tales that are distributed over all the Old World; we can be certain that many motifs, and even entire tales, have come from outside, for the factor of cultural borrowing is one of the most widely recognized mechanisms in the dynamics of cultural change.

Within this process of borrowing, and at the same time complementary to it, is found both the conscious and unconscious reworking of what is newly taken over to bring it into congruence with the ways of the group. The degree of mutation under this reworking depends in part on the skill and inventiveness of the innovator, but more decisively on how the tale fits into the tradition of the borrowing people. And it is this tradition, as a describable body of behaving and valuing, that sets off one culture from another, no matter how many elements they may historically have in common.

We perceive this when we focus on certain familiar Old World tales and see what, in their particular versions, gives them a special Dahomean character. In the world of gods or men, no one is of such high station that he is set up as all-wise, all-knowing, all-masterful. There is none who is not subject to the foibles, vexations, and doubts experienced in the world as the Dahomean knows it. Thus the Creator, Mawu, does not entrust any of her children with the formula for creating. In No. 1 we see the problems her youngest child, whom she has never disciplined, presents to her; in No. 6 she tries to right an error of creation. No. 4 shows us Mawu is not omniscient, since we are told that the feud between Earth and Thunder, her sons, was not known to her. No. 12 shows Mawu succumbing to the frailty of accepting praise but passing on blame to Legba.

If we take the symbol of the father in this collection, leaving aside the Oedipal motifs, which we will discuss later, we see that a father can be outwitted by his youngest son, or can be shown as violating interdictions at a tragic cost. Even the love of a mother can falter when the supreme sacrifice is asked (No. 103). And a king can be commanded by a poor stranger (No. 101), or a king's son defy his father's wishes and bring misfortune on the kingdom (No. 99).

In all this, it is important to note that neither gods nor men are pawns in an all-ordering system. Where individuals are endowed with supernatural powers, they derive these from spiritual helpers who respond when they are called on, but the individual is not moved like a marionette by these powers. And while among gods and men there is an element of unpredictability, the role of the ancestors, the dead, is less qualified and never satirized; their powers are never questioned. It would be unthinkable in terms of Dahomean values to blame the ancestors for the conquest of Dahomey or for some evil in the land. The explanation is rather the failure of the living to follow the ancestral code, thus bringing punishment on themselves. The power of the ancestors is symbolical and is not to be challenged. No narrator would tell a tale wherein one of the dead was outwitted by any other supernatural agent; and no tale involving incest, as culturally defined, could have a happy ending, since this would contravene deeply set ancestral moral sanctions.

One complex of values that also comes out with great clarity in the narratives is the importance of realism in all relationships, of discretion in speech, of resilience in social situations, of taking steps to meet difficulties previsaged. We find these variously expressed. Thus, in No. 7, Mawu, the Creator, sends a chameleon to earth with the first pair of human beings, so that "those who would conspire against them," as they spread the teachings of Mawu, would be seen in the smooth skin of the chameleon's back, as in a mirror, and the pair could protect themselves.

The lesson that at all times one must be discreet is driven home again and again. "Softly toward the mouth of the great," says Goat as he places honey in the mouth of Hyena (No. 34). The phrase is repeated as Goat placates Lion, in No. 124, a story whose moral is, "That is why, in this life, one has to have cunning." A man does not tell when he has become rich, lest he lose his possessions (No. 26); he is cautious in what he says, even with friends (No. 85); there are things which one does not discuss with one's wife or any other woman (Nos. 46–48, 97), especially since, as taught by No. 109, "women never kept their husbands' secrets"; and he who reveals a secret will pay the penalty for his indiscretion (No. 49). A good deed may be rewarded by ingratitude (No. 110); and lack of self-control when seeing the unaccustomed brings embarrassment or punishment (No. 69).

The narratives reveal correlative values. Thus, in No. 33, we learn that astuteness is more advantageous than strength. As pointed out in No. 142, it is not good to make any commitment without first exploring its implications. The lesson is taught in No. 44 that even oaths may not be taken at face value, for words are not to be trusted, and men do not readily change their character. This refrain of not taking appearances for granted is repeated, among other instances, in Nos. 88 and 89, where the action turns on the fact that when a choice of animals is to be made sight unseen, the steer is found to be attached to the thin rope, the goat to the stout one.

A further variant on the same theme is found in No. 122, where Asogbwa watches at a distance to see whether the animals who engage to kill his mother, who is pursuing him, are successful. The end of this same story, returning us once more to the basic theme of the need for discretion, but on a more positive note, points the importance of being diplomatic in relations with others. The necessity of having witnesses to any important event, shown in No. 107, or of being able to back up an assertion with deeds, as in No. 143, also makes the point that too hasty commitment to a position is imprudent.

Another set of values derives from, and at the same time supports, institutional and individual aspects of the Dahomean social system. They are values that, incidentally, we have not seen associated with the same tales as told in other Old World versions. No. 139 carries the moral, "No man can quarrel with another who has a large family." In this tale of the Relay Race, Horse unwittingly competes against a great many frogs posted along the route and dies of exhaustion before he reaches the goal. Or, in No. 53, on the Chosen Suitor theme, the story explains why "a woman takes the husband her father chooses for her."

That respect for parents and a willingness to serve them is essential for success is explicitly stated at the end of No. 64: "That is why, if you want to become rich, you must obey and serve your father." A number of tales, of which Nos. 68 and 69 are examples, drive home the closeness of the relation between mother and child within the polygynous family constellation. This is an important point, as we shall see, for understanding the adjustments that must be made in this powerfully patrilineal society, for it is a relation that is held to persist after death. In the emphasis laid on the protection the spirit of a dead mother gives her surviving child, moreover, these tales clearly give the rationale for the principle that orphans must not be mistreated, a principle that, by extension, is but one manifestation of a more general value, that the weak and powerless must be cared for, as a safeguard against their invoking supernatural vengeance for ill treatment. In one of the incidents of No. 15, it is, however, made clear that a child who is a threat to its parents must be struck down. For here the Messenger of Mawu, the Creator, destroys a child, saying, "This one . . . could not be allowed to spoil . . ." the lives of its father and mother.

Canons of conduct governing the relationships between individuals enter into a number of stories. No. 110, already mentioned for the lesson it teaches in discretion, is based on the theme of ingratitude and its ultimate punishment. No. 52 underscores the value of reciprocity in giving aid, presented in the negative sense of "nothing for nothing" and, in a more cynical vein, suggests that it pays to care for those who may in the future prove useful. In positive terms, No. 57 stresses the importance of repaying a favor, of giving full recognition for a service rendered, whatever the cost. Emphasis is also laid on gratitude in No. 147 where, as in other myths of clan origin, it is recounted how clan taboos and prescribed forms of behavior represent repayment for services rendered to the ancestors in their time of need. We also find, in No. 19, the need to hold to the terms of a bargain made explicit by the protagonist's return to poverty.

Insights into Dahomean standards by which the individual is evaluated are also to be had from these narratives. Thus, in No. 140, the moral, "You must know a thing before you talk about it," is a warning against superficiality. Astuteness is held in high esteem, as we see from No. 154, when the condemned man saves his life by performing a seemingly impossible task; in No. 76, where the trickery of Yo is justified by its successful outcome; in No. 124, with its ending, "That is why, in this life, one has to have cunning"; and in No. 128, we are told that a man chooses his most astute son to confide in, and "leaves the stupid one alone." This is also apparent in No. 33, in which the small bird, Titagweti, outwits Elephant, so that, "when they kill Titagweti they must perform as great a ceremony as for the largest animal"; and again in No. 35, where Fa profits by outwitting his creditors when, by trickery, he causes them to kill off one another.

Yet the one who has qualities that are held in esteem, or who has many possessions must not be overbearing. "When a person is strong, or brave, or rich, he never talks about it," we learn from No. 56. Or, as we have mentioned earlier, in No. 108 wives effectively deflate their braggart husband. Even Yo, the boaster *par excellence* in the Dahomean repertory of characters, is shown in Nos. 82 and 83 to have less wisdom than a young boy, and in this case, at least, is forced to admit that "the young are more cunning than the old." But though cunning may be valued, it is to be noted that in No. 36, in which Rabbit tricks Death and thus gets out of paying his debt to him, the moral, curiously inverting the seeming intent of the tale itself, is that, "If a person owes, and pays, he will be happy."

The importance of wealth is marked in the tales, and provides a clear and undistorted reflection of one of those aspects of life of the Dahomeans that finds repeated expression in daily life. For one cannot live in Dahomey for any length of time without being made aware of the important place pecuniary motivations have in thought and behavior. Thus, in No. 26 we see how rudeness is punished, when the riches that would have come with proper conduct are withheld; and, in this same story, as we have already seen, how failure to keep a secret exacts the loss of what had been richly given as a penalty. In No. 39, the point of the tale turns on the degradation of poverty, while in No. 27 there is the revealing passage where the protagonist, a hunter, is mocked by those at the court of the king, "because he had no clothes, nothing."

In the Yo tales, a number of incidents show the stress laid on obtaining riches. The first tale of this category, No. 75, explains why a man must have much money before he can marry; while, in No. 78, Yo is rewarded by the king for capturing a live hyena by being given the king's daughter, and in consequence becomes rich. In one of the tales, No. 109, where the theme that women cannot be trusted is emphasized, the reward for the wife's betrayal is money. In No. 112, Egret hovers over the cattle herds because he has advanced money to Bull as marriage payment for a daughter he is never to receive; in No. 155, the action turns entirely on the desirability of acquiring wealth.

Of more than usual interest is the love theme. Tales Nos. 103, 104, and 105 show the love story handled with sensitivity. In both Nos. 103 and 104 the great lovers are women. Here, indeed, is a countervailing theme to the faithlessness of women. For in these tales the women defy the gods, the ancestral code, and Death itself, and by their selflessness win the admiration of the deities.

In No. 105, Degeno, the hero, whom one of his father's wives tempts into violating an incest taboo, tells Death "he would rather die beside the body of the woman he loved so much, than to let her be devoured by vultures." Brought back to life, however, she yields to the powerful King of Adja, and betrays Degeno's secret. "His wife . . . ordered that Degeno's head be cut off and brought to her." In a scene which recalls the motif of Salome and John the Baptist, she mocks Degeno's skull. She sings,

> *Gather up for me his fat*
> *With which to light my lamp*
> *Give me his bones*
> *To use as firewood*

The King of Adja hears his rival mocked with displeasure.

Women are strange
Do you remember the watch Degeno kept
over your dead body?
Do you recall how he watched during
those days?

But when Degeno is restored to life, he bears no rancor toward the King of Adja. "I, Degeno, would do the same for a woman as beautiful as she."

Insights into attitudes toward the structure of power that held together the Dahomean political order are gained from No. 6, where we are told that Aido-Hwedo, who accompanied Mawu when she created the world, lives in the sea but does not rule over it. "It is Agbe, a son of Mawu, who commands there, because those who command must be of royal blood." But there is social mobility, and an open path through initiative to high position, as in No. 10, where the dog, who solves for Legba and his two sisters the dilemma of the odd cowry, is rewarded with a new position in society. "You will lead all men. You will never let them lose their way." Since leadership must depend on the good will, or faith of those led, a rationalization for hypocrisy in high places is given, as in No. 12, where Mawu places blame for all that goes wrong on Legba, "Mawu said to him that in a country it was necessary that the master be known as good, and that his servants be known as evil." But, as we have seen, Legba evens scores by tricking Mawu, in the same way as, in No. 100, King Agadja is tricked by his daughter. The wry assertion, in No. 97, where the king alone survives the magic that kills his soldiers ("the king is never in front"), gives us insight into Dahomean unadorned realism.

Social conformity as a good is stressed. No. 27 ends with the advice: "In Dahomey, what others cannot do, one does not oneself do." No. 43 shows the need for deferring to experience, in the penalty exacted of the young hunter for killing an animal endowed with magic powers too great for one of his age and status to cope with. And, as mentioned above, both the Chosen Suitor Theme and the Flight up the Tree, in some of their variants, teach the value of conformity to culturally approved patterns of marriage.

In the case of certain stories, we see that those who formulate and tell them are not beyond employing them as instruments to heighten their own prestige, as they reaffirm the sanctions that give them their authority in Dahomean society. Outstanding among those who use this device are the Fa diviners who call on the tales which are associated with each constellation of the fall of the divining kernels as parables for problems faced by the consultant. They either incorporate separate motifs, or shape a story into a homily about the success of the one who consulted the diviner, as against his antagonist who did not consult.[1] No. 90 underscores the importance of divination in planning: "This is the reason why, in Dahomey, when you are going to do something, you must first divine."

It is also important that the diviner, like any diagnostician, be given the facts of the case on which he is consulted. Failure to do so can be seen from No. 30; and if the point is not clear from these happenings, it is driven home by the moral: "That is why, in Dahomey, a person does not deceive his diviner." Even in the face of the control of supernatural forces represented by the diviner, the Dahomean does not lose his sense of realism, however. "When the diviner asks for something, a person gives it to him," is the final sentence of No. 31, so that with the affirmation of the need to conform and provide whatever the throws of the Fa seeds indicate as necessary, goes the suggestion that unless the diviner is given what he names all may not go well.

The power of the diviner is not made any the less important by No. 23, a myth which tells of the relationship of Fa to the other forces that rule the universe. Here, stated quite explicitly, we find a clear expression of the Dahomean principles of social and moral flexibility, exemplified in Legba who, "if he wishes, can change things about," as the "way out" in a universe ruled by Destiny. While in this myth we learn of the introduction of the Fa system of divination, the "writing of Mawu," by prophets who came down from the sky, No. 24 tells that it was taken over from the neighboring Nago (Yoruba) in the reign of Agadja, to counter the influence of the type of divination used by the autochthonous

[1] For details concerning the nature and functioning of the Fa cult in Dahomean culture, cf. *Dahomey*, Vol. II, pp. 201–222.

inhabitants. "They plotted against the King. So the King looked for something which was truly of providence itself." Today the Dahomean conforms, but he is skeptic enough to call on three Fa diviners for any important decision.

We may finally mention certain personal qualities that are esteemed. Thus, in No. 40, the value is stressed of using intelligence in resolving a difficult situation. Here the large and powerful animals are frightened away from the stream at the command of an unseen being. Pig throws his spear in the direction of the voice that issues from the water, and discovers that the command came only from Frog. "And that is why today the animals of the bush do not kill pigs." No. 133 focuses on the qualities of the best friend, setting up in contradistinction the less disinterested loyalty of the diviner and father-in-law. Industry is also held in high regard, as is seen in numerous stories, such as Nos. 138 or 116. The virtue of utilizing what is at hand in seeking a given end is implied in the first episode in No. 75, when Yo gathers grasshoppers with which to feed the chickens he will use to initiate his series of exchanges that allow him to execute his assignment of finding a wife for Dada Segbo with the expenditure of but one cowry shell.

A CROSS-CULTURAL APPROACH TO MYTH

1 *Some problems in the study of myth*

The presentation of a body of oral literature from a cross-cultural point of view throws new light on the many debated approaches to myth. As a point of departure, we may define a myth as a narrative which gives symbolic expression to a system of relationships between man and the universe in which he finds himself. And since we observe that in the myths men tell, the gods for all their macroscopic dimensions are set in man's image, we may posit further that the myth-making process, in its fundamental derivatives, is psychological and cultural.

On another level, we may define myth as those narrative forms that embody a system of symbolized values which, in each separate society, phrase the philosophy underlying its concepts, ideals and ends, and mark off its culture from all others as a way of life. Myth, in these terms, implies a social acceptance of approved symbols that, by transcending the generations, are at once the instrument of identification with the past and with the continuities of present and future. That is to say, like all manifestations of culture, myths draw their deepest sanctions from the fact that for the individual of a given society they existed before he was born, and that he carries the conviction they will continue after he is dead. Herein lie both the social and psychological importance of mythic symbols. Of significance also is the fact that, allowing for regional or sectarian variants involving points of emphasis, myths have the same meaning for all members of a society, whether in terms of a conceptualization of the powers that rule the universe, a system of institutions, a moral code, or the rituals of worship.

Let us sketch briefly those definitions of myth that have gained wide currency, before proceeding to their fuller analysis. Some define myth variously and vigorously as the negation of truth, as a consciously contrived ideology. Others hold that, from the point of view of any given people, their myths are their affirmations. Again, myth is held to provide an explanation of rite, which in these terms is held to derive point and meaning from it; or, with equal conviction, that it is the source of ritual, having given birth to mystic representations of gods and the forces of nature in the magic act. It is stated that the essence of myth lies in its magic power; this is denied by others, since for them myth, being the validation of belief, is identified as a phenomenon lying in the field of religion, which they differentiate from magic.

Theories of the origin of myth also abound. Myth is held to arise from the unconscious desires of individuals, from the collective unconscious, from the inspiration of ritual, from the need of early man to explain the movements of the heavenly bodies, from a tendency to clothe an idea in imagery and allegorical design.[1]

As regards any ascription of origin to myth, we reject, on well-

[1] For discussions of these approaches, see "Myth: A Symposium," *Jour. of American Folklore*, Vol. 68 (1955), *passim*.

established grounds of methodology, attempts to explain beginnings by the use of the traditions of living peoples as a referent. We know that culture is dynamic in character, however variable in degree of change, and that change is channeled by the uniquely human ability to transmit ideas cumulatively through the medium of language. We know, moreover, that this measurable equation of change is found in every society, without regard to size, or numbers, or to such features as a complex or simple technology, or a habitat that makes for much intercultural contact as against an isolated one. From this the principle derives that every manifestation of human culture is the result of the particular historical experience of the people who live in accordance with it, and that it represents in its present form the end result of a continuous process of internally generated, or externally transmitted change over the generations it has been in existence.

Similarly we support the criticisms lodged against theories of origin that attempt to relate specific forms of myth to particular psychological mechanisms, analagously calling on living nonliterate peoples to support the argument or, at the other extreme, restricting documentation to a single cultural stream. Until a completely new system of mythology can be found in the making, we must be on guard against any kind of reasoning, however impressive its logical appeal, that cannot be referred to the ultimate test of observed data. But even were it possible to find a mythological system in the making, we should still be faced with the problem of generalizing from one instance for all of human culture, as it has come down to us through time, and is found distributed in space.

It is thus inadmissible to posit a unilineal genealogy for the origin and development of myth. By acknowledging man's propensity to seek and order metaphysical systems that give a rationale for a way of life, and his flair for expressing the unrealized wish, we focus again on the creative process in human societies. Whether it emerges in newly devised symbols or in the incorporation of borrowed ones, it attests to man's receptivity everywhere to the symbolization of the Unknown according to the pattern of the known. As a consequence, we hold that comparisons on a cross-cultural basis must be cast in terms of processes rather than in those of form. By thus reaching the universals in human experience, we are freed to concentrate on the historically distinguishable manifestations of this symbolizing process as it is expressed in the mythologies of the diversified societies of the earth.

Another aspect of the discussion of myth concerns its role as narrative. From the social and psychological point of view, myth may be regarded as a stabilizing factor that makes for the adjustment of the individual in a world that is brought within his powers of comprehension. Myth as literature must be looked at in terms of patterns which provide a frame for the exercise of fantasy, within the limits set by cultural imperatives. Here we come to a point of great importance, the more so since it has been overlooked in most discussions of myth by students of literature. We refer to the phenomenon of diffusion, particularly the fresh materials from other peoples, which supply the story-teller with new themes or ways of combining or resolving themes that already exist in his own culture. The innovating story-teller incorporates a new motif thus acquired into a much told myth or tale, changing incident or plot structure to express the effect of contact, or a changing order, or newly introduced values. The influence, moreover, can be relied on to go beyond thematic additions or mutations, to include stylistic devices in narration and new imagery.

We emphasize this factor of cultural transmission because it not only has bearing on a discussion of the sources from which myth originally came, but is also critical for understanding the nature of its functioning within a given society. We shall treat of diffusion more fully in our examination of certain specific theories of myth. Here we need only indicate that many of the myths that have been called on to illustrate theories of origin or function, and have been classified from the comparative point of view as distinct units, are in effect themes that draw on the common store of a single historical stream.

The point of view of the approach which holds that myth is fixed and invariant gives rise to the question of where the similarities in the mythologies of nonliterate peoples have come from. This question has not been seriously faced since the days of the classical evolutionists who, at the turn of the century, followed the logic of their position, holding that resemblances in mythologies even of peoples living not too far apart were to be accounted for by similar reactions to similar environments. For reasons that are not germane to the discussion here, the position of the classical evolutionists has been refuted many years ago. But certainly no better explanation has been offered since by students of mythology.

Why the factor of diffusion has not been faced is due to the preoccupation of many students with the myths of peoples whose cultures are no longer living, or with the application of prinicples, theoretically derived, as they are held to relate myth to contemporary literature. The broad comparative view has in both cases been lacking. But we have come to know that if we are to establish general principles for any facet of human experience, we can no longer operate from so limited a methodological base. And even though our analysis of these Dahomean narratives cannot at this stage be extended into a comparative study, we will in later pages give attention to the historic contacts, not of Dahomey alone, but between peoples living in all the Old World, as evidenced in the close correspondences found in the narratives recorded from this great land mass. These correspondences show how myth, like all other narrative forms, represents a fusing and reworking of materials which have travelled great distances, taking on or sloughing off elements as they touched each individual society.

2   Sibling rivalry and the Oedipus theorem [1]

Let us, first of all, consider the Freudian approach to the problem of myth, and its emphasis on the unconscious wish to kill the father or father-surrogate. If we look at the myths commonly used in these discussions, from the point of view of enquiring into the problem of motivations from other possible perspectives, we discover the initiating act of hostility to be that of the father. It is the father's fear of an untimely challenge from his son, usually as made known to him through the instrumentality of some form of supernatural revelation, that eventuates in the order to have the son

[1] This discussion, with certain of the relevant tales reproduced in their entirety, appeared as an article in the *Jour. of Amer. Folklore*, Vol. 71 (1958), pp. 1–15, under the title "Sibling Rivalry, the Oedipus Complex, and Myth."

exposed, or killed outright. Where the threat is to a ruler, the command is to have all the sons born of a given category of mothers done away with.

This comes strikingly to the fore when we examine the development of the Oedipus thesis in relation to myth and myth making in Otto Rank's *The Myth of the Birth of the Hero,* the work which has long been the standard presentation of this approach, and to which, therefore, we will confine our comments. Carrying the subtitle, "A Psychological Interpretation of Mythology," the book is a well-documented, closely reasoned exposition and defense of a thesis. These qualities emerge particularly in the skilfull reconciliation of antithetical motifs in order to weld the core synthesis of the Freudian formulation. It is clear, however, that the dominance of this hypothesis over the data has made for the manipulation of these motifs to the neglect of possible conclusions from them that, as we shall show, Rank himself adumbrated in his discussion.

Let us follow Rank in his rich documentation, bearing in mind the principle that guides his analysis: "We are convinced that the myths, originally at least, are structures of the human faculty of imagination, which at some time were projected for certain reasons upon the heavens, and may be secondarily transferred to the heavenly bodies, with their enigmatical phenomena." [1] We may note here, without further comment, the earlier influence of Max Müller and the other proponents of the so-called "solar school" of mythological interpretation, who held that the origin of myths was to be explained in the efforts of early man to interpret the movements of the heavenly bodies. [2] This has waned to the point where it no longer enters in the thinking of students. Rank, it may be remarked, makes no further mention of this mode of interpretation, but turns to his data—the hero myths of King Sargon of Babylon, of Moses and Abraham, of the Hindu Karna, of the Greek Oedipus, Paris, Telephos and Perseus, of the Babylonian Gilgamos; followed by a more extended discussion of Kyros who, as king of Persia, reigned over Asia. The series continues with the Iranian myth of

---

[1] Otto Rank, *The Myth of the Birth of the Hero,* New York, 1952, p. 8.
[2] For the rise and fall of the "solar mythology" school, cf. R. M. Dorson, "The Eclipse of Solar Mythology," *Jour. of Amer. Folklore,* Vol. 68 (1955), pp. 393–416.

Feridan, with the Tristan saga, and the adventures of Romulus and Remus, followed by another extended analysis, this time of the Jesus story, and concluding with the tale of the Norse Siegfried and Lohengrin.

Rank summarizes the common thematic components as follows:

The hero is the child of the most distinguished parents; usually the son of a king. His origin is preceded by difficulties, such as continence, or prolonged barrenness, or secret intercourse of the parents, due to external prohibition or obstacles. During the pregnancy, or antedating the same, there is a prophesy, in form of a dream or an oracle, cautioning against his birth, *and usually threatening danger to the father, or his representative*. He is then saved by animals or by lowly people (shepherds), and is suckled by a female animal or by a humble woman. After he has grown up, he finds his distinguished parents, . . . takes his revenge on his father, on the one hand, is acknowledged on the other, and finally achieves rank and honors.[1]

It is not necessary for us to follow the course of the argument whereby Rank, employing the techniques of dream interpretation and utilizing the mechanisms of identification and projection, builds up the psychoanalytic documentation of the ultimate origin of myth in fantasy. What is of importance is that Rank continuously focuses his interest and lays his stresses on the experience of the hero, without reference to the fears of the father because of a certainty that he will be replaced by this child.[2]

When attention has been called to the motif of the father's fear of his son, it is impressive to see the degree to which this theme appears in Rank's own abstracts. Without citing all such instances, we may note that even the Oedipus tale turns on the incident wherein the Delphic Oracle tells Laios that "he may have a son if he so desires, but fate has ordained that his own son will kill him." In view of the consistency of this theme in Rank's materials, it is strange that

[1] Rank, *op. cit.*, p. 61 (italics ours).

[2] In this context, attention should be called to the well known critique of the Oedipus theory by B. Malinowski in *The Father in Primitive Psychology*, London, 1927, and in papers by W. A. Lessa, "Oedipus-type Tales in Oceania," *Jour. of Amer. Folklore*, Vol. 69 (1956), pp. 63–73, and W. R. Bascom, "The Myth-Ritual Theory," *Jour. of Amer. Folklore*, Vol. 70 (1957), pp. 104–114, esp. pp. 109–110.

he did not develop the insights regarding the father's fears that are foreshadowed in his discussion, as where he says, "The hostility of the father, and the resulting exposure, accentuate the motive which has caused the ego to indulge in the entire fiction"; or tells us, "The child simply gets rid of the father in the neurotic romance, while in the myth the father endeavors to lose the child." [1]

Just as Rank was aware of the father's initiating role of hostility, he was also not oblivious to the motif of rivalry between brothers. As a matter of fact, we have the impression that he was troubled by this unresolved factor in his equation. Thus he says, "The duplication of the fathers, or the grandfathers, respectively, by a brother may be continued in the next generation, and concern the hero himself, thus leading to the *brother myths*, which can only be hinted at in connection with the present theme." [2]

The focus by Rank, and those who have accepted his position on the genesis of myth, is a prime example of the influence of cultural background on a student who is not accustomed to think in comparative, cross-cultural terms. This focus is on the hostility of the son toward his father, to the neglect both of the fear which, in the very tales Rank cites, the father is found to have of his son, and the hostility between brothers. For when we turn to the Dahomean tales, we find that the classical Oedipus formulation can be reached only by distorting the intent of the myths, whereas the factor of the father's anxiety in the face of challenge by the son, or of rivalry between brothers, stands out in bold relief.

The reason for this is clear when we look at the social structure of Dahomey from the point of view of the relation of the child to his mother and to his brothers and sisters. To the extent the economic pattern allows, the infant is constantly with its mother. It is fed when it cries. The mother carries it on her back as she goes to market; while she pounds grain in the mortar, or performs other duties in the compound; when she dances. It lies close to her on the sleeping mat at night. With the appearance of her next child, this intimacy is no longer possible. During the initial period, the child may be taken by a maternal grandmother, if the compounds are close enough, though most often it remains with its mother.

[1] *Op. cit.* pp. 68, 69.
[2] *Op. cit.*, p. 87. Italics as in the original text.

If there is no older child of its mother to care for it, a little girl who may not be more than seven or eight years old is brought into the mother's household to help with the task. It is not difficult to see that however good the adjustment of the child to this new situation, a sense of rejection and neglect is an inevitable concomitant. If in addition to this we consider the situation within a polygynous household, we see how rivalry between siblings has a firm base in the early experience of the child.

When we turn to the expression of this in the Dahomean narratives, we find, as we have noted, the recurrent theme of fraternal jealousy. It is present in myths Nos. 2, 3, and 4; in such myth-chronicles as Nos. 92, 93, and 94; and in such a tale as No. 138. A point that is of some importance for the Freudian theory of myth, when this is considered against the background of Dahomean family life, is that jealousy between siblings never involves the youngest child in relation to the oldest. It is always the eldest and the one next to him who are at odds, and in this situation the youngest, in accordance with the accepted cultural formula, plays the role of conciliator. This, for example, is the role of Legba, as told in myth No. 4, in the fraternal strife between Hevioso and Sagbata, or that of Kpelu, in tale No. 60, where there is controversy between the royal *tohosu*. The motif of jealousy which occurs in the relations between parent and child, as in No. 16, usually manifests itself as an attitude of a father toward a son who is destined to surpass him, and in this particular instance, is at bottom a contest between two rivals, Dada Segbo and Lisa, and not the son at all.

The theme of rivalry between brothers, as may be inferred from the examples which we have just given, are found in all categories of Dahomean narrative. As mentioned, tale No. 60 recounts the strife among the abnormally born offspring of the royal family. Another type, of which No. 26 is an instance, tells how an older brother leaves his ancestral home to seek his fortune. Aided by supernatural power he attains wealth and high position. His younger brother finds him, forces him to disclose the secret that has given him good fortune and brings ruin on both of them. In one tale of royalty, No. 96, which includes such elements of the classical Oedipus motif as the attempt to do away with the future king

(in this case by throwing him into a river from which he is res-
cued by a boatman and nurtured until his return to his father's
palace where he reveals his identity), it is the elder brother, and
not the father, who initiates the action. In various versions of the
origin myth of the royal family which we give, the theme of
fraternal strife enters repeatedly. Thus No. 93 tells how the children, born of a union between a leopard and a royal wife of Adja,
who fled to Allada and established their rule there, part to found
separate kingdoms because "the three brothers could not live together without quarreling."

The infrequency with which the Oedipus theme—the hostility
of son toward father—is found in Dahomean narrative brings us
back to certain significant elements in the culture that shape Dahomean thinking on this point. In summary, the structure of Dahomey
is patrilineal and patrilocal, with a system of clans, each of which,
as we have noted, is conceived of as being supernaturally controlled
by its *tohwiyo*, the spirit of the first human offspring of a non-
human totemic father and a human mother. The family is polygynous, inhabiting a compound headed by the oldest living male. Of
primary importance in the development of the emotional life of the
child is the fact that each wife of the compound head, and of
his married sons, or brothers, if they are living in the compound,
has a separate dwelling. Cohabitation takes place during a Dahomean four-day week, when each wife in turn leaves her own house
at night and sleeps in the house of the common husband. Her children remain in their mother's house, so that they do not witness
the sexual act of their parents. During this week, the mother also
cooks for her husband, and the young children, who take their
meals with her, join the father, who eats apart. They receive tidbits
from him, so that the feeling established from infancy toward him
has a strong positive emotional tone.

The relations between members of these polygynous households
introduce complexities. There is first of all the degree of adjustment between the father and mother, which must be projected
against his attitude toward his other wives and their children. This
in turn is related to competition between co-wives, often motivated
by the desire to achieve the most favorable treatment for their own
children, particularly as regards inheritance. Though seniority is

important, the principle incorporates a high degree of plasticity. For everyone is senior, actually or potentially, to someone else, so that there is ample play for compensation where a person junior to one man is at the same time senior to another younger than himself. It is this complex which gives rise to the common belief, found not only in Dahomey but widely throughout West Africa, that the youngest child is the cleverest of his siblings.

As critical in assessing the classical Oedipus theorem, it must be recognized, moreover, that not only does the Dahomean child not witness the sexual act of his parents, but that the father is far from being the sole punishing agent or the court of last resort in making decisions. The earliest punishments, and the most frequent, are received from the mother. Though the father is called in to punish serious offenses, a mother will at times hide certain of her son's misdeeds from her husband, and punish her son herself during the early formative years, before he begins to assume male tasks and to follow his father to the fields. Moreover, a child may be punished by any man or woman of his compound who sees him misbehave, and the compound head, who is perhaps the father's older brother or an irascible old woman who has returned to her paternal residence from her husband's village to look after the family ancestral rites, may be far more important in fulfilling the symbolic role of authority than the young father.

The world-view, as reflected in the mythology, is predictably quite in harmony with the social structure. We see it ruled by a hierarchy of deities, who stand in family relationship to one another as children of the androgynous god, Mawu-Lisa. Her offspring, who are the protagonists of the myths, are the principal deities, organized in pantheons of nature gods. Legba, the youngest son of the Creator, however, heads no pantheon. For, as we have seen, Mawu, in apportioning the control of the Universe among her children, with the astuteness that characterizes Dahomean thinking, gave each a different language. What is significant about this procedure, in the present context, is the fear of generational supersession that so clearly emerges. Legba, alone, her youngest child and her messenger, shares with her a knowledge of the speech of all the domains, nor has she permitted any of her offspring access to ultimate power. They may destroy, but they cannot create.

The gods, in the Dahomean world-view, moreover, are not separate from man. There is no rigid dichotomy between heaven and earth. Both are parts of a complex overriding unity. The ancestral cult ties living man actively into the world of the supernatural, while the personal forces in man, such as destiny, Fa, or the concept of fortune and power, Dã, place him in continuous interaction with the highest beings. Man calls on magic for protection against malevolent powers; so do the gods, whose shrines, like the dwellings of man, have magic charms. Of the three souls of man, one, the inherited component, is ancestral; another incorporates "a bit of Mawu," so that every man has in his own being something of the Creator; the third is the man's own personality, the essence that individualizes each human being, and at death is held to account for the way he uses the powers of the other two. Nor, as we have observed, is Destiny, in the Dahomean sense, fixed as in the oracles of classical mythology. Within the ultimate limits of fate, as set by Mawu when a man is born, there is latitude for the play of experience. Man in the Dahomean universe, therefore, is not a passive figure. It is noteworthy that before a man embarks on any project of importance, he gives offerings to his own head—his intelligence, which he calls on for decisions and choices—as well as to the ancestors and the gods.

Against this background, then, let us return to the question of intergenerational rivalry. There are, in the Dahomean system of values, explicitly institutionalized rejections of specific categories of children, especially those born with abnormal traits.[1] Hemaphroditic and deformed infants are always exposed. They are believed to threaten the lives of either of their parents, usually the father, and to be an ill omen for the entire group. Children born with four fingers, when divination so indicates, may be "sent back" to the river, since they are regarded as powerful river spirits. Where this is not done, the child will be reared by his parents only reluctantly. Other parental fears are projected upon children who are either born with teeth, or whose upper teeth come before the lower. If the infant is male, it is believed that the father will die—"will be replaced," as the Dahomean phrasing goes—or if a female, the mother.

[1] Cf. *Dahomey*, Vol. I, pp. 262–275.

Twins, thought to bring luck, yet feared for their supernatural power, are prized, though in certain other parts of West Africa they are done away with. The child born after twins, the *dosu*, however, "is held in aversion . . . because it is believed that these children are avaricious and grasping; that they never share their possessions with another; that they are not to be relied on by friends or relatives to be of assistance in time of adversity." [1] And the Dahomean attitude toward yet another phenomenon of child-hood likewise reveals a patterned hostility:

The appearance of teeth before the child is able to sit is . . . an un-welcome occurrence, the feeling being that such children will always be sickly. Such of these children as do survive, tradition tells, will be well-to-do, for they come from the serpent spirit who is the giver of riches. In spite of this, and though credited with being highly intel-ligent and able, they are disliked, for they are said to be thoroughly 'bad' and are reared by their parents without affection. When they at-tain maturity and gain wealth and position they are liked none the more, since belief holds that the greater their riches, the greater the misery and poverty of their parents. [2]

What on the other hand, does Dahomean mythology show as regards the hostility of a child toward its parents? We may, as a first example, return to No. 12, which tells how Legba, irked at being blamed for all that went wrong, when Mawu was at fault, steals her sandals and wears them as he takes yams from her garden. When a search is made for the culprit, it is revealed by the match-ing footprints that Mawu herself was the thief. Shame at being humiliated by her own son causes Mawu to leave the earth. From the point of view of the Freudian theory of myth, it will be noted that Legba tricks his mother because of pique against injustice. But more significant is the fact that redress is achieved through the instrument of ridicule, and release from close supervision by the use of subterfuge.

We may take No. 16 as a further instance. Here we have the theme of the son who is destined to surpass his father, one that, as we have seen in discussing the development of the Oedipus theory

[1] *Dahomey*, Vol. I, p. 275.
[2] *Ibid.*, p. 275.

of myth, has not received the consideration it merits. The father attempts to destroy the son, whose final victory is achieved when, through the instrumentality of the son's maternal grandfather, the father is transfixed into a mountain, a penalty in which, it is to be noted, the son has no hand. When the son, who has been transformed into the Thunder god, charges through the heavens, wanting to kill, presumably because of the trials he suffered on earth, his mother in the rumble of the more distant thunder, admonishes, "Take care, take care, he's your father."

Our materials make it clear that the emphasis laid in discussions of myth on the theme of the son's hostility, as embodied in the Oedipus tale, has caused to be overlooked such other major psychocultural factors as rivalry between brothers. We are, in fact, faced here with one of those distortions of perspective that result from overemphasis on a single element when searching for explanations of a complex phenomenon. In this case, perspective can be corrected only by taking into account the more inclusive mechanisms of generation and sibling counterposition. More than this, the materials call attention to an essential need to submit generalizing conclusions about the Oedipus myth to the test of cross-cultural comparison.

A reading of the Dahomean myths in cultural context makes it apparent that the Freudian hypothesis, or any other explanation of myth that is based on a single causal factor, does not hold. We have come to recognize that the theme of rivalry between siblings, hitherto disregarded in discussions of myth, is to be taken as basic to an understanding of patterns of interaction. In analyzing the motivating forces underlying the myth clusters that fall into the Oedipus category, we must take into account not only the son's jealousy of the father, but also the father's fear of being displaced by his son. Parent-child hostilities, that is, are not unidirectional. As manifest in myth, and in the situations of everyday experience, they are an expression of the broader phenomenon of intergenerational competition. These tensions, moreover, begin in infancy in the situation of rivalry between children of the same parents for a single goal, the attention of the mother. This rivalry sets up patterns of reaction that throughout life give rise to attitudes held toward the siblings or sibling substitutes with whom the individual was in competition during infancy, and it is our hypothesis that these attitudes are later projected by the father upon his offspring. In myth, if the psychological interpretation is to be granted validity, we must posit that the threat to the father or father-surrogate is to be seen as a projection of the infantile experience of sibling hostility upon the son. It may be said to be the response to the reactivation of early attitudes toward the mother under the stimulus of anticipated competition for the affection of the wife.

This does not argue the rejection of the hypothesis of the Oedipus mechanism as a functioning causal factor in influencing the themes of the myths that man has produced to explain the world in which he lives. It is, however, only one of the causal factors, and not *the* causal factor. Again, in terms of our earlier discussion, it is essentially an explanation based on form and not process, for it is the form of the Oedipus response that is stressed, and not its functioning as one of a number of psychological responses that comes into play. Another methodological point of importance is that a minimum of cross-cultural referents have been used to put the Oedipus hypothesis to the test. As we have seen here, the comparative materials that were called on were ranged so as to focus on the Oedipus theorem. The Oedipus complex has thus emerged as an article of faith rather than as a tool to aid investigation, as is clear from the statement by Freud, that, "Recognition of it has become the shibboleth that distinguishes supporters of psychoanalysis from their opponents." [1]

3   *The* mystique *of the archetype*

It is necessary to examine here the influence on students of literature of the concept of the archetypal mythologem, a kind of living psychic fossil preserved in the collective representations of "primitive" peoples, and the assumption in this context, that archetypes are universal. Of special pertinence are certain of its methodological implications.

---

[1] This quotation from Freud's *Collected Works* is cited by Ernest Jones, *Sigmund Freud, Life and Work*, London, 1955, Vol. II, p. 326.

Let us see how C. G. Jung, with whose name the concept is primarily associated, himself defines the archetype. Moving from the base of his system of analytical psychology, which revealed certain consistent themes that, he asserts, are akin to mythic motifs, he says, "These products are . . . mythological components which, because of their typical nature, we can call 'motifs,' 'primordial images,' types or—as I have named them—archetypes." These mythic manifestations in individual psychology are to be differentiated from myth itself: "In the individual, the archetypes occur as involuntary manifestations of unconscious processes whose existence and meaning can only be inferred, whereas the myth deals with traditional forms of incalculable age. They hark back to a prehistoric world whose spiritual preconceptions and general conditions we can still observe today among existing primitives." [1]

It is unnecessary here to enlarge on Jung's definition and point of view with further citations from his work; it is more important to consider his ideas on the psychology of the "primitive." From his discussion, we infer that he was influenced by the concept of the *elementargedanken* of Bastian, those fundamental ideas of all mankind that find their specific manifestations in the *völkergedanken*, the parallels that have been recorded from all peoples, and which, thus early in the history of the scientific study of man, posed the problem of origins with which Jung is concerned. Another influence that is discernable in his approach and phrasing is that of the French philosopher and anthropologist Lucien Lévy-Bruhl.

To those who have had first-hand experience with nonliterate peoples (or, in the specific case of Dahomey, have gained from the preceding pages an impression of how hard-headed, realistic, and logical Dahomeans can be), the passages we quote from Jung take on an air of fantasy. "Primitive mentality differs from the civilized chiefly in that the conscious mind is far less developed in extent and intensity," he says. [2] "Functions such as thinking, willing, etc., are not yet differentiated; they are pre-conscious, a fact which in

---

[1] C. G. Jung and C. Kerenyi, *Essays on a Science of Mythology*, New York, 1949, pp. 99–100. We use citations of the most recent relevant publications to document the current Jungian position.

[2] *Ibid.*, p. 100.

the case of thinking, for instance, shows itself in the circumstance that the primitive does not think *consciously*, but that thoughts appear." From this it follows logically, in terms of Jung's frame of reference, that "primitive mentality does not invent *myths*, it *experiences* them." In other words, "Myths are original revelations of the pre-conscious psyche, involuntary statements about unconscious happenings, and anything but allegories of physical processes." Myths, indeed, "not merely . . . represent, they are the mental life of the primitive tribe, which immediately falls to pieces and decays when it loses its mythological heritage, like a man who has lost his soul." Finally, as regards the problem of the processes that are the causal factor in the creation of myth, we are told that "Many of these unconscious processes may be indirectly occasioned by consciousness, but never by conscious choice. Others appear to rise spontaneously, that is to say, from no discernible or demonstrable conscious cause." [1]

The breadth of these assumptions, with their assurance of universal validity, and the certainty that they provide an answer to one of the most complex questions faced by students of man, account in large measure for the conviction they have carried. Yet the fact remains that the "primitive" automaton, as pictured by Jung, ignores the most elementary lessons that have been taught us by the scientific study of man. It is, indeed, sheer mysticism, and lies on a different plane, conceptually and methodologically, from those attempts to understand human beings everywhere which use the methods of induction. Any search for supporting facts from cultures that have been studied in the field becomes an exercise in frustration, for there is little with which to come to grips except in terms of bare assertion and denial.

There is no question but that the problem that gave rise to Jung's theory of the archetype is a real one. It has been recognized ever since there has been contact between peoples of differing ways of life. In essence, all these enquiries represent attempts to account for the resemblances found in the cultures of man which, though exhibiting wide variation, manifest unities that give them their common human base. There are two possible answers: One ascribes these similarities to the historic experience of humanity,

[1] *Ibid.*, pp. 100–102, *passim;* all italics are in the original.

holding that they represent the working out of inventions made in the early days of man's experience as a culture-building species, and the interchanges of contact since then. The other relates these similarities to tendencies inherent in man, and as in the instance we are considering, bases its formulation on some not very well defined idea of unilineal evolution, with an overtone of invidious comparison between the various "stages" of presumed development.

Bearing in mind this theoretical orientation we may quote again from Jung, giving his comments on a collection of American Indian trickster tales that date a decade and a half after the passages cited above were published. The figure of the trickster in mythology, we are here told, "is obviously a 'psychologem,' an archetypal psychic structure of extreme antiquity." This being the case, "When . . . a primitive or barbarous consciousness forms a picture of itself on a much earlier level of development and continues to do so for hundreds and even thousands of years, undeterred by the contamination of its archaic qualities with differentiated, highly developed mental products, then the causal explanation is that the older the archaic qualities are, the more conservative and pertinacious is their behavior." This "senseless appendage" as Jung calls it, in terms reminiscent of the nineteenth-century concept of the survival, "still 'functions' provided they have not been spoiled by civilization." [1]

Inherent in this thinking is an assumption of the conservatism of the "primitives" to a degree that goes beyond the postulates even of those who, as we shall see in later pages, hold that nonliterate peoples lack any of the curiosity that leads to innovation and creative expression. Yet the germ of validity in the approach remains, and in constructive terms this is what concerns us here. In this context, we return once again to the problem of universals.

If we take trickster tales as a case in point, we know that peoples all over the world, having the most diverse customs, include them in their repertory of narrative. Nor can there be any question that those trickster tales reflect unities in human experience. Who,

---

[1] C. G. Jung, "On the Psychology of the Trickster Figure," in Paul Radin, *The Trickster, a Study in American Indian Mythology*, New York, 1956, pp. 200–201.

in his personal life, in no matter what society, has not known the man who evades the unpleasant task, or gains a desired end by using his wits, or by playing the fool? Or one who just skirts the limits of acceptable behavior? We know empirically that the anthropomorphizing habit of man—of all men—is strong. It is consequently not difficult to conceive the transfer of these human experiences to the animals, each of whom, from observable behavior, responds differently to the same situations.

This is, of course, speculation, for we cannot repeat too often that we have no means of arriving at certainties about origins. What is important for our analysis is not the question of unities, as such, for there is no gainsaying the unities of human psychology, and insofar as these unities form the basis for theories of similarities in the cultures of man, their cogency is patent. But there is a vast difference between assuming tendencies in the human psyche, on a genetic basis, that manifest themselves in specific forms; and holding that similarities in response arise out of similarities in adjustment to social situations, and in meeting the demands of the natural environment. The first inevitably leads to a *mystique*, such as the concept of the collective unconscious that, in Jungian terms, forms the basis for the archetype. It is reminiscent of the long discarded concept of the group mind advanced by Tarde which, like it, was incapable of empirical proof, and therefore, acceptable only as an article of faith.

The very anonymity of authorship in societies where narrative is common property, and where artistry lies in the stylistic incorporation and transmutation of new narrative elements, has served to lend credence to such a concept as the collective unconscious. But, significantly, it was reached without first-hand acquaintance with the peoples whose cultures were used to formulate it. In the final analysis, however, there are only individual human beings. All mankind belongs to the same species, with the special proved ability to establish and continue those bodies of tradition we call cultures. It is thus not strange that the similar problems that human beings, as members of their societies, must face should eventuate in solutions that, in broad line, are similar.

What we find is that man everywhere has faced the psychological challenge of forces greater than himself, whether of nature, or of the animal world, or of man. As a consequence, it may be postulated that the spoken symbolizations of these challenges have found wide appeal through the contact of peoples, from the earliest days of man on earth. This in turn has made for a universalizing of symbolic experiences, by devising a system of meaningful relationships with these forces, in categories that range from the just and beneficent to the mischievous and hostile. Under the play of man's fantasy, whatever mechanism may underlie this, his constants of experience have been projected, elaborated, exaggerated to endow these forces with the powers and personalities that we read of in world mythologies.

An important point is that man has not done this everywhere in the same way. What may seem to be identical expressions of mythic concept are by no means the same when subjected to intensive analysis. It is very well to speak of "the trickster," yet one need but compare the Winnebago trickster, as discussed in the volume that gives rise to the comments by Jung which we have cited, with Legba and Yo in Dahomey to find that the specifications for the first by no means fit the second. It is not necessary, as a matter of fact, to do more than quote from the description of the trickster in the prefatory note to these American Indian tales to see how slight, except for the fact that he is a trickster, is his correspondence to what, on the surface, would seem to be his Dahomean counterparts.

In what must be regarded as its earliest and most archaic form, as found among the American Indians, Trickster is at one and the same time creator and destroyer, giver and negator, he who dupes others and is always duped himself. He wills nothing consciously. At all times he is constrained to behave as he does from impulses over which he has no control. He knows no values, social or moral, is at the mercy of his passions and appetites, yet through his actions all values come into being. But not only he, or so our myth tells us, possesses these traits. So, likewise, do the other figures of the plot connected with him: the animals, the various supernatural beings and monsters, and man.[1]

When we compare this American Indian trickster with the Dahomean Legba we find that Legba is neither creator nor de-

[1] *Ibid.*, p. 9.

stroyer; that what he gives and takes away is far more often individual than cosmogonic; that while he dupes others, he is rarely duped himself. His activity, again, is calculated, highly conscious. His acts are rarely impulsive, but for the most part are directed toward the achievement of a well-defined end. He knows socially accepted values even when he behaves contrary to them; he is in no wise the source of them.

Again, Legba is not the only Dahomean trickster; we also have Yo. Yo, however, while he "dupes others and is . . . duped himself" is hardly what would be called a mythic figure, if by this we mean a being with power over some aspect of the Universe. As the protagonist of the humorous tale, he is the symbol of comedy, and, as we are told in No. 76, he gives his name to these tales. He is far closer to the type that the common meaning of the term "folkloristic" would fit. The tales in which he figures are by no means always explanatory, and when they are, the phenomena they explain are simple and direct—why a man must have much money to marry (No. 75), why the lizard beats his head on the ground when he wants to say something (No. 80), why dogs that harm people are killed (No. 81), why there are leopards (No. 82), why one hears echoes in the forest when a tree is struck (No. 84), why the body of a dead rabbit is not buried (No. 87), why one must divine before starting any proposed course of action (No. 90), why a particular kind of butterfly is the child of Yo (No. 91). Out of the seventeen Yo stories we give, only eight can be regarded as in any sense ascribing to the personality or acts of this trickster qualities that might be termed mythic, and even these acts scarcely deal with matters of cosmic importance.

We could also perform this same exercise for what is termed the archetypal character of the child-god, discussed at length by Kerenyi in the volume from which our first quotations from Jung have been taken. In this discussion, however, we find the same absence of cross-cultural reference whose implication for a general theory of myth we have discussed in connection with Rank's work. For Kerenyi, who draws exclusively on the Graeco-Roman tradition, maintains he is discussing "the primordial child in primordial times." As has been done for the trickster figure, we could compare characters and roles of the beings he discusses with

the Dahomean *enfant terrible* category, which comprises the abnormally born *tohosu*, the twins, the orphans, all of whom are
endowed with supernatural powers, or enjoy supernatural guardianship.

But it would be pointless to do this. Because just as there are
those circumstances in the life of men in all places, and presumably
at all times, when they must cope with a vastly superior force or
superior intelligence, so at all times and in all places children enter
into this experience as an ever-present factor. Fantasy is a part of
the development of the growing child. Contrast in precocity, in
physical or mental or artistic endowment, perplexity at or be-
wilderment by deviance, encourages symbolization of differences.
We are not here concerned with the validity of explanations that
the fantasies of the adult creative artist who weaves the tales
about precocious children, or gives them the powers and status of
gods, may well be repeating his own childhood fantasies of counter-
ing the power of the adult.

These, whether as explanations or speculations, are phrased in
terms of the universal experiences of mankind; they do not require
us to postulate a metaphysical concept such as a collective unconscious that, through the operation of a sort of racial memory,
accounts for highly generalized unities found among the peoples
of the world. We have seen how essential it is to take into account
the mechanism of diffusion through which innovations come to
one people through contact with another. In terms of the hypothesis advanced by Jung and his followers all these derive from the
earliest times of man—that is, are "primordial" in the conceptual
sense—and consequently no data of scientific relevance can be
brought to prove or disprove their fundamental character. Reference to living nonliterate peoples, the "primitives" in discussions
of the archetype, will prove nothing at all except that at the present
time men everywhere exhibit broad underlying similarities in their
ways of life.

We can but repeat that since *homo sapiens* is a single species, it
follows that no living group has less time behind it than any
other, and what we know of the dynamic nature of all culture
teaches us that no body of tradition lies inert and unchanging,
producing the human automaton we have seen described. In actu-

ality, then, the *mystique* of the archetype falls into that large body of theoretical formulations that explain universals in human behavior without the benefit of empirical proof; formulations that, as we have said, must be taken on faith or not at all. The "proofs" offered are those which fall within the framework of the theory; the exceptions, the complexities, the inexplicable elements are disregarded. The vitality of all such theories is due in part to the fact that they represent attempts to explain fundamental problems in human behavior and to account for recurrent themes in the creative efforts of man. But in part, also, they tend to be well received because they give simple answers to questions that remain to challenge those willing to face the complexities of objective enquiry.

4 Functional and ritualistic approaches to myth

There remain three other approaches to the study of myth that have wide currency. Each of these has its particular emphasis, but they have so influenced one another that for purposes of discussion they can best be grouped together.

Despite individual orientations, all three share certain points of view. First of all, psychological considerations play a minor part in their analyses, so that the factor of individual creativity does not enter into their theories of the origin or development of mythic narrative. While the idea of the group mind is not a part of their conceptual apparatus, the myth is taken somehow as a kind of extra-individual "given," and tends to be reified in their discussions as a *ding an sich*. In the second place, they share a strong anti-euhemeristic position, being agreed that myth—and, by extension, any narration of events that has not been reduced to writing—must be refused any measure of historic credence. Finally, all of them are "anthropological" in the sense that the mythologies of non-literate peoples, usually denoted in their works as "primitive" or "savage," figure importantly in their argument and documentation.

Chronologically, the first to appear was the group termed the Cambridge School, whose best-known representatives were Sir

James Frazer and Jane Harrison. This group draws its data and its conclusions primarily from Greek mythology, and its members have made outstanding contributions to classical scholarship. More than any others, they have urged the ritual theory of myth, their basic assumption being that since myth explains ritual behavior, it can have come into being only after the rituals they explain were fully established. This view is most energetically espoused in the United States by the literary critic Stanley Edgar Hyman.

The functionalist explanation of myth, the second of these approaches, was advanced by Bronislaw Malinowski, who based his theory on the anthropological field research he carried on from 1915 until 1918 in the Melanesian Trobriand Islands. The influence of the Cambridge School on Malinowski's thinking came principally through Sir James Frazer's major work, *The Golden Bough*. This is stressed in the Preface to the essay in which Malinowski states his theoretical position on myth, the text of an address delivered at the University of Liverpool in 1925 in honor of Frazer.

The relationship between these two points of view is not as close as later students of literature have suggested. For Malinowski was, first and foremost, the fieldworker; he dealt with living people. He did not confine himself to texts either handed down from cultures no longer existent, or sent to his study by those in first-hand contact with "savages," as was the case with Frazer, who, like the other members of the Cambridge group, had no first-hand experience outside his own society. But resemblances, along the broad lines we have indicated, are present.

The third approach, while fully accepting the ritual theory of the origin of myth, lays its major emphasis on the unreliability of oral tradition as history. It was propounded by Lord Raglan, its exponent, in his work *The Hero*, first published in 1936, a book showing the influence of both the Cambridge School and of Malinowski. Raglan's interest in testing the historical adequacy of oral tradition seems to have arisen from his study of the degree of truth and untruth to be found in the stories about various heroes. To his shrewd assessment of how the play of fancy can distort any historic reality, he brings many arguments from the accounts of recent events, in literate cultures, that have moved into the realm of folklore. His conclusions reflect the influences of the currents of thought that have stimulated his thinking: ". . . that the folk-tale is never of popular origin, but is merely one form of the traditional narrative; that the traditional narrative has no basis either in history or in philosophical speculation, but is derived from the myth; and that the myth is a narrative connected with rite." [1] A biographical item that may be of relevance is that, unlike the Cambridge group, and like Malinowski, Raglan did have first-hand contact with "savages," as he consistently terms nonliterate peoples. What influence this may have had on his thinking is difficult to say, but to the anthropologist approaching his theory of myth, it seems relevant that this first-hand contact was with a nomadic herding people of the Sudan, where for a number of years he was an officer in the British colonial service.

Hyman, whose excellent summary of the development of the ritualistic approach to myth [2] may be drawn on here, speaks of 1912 as "the watershed year" in which this position was fully enunciated. This was in Jane Harrison's *Themis*, where, he tells us, these points were made: "that myth arises out of rite, rather than the reverse; that it is 'the spoken correlative of the acted rite, the thing done' . . . and that it is not anything else nor of any other origin." This was long before Malinowski's demonstration, for the Trobrianders, that myth is to be thought of as an essential component of ritual, and associated with it; that while "there is . . . no ritual without belief . . . ," the rites themselves "are regarded as the results of mythical events"; that they are the "statement of a primaeval, greater, and more relevant reality . . . the knowledge of which supplies man with the motive for ritual and moral sanctions, as well as with indications of how to perform them." [3]

Yet before this point of view was enunciated, Harrison had been rethinking her materials, especially in the light of the developing currents of psychological theory, to revise her position to a degree not customarily recognized when her contribution to the theory of myth is discussed. "Man, the psychologists tell us, is essentially an image-maker. He cannot perform the simplest operation without

[1] Lord Raglan, *The Hero, a Study in Tradition, Myth and Drama*, London, 1936, p. 144.

[2] Stanley Edgar Hyman, "The Ritual View of Myth and the Mythic," *Jour. of Amer. Folklore*, Vol. 68 (1955), p. 463.

[3] B. Malinowski, *Myth in Primitive Psychology*, New York, 1926, pp. 29–30.

forming of it some sort of correlative idea." Then, moving to ritual, she remarks,

> A rite is not of course the same as a simple action. A rite is—it must never be forgotten—an action *re*done (commemorative) or *pre*done (anticipatory and magical). There is therefore always in a rite a certain tension either of remembrance or anticipation and this tension emphasizes the emotion and leads on to representation. . . . If we were a mass of well combined instincts, that is if the cycle of perception and action were instantly fulfilled, we should have no representation and hence no art and no theology. In fact in a word religious presentation, mythology or theology, as we like to call it, springs like ritual from arrested, unsatisfied desire. We figure to ourselves what we want, we create an image and that image is our god.[1]

This quotation from Harrison takes on added importance because, among many students of literature, the derivation of myth from ritual is unquestioned. Thus Hyman asserts that "the important relationship of art literature to folk literature lies, not in the surface texture of folk speech, but in the archetypal patterns of primitive ritual, the great myths." [2] Elsewhere, he states, "a ritual origin for the blues constitues a fascinating problem, although not a critical issue (too much obviously convincing ritual interpretation has been produced for the theory to stand or fall on any single form)." [3]

Yet if we move away from dogma to the realism of empirical analysis, we realize, as we have seen before, that assumptions of this kind concerning absolute origins are no more amenable to objective proof than any others. The concept of the survival, in its classical sense, as against its later meaning of a socially reinterpreted act, has long been shown untenable. We know enough about the ease with which new forms are assigned old meanings, or old forms given new ones, to refuse credence to the act that has no meaning, essential to the myth-from-ritual hypothesis. If ritual is symbolic action, then symbolism is the essence of myth. It is thus incon-

[1] Jane Ellen Harrison, *Epilegomena to the Study of Greek Religion*, Cambridge, 1921, pp. 27–28.
[2] Stanley Edgar Hyman, *The Armed Vision*, New York, 1955 (revised edition), p. 122.
[3] *Journal of American Folklore, op. cit.*, p. 471.

ceivable that any rite should have been initiated without there having been some antecedent idea of what it was intended to achieve, and what forces might be called on to bring this about.

Here, if anywhere, we must have a formulation of the precondition for understanding the relationship between myth and ritual. In the beginning, we may assume with Harrison, was the word, *not* the act. A myth, in these terms, is either a rhetorical form that represents an elaboration over time of a core concept, or is part of a myth-rite complex borrowed wholly from another people. But whether originating within a culture or introduced from outside it, what is added by way of elaboration and accretion to the first category of myths, and what is changed in the second, will be governed by its congruence with the cultural base where it is to have a functioning role.

The proposition that ritual is the basis of myth presupposes random, unthinking behavior by human groups, behavior that becomes standardized before it is translated into belief. And here we are faced by a fundamental inconsistency in the argument. For many of those who hold to the myth-from-ritual theory are also those who insist most vigorously that but few men are interested in explaining the world about them, a point to which we will return shortly.

As students of classical mythology, the Cambridge School could scarcely be expected to evaluate myth in the more specific terms of its living reality. Who narrated the Greek myths can only be conjectured—or why they were told, to say nothing of how they originated. Let us read a lesson from the Dahomean materials. We have seen how on two occasions, at least, Dahomean kings are reported to have summoned the clan elders so that the myths of clan origin that sanction clan prerogatives, and the rituals of the clans, could be regularized. We have indicated something of the political exigencies that dictated this move, and have suggested that the popular and the official versions of these myths do not necessarily coincide.

If we refer to No. 24, which tells of the introduction of the Fa divining cult, we see that political exigency also dictated this move. In No. 23, however, we are told that the Fa system of divination came from the teachings of prophets who "came down from the sky." And No. 22 introduces us to Gbadu (a hermaphroditic child of Mawu, born after the twins who were to rule the sea), and we learn that Gbadu is also known as Fa. It is interesting, however, to note that the myths as told by the *vodun* priests make no mention of Gbadu as a child of the Creator. We may surmise that this was a revision to give status within the existing cosmogony to a newly introduced cult.

Or, if we take the role of Aido-Hwedo in No. 16, we are told, "Aido-Hwedo, the serpent, is a *vodun*, but is not of the family of the gods. They say he is not the son of the Great Mawu, because he existed before any of the children of Mawu, before Sogbo." It is clear that we are seeing a deity of an autochthonous group made subject to a pantheon that, again, if we may rely on oral tradition, tells us in No. 20 that Agadja was instrumental in bringing the worship of the Sky Pantheon to the plateau of Abomey, where was located the seat of the Dahomean kings after they had conquered their way north from Allada.

We have determined all this by going to the Dahomeans, recording variants, and finding out why they are countenanced. But how, in the case of the Greek myths, could this be done?

Thompson, in summarizing the currents in the stream of ideas regarding myths and myth-makers, phrases the point admirably: "At journey's end, we come to the ritual origin and observe something that no anthropologist has told us about—that all rituals in the world have a single pattern and a single purpose, and that the only way a story could be made up originally was in imitation of a ritual. But though they show some undoubted instances of this occurrence, none of these writers tell us how the ritual itself evolved and how the inventive process which moved from ritual into a story about the gods and heroes is any easier than any other form of invention." [1]

In entering our reservations, we of course do not reject the proposition that the retention in narrative form of specifications for a rite no longer performed does occur on occasion. But however valid this revised version of the theory may be, it cannot replace the more realistic principle that recognizes the *association* of myth

[1] Stith Thompson, "Myths and Folktales," *Jour. of Am. Folklore*, Vol. 68 (1955), p. 483.

and rite, without assigning priorities, or insisting on either one as the primary causal factor in shaping the other.[1]

If we turn to the discussion of myth by Malinowski, we see how first-hand contact with societies where myth has a functioning role makes for a more sober point of view. Focusing on the life of the Melanesians, Malinowski tells us at the outset of his little volume, "I propose to show how deeply the sacred tradition, the myth, enters into their pursuits, and how strongly it controls their moral and social behaviour. In other words, the thesis of the present work is that an intimate connection exists between the word, the mythos, the sacred tales of a tribe on the one hand, and their ritual acts, their social organization, and their practical activities on the other." [2] In this passage, he summarizes the experience of all who have studied myth in the field, at first-hand. Without laboring the point, it is precisely this that we have tried to sketch in the preceding pages where we have indicated how the various forms of narrative in Dahomey relate conduct to belief, and function as a powerful enculturative factor from the earliest days of childhood, stabilizing social behavior, giving meaning to acts in every sphere of life, and stimulating self-expression in the spoken arts.

It was, indeed, Malinowski's essential contribution to sharpen and bring into focus this concept of the association between narrative and behavior, between myth and ritual. "Mythology," he says in another passage, "is . . . a powerful means of assisting primitive man, of allowing him to make the two ends of his cultural patrimony meet." Again and again he speaks of the "pragmatic" character of mythology among the people with whom he worked. And he reads a lesson which exponents of the myth-from-ritual school, whose enthusiasm for Malinowski's work exceeds their mastery of what he has written, might do well to ponder. For in placing myth in the total context of the culture, he shows that to think either of myth or ritual as entities outside this cultural whole leads to distortion. We may even remember that, in discussing one particular form of myth, he tells us that it "shapes the ritual," that it

---

[1] This point has been well made by C. Kluckhohn, "Myth and Rituals: A General Theory," *The Harvard Theological Review*, Vol. 35 (January, 1942), pp. 45–79.

[2] Malinowski, *op. cit.*, p. 11.

"vouches for the truth of the belief in supplying the pattern of the subsequent miraculous confirmation." [1]

Let us now examine certain other aspects of Malinowski's position on oral literature. If the Cambridge School draws its generalizations from Greek mythology, Malinowski is equally centered on the Trobriands. In his case, this is the more serious, since in his study of myth, as in all his works, he sets up general principles that he asserts are valid for "savage" or "primitive" society in general. Now, it was well recognized, even at the time Malinowski wrote, that the cultures of peoples without written languages are of such great variety that to group them as a unit in contrast to "civilized" cultures is to mask reality. Specifically, a principle that might apply to the Trobrianders would not necessarily be valid for the Dahomeans any more than it would for the Danes.

This is evident when we reread certain of his statements, which he makes without qualification, regarding the nature of myth, and project them against the Dahomean materials as a test of their universality. For example, he writes, "As to any explanatory function of these myths, there is no problem which they cover, no curiosity which they satisfy, no theory which they contain." [2] The logical conclusion would seem to be that the theory holding myth to arise from a desire to explain natural phenomena, and which assumes a certain curiosity among "primitive" peoples concerning the world in which they live, is valid in no society. Now it is true that theories of myth that ascribe the derivation of all mythology from attempts to explain the movements of celestial bodies have long been refuted, but we do not resolve the difficulty by substituting one untenable generalization for another.

We have seen how Dahomean mythology not only incorporates explanatory elements, but how it also gives important roles to the Moon and to the Sun. It would not be impossible, with a degree of emphasis that ignored other elements of reference, to utilize the collection of narratives we give to bolster either the position that myths are essentially explanatory, or that they are essentially of the solar-lunar type. But our point is precisely that just because neither

[1] *Ibid.*, p. 35.
[2] *Ibid.*, p. 59.

of these, as over-all theories of myth, applies to the Dahomean narratives, this does not mean that the insights they give cannot illumi-
nate some aspect of myth in Dahomean culture.

As a matter of fact, if Malinowski had not been so intent upon
controverting certain of those extreme theories of myth that at
the time were prevalent and accepted, he would have recognized
how many of the examples he himself gives contradict the position
he took. For he was too good a field-worker not to present his
findings in cultural context, and it is here that he provides us many
instances, even in the short abstracts he gives, that show how lively
is the interest of the Trobriand Islanders in accounting for certain
elements in their culture. On pages 61–62 of his book we read their
explanation of why human beings die; on pages 65–66, how black
magic came into being; on page 70, "why the spirits are invisible";
on page 71, how the seasonal feast called *milamala* was instituted.
And while Malinowski is entirely correct in asserting that these
explanations do not explain the reason for these phenomena to the
student, that is to say, to Malinowski himself, he overlooks the fact
that, in the ethnographic sense of the word "explanatory," they
do explain them to the Trobrianders.

These observations are also applicable to much of Raglan's position, valuable though his strictures are in revealing the untenability
of certain ideas that have been taken for granted among too many
students of myth. His attack on euhemerism is an example of this,
for much undisciplined writing has been done on the assumption
that the heroes of tradition must have had historic existence; that
unwritten narrative can be employed to establish actual historical
happenings. Yet, here again, a good argument is pushed much too
far. In principle, the point has been accepted for decades by students of nonliterate peoples; but one does not go to the other extreme, as he does, in asserting, "When, therefore, we attribute to
the savage an interest in the past comparable to our interest in the
history of England, we are attributing to him a taste which he
could not possibly possess, and which if he did possess he could not
possibly gratify." [1] In terms of Raglan's definition of history,[2] he is

[1] Raglan, *op. cit.*, p. 6.
[2] *Ibid.*, p. 2.

entirely correct; but his definition bristles with ambiguities, many of an ethnocentric nature which assure their inapplicability to peoples of a predominantly oral tradition.

If the narratives in our collection tell us anything, it is that the Dahomeans, at least, who have no written language and therefore come into Raglan's category of "illiterates," show an interest in their past that, were there any possibility of drawing valid comparisons, might well be found to be "comparable to our interest in the history of England." Indeed, the portrayal Raglan draws of the attitude of "the savage" toward past events is little short of caricature. "He may remember," goes one passage, "that there was a war with the next village in his father's time, because it led to a blood-feud which has not yet been settled. But when all the participants have died, then the war is forgotten. There is no inducement to remember it, and no machinery by means of which its memory could be preserved."[1] However true this may have been for the Sudanese people Raglan knew, Dahomey had its royal "remembrancer," who recited the genealogy of the kings, a genealogy that compared very well in its unwritten form as given us in 1931 with the names of the Dahomean kings, and when they reigned, given by early travelers in West Africa—works to which our informants could not possibly have had access.

To say that tradition cannot be taken at face value, as Raglan in his excellent discussion of the tale of Troy shows certain classical scholars have done, does not justify the assertion that *no* tradition can have *any* basis in fact. The arbitrary figure of one hundred and fifty years as the maximum for which "an incident which is not recorded in writing can be remembered," is negated by the Dahomean materials, as in No. 96, which in certain cases can be documented as having been carried by oral tradition for more than twice that time. Similarly, the ethnohistorical study by Fuller of the Gwambe of southeastern Africa[2] shows how, in this case, at least, traditional accounts of the tribal past have a far greater degree of verisimilitude than even those whose position on the

[1] *Ibid.*, p. 7.
[2] Charles Edward Fuller, *An Ethnohistoric Study of Continuity and Change in Gwambe Culture*, Ph.D. Dissertation (Microfilm, 1955), Northwestern University. Bascom (*op. cit., Jour. of Am. Folklore*, 1957) in his critique of Raglan's theory, discusses Fuller's data.

historical validity of myth is less extreme than that of Raglan might think possible. Nor can we disregard the lessons that are being learned from research in West Africa, where traditional and written historical accounts are being carefully analyzed and collated, and where oral tribal histories are being utilized under effective controls.

Another instance of beginning with a good critical point and expanding it beyond tenable proportions is found in Raglan's discussion of the absence of creativity in the telling of tales. No statement could be more explicit than his dictum: "No popular storyteller has ever been known to invent anything"; nor be more in need of clarification than his comment that "the exercise of the imagination consists not in creating something out of nothing, but in the transmutation of matter already present in the mind." [1] If the first is valid, it is difficult to understand how, in those earliest societies of man where there was no writing, any story could ever have been told. As for the second statement, one cannot but wonder whether Raglan is doing more than repeating the axiom that most invention consists in reworking pre-existing cultural materials; that in any particular case the new is far outbalanced by the reinterpreted old.

Now it is quite true that the role of the artist as innovator has tended to be overstressed, and that, as Raglan is saying, the innovator does not create *de novo*. Yet this evades the essential fact of innovation, which is that any exercise of the imagination that builds on past experience to produce something that has not existed in this same form before is an exercise of the creative faculty.

We have seen how the culture of Dahomey affords institutionalized channels for self-expression in the spoken arts, provided first of all by the prerogative of new songs for the annual rites in the worship of the Earth Pantheon, and by the comparable prerogative exacted by the human rulers in the worship of the Royal Ancestors. The two types, one on religious themes, the second on secular, often draw on the proverb for opening statement and moral. Whether in praise of gods or men, a favored vehicle is social satire. The comment is by indirection, and the imagery is metaphorical. More pronounced still is the outlet for social satire

[1] *Op. cit.*, p. 133.

afforded by the opportunity to improvise songs and recitatives in criticism of the reigning king—or at present a chief—during his celebration of the rites to his head, which is to say, to his own Destiny, and by extension the Destiny of the land. Again, social dances, held in rotation by competing groups, such as the Abomey *avogan* which is given successively by each quarter of the city, afford widest opportunity to young people to develop virtuosity in composing new words to songs.

On the enculturative level, there are the children's story-telling sessions which are presided over by a leader chosen by themselves from their own group, where riddling and story telling serve to entertain, but, according to the Dahomeans, also to train in expression and, later, self-expression through the medium of traditional lore. This is continued into maturity and throughout life by the use of myths and tales in divining, wherein the individual ponders the bearing on his own life of the parables he had heard. But the outstanding example of artistry in narration is experienced when the Dahomean participates, whether as narrator or listener, at wakes for the dead. These story-telling sessions are performances to please the connoisseur, the dead, whom it is important to regale with the best at hand. As mentioned, there are no digressions to moralize. It is, in fact, on these occasions that incidents of the most deft caricature, of the widest play of fantasy, of the most daring assault on the inhibited and the socially inexpedient are introduced and developed; this is when the narrator of creative bent has full cultural approbation to introduce variant themes and explanations.

The problem, then, is not whether the story-teller "creates" something that is entirely new—"imagined," to use the word Raglan uses—in all of its elements, unlike anything heard before. The need is rather to balance and give full weight to the degree to which creative expression, as an exercise of the imagination, can be recognized in oral literature when at present our essential comparative materials from most world areas are so lacking in time depth. We can only collate variants, and compare synchronically what we find. In our own cultural stream, we are quick to recognize and react to change, but even a stylistic innovator like Joyce gave us recognizable Dublin in dress, in speech, in ritual observance, and in the tensions that well up from political and religious differences.

How daring was the narrator who, functioning within the framework of Dahomean culture, and the role assigned in it to the person and office of the king, told story No. 101, where the poor stranger refuses all worldly bribes so that he might enjoy the beggar's satisfaction of commanding the king? According to the narrator who told us the story, the shift in the plot to place the king above morality and the execution of the beggar were the only acceptable resolutions. But we are nevertheless led to speculate both as to the creative act of the first teller of this tale and, if the "intentional fallacy" may be forgiven us, cannot but wonder what occasioned its telling. It might have been during the ritual to the king's head, or it may have been brought to Abomey by a professional *ahanjito*, who wandered through the land as entertainer, stopping at the gates of the great compounds to beg entrance, and once invited enjoyed immunity from recrimination for the songs he sang and the tales he told. For his reputation—and his rewards—depended not only on the felicity with which he rendered the familiar, but also on the appeal of the new that he brought.

If we say that Euroamerican tradition tends to lay emphasis on innovation and to underplay the unchanging elements, then the antithesis is not the stereotype of the static "primitive" culture that Raglan depicts. As we have come to understand, in a cross-cultural situation the attention of the outsider seizes on the most common forms, and fails to recognize the variations. For variant forms are masked by the semblance of uniformity to an eye not fixed on the delicate gradations in response that produce deviation, and result in new forms.

This is why, whereas the role of the artist and writer as nonconformist has been stressed in our own society, in the so-called "savage" cultures the artist-narrator is conceived as being held to fixed traditional forms, with neither the urge nor the latitude to experiment. It is to the credit of Raglan that, in extending this admittedly extreme point of view to his own culture—though only for the peasants—he has to that degree injected a note of realism into stereotype. But this does not alter the fact that the concept of the fixity of the "primitive" tale or myth, as in Raglan's thesis, does not hold. The Dahomeans, it will be recalled, distinguish between the singer-narrator of good memory, and the one of great understanding. In effect, once improvisation is not only culturally tolerated but assigned a prestige role, the factor of innovation becomes a cultural reality.

There are, to be sure, good reasons why the idea of "primitive" uninventiveness has seemed so plausible.[1] If we consider that among peoples without written languages the innovator is anonymous, the reasonableness of the proposition that there is no creative individual among these peoples is compounded. Here, in truth, we have the explanation why students of literature have been so beguiled by the mysticism of Jung's idea of the collective unconscious, or have so readily accepted such a concept as that of prelogical mentality advanced, but later rejected, by Lévy-Bruhl.[2]

A fundamental difficulty with all theories of myth, when judged in terms of the available data, is that the nature, extent and significance of internal innovation is ignored. Neither Raglan nor Malinowski give the study of variants any place in their discussions. Yet we know that in all societies, the literate ones of Europe, America, and the Near and Far East, as well as those that do not possess writing, variants constantly appear to tales orally told, and by this very fact reshape their form and, over time, their point and meaning.

This is not the place to repeat the conclusions of the many students of myth in nonliterate societies who have recorded and commented on the multiplicity of these variants and their significance, and have remarked how differences in personality, age, sex, and status can influence the form of a given myth or tale. Serious students of myth who are steeped in the writings of humanistic scholarship and accept the doctrine of the uninventiveness of the "primitive" might well study the extended analysis of the myths of the Wintu Indians of California by Demetracopoulou and du Bois, to which an entire issue of a major periodical in the field, the *Journal of American Folklore*, was devoted in 1932.[3] In this "study

---

[1] For a full discussion of this problem, especially in the field of technology but by no means this alone, see H. G. Barnett, *Innovation, the Basis of Cultural Change*, New York, 1953.

[2] Cf. L. Lévy-Bruhl, *Les Carnets de Lucien Lévy-Bruhl*, Paris, 1949.

[3] D. Demetracopoulou and Cora du Bois, "A Study of Wintu Mythology," *Jour. Amer. Folklore*, Vol. 45, No. 178, Oct.–Dec. 1932.

of change and stability in Wintu mythology as it exists at the present day" to name only one of the many relevant points discussed in it, we find, for example, fifteen versions of the single tale of Coyote and Death. Yet neither this collection nor any discussion of its conclusions nor those of any other comparable researches,[1] as far as we have been able to ascertain, has entered into the analyses of myth by scholars who have proposed broad overall formulations for a general theory of mythology.

5   *Toward a general theory of myth*

Before turning to the narratives themselves, we may briefly consider a point that has entered into our discussion a number of times, but whose significance has thus far not been analyzed. This has to do with the fact that Dahomey, like other societies of Africa, represents a particular manifestation of what we have termed the Old World Culture. In this vast region, the basic themes of narrative show a remarkable correspondence, a fact that has direct bearing on the theories of myth that have just been explored.

We turn, first of all, to a quotation from the Preface to the abridged edition of *The Golden Bough,* a work that has so impressively influenced thought on the nature and sources of myth: ". . . It is no longer possible to regard the rule of succession to the priesthood of Diana of Aricia as exceptional; it clearly exemplifies a widespread institution, of which the most numerous and the most similar cases have thus far been found in Africa."[2] It is of no consequence for our discussion here that, as the argument progresses, Frazer has recourse to the outmoded classical form of the comparative method, which consisted essentially of bringing together phenomena from peoples over the world, which on the

[1] Some examples of these are R. Benedict, *Zuñi Mythology, loc. cit.;* E. C. Parsons, *Folk-Lore of the Antilles, French and English,* Memoir XXVI, American Folklore Soc., New York, 1933–1943 (and other works by this author); E. Goldfrank, "Isleta Variants: a Study in Flexibility," *Jour. Amer. Folklore,* Vol. 29 (1926), pp. 70–78. In the study by Daniel J. Crowley, *Tradition and Individual Creativity in Bahamian Folktales,* Ph.D. Dissertation (Microfilm), Northwestern University, Ch. I, and folios L 279–289, this problem is considered at length.

[2] Sir James Frazer, *The Golden Bough* (Abridged edition), New York, 1942.

surface seem to be similar, but which have been torn from their
cultural context and utilized without regard to the meaning which
provides them their essential, and often quite different, cultural reality. What is important for us is that, of his comparisons, the
"most numerous and most similar cases" to the ancient Greek rite
he uses on which to base his argument have been found in Africa.

It is impossible to read the narratives that follow without recognizing the many themes which they have in common with Old
World lore. The fact that parallel animal stories are found in all the
Old World is only one general expression of this—the resemblances between numerous African tales and Reynard the Fox, of
Mediaeval Europe, the Aesop fables, the Panchatantra of India,
and the Jataka tales of China have long been remarked. But beyond
this, many motifs with human and non-human protagonists, found
elsewhere in the Old World, are present in this Dahomean collection. These include variants on the Oedipus theme (No. 16), the
Prometheus theme (No. 17), William Tell (No. 27), Lohengrin
(Nos. 48, 49, and 132), Cinderella (Orphan tales, Nos. 68, 69, and
70), Delilah and Salome (No. 105), Ali-Baba and the Forty
Thieves (No. 155)—all these, but in forms shaped by the configurations of Dahomean culture, which, when stripped away,
reveal the underlying unities.

The significance of facts of this order for the various theories of
myth that have been propounded cannot be overestimated. For it
will be recalled that, in most of the cases we have cited—Rank and
Jung, the Cambridge School and Raglan—the examples that have
been called on to "prove" the position taken derive predominantly
from Old World Cultures. This means that, once we recognize the
historical interrelationships of the entire area, we discover that in
accounting for the basic unities we are dealing with historical
phenomena, and not with causalities that inhere *ipso facto* either
in the nature of man, or in the nature of myth.

In a very real sense, these comments are a *caveat* against the use
of these Dahomean materials to "prove" any general theory of
myth that calls primarily on Old World materials for its documentation. We agree with the position taken by Graves, when he says,
"Let me emphasize that my theory is intended to cover only the
area from which the myths I quote are drawn—not, for instance,

China, Central America, or the Indus Valley—that any statement here made about Mediterranean religion or ritual before the appearance of written records must necessarily be conjectural; that I regard my intuition as by no means infallible; and that if anyone can make a guess that rings truer than mine I shall be the first to applaud it." [1]

The question why men make myths remains to challenge us to account for a universal human response in its most significant, because its most imaginative, expression. And related to this is why such different explanations of the myth-making phenomenon, each so reasonable to its proponents, have called forth so much disagreement among students of myth and why the various positions are so hotly debated.

We turn once again to certain patterns of thought, germane to our discussion, that are characteristic of Euroamerican culture. These may be subsumed in the tendency to dichotomize experience, a tendency which reflects one of the most deeply set constellations in the cultures of Europe and America. It is of great antiquity in this vast cultural stream. It was present in the functioning religions at the beginning of the historic period, when writing was first discovered. It was given philosophical formulation in classical Greece.

This mode of thought gives rise to what we may term the *all-or-none fallacy*, the operation of which we saw exemplified in Rank's formulation based on the Oedipus complex, or in Malinowski's exclusive stress on the sociological role of myth. It needs no great psychological sophistication to recognize that responses of this order move on the unconscious level, especially where a given proposition is ordered under the rubric of scientific analysis. This is why, for example, the concept of variability, when advanced in the nineteenth century, brought on a revolution in scientific thought; why it is still a concept difficult to grasp for those in our culture unaccustomed to working with quantitative data.

Recognition of the fact that this tendency to dichotomize is culture-bound could not have come until the researches of anthropologists were available for comparative purposes. For to one trained in a system of thought based on polarities, the idea of a continuum which extends to unspecified terminal points on both

[1] Robert Graves, *The Greek Myths*, London, 1955, Vol. I, p. 23.

sides of a norm represents a major and often a painful reorientation in point of view. The proved validity of this approach in the natural and exact sciences, together with the anthropological findings, that show the dichotomizing pattern to be only one of a number of possible means of structuring thought, has opened the way to the reordering of concepts that had come to be more or less taken for granted. In essence, this approach cuts under the all-or-none fallacy, permitting us to examine accepted positions in terms of possible complementary elaborations.

We suggest that this is precisely the approach to myth that will be most fruitful. For a valid general theory of myth cannot be developed except in terms of a general theory of human culture. In essence, this recognizes man's endowment as a culture-building animal, through his ability to manipulate the symbolisms of language, and extend his personal powers through the use of tools. It stresses the exploratory aptitudes in man which, while always finding expression within the limits of a given body of tradition, yet interact with these so as to bring on change in them. Of this process, myth is but a part. But as a part, it cannot go beyond the terms of reference set by the overall concept, and must be ordered within this frame.

In demurring at the generalizing nature of the various theories we have discussed, we grant each what measure of validity it holds. It is for this reason we have recognized that though the Oedipus theorem as at present formulated needs to be broadened, it is not to be denied its place as one important segment of mythic conceptualization. This is why, too, though we could not accept the *mystique* of the collective unconscious, we have pointed out that the universals in human *experience*, and the historic factors that have played on these, may be held to account for the presence of similar broad themes in the narratives of peoples living all over the world. In rejecting the thesis that myth arises out of ritual, we have in no wise denied the importance of the relationship between the two. As concerns the sociological theory of myth, we do not disavow for myth its sanctioning role in social organization; nor, in our attempt to isolate the factors that in Dahomey encourage creativity, have we overlooked the influence of preconditioning and cultural imperatives, even when the narrator, or singer-poet is most creative.

We recognize all of these; but we are led to conclude that none of them provides a full answer. There is no easy theory of myth. We repeat, myth is a manifestation of human culture and must be treated as such. This means that it does not exist of itself. Mythic symbolism, in any age, and at all levels of abstraction, is a cultural fact. Mythic themes are not emanations of images engraved on the unconscious in primordial times. As a cultural fact, myth is seen as deriving from human language skill, and man's fascination with symbolic continuities. But as a cultural fact, it also finds dynamic expression in the play between outer stimulus received by a people, and innovation from within.

We advance, in essence, as far as causation is concerned, a pluralistic theory of myth, recognizing the demonstrated universal fact that men everywhere have felt impelled to symbolize metaphorically the relationship between man and his world. The answer to questions about the genesis of myth and mythic themes is no simpler, or more difficult, than the question why in Dahomey, in the rites for the ancestors, the boasting pattern of song and invocation does not cause the family singer to list the number of wives and children and palm groves and, in earlier times, the number of its slaves. Instead, he disposes of the pretensions of a rival by singing:

> *The serpent does not measure its shadow*
> *against the rainbow,*

or

> *This river and that river,*
> *It is the Sea who is their king.*

As we see it, the most important elements in the scientific approach to myth—and the literary approach as well—are the cumulative reality of culture in human experience; the factor of borrowing, whether achieved or in process, and over time and in space; and the creative drive in man. The origin of the symbolic intangibles of an oral tradition cannot be illuminated by carbon dating, even though archaelogical findings have given us, and are giving us, important leads to relationships between peoples. Nor can one speculative system which attempts to explain genetic relations do more than another.

There remains the challenge to take concepts and hypotheses into the laboratory of the cross-cultural field, and test their generalizing value, or arrive at new generalizations. Perhaps "challenge" is too austere a word for our implicit meaning. In the tradition of humanistic scholarship, it is an invitation to discover for world literature and thought vast resources which will inform and delight us.

As spoken forms, the stories should preferably be read aloud.

I

Exploits of the gods

Exploits of the gods

1

To each is given his dominion [1]

Sagbata comes from Mawu and Lisa. Mawu is one person but has two faces. The first is that of a woman, and the eyes of that part which belongs to the woman is the Moon. That face takes the name of Mawu. The other side is the side of a man. That face has for its eyes the Sun, and it takes the name of Lisa. The part called Mawu directs night. Where the Sun is, Lisa directs the day.

Since Mawu is both man and woman, she became pregnant. The first to be born were a pair of twins, a man child called Da Zodji, and a woman child called Nyohwè Ananu. The second birth was So, who had the form of his parent, man and woman in one. The third birth was also of twins, a male, Agbè, and a female, Naètè. The fourth to be born was Agè, a male, the fifth Gu, also male. Gu is all body. He has no head. Instead of a head, a great sword is found coming out of his neck. His trunk is of stone. The sixth birth was not to a being, but to Djo, air, atmosphere. Air was what was needed to create men. The seventh to be born was Legba. Mawu said Legba was to be her spoiled child, because he was the youngest.

One day Mawu-Lisa assembled all the children in order to divide the kingdoms. To the first twins, she gave all the riches and told them to go and inhabit the earth. She said the earth was for them.

Mawu said to Sogbo he was to remain in the sky, because he was both man and woman like his parent. She told Agbè and Naètè to go and inhabit the sea, and command the waters. To Agè she gave command of all the animals and birds, and she told him to live in the bush as a hunter.

To Gu, Mawu said he was her strength, and that was why he was not given a head like the others. Thanks to him, the earth would not always remain wild bush. It was he who would teach men to live happily.

Mawu told Djo to live in space between earth and sky. To him was being entrusted the life-span of man. Thanks to him also, his brothers would be invisible, for he will clothe them. That is why another name for *vodun* is *djo*.

When Mawu said this to the children, she gave the Sagbata twins the language which was to be used on earth, and took away their memory of the language of the sky. She gave to Hevioso the language he would speak, and took from him the memory of the parent language. The same was done for Agbè and Naètè, for Agè, and for Gu, but to Djo was given the language of men.

Now she said to Legba, "You are my youngest child, and as you are spoiled, and have never known punishment, I cannot turn you over to your brothers. I will keep you with me always. Your work shall be to visit all the kingdoms ruled over by your brothers, and to give me an account of what happens." So Legba knows all the languages known to his brothers, and he knows the language Mawu speaks, too. Legba is Mawu's linguist. If one of the brothers wishes to speak, he must give the message to Legba, for none knows any longer how to address himself to Mawu-Lisa. That is why Legba is everywhere.

You will find Legba even before the houses of the *vodun*, because all beings, humans and gods, must address themselves to him before they can approach God.

[1] For another version of this myth, cf. *Dahomey*, II, pp. 129–131.

2

The rule of sky and earth delimited

Originally Sagbata was not called Sagbata. He comes from Ananu and was called Azõ. He was always disobedient. His parents sold him. At the place where he was sold, he behaved as always. He never obeyed. Those people took him and sold him to Death. They said when they sold him, "Now if Death buys you and you begin the same tricks, if you refuse to obey him, then we will see what happens to you."

So Death bought him. He said, "Now, I will show you how

people behave here." He said, "We never permit insults here." So Death planted millet. Death said when the birds came to eat this millet, he must drive them away.

He said, "I, I don't want to do this. I am not one to drive away the birds who come to eat millet."

Death said, "You are my slave. Why don't you want to go?"

Then Death and he began to quarrel. So Azō said, "Here's a man with long eyelashes who insults me."

Death asked, "Do you know what we do here with a man like you? You shall see."

He said, "What will you do to me? Nothing."

At night Death put him in a locked room. He said, "Now you will eat nothing. You will die here of hunger."

Now, it was settled that the moment Azō fell asleep, he would be killed by Death. So he did not sleep. He knew it. He did not sleep for seven days. The seventh day Death came to open the door. He thought the man was asleep. But he was not asleep. Death said, "This man cannot stay here. He will destroy my house if he stays." He went and sold him to another.

So Death sold him to another country, and this country was quite close to Azō's own home. So Azō escaped and went home.

Now, as no master would keep him, but bought him and sold him, bought him and sold him, he had sores all over his body. People said, "Ah, Azō, why have you sores like this?"

He said, "It is because they sell me and resell me."

So his brothers said to him, "You have become like a mound of earth that is gradually worn down and down until it is all flattened out." They mocked him. But they were not sold like he had been sold.

As they were in the house, he joked with his brothers, and one day he said to them, "One does not insult Death. But I, I insulted him. Now I am called Keledjegbè Kutō. I am greater than Death. Death has millet, but he cannot chase away the birds."

Before he was sold, Hevioso was his friend. When he was away, they took Hevioso, his friend, and made him family head. After he came home and all the sores were healed, he was a fine looking man. He was asked to become king. So he and Hevioso began to quarrel. Hevioso said, "Now, what they gave me, you cannot take away from me." But he took away the kingship from Hevioso, and he became king.

So this happened when he became king and Hevioso was nothing. He commanded a field to be cleared, and he told his people to cultivate it for him. They planted corn. When the time came for the rains, so that the grain might come, Hevioso stopped all rain. There was no longer any rain. So the season became dry. The animals died; men died, too. There was no water to drink.

Everybody began to berate Sagbata. They said, "So, that evil man has come back again to us."

So he had all the people come. The people came and the animals, too, Eagle, Vulture, Cat, Chameleon. Sagbata had much magic. He had white cotton and black. He took the white and black cotton to his mouth, talked to it and had it ascend to the sky.

He said to the creatures, "I'm going to send you to Hevioso to ask for water."

He asked who would be the first to go. Eagle said, "I." When Eagle climbed up half way to the sky, Hevioso killed him.

The cat said, "Now it is my turn." He almost reached the same place, when lightning crushed him. So Chameleon, who belongs to the Sun-god Lisa, said, "Now it is my turn." He left.

Sagbata said to him, "Now go to Hevioso and tell him to send water that the people and animals and the harvest may thrive. Here on earth all are almost dead."

Chameleon went slowly, slowly. He went almost half way. When Hevioso wanted to kill him, he curled up and hid under the thread.

Now Hevioso sends his thunderbolts, then goes into his house. He returns and sends another, then goes back to his house. So when he hurled the thunder and went in, Chameleon was at his door. Now there were guards there, and they asked Chameleon, "What do you want here?"

He said, "I am looking for Hevioso." So one guard went to tell Hevioso that there was a man to see him.

He said, "Who sent him?" The man said it was Sagbata.

Chameleon said, "Sagbata sends me to tell you that pigs, goats, men, homes, harvests, all are dying." He said, "He begs you to send water that man might find water to drink."

Hevioso said, "All right. I'll send him water." So he led Chameleon behind his door and gave him a new jar and a new calabash. He said, "Now, give these two things to Sagbata, and tell him to bring all his people together before his door. He must make a hole, and put the jar inside." He said also, "All right, I'll send him water. But tell him beginning today, he is not to command the people in the sky, and I will not command the people below." He said, "All right. Now that I shamed him before his people, I do not ask any more to rule below."

When Chameleon came before Sagbata and said all that Hevioso had said, they had all the people assemble. So they made the hole and put in first the closed calabash, and then the jar on top. So they put earth over this and said, "If someone goes for water, the first water he finds, he must throw over this mound of earth."

Before this there was no earthen mound which they call Aizan. If Hevioso had not ordered Sagbata to make this earthen mound, the rain would not fall. From then on, when it did not rain, one put water on Aizan, and the rain fell. Before this quarrel, there was no trouble, because Hevioso gave water.

3

Sogbo becomes master of the Universe [1]

Sagbata and Sogbo are brothers. We are told that the Creator did not work any more after she created the world, but delegated her children, Sagbata and Sogbo, to rule the world for her. The two quarrelled. Sagbata, the elder, decided to leave the sky and go down on earth. He took with him, since he was the eldest, all his heritage, which included everything of his mother's. The younger brother, who was the more brutal, remained in his mother's kingdom, and he took the name of fire—Miyomiyo, or Sogbo.

Before leaving for the earth, their mother said to them, she would not justify the claim of either in a quarrel. They must be together like a closed calabash and the world must exist inside them. She said that since Sagbata was the elder, he should be the lower part and that Sogbo should be the upper. The mother told them both to go and live in the world. Sogbo refused. He would not leave his mother.[2]

When Sagbata descended, he could not get back on high. He, therefore, descended lower and lower. Sogbo, who was near the mother, won all the confidence of his mother and of the gods who surrounded her. Then one day Sogbo caused the rains to stop. Rain came no longer.

Now in the world below, Sagbata had had himself chosen as king, and the people came to him and said, "Since you came among us and we made you king, there is no longer any rain. We are dying of hunger." He said, "Yes, it is so, but in a few days you will have rain."

A year went by and no rain. Two years went by and no rain. For three years, no rain. Now, two men came down from the sky. Those men fell down in a country called Fe. They preached. They preached the writing of Fa, Destiny. They traveled everywhere.

It is said that at that time the world had no more than a thousand people.

Now, people came to tell Sagbata that two men came from the sky and preached something called Fa. He said they should come. When they came, they spoke to Sagbata the language spoken in the sky, and Sagbata knew at once [that they told the truth]. He asked them why there was no rain.

They said they did not know. Their errand was to preach Fa. What they did know was that his little brother was angry.

Sagbata asked, "Why is he angry?"

They said they did not know, but with Fa, which was the writing of Sagbata's mother, they would know at once. They took the divining seeds, and, throwing them, asked why the rain did not fall in this country? The first combination of Fa that fell was called *Yeku Gbuloso.* At once they told Sagbata that there was a dispute between two brothers, who both wanted the same thing, and that the elder should submit to the younger to bring about a reconciliation.

Sagbata said that now the sky was too far away and that he no longer had the power to climb up. He said that before going down to earth, his mother had given him the right to take with him all the riches. These he put in his sack. He said that it was he himself who had refused to take along water, because he could not take it in his sack. But arriving on earth, the water which he had left behind had become very necessary. The two men said that water was now under control of his brother. Sagbata asked these men what was to be done to have the rain fall.

The two men then said to him if he wished to make the sacrifice, he must give a portion of all the riches on earth and confide this to the bird Wututu, the great friend of Sogbo. They said, "When Wututu goes up there to talk to Sogbo, Sogbo will never refuse her."

Sagbata heard. He gathered up a portion of all of his riches, and he had Wututu called. He said to Wututu, "Go tell Sogbo that now I, Sagbata, surrender the Universe. I shall let him have the country, and the compounds, and the houses. He may take the sons and the father; the children and the mother. He, Sogbo, is to dwell up high and guard those below."

Once she was up high in the air, Wututu, in a voice which Sogbo knew at once, began to sing. "The earth, Ai-Sagbata, charged me with a commission for you. Do you hear, So?" And Wututu sang, "He said that he leaves you the Universe. He leaves you the country. You are to have the compounds and all the houses. He lets you have the sons and the father; the children and the mother."

When he said this, Sogbo recognized the voice of Wututu from on high. He told his sons to behave, that a stranger was coming. He sent a bolt of lightning. As the lightning flashed, he saw it was Wututu. Sogbo said to let him come.

When Wututu came up, Sogbo said, "Go and say to my elder brother Sagbata that though he is the elder who inherited all the wealth of our mother, he had been foolish to leave behind the two things that are the power of the Universe. With these two things, I, the younger, can control all the wealth of Sagbata."

Those two things are water and fire.

He told Wututu to return, and before even reaching earth, he would see what followed. Wututu flew away toward the earth. When he reached half way between sky and earth, a great rain began to fall.

Wututu arrived. Sagbata was very happy. And he commanded that Wututu was never to be killed. Should someone kill him by accident, a great ceremony is to be given. This ceremony consists of removing the head-pad, because it was he who had carried on his head the message from Sagbata to Sogbo.

That day the brothers were reconciled. And that is why each year Thunder visits the Earth. On that day Hevioso gave himself the new name *Djato-gbedji-gbezō Djato-megi-mete Kutjo-amu-susu-nokloso*.

> *Fallen on the grass, the grass puts forth shoots;*
> *Fallen on mankind, mankind becomes fertile,*
> *The sprinkling dew gives glory to So.*

[1] For another version, cf. *Dahomey* II, pp. 132–134. Another name for Sogbo, used in this myth, is So; Sagbata is also referred to as Ai.
[2] The narrator used the French "he" and "she" interchangeably.

4
Sagbata's control of earth stabilized [1]

When they were about to choose the child who was to rule the earth, Hevioso was the first to offer to go. Mawu said as the earth was too far from the sky, the oldest had better go. So Sagbata went. When he came there, Hevioso stopped rain from falling. He waited for men to entreat his mother to send him instead. The people complained. They said [of Sagbata], "This king is not good for the earth. Since his coming, we find nothing to eat; we find nothing to drink. We have nothing."

One day Mawu sent Legba to earth to see what was happening. He went to see Sagbata, and Sagbata told him Hevioso was keeping the rain from falling. Legba said, "All right. That is nothing." He climbed back into the sky, promising Sagbata to send him a bird who would tell him of Mawu's decision. On his arrival there, Legba sent a bird named Wututu to Sagbata with the message that a fire, so great that the smoke would mount on high, should be kindled at once.

Now Legba had himself suggested that Hevioso cause the rains to stop. To accomplish his purpose, Legba had gone to Mawu with a tale that there was no water in the sky, and that everyone was dying of thirst. Mawu, on hearing this, had given orders that not a drop of rain should leave the sky, so that all the water might be retained there for those in the heavens. But now, after visiting Sagbata on earth, Legba had told the bird Wututu that when Sagbata lit the great fire and the smoke began to rise on high, Wututu should begin to sing.

Thus when Wututu came to earth with his message, Sagbata kindled the fire he had been told to light and, as the smoke rose, Wututu began to sing. Legba then hurried to Mawu and said that he had not been able to go to earth himself, but had sent his "little assistant," Wututu, who, because there had been no rain on earth and the heat had so dried everything that the trees and all else were burning, was on the verge of being consumed. He said, also, that all the sky risked being destroyed in the flames, if rain was not at once made to fall and extinguish the fire. Mawu at once gave Legba orders to command Hevioso to cause the rain to fall, so that Wututu should not be burned. And rain fell abundantly and the earth was saved.

All this time Mawu did not know about the quarrel between the brothers, Sagbata and Hevioso, and to this day knowledge of their quarrel has been withheld from her. Because of what occurred, however, Mawu decreed that all rain should be regulated from the earth, since the danger of a universal conflagration lies there. For this reason Wututu was sent to live on earth, and when this bird finds that the ground is too hot, he cries out, and the rain comes down. Later, Legba effected a reconciliation between the two brothers, so that today man lives without fear of another such severe drought.

¹ Narrated by a priest of the Sagbata cult. For another version, cf. *Dahomey*, II, pp. 131–132.

5

Sun god brings iron to man ¹

I do not know if Mawu is a man or a woman. History tells that Mawu created the world. Then when the world was created, Mawu withdrew from the earth and went to live in the sky. After living in the sky, Mawu did not care to come down and live on earth again. But on earth nothing went well. Human beings did not understand how to do things for themselves. They quarreled. They fought. They did not know how to cultivate the fields, nor how to weave cloth to cover their bodies.

So Mawu sent her only child down to earth. This child's name was Lisa. Now, Gu is not a god. Gu is metal. Now, to her son Lisa, Mawu gave metal, and she told Lisa to go down to the earth and cut the bush with this metal, and teach men how to use it to make useful things.

So he came down, and with him he took Gu, this metal given by his mother. With the help of Gu, Lisa cut down trees, and cleared the bush, and got the fields ready. Then he built houses. And when all was done, he said to all men that his mother's words were: "Without metal men cannot live." So Lisa remade the world; and he told all men, "To overcome obstacles, you must learn to use metal." When he said this, he went back to the sky.

Lisa returned to his mother and gave her back the cutlass called *gugbasa*, which was made of iron.

Mawu said, "Gold is a costly metal. All other metals are dear, too. But iron must serve all mankind." And Mawu said that as Lisa was a good son, and had carried out his mission well, he would have as his reward the Sun to live in. From there Lisa keeps watch over the Universe. Gu went with Lisa to the Sun, to serve as his sword. This was a gift from Mawu to Lisa so that Lisa might do his work in the world.

From that day onwards this cutlass has been called *Ali-su-gbo-gu-kle, The-road-is-closed-and-Gu-opens-it.*

[1] Cf. *Dahomey*, II, pp. 106–107, for another version.

6

Serpent as head-rest for an overburdened earth: Why mountains hold riches: Reason for earthquakes [1]

There are some who say the world is a machine. Somebody made it, but if there was one Mawu or many, history does not tell us. Aido-Hwedo, the serpent, is a *vodun*, but is not of the family of the gods. They say he is not the son of the Great Mawu, because Aido-Hwedo existed before any of the children of Mawu; before Sogbo. They say that Aido-Hwedo came with the first man and the first woman of the world.

Now, when the Creator made the world, she had Aido-Hwedo with her as her servant. Aido-Hwedo carried her in his mouth everywhere. We do not know if the world was there already. We know the earth was the first created, because the world is like a calabash. The top is put on last.

Wherever the Creator went, Aido-Hwedo went with her. That is why the earth is as we find it. It curves, it winds, it has high places, and low places. That is the movement of the serpent Aido-Hwedo. Where Mawu and Aido-Hwedo rested there are mountains, because the mountains were made by the excrement of Aido-Hwedo. That is why we find riches inside mountains.

Now, when the work was finished, Mawu saw that the earth had too much weight. There were too many things—too many trees, too many mountains, elephants, everything. It was necessary to rest the earth on something. So Aido-Hwedo was told to coil himself into a circle and rest as a carrying pad underneath the earth.

Now, Aido-Hwedo does not like heat, so Mawu made water for him to live in. So he is in the sea. But it is not he who commands the sea. It is Agbè, a son of Mawu, who commands there, because those who command must be of royal blood.

Now, when Aido-Hwedo stirs, there is an earthquake.

[1] For a variant of this myth, cf. *Dahomey*, II, pp. 248–249.

7

The first human family: The people who descended from the sky [1]

Tradition tells that in very ancient times, a man and a woman came down from the sky to the district of Somè in Adja. This was the first family on earth. The man and woman brought with them a long wand and a calabash. They wore long shirts, much longer than those worn today.

It rained the day they came from the sky, and it rained for seventeen days more. All this time they did not speak. They only called out "Segbo, Segbo, Segbo . . . !" [2] This was the name of the one who had sent them on earth. After seven days, another man and woman came down from the sky. This man and woman wore the beads we know even today as *lisaje*, "Lisa's beads."

Then they began to teach the worship of Mawu and Lisa. We are told that the first temple they raised for Mawu-Lisa still exists in Adja. On the day they were to offer sacrifices to Mawu and to Lisa it rained once more. Many people came down from the sky with the rain to help them carry out the ceremony. But as soon as the ceremony was over, these went back to the sky.

This ceremony of giving offerings to Mawu and Lisa was carried out three or four times. Then the man and the woman who had brought the beads returned to the sky. They left their beads behind them. They also left a daughter on earth. Four shrines had by then been established, one for Mawu, one for Lisa, one for Gu and one for Agè. For Mawu they killed a sheep, for Lisa a white goat and a white chicken. For Gu they gave a white cock, and to Agè a dog was given. We make the same sacrifices today, because that is what these people had done who came from the sky to teach the worship of Mawu to man.

Then the woman gave birth to two children, the first a son and the second a daughter. Each child was born with a small wand in the hand, and the wand grew as the child grew. The children always had their wands with them. They were never lost. Then seven years later, the mother and father of the children returned to the sky. The children carried on the teaching of the worship of the Sky-gods. Since what they taught was good, the worship of these gods spread everywhere in Dahomey.

The first pair who came from the sky was accompanied by a chameleon. The chameleon went everywhere the man and woman went, just as a dog goes with his master. The chameleon was sent by Lisa to protect them. Lisa knew that when they taught about Mawu and Lisa, there would be people who would refuse to receive their teaching, and who would conspire against them. But the chameleon, who was always in front, reflected on his smooth skin everything that happened behind their backs as they went about.

Any move by an enemy to strike them from behind was mirrored on the body of the chameleon. For the chameleon's body is like Lisa's, smooth as a mirror. This is why the chameleon is the animal sacred to the god Lisa.

[1] Cf. *Dahomey*, I, pp. 174–176.
[2] Segbo is not to be confused with Sogbo, the god of Thunder.

8

Origin of the people of the Agblo quarter [1]

This was in very ancient times. There was a heavy rain. A great cloud of smoke came up from the earth. In those times, the region of Abomey was all big bush. There were no people living there.

The cloud of smoke came from inside this bush. When the smoke cleared, a man followed by a woman were visible. Each carried a sack of okra seeds.

The following day it rained again, and again smoke came from inside the bush. When everything cleared, there were sixty-six people there, thirty-six women and thirty men. These people began to cut down the trees and to clear the land for planting. They prepared the fields and planted the okra seeds they had brought in their sacks.

The name of the first man was Agblo. Agblo mated with the woman who accompanied him. The people who came with the second rain also mated. They had children, and these grew up and mated, and in time their descendants peopled the region.

Agblo and his wife died, he in the morning, she the same afternoon. The others mourned the two who, they said, had founded their family. A ram was sacrificed to their spirits, and this was buried with them in the hole in the earth from where they had come.

When the founders of the family were buried, and the hole from which they had come was filled in, these people had no gods to worship. Then later, a man named Cheyi began to dig a well. When he had dug to a depth of twelve to fourteen meters, he saw a road along which many people were passing.

He followed along this road, and soon met an old woman. The woman asked him why he had come. He said he was digging a well and had found this road. The woman said the place where he had been digging was sacred to the Earth. She said he must come before the ruler of this place.

Cheyi was brought to a temple where he heard a voice say he was now in the house of Sagbata. He saw no one, but the voice went on speaking. The voice said Sagbata had caused him to choose the spot for the well to bring him to this country so that he might learn how to worship the Earth gods and take this knowledge back to his people.

Then Cheyi was told to return to his home. He was instructed to close the hole where he had dug and build a temple for Sagbata over it. He was told to raise another temple for Mawu and Lisa, the gods of the Sky, not far from the Sagbata temple. Then he was commanded to tell his people to worship these three deities as their *tohwiyo*.² He was told how Sagbata "eats" the male goat, Lisa the female goat, and Mawu the sheep. He was taught the cult of these three gods.

Cheyi did as he was told. He closed the hole he had dug, and built the house for Sagbata over it. Then he built the houses for Mawu and Lisa. He called all the people together to tell them what had happened to him and what he had been told. Then the first ceremony was held. Everything Cheyi was told to do he did. The first sheep and goat sacrificed to Mawu and Lisa were accepted. A heavy rain fell, thunder was heard, and in an instant the animals disappeared. When the goat for Sagbata was brought to the house of Sagbata, the earth opened and swallowed it.

Cheyi knew the animals to sacrifice to these gods, but he did not know how to worship them. That is why, later, a man named Agamu came out of the earth to teach Cheyi how to "establish" the gods, how to sprinkle their altars with the blood of the animals sacrificed to them. For sixteen days he stayed with Cheyi teaching him about the gods.

Cheyi was the first human to learn about the cults of the Great Gods. He became the first priest of these gods. When he was very old, the earth opened and he disappeared. But he had taught what he knew to others, and the worship of Sagbata and Mawu-Lisa has continued.

¹ For another version, cf. *Dahomey*, I, pp. 172-174.
² That is, the founders of their clan.

9

How Legba became chief of the gods: How
magic became a human skill: Man against
Creator: How magic spread ¹

Long ago, Legba was the last of the gods. One day Mawu said to the gods he would show them something. He would show them who would be their chief. Mawu then gave them a gong, a bell, a drum, a flute, and said whoever took all the instruments, and played the four together and also danced to them would be their chief.

Hevioso said, "I am very strong. I can do all." So he tried. But he failed.

Mawu called on Gu and Agè to try. Agè said, "I am a hunter. I have great strength. I can do everything." He tried and failed. Gu came. He said he had much strength. He had fire. He made many things. He would do it. He tried, and he, too, failed.

Now Mawu called all the gods together and asked Legba to try. Legba tried and did all. He struck the drum; he played the gong; he rang the bell; he blew into the flute, and [at the same time] made all the gestures of the dance. Mawu said to him, "Now I will give you a woman whose name is Konikoni." And Mawu said to the other gods that Legba was to be first among them.

Now Legba said he would sing, and he sang

> *If the house is peaceful*
> *If the field is fertile,*
> *I will be very happy.*[2]

Now Legba had knowledge, and he began to make magic charms. He was the first to make them. He made a serpent. Then he put the serpent down on the road to the market, and he commanded the serpent to bite the sellers and the buyers. Once the serpent bit them, Legba came and said to them, "Give me something, and I will cure you." If they gave him something, he went away to buy *acasa*, and palm oil, and drinking water. Then he ate all and drank all.

One day someone asked Legba, "What is that," pointing to the serpent, "that which bites people?"

Legba answered him, "It is magic." Legba said to this man, "Bring me two chickens and eighty cowries and some straw, and I will make one for you." So Legba began to make magic charms for this man.

Legba led this man down the road to the market, and he told him all that had to be done to make this magic charm. When Legba said to throw the liana, the liana became a serpent, and began to bite people. Then, Legba gave him the medicine to cure these people. This man was called Awè, and it was Legba who gave magic charms to Awè.

Now magic charms spread everywhere. Legba began to give him other charms so that if someone needed a charm he came to Awè, and Awè called Legba to his house. They made the charms inside the house, and then carried them outside to give to those who came for them.

Now, Mawu was angry. She called Legba and said to Legba, "Now if someone does not see you,³ you will not do this again."

Now, Legba is forever a *vodun*. Awè is a man. So he continued to make charms. Awè became chief of magic. When someone wished to make a charm, he came to him and brought all that was needed, and Awè took the place of Legba. So Awè went everywhere and asked who wanted to make charms? Then he gave them charms and disappeared.

He gave the magic charms to everyone. He also gave charms to those who do evil. He gave charms to pregnant women that the child should not come. Then when the woman was having a difficult time, they called Awè, and they had to give him many things before he was satisfied. Then only would he give medicine that the child might come.

The kings of many lands came to Awè to ask for charms. If Awè met a child he would drop medicine on its body, and the body of the child became a ball.

Awè now said, "I am going to see the world. Now there is enough magic." One day he bought cotton thread and silk, and all one night he rolled the cotton into a ball. He did this from six o'clock in the evening until six o'clock the next morning. He left it. During the day he took the silken thread, and he rolled it until night. He measured both and he discovered that they were both the same length.

One day he climbed an ant-hill, and he threw the cotton and silken threads toward the sky. Mawu caught both threads. Then holding on to these two threads, Awè reached the sky. Mawu said to him, "What are you looking for here?"

Awè said to Mawu, "My knowledge is great. I now seek to measure my knowledge with Mawu."

Mawu said, "Show me what is your knowledge." Awè cut down a tree. He began to make a human figure. He made the head very well, the face, the hair, the arms, all the members. But the statuette could not talk. It did not breathe. It could not move. Mawu said to him, "Your knowledge is not enough. Wait, I'll show you."

On the same day Mawu took a grain of corn, traced a row and sowed it. The grain sprouted, and the same day they ate the ripe corn. They removed the corn from the cob, put it in the mill, brought the flour home, and prepared the dish that Awè ate.

Mawu left Awè, and Awè went back to earth. But Mawu sent Death to follow him. Mawu said to Death, "Men are evil. If someone does evil, it is necessary to kill him."

Awè tried a charm, and attacked Death. In those days, wood would not burn, for there was no fire. It was impossible to cook. So Mawu said to Death and Awè, "If you, Awè, attack Death then whoever will prepare his food will find that food raw again." So Awè let Death go, in order that, among men, one could put food to cook, and it would cook quickly, and people could eat. Mawu said to Awè, "If someone is ill, you are to take good care of him. But if I like, I will send Death to kill him."

Awè mastered Legba's knowledge, and he became a practitioner of magic. Awè and Death are the two friends of the world.

[1] Cf. *Dahomey*, II, pp. 257–259.
[2] Record No. 90–1.
[3] That is, Legba was given invisible form.

10

How Legba became guardian of men and gods: Why the dog is respected [1]

There were three children of Agbanukwè and Kpoli. The first was a sister whose name was Minona. The second was called Aovi, the third Legba. These three formed a little funeral band. And so, one day, when a great man died in the faraway country of the man

Adjaminako, they went to help at the funeral. Each of the three had been married, and each had killed his mate. When Minona killed her husband, she cut open his stomach and ripped out his intestines. When Aovi killed his wife, he cut off her head. And Legba killed his by giving her a blow on the head with a stick.

Now, when these three came to the funeral, they played their drum, and made up funeral songs, and people liked what they did. So they were given many, many, many gifts, many, many cowries.

Now, King Metonofi was also at the funeral. He had married his eldest daughter to the King of Adja. But this king was impotent, and had not been able to lie with her. This gave the king much shame. So he gave the girl to his eldest son.

Now, at the burial they met Fa, Legba's master. Before Fa could speak, it was necessary that Legba be at his side.[2] The son of the king of Adja had come to find Fa, and he told him all that had happened between his father and the daughter of Metonofi. And he told that his father had given him the girl for his wife. He asked Fa for a powder that would make him potent, and would remove the shame from his family.

Fa told him to go home. In three days he would send him a good powder. But Legba, who kept the sack that contained Fa's medicines, said, "Your sack is here. I can take the boy behind the house and give him the powder immediately."

So Fa said, "Yes," and instructed Legba to give the boy some of the white powder. For Fa had two powders, one that was white that gave potency, and one red, that rendered men impotent. But when Legba got the sack, he gave the boy some of the red powder.

The burial over, Legba and his two brothers[3] started on their way home. When they came to a crossroads, they sat down to divide the gifts they had received. They divided the cowries into three piles, each of equal size. But, one cowry remained over. They tried again and again to divide the cowries equally, but no matter how they divided the pile, one remained.

So Minona said that, since she was the eldest, she would take it. But Aovi disagreed, and said that, since he was the second, it should go to him. Legba also laid claim to it, saying that the others had had much to eat before he was born.

There was a great discussion, but the three could not agree.

While they were talking, along the road came a woman who had been collecting wood to sell in the market-place, and she carried a bottle on her head. They called to her, and asked her to divide the cowries equally. She tried and tried, but every way she tried there was always one over. So finally she asked, "Who of you is the eldest?" Minona replied, "It is I." So the old woman said that in her country when three divided something and there was one over, this went to the eldest. So she gave Minona the extra cowry. In an instant, Aovi cut off her head, and Legba struck her with his cane. Then they threw her body into the bush. But Legba went off into the bush where the body was, and lay with the dead woman.

When he returned, they resumed their quarrel, until a woman came down the road on her way to the well to get water. They called to her and asked her if she would divide the cowries for them. She tried and tried, but always one cowry was left over. So finally, she asked, "Who among you is the second?"

Aovi replied, "It is I."

She said, "In my group, when there are three among whom something is to be divided, and one is over, the first doesn't take it, or the last, but the middle one." And she gave the extra cowry to Aovi. Instantly, Legba struck her with his stick, and Minona slit her stomach and ripped out her intestines. And, when they had thrown her body into the bush, Legba again went where the corpse lay and had intercourse with it.

After a time, a third woman came, this time on the way home from the market. They invited her to distribute the cowries. She tried and tried, but always after an equal division had been made, there remained one. So she asked, "Who is the youngest?" Legba said, "It is I." So she gave the extra cowry to Legba, saying, "In my group, when three divide something and there is one over, we give it to the youngest, for the older ones have eaten before he was born." At this, Minona ripped open her intestines, and Aovi cut her head off, while Legba took her body into the bush, and he lay with the dead woman.

By now Legba had had enough, and so he told his brothers he was going into the bush to look for something. Legba was a great singer, and he still carried with him the sack of his master, Fa. In this sack he now found a carved figure which he turned into a dog. He whispered to the dog to go past the brothers, who were still trying to divide the gifts from the funeral, and he told him what to do. Then he rejoined them.

Now, no sooner did he come back, than a dog came down the road. So they invited him to divide the cowries. He tried and tried, but always there was one over. So with his paws he scratched a small hole, and said, "In my group, when three divide something and one is left over, it is for the ancestors." And he buried the extra cowry in the hole.

Now, all three of the brothers were satisfied, and they blessed the dog. Na said, "You will lead all the *vodun* that I command. You will always be in the lead." And Legba said, "You will lead all men. You will never let them lose their way." They blessed the dog again, and he went on his way. But Legba went into the bush, where the dog came to him and was changed once more into the statuette.

When they came home, the son of the king of Adja, to whom Legba had given the red powder, was there with Fa. He said that he, too, had become impotent.

Now, in those days, everyone had to come and consult Fa before he did anything. And so, when Metonofi announced that any man who could have intercourse with his daughter would be given half his kingdom, all the men came to consult Fa. But Legba gave them all the red powder, and made all the men of the kingdom impotent. When the men complained to the king that Legba had rendered them impotent, Metonofi looked for him to punish him. But he ran away to the house of Ayo, his mother-in-law.

It happened that his father-in-law was away, and Legba had to sleep in the same room with her. During the night he lay with her, and in the morning he returned to his village.

There they arrested him at once, and brought him before the king, who now summoned all the men of the kingdom to come and make their complaint. When the men of the families of the three women who had been killed by Legba and his brothers at the crossroads saw Legba, they accused him before the king of their deaths. And Legba's father-in-law also made complaint that Legba had slept with his wife. And all the men of the kingdom accused Legba before the king of having given them the red powder.

Now, the first case was up for trial. The king asked Legba if he had killed the three women. Legba replied, "No, it was Aovi." He said he had intervened and had helped to divide the cowries so as to save other deaths. But the brothers denied the guilt of Aovi, and said that a dog had finally settled the matter. At this, Legba said that he was the one who had commanded the dog. He told that he had changed a carved figure into a dog, and to prove his words, he took the carving and, before the eyes of everyone, changed it into a dog.

Now all the people saw that Legba had spoken the truth, and Metonofi ordered that Legba be guardian of men and women, and of all the gods. He told Minona to return to her home, and henceforth live in the houses of women, whom she would command. He told Aovi to live among the gods. But Legba, he told could live anywhere he wished. So Legba came into the houses.

After this, there was the second complaint to be disposed of. The trial took place after two days. Legba was asked, "Did you lie with your mother-in-law?" [4]

And to this he answered, "Yes." But he explained that she had slept in the place where his wife usually slept. And so judgment was given in this case. Metonofi said that since he had already made Legba guardian of all, he could not revoke this. But because Legba always created scandals, he was not to live in houses, but that his place would always be in front of houses.

After two days, the third complaint was brought before the king for judgment. It was the complaint that Legba had given the men of the kingdom the powder that made them impotent. "Did you give the good powder?"

Legba replied, "Yes." So they told him to bring the powder he had given the men that they might see.

While he was gone, Legba mixed the blood of a pigeon with the good powder, making it red. In the red powder he put water in which caolin had been mixed, thus turning it white. When he came back with the two powders, Metonofi asked the men, "What color was the powder given you?"

All cried out, "The red, the red!" So they told Legba to take the red powder himself, and Metonofi told everyone to return in two days, when they would see whether the red powder had made Legba impotent.

When all had reassembled, they found that Metonofi had caused a little house to be made, and in it he had placed his daughter, the wife of the King of Adja. The men were told to enter, one by one, to see if they could lie with his daughter. None of them could accomplish sexual intercourse, and one by one they left her. They were sad, because they were impotent. But there were some who said that it was not good to try it this way. With everyone waiting anxiously, they could not be expected to accomplish what was desired of them.

Legba, however, told the king that these men knew nothing. He, Legba, would have intercourse with the king's daughter in public, if they wished it. And so, it being his turn, Metonofi told him to enter the house, and that if he accomplished intercourse with his daughter, he would reward him well.

Now Legba had made drums, and these he caused to be played as he entered the house where the girl lay. No sooner had he entered, than he deflowered the king's daughter. There was blood all over the house. This done, he came out of the house still naked, with his penis erect, and when he approached anyone, he went through the motions he had made when he was with the girl. And all this time his drums were being played.

Metonofi was very pleased with what had happened. He told Legba to take his daughter as his wife. And he ordered that from that day on, this drum should be played everywhere in remembrance of his daughter. He also said that Legba might sleep with any woman he chose, without any distinction. And as Legba was wise, he named him intermediary between this world and the next. This is why Legba dances in the way he does everywhere.

Legba gave Metonofi's daughter to his master, Fa, and Fa invited all the men of the country to his house to celebrate the marriage. When all were there, Legba gave everyone a drink, putting the good powder in the liquid. And at once each recovered his potency.

On that day, Legba was named Aflakete, meaning, "I have deceived you." And he gave the name Adje to the girl. The name means cowries, since it was for cowries that they had killed the women.

That is why Legba is now found everywhere. To go to a *vodun*, one must first pass Legba. To make Fa, one must pass by Legba. And all men and women must have their Legba as a personal guardian. And this is also why the dog is respected as the animal of Legba.

[1] Cf. *Dahomey*, II, pp. 225-229.

[2] Legba is spokesmen for the gods. His role corresponds to the African political official known in the literature as "linguist."

[3] This word is used for both male and female siblings.

[4] An act hateful to ancestors and gods.

II

Why Legba may take all women

Legba had one wife, called Nunde. When Legba left home, Fa came to his house, and deflowered this wife, for she was still a virgin.

One day Legba asked his wife, "Why do you behave so badly, in my absence?"

Nunde replied, "Your penis is not enough for me. That is why I look everywhere."

Now, Legba went to his house, and ate a great deal. Then he called his wife, Nunde. He said, "Today you will get plenty." Legba brought together all the people of the country. He made his wife lie down before everyone.

And he said, "My penis is strong. Today I will succeed." So he lay with his wife before everyone. She said, "Now I am satisfied." But Legba said, "Today I will have intercourse with you until you are tired." The people began to beat the drums, and Legba sang:

> *Gudufu,*
> *The path of my destiny,*
> *Is large;*
> *Large, large*
> *Like a large penis.*
> *Oh, Gudufu,*
> *You are large.*[1]

He did this to make his wife ashamed. He said to everyone, "Fa is my friend, and we are gods of the same quarter. Fa is the first, and I, Legba, am second." Legba said, "In my absence, see what my wife has done! It is because of this that I shame her."

Legba said to Fa, "Now, you must not go out. You are always to remain in the house. And we, the others, will walk about everywhere. If we find something good, we will share it with you."

After this when Legba went out, he went with his wife. He did this so that Fa might not have her again. And Legba said, "If I find any woman, I will lie with her, no matter whose she may be."

It is because of this that to this day, when someone beats the drum for Legba, he comes and he dances joyously. He does all he wishes. And Konikoni is always with him when he goes out. Nunde and Konikoni is the same woman. She has many names.

It is also because of this that Legba comes first, before Fa.

[1] Record No. 90–2.

12

Why trickster has a bad name: Creator tricked: Why the sky is high

Legba did good towards everybody, and he was always with Mawu. When he did a good deed, people always went to thank Mawu. Now Legba said to Mawu, "What you tell me to do, I do, and no one says thank you to me."

Now, it is said that in those days Legba did nothing without instructions from Mawu. But when there was evil, and the people cried out and went directly to Mawu, Mawu said to them, "It was Legba who did that." All the people began to hate Legba.

One night Legba went to see Mawu to ask her why when there was evil, she called his name? Mawu said to him that in a country it was necessary that the master be known as good, and that his servants be known as evil. Legba said, "Very well."

Mawu had a garden in which she planted yams. Legba went to tell her that thieves were planning to go to that garden to gather all the yams and divide them. So Mawu assembled all the people of her kingdom to say to them that the first one who went to steal in this garden would be killed.

That night rain fell. Legba passed behind Mawu's house and stole her sandals. He put on Mawu's sandals and went into the garden. He stole all the yams. In the morning the theft was discovered. At once Legba said all the people must be assembled to see whose feet these were. All the people came. They measured the feet. But they did not find a foot to match the footprints in the garden. Now Legba said, "Ah, is it possible that Mawu herself came at night and has forgotten it?" Mawu said, "What, I? That's why I do not like you, Legba. I will measure my foot with that footprint." Mawu put down her foot. It was exactly the footprint.

Now everybody shouted, "There is an owner who is herself the thief." Mawu was humiliated. She said to all the people that it was her own son who had played her this trick. Now, she would go up above, and leave the earth, and every night Legba would come to her to give her an account. Until then Mawu was on earth. Mawu now went up towards the sky.

It is said that in those days the sky was quite near, only about two meters from the earth. Now, when Legba committed a fault, Mawu saw him and reproached him. Now, Legba was irritated by this, so he went to conspire with an old woman. He told the old woman to throw water at the place where Mawu was, two meters from the earth. The old woman, after washing her plates and pots, threw the dirty water where Mawu was. Mawu was angered. She said, "To stay here is troublesome. It is necessary to go farther away." And so Mawu departed from here on high, and left Legba here on earth.

13

The first humans: Missionary version of Legba rejected

History tells that in early times all of Africa was desert. A man named Zogbo crossed the Duwaya [the Niger], and came to establish himself here with two women. The first woman was called

Hetī, the second Heto. It is after his arrival with his family that the five prophets who came down from the sky to explain Fa were here.

Before this time, men lived a long, long time. They lived to four hundred years, six hundred years, and when they lived so long, they bore many children. Yet it is only after the arrival of the five prophets that the people really multiplied.

In the beginning, there were first just a man and a woman. It was they who peopled all the world. He was called Adanhu and she Yewa. The Creator used earth, and he made four human beings, two men and two women. They were there, but they were not yet given life. Legba went and changed two of these beings. Since he did this without the knowledge of Mawu, and he did not know how to do this work, these two were monkeys. All monkeys are descended from these two. The other two God made into Adanhu and Yewa.

The story the missionaries tell about the fruit does not exist here. That Legba gave this fruit, that we do not know. All we know is that the man who came here was called Zogbo. The proverb says: When one says he is greater than the other, ask him, "Are you Zogbo?" But the missionaries, when they heard our name of Adanhu and Yewa, said our gods and theirs were all the same. They tried to teach us the rest about the beginning of man and woman, but the Dahomeans do not agree. They say this is not their story. They know nothing about Legba trying to give fruit.

14

Why monkey did not become man

Now Mawu created all the animals. But they had no names as yet. Mawu said, "A little later I will give you each a name. In order to give you a name, though, you must first work the clay for me." For Mawu had not yet finished making all the creatures she wanted to make, and she needed this clay out of which to mold them.

They began to work the clay. Mawu said to what is now Monkey, "As you have five fingers on each hand, if you work well, I will put you among men, instead of among the animals."

When Mawu had said this to him, the animal who is now Monkey boasted before all the animals. "Well, me! . . . Now tomorrow, I won't be among you animals. I'll become a man."

First he told this to Lion, then to Hyena, then to Elephant. And then he called each animal in turn, and said he had a secret to tell him. When they came, he told them the same thing.

Now, Monkey was so busy telling this, and clapping his hands with joy at his fate, that he did not work at all.

Now, while the animals were working, Mawu came to see what they were doing. She came to observe those who were working well, those who were lazy. As Mawu approached, she saw that the animal they now call Monkey was happier than all others. He continued to sing, clapping his hands, "Tomorrow I change into a man. Mawu herself told me that."

Mawu heard this. She ordered him to come to her. Then she kicked him and said, "You will always be Monkey. You will never walk erect."

15

Mawu's ways are just

In ancient times Mawu sent a messenger to earth daily to travel from sunrise to sunset.[1] He did this all the time; every year.

One day, while on his errands, he reached Adjala, and in Adjala it was already night. He could go no more and so he went into a house. There was a man who was also on the road. As night fell, he, too, went into this house.

They gave them a place in the same house, the two strangers together.

Mawu's messenger asked the other, "Where are you going?"
He said, "I am going where the sun sets."

Good. Mawu's messenger said, "It is life that gives a companion. I myself am going to the same place."

The following morning, at first cockcrow, in a house beside theirs where a sick child slept, the parents were crying.

Mawu's messenger went to ask them, "Why haven't you slept all night?"

They said, "We have a child here who is very sick."

Very well. Now, Mawu's messenger had a sack in which he carried some powder. He gave some of that powder to a man to give to the sick child.

And he went back quickly to the man who was sleeping in his house, and said, "Wake up! Wake up! We are leaving."

They took but a few steps away from the house, when all at once the people in the house began to shout, "Where is the stranger? Where is the stranger?"

The child was dead.

So they went away. They went till . . . they came to Savalou. There in Savalou they spent the night. They took shelter in a house beside the road. At first cockcrow, Mawu's messenger took some flint and made a fire. And this fire he put to the straw of the house where he had slept. He said, now, to the other man, "Wake up, wake up! We must be going."

After they left, the house took fire. The people asked, "Where are the strangers? Where are the strangers?" But they were gone.

They ran away and continued their journey. As Mawu's messenger did that, his companion, who was a human being, was astonished. He did not know that the other was a *vodun*. So they reached Badahwedji where the sun sets. That is, they were almost there.

Now, there was a river that separated Badahwedji from where the two travelers were. In order to cross the river, one must put down a raft and pass on it. There was an old man from Badahwedji who was in the habit of coming to the river bank for leaves. He gathered them and went back. Now he was crossing the river for the second time. So Mawu's messenger followed the old man. The old man went ahead. He went slowly, cautiously. Mawu's messenger came behind him and pushed him, so that he fell into the water.

When he did this, the man who came with Mawu's messenger ran away. Mawu's messenger saw him run and he called him back. "Come, come here," he said. He said, "That's not where you are going. You are going to this place. Here it is."

The other said, "What I saw on the road here is too much. I am running away from it."

Mawu's messenger said, "Now, I'm not a man. I know you are astonished at all I did. But I'm not a human being. In the house where I killed the child, if that child had not died, its mother and father would have died when it took its first step. It is Mawu who sent me to destroy that child." He said, "In that house this mother and father have borne many children, and this one child could not be allowed to spoil their lives."

He said, "The family where I burned the house has rich relatives among them. But they buried all their money and their children are poor. So I burned the house, so that when they break the walls to make them anew and begin to dig the foundation, they will find the money."

He said, "I had the man fall into the river, because the king of Badahwedji is dead. To replace this king, a young man should be named. If that old man were alive, a young man could not be named. That is why Mawu sent me to throw him into the water. The people still think the old man will be their king. But if that man became king, there would be no more goats, no more cattle, no more children in that kingdom. Sagbata would come to their kingdom and kill them, because Mawu had ordained that one could not be king. With a young king, they will have goats, pigs and children also."

Then he said, "I, I look into the hearts of men,[2] and Mawu sends me to look at things. You must not be astonished. Year after year, if I do not change into a man, I change into headache and kill men. I change into serpents and burn houses. And when, in the course of life, you see such things, you will know that it is Mawu who sends them."

[1] This is idiomatic for "from east to west."
[2] Lit., "into men's stomachs."

16

The son who surpassed his father: Why a faint
rumble succeeds loud thunder

Lisa had a daughter called Maho. One day Lisa said to her he would give her a new name.[1] He would call her Gbemende, which meant that she would overcome all obstacles.

Now, the great Segbo heard this, and he said, "Ah, we shall see." He asked Lisa for his daughter, and Lisa gave him Gbemende.

One day Segbo called all his wives together. He had twelve besides Maho. He said to them he would give them each some millet to make beer for him. And he said that she who failed to make good beer would be killed. Now, millet beer is made this way. Millet is put into water and allowed to stand overnight to ferment. When at night the wind comes, he changes it, and it becomes beer.

Segbo then gave millet to his first twelve wives, but to Maho he gave okra. Maho took the okra and began to cry. She cried and cried until Lisa heard her and asked her what was the trouble. Maho told her Segbo had set all the wives the task of making millet beer for him, and that he said she who failed to make good beer would be killed. But instead of millet, he had given her okra.

"That is nothing," said Lisa.

At night a great wind came up, and blew and blew. In the morning Segbo called his wives together and asked them to give him the beer. He went to Maho first. Maho gave him some excellent beer. When the other women looked at their beer, they saw okra.

Segbo said, "All right. That is the work of her father Lisa. Well, we shall see."

Now, these twelve women had already borne children to Segbo, and they were again big with child. It happened that whenever these women gave birth, it was on the same day. Now, one day Segbo called all his women together, and he said to them that in two days their children would be born.

Now, Maho was not even pregnant. So she began to cry. And

she cried and cried, until Lisa heard her. Maho told her Segbo had said that in two days they were each to bring a child into the world, and that she who failed him would die. She said since she, Maho, was not even pregnant, she would surely die in two days.

Lisa said, "Stop crying. It is nothing at all." He told her to go home and go to sleep. Then when she heard the others being delivered, she had but to strike the earth three times with her foot if she wanted a son, and three times with her head if she wanted a daughter.

So when Maho heard the other women being delivered, she knocked three times with her foot and at once a man-child appeared. He was handsomer and stronger than all the other children.

Segbo went first to all the other wives. And then he came to Maho.

"Where is your child?" he asked.

Maho lifted the cloth under which she lay, and there Segbo saw a child who was handsomer and stronger than any of the other children.

Segbo said, "That is all right. Again this time Lisa has won. But we shall see."

Now, Segbo had a medicine that could make a child of ten days grow so that it could walk and talk. To all the other twelve sons, he gave this medicine. But he did not give it to Maho's son. "In twelve days," said Segbo to his wives, "I want to see all my sons walking and talking. If any child is unable to do this, I will kill him and kill his mother."

Maho went back to her house, and again began to cry. Lisa heard her, "Why are you crying now?" asked Lisa. And Maho told her all. "Ah, that is easy." And she said, "When the others start walking and talking, you have only to tap the child's head seven times and he, too, will walk and talk."

On the eleventh day, all the other children walked and talked. Maho tapped her son on the head seven times, and at once he stood before her taller than all the other children, and stronger and livelier.

Segbo called for all of his children. He saw Maho's son among them, but taller and finer looking than all the rest. "This time, again, Lisa has had the best of me. But I shall try something else."

A day came when he called all his sons to him. He asked each to tell him his name. For the children had no names as yet. Each child gave himself a name. The great Segbo said to each that it was good. When he came to Maho's son, he asked him his name.

The boy said, "My name is *Agba-gugu-teso-teno-maye-vidogbe-nada-uku*—Energy-Itself: The yam is pregnant, but its owner does not know it. If the child lives, it will surpass its father."

Segbo was angry when he heard this. He said, "That day will never come!"

He found twelve horses and one sheep. To the sons of his other wives he gave the horses, and to Agbagugu he gave the sheep. "Go to the field with this sack of corn," said he to each. "He who is last will be killed."

Maho began to cry. How was her son to race on his sheep against the sons who had horses?

Lisa heard her and asked her what the trouble was. Maho told her what Segbo had done. Lisa gave her a white powder, and said to let the sheep inhale this powder. Then they should see what would happen. When they did this to the sheep, the sheep changed into a fine horse, and this horse galloped faster than all the other horses. Agbagugu was the first to reach the field with his sack of corn. And he was the first to reach his father's house.

The great Segbo said, "All right. But sooner or later we shall see." Segbo now asked Agbagugu to go and get the scythe which Death carries. Now, no man can go to see Death and come out alive. Maho went crying to Lisa, and Lisa gave her seven peppers. Lisa said Agbagugu was to break them one by one, beginning with the moment he left his father's house.

Agbagugu broke the first one, and he found himself in the midst of a great crowd of people whom he had never seen before. He broke the second, and he stood before a closed door, which was watched over by two dogs. He dropped the third, and the dogs fell asleep. The door opened. He dropped the fourth, and he found himself before the chamber of Death, where bees circled round and round and kept him from entering. Through the thick veil formed by the swarming bees, Agbagugu saw Death seated. Death was a terrifying creature, with four eyes, and the scythe was in his hand. Agbagugu dropped the fifth. Death went to sleep, and the bees went off peacefully to rest inside a nearby tree. He dropped the sixth, and he found himself beside the sleeping Death. He then took the scythe out of the hand of Death and dropped the seventh. When he had done this, he saw himself back in his mother's house. But the scythe was in his hand.

When Death awoke and saw that his scythe was gone, he sounded an alarm, and ordered his hammock carriers to take him at once into the world to search for his scythe.

Now, when Segbo saw Agbagugu come with the scythe of Death, he said to himself, "His grandfather tricked me again. But we shall see." He said to the boy, "Death is very angry. You must return to the house of Death, and give him back his scythe."

Maho began to cry again, and she cried and cried until Lisa heard her. Lisa gave her seven more peppers for her son. When Agbagugu dropped each of the peppers, the same thing happened to him as had happened before, except that instead of taking the scythe out of the hand of Death, he replaced it.

When Segbo saw his son returning alive, he called Maho, and he said to her that now he would admit that the name Lisa gave the boy was right. For he was indeed invincible. He said he would, therefore, give him his other wives and the children of his other wives as slaves. And he would let her and her son rule the world. He himself would change into sand and rest on the earth. And when the mother wanted to make men and women, they could use his remains to mold the bodies of these men and women.

Maho and Agbagugu believed him. But at night Segbo tried to kill Maho and her son. Lisa was watching over them. When Segbo came to kill them, he took his little finger and pushed Segbo. At once Segbo turned into a mountain on earth.

All of Segbo's possessions now went to Agbagugu. And Agbagugu took some white thread, intertwined it with black thread, and out of that made a ladder for himself and his mother. Then they climbed up high into the sky. He also took with them his father's other wives and his twelve brothers.

Agbagugu, who is Sogbo or Hevioso, shouts and shouts in the sky. He always wants to kill. People say when they hear thunder and then the low rumbling from a distance, that the first is Hevioso's anger. The second, is his mother's voice, which says, "Careful, careful, he is your father."

After some time Lisa, too, left all his domain to him. That which he inherited, he divided among his twelve brothers.

It is said that at night Hevioso comes down to earth with the dew and the mist. For his brother, who is King of the Earth, has a wife whom Hevioso loves. And nightly, he steals down to lie with her.

[1] New names are traditionally given to celebrate new status, or a special achievement.

17

Stealing fire from the Creator: Why Chameleon and Tortoise are respected

When Mawu created the world, there was no fire. So, in the space that separated the earth from the sky, Mawu lit a great, great fire. But she forbade all the people of the sky and all the people of the earth to go there.

Mawu gave the guardianship of this fire to a man called Agbakankan, and she told Agbakankan never to allow this fire to be taken by anyone. To fulfill his task, Agbakankan went to Mawu to ask her for two birds called *chachuè*. Now, the *chachuè* is a bird that eats only roasted food. So, Agbakankan left the birds beside the fire and himself stayed at home.

Now, this was the time of rain on earth. In those days, the animals lived in houses like men. There was no distinction between animals and men. All spoke the same language. One day they held a council to discuss how to get this fire, because the earth was too dark. Lion said he would go to get the fire. So all the people saw him off, and he went on his way. When he approached the fire, he took two good coals.

The two birds began to sing,

> *Agbakankan o!*
> *Lion took some fire;*
> *Agbakankan o!*
> *Son of Segbo,*
> *The male Lion took some fire,*
> *To give to the world below.*[1]

The birds repeated their song, "Oh, son of Segbo, we tell you that the great Lion took some fire for the earth." Agbakankan came carrying two sticks, and when he spied Lion running toward him, he threw the two sticks at him. Lion tripped, and dropped the two burning coals. So Agbakankan put back the two coals.

When he returned, Lion reported it was impossible to take fire, and bring it to earth. He said, "The man who guards it is a very clever man."

Elephant, Panther, Antelope—all the large animals tried. And it was the same thing.

The next day Tortoise and Chameleon came. Tortoise said, "Now to get fire, one must first have straw and firewood. With these, it will be possible to come near the fire, light these and leave the fire of Agbakankan undisturbed."

In those days there was no straw on earth. Mawu had put some straw under a special tree, and this tree was watched by Gedè. They asked which of the animals could go for the straw. All the animals promised to go. But when they came to the tree, they were driven away and beaten by Gedè. Now, under this tree, there was a man with a flute who signaled to Gedè the arrival of the animals.

This time, it was Elephant who was the first to go. When Elephant came, the man's flute sang,

> *Gedè o!*
> *Elephant took away straw;*
> *Gedè, son of Se,*
> *Elephant took straw away*
> *To steal fire for the earth.*

At once Gedè appeared to beat Elephant and take back the straw. Panther, Antelope, Rabbit, Fat-tailed Sheep, Porcupine and Mole all tried, but it was the same thing.

Now Chameleon said he would go to find the straw. No one believed he could do it. Just to reach the place, he had to spend three days. When he arrived there, he took the straw. The man with the flute signaled. Chameleon climbed the tree. Gedè came and looked and looked for the one who took the straw, but he could not find him. So now Gedè was angry. He told the man he was going home to eat.

Now, when Gedè went back to his house, Chameleon climbed down, and went on his way, with the straw on his head. Again the man with the flute whistled for Gedè to come. When Gedè arrived, Chameleon climbed up another tree. This time Gedè beat the guardian for having deceived him.

The Chameleon took three days to get back, but he came back with the straw.

There Tortoise took it. Before reaching the fire, he also spent three days. When he came there, he put the straw on the fire. The straw caught fire, and he lit the wood with this straw. Then he put this inside his shell. The two birds cried out, singing,

> *Agbakankan o!*
> *Tortoise took some fire;*
> *Agbakankan o!*
> *Son of Segbo*
> *Tortoise took some fire,*
> *To give to the world below.*[2]

In those days Tortoise was called Logo. When Agbakankan came, he found Logo. But Logo said he had no fire, he was just passing by. So Agbakankan said, "All right, go. The birds lied to me." And Agbakankan went back to his house.

A little later Tortoise took out the fire, and the birds again began to cry their warning, singing their song. This time, when Agbakankan came he himself saw the fire from afar. But when he caught up with Logo, he saw nothing. He said the birds bothered him too much. But when Agbakankan returned, he again saw the fire from a distance. So he cried aloud to the sky, telling Mawu to look down on earth and see the fire that had been taken.

Immediately Mawu ordered rain. When the rain fell, Logo put the fire inside his shell. He continued on his way. Arrived on earth, he waited till the rain stopped. When the rain was over, he gave the fire to everybody.

So Metonofi [3] said, "Always recognize Chameleon and Tortoise as sacred animals." And the people who had fire, added the name Zo [4] to Logo. History tells us that is why Tortoise exists today. It is the custom to put Tortoise into water, and give him black coal to eat. He eats only charcoal. [5]

[1] Record No. 118–4.
[2] Record No. 118–5.
[3] Storyteller: "According to some histories, Metonofi is Death."
[4] Fire.
[5] Cf. No. 118, for this same explanatory element arising out of an animal trickster tale.

18

The good child: The tail that talked: Changing to stone: From animal to thunder-god

There was a bird called Vulture who was raised by an animal called Sewanla, an animal like an antelope. When Vulture was born, he was born with a rope to climb a palm tree, and an axe. The one who cared for Vulture during his infancy was called Tetelidja.

Sewanla had a father. In those days, when a man died, before they could bury him they had to find the tail of a *tetelidja*. And so the father of Sewanla died. Sewanla had an elder brother, and this brother said to him, "Before we can bury our father you must find the tail of a *tetelidja*." The place where a *tetelidja* was to be found was as far as from Allada to Abomey. [1] And so Sewanla departed to find a tail of *tetelidja*. He had with him three cooked eggs. He went on his way until he came to the house of an old, old woman who lived in the bush.

The woman asked him, "What are you looking for, that you came all the way here?"

He said to the old woman, "I am looking for the tail of a *tetelidja*." As a present for the old woman, he gave her one of the eggs.

The old woman took it and ate it. She said, "If you have another, give it to me, and you shall have what you are looking for." He gave her all three. And the old woman ate one after the other. She said, "The *tetelidja* sleep here. But, now they are away eating. You hide behind this tree. When they come to sleep here, you seize one and cut off its tail."

With the approaching night the *tetelidja* came. One after another said, "There is a living being here. I smell a man here." They began to look about.

The old woman said, "Silence! No one is here." When they heard this, they all went to sleep.

At midnight, Sewanla found the largest of the birds and cut off its tail. And no sooner did he cut it off than he escaped, running as fast as he could. Good. He ran until daylight, and had not yet reached his house. The next morning, when the *tetelidja* awoke, the largest *tetelidja* missed his tail.

He said to the old woman, "I said yesterday there was a man here.[2] Now my tail is missing." Tetelidja said now, "Be my tail in the hands of a man, or in the stomach of an animal, let the tail speak."

The tail answered, "Here I am."

The man who carried it was very much astonished. He carried a tail, and the tail talked. The moment the tail spoke, Tetelidja took to the road to catch the man who had carried away his tail. Now as Tetelidja continued in pursuit, he no longer heard the voice of his tail. He said again, "Be my tail in the hands of a bird, an animal, a human, no matter where, let me hear its voice."

The tail said, "I am still in the hand of this man."

Sewanla began to run all the faster. Tetelidja also ran. Now, there was only a distance of six kilometers between where Sewanla found himself and his home. But between him and his house there was a river. There he could go no farther. So he changed into a stone, and he changed the tail into a stone, too.

The *tetelidja* came to the river, but they saw nothing. *Tetelidja* are creatures who never go into the water. There was one of them who said, "Ah, if I saw the man, I'd take up this stone, and I'd throw it at him." He picked up the stone and threw it across the river. When the stone fell on the other side, it changed into a man. The man held up the tail and showed it.

The animals seeing it wanted to go across, but there was no way. So Sewanla brought the tail home. And the *tetelidja* could do nothing but go back to their home. He [Sewanla] said to his brothers, "Here is the tail of a *tetelidja* which is needed to bury our father. I found it, but I am not in agreement with the king of this country."[3]

After the burial, the king had Sewanla come to him. He said he had an oil palm, and he wished Sewanla to go and get the nuts. Now, he sent him not because he wanted the palm nuts, but because he wanted to kill Sewanla. When Sewanla climbed the palm tree, the king had many men come there, and these brought dry straw and oil. He told them to put these down under the palm tree.

In order to climb the palm tree, Sewanla borrowed the cord that Vulture had. Now, the king ordered his men to make a fire underneath the palm tree. Sewanla could not climb down. So, since he could no longer climb down, he took the cord and climbed into the sky. There he changed to Hevioso.

Then the lightning came, and he gathered up all his brothers.[4] He said to one brother,[5] "You will always follow me. If I want to do evil, you will do it with me." That is why there are two Hevioso heard whenever there is thunder. The man is called Hevioso. The woman is called Bade. She does not want them to do harm to men. The most cruel of all the brothers is Hevioso himself. If he wishes to do some evil, the woman says to him, "Let me go first, and see if the man deserves punishment." Hevioso never does anything without the advice of Bade.

That is why Vulture is a thief. When they departed to become

Thunder Gods, some changed into vultures. They are always flying about, and never find a place to rest.

¹ A distance of about 45 miles.
² Lit., living person.
³ *I.e.*, because the king named this as a condition for allowing burial.
⁴ This is generic for all kinsmen of his generation, male and female.
⁵ Actually "sister," as the text shows.

19

Why a promise to the *vodun* must be kept

This is about a man whose name was Kakpo. This happened in Tendji.¹

In the early days Loko was an ordinary tree. There was this poor man who made hoe handles. He used to go to the bush to cut down the trees to get wood. Once he found a good tree to cut. He cut at the Loko.

Then Loko said to him, "Do not cut me down. No man must cut me down."

Now, there are three *vodun* who live in the Loko tree. Dã is the first, Dangbe is the second, and the third is the *tohwiyo* of the Ayato clan.²

Now, Loko had seven kinds of small double calabashes. Good. Now Loko said to the poor man, "Turn your back to me." Loko said to him, "If I give you wealth, will you do what I command you to do?"

Now the poor man said to him, "Yes."

Loko gave him seven of the little double calabashes and said to him, "Find a good place, and break one on the ground." He said, "If I give you riches will you give me an ox yearly?"

Now, that place where the poor man had broken the first calabash became sacred. He then broke a second one. Many houses appeared. When he broke the third, the houses were surrounded by walls. With the fourth, hammocks appeared and the stools for the needs of a king. He broke the fifth, and he saw many people inside the houses. He broke the sixth, and he saw horses appear. He mounted a horse. He broke the seventh and he found Fa and Legba. Now he became king. These were the men themselves, Fa and Legba, and not just the things for worshipping them.

But Kakpo did not give to Loko the ox which he had promised him.

Now Loko changes into a man. He is wearing a raffia cloth,[3] and he comes to this man to ask him for a drink of water. He found the Mingã of this man who had become king. Loko asked for the master. The Mingã said, "Get out of here. What kind of man is this who wears a raffia cloth?"

Good. Now Loko went away. He came back a second time. The Mingã beat him, beat him with a whip. He went away. And now he came back for the third time. The villagers were busy cultivating for the chief. They beat him again. Now, Loko began to sing a song,

> *Put down the hoes,*
> *Come at once, and dance for me,*
> *You dancers who dance well.*[4]

Good. Now Loko sang so, and as he sang, all at once all the people who were cultivating disappeared. The chief became poor again. Loko left him only a raffia cloth. Now, Fa left to return to the kingdom of Fè.

Now the poor man went again to Loko. He went down on the earth before him and put dust on his forehead. He begged and begged him to forgive him. "I will give you the ox which I promised you."

Loko refused. That is why there are poor people among the black people.

---

[1] A village near Abomey.
[2] The founder of a clan of Yoruba origin.
[3] Native cloth worn by the poor.
[4] Record No. 109-3.

20

How the *vodun* came to Dahomey

The *vodun* came into the world because of Agadja. The *vodun* came from Adja.[1] There was a woman who was called Hwandjelè. She brought all the *vodun* from Adja. In those days there were no *vodun*. If a woman was pregnant she could bear a goat, and a goat could give birth to a man.

Ahwandjelè, who came from Adja, sold indigo. She saw many times men behind goats. She saw goats behind women, and she asked who bore these? They said that a woman bore them.

There was a wife of Agadja who was called Naè Adono. The life of Agadja with this woman was not yet happy. After market, Naè came to tell her husband that she saw a woman from Adja in the market who said she knew the sacrifice to make so that men will bear men and goats bear goats.

Agadja sent a man to call Hwandjelè of Adja. Now Hwandjelè was married to a man in Adja, and she had borne him a male child. When this woman heard that Agadja called her, she came to Agadja and she said, "In our village, women give birth to human beings, and animals bear animals. Agadja asked her what they did in their country so that this happened. She said, "In our country we have *vodun*. You have no *vodun* here."

Agadja said, "Bring us these *vodun*, too." She asked him for all that was necessary, and she brought Sagbata, Hevioso, Ogu, Lisa, Dã, Aido-Hwedo, Nesuhwe, Tovodun, Fa, Minona, Boko Legba. She brought all these for Agadja.

Now Agadja asked Naè Hwandjelè to become his wife. Hwandjelè gave birth to a boy called Tegbesu. In those days, just as today we give soldiers to the whites, the Dahomeans gave men to the people of Oyo called *ayogban*,[2] which means the load given to the Ayo. To give those people to the Ayonu, each of the chiefs had to give his own son, as well as many others of his village, and Agadja himself had to give a son, too.

When the boy Tegbesu grew up and the time came to give the men to Ayo, Agadja's wives said to him, "Now you must send your son Tegbesu." They, too, had sons but they refused to give theirs. Agadja was angry and said that Tegbesu must not go. Hwandjelè went to see her husband and said that he was to send Tegbesu. She did not want her son to break [3] the kingdom.

Good. Tegbesu then went with the others. When the king of Ayo wanted to send a message to Agadja, he always sent Tegbesu with the message. One day Tegbesu was on his way to give a message to Agadja from the king of Ayo. On the road he met a diviner with the white head of a bull. The *bokonon* asked him, "Where does this boy whom I always meet on the way come from?" The *bokonon* said, "When you go to see your father, I will go with you." Tegbesu went and told this to his father. His father said, "Go and bring him." He brought the *bokonon* there. The *bokonon's* name was Djiso, the second was called Gongon. They both had their Fa. Agadja gave them a place to make Fa.

As Agadja's death was approaching, he said, "Why is it that you do not like my son Tegbesu?" He said this to his other sons and wives. "My life and Dahomey belong to Tegbesu and Fa."

[1] A region of present-day western Dahomey.
[2] *I.e.*, tribute.
[3] Idiom for "destroy."

2 1

Cult separatism and the great gods [1]

Formerly we and the people of Djena were together. In those days everybody followed the cult of Djena. Then when the worship that came from Hwala [Grand Popo] and Hevie began to spread, they separated. Because, before, *So* existed at Djena.

Now the religion of Hevie and Grand Popo says Sogbo is master of all. Sogbo created all, the Hevioso people say, and his brother, the Earth, does not command. He is but the riches of the earth. The people of Djena do not agree. They say two gods existed who disputed the kingdom of the sky, and one of them came down to rule the earth. In addition, there are the two above them, Mawu and Lisa, who created the Universe and are above Sogbo and above the god of the Earth.

But the Hevie people say that Mawu is Sogbo, that Lisa is Agbè.

Djena denies all that. They say Agbè exists separately, Sogbo separately; that Agbè, Sogbo and Sagbata are sons of Mawu.

This is a dispute that will never end.

[1] Told by a Hevioso priest. Cf. *Dahomey*, II, pp. 158–159 for a statement of the setting of this controversy.

II

Divination

Divination

DRAMATIS PERSONÆ

FA, destiny; system of divination, personified as Gbadu

GBADU, personification of Fa

MAWU, the creator

LEGBA, youngest son of Mawu; divine trickster

MINONA, daughter of Gbadu

AOVI, ABI, DUWO, KITI, AGBANUKWÈ and ZOSĚ, sons of Gbadu

KODA, first man to descend to earth

CHADA, his companion; a prophet

ADJAKA, Oku, and Ogbena, three later messengers of Mawu

ALAUNDJE, first Fa diviner

DJISA, pupil of Alaundje

AGADJA, Dahomean king

GOGO, early bringer of Fa

HUNSU, son of *vodun*

AMUSU, son of Fa

LOKO, sacred tree; a deity

SEGBO-LISA, another name for Mawu-Lisa

AZIZĀ, in this section, sea-monster

DADA SEGBO, early king

YEHWÈ (Yehwe Zogbanu), thirty-horned, fire-breathing mythological monsters of the Dahomean forest

TORTOISE (LOGOZO), diviner for the animals

AWELÈ, a small bird

MONKEY, BUFFALO, LEOPARD, ANTELOPE, ELEPHANT, LION, HYENA, DOG, PIG, RABBIT, GOAT, LAMB, and other animals

AYOHOSU, king of Oyo

HWEGBADJA, king of Dahomey

KPANUHWÈLÈ and HWELÈAGO, two doves

TITAGWETI, sacred bird

HUNTER

SERPENT

DEATH

NUNDE, KONIKONI, wives of Legba

AGBOGBO, "the largest bird of all"

AGBÈ, a small spotted animal

VULTURE

SOSOGLOSÈ, a fish

CROCODILE

CROW

ADJAHOSU, king of Adja

22

The origin of Fa [1]

Gbadu came after Agbè and Naetè. She has sixteen eyes, and like Mawu is both male and female. She was told to live on top of a palm tree in the sky in order to observe the kingdoms of the Sea, the Earth and the Sky. Mawu said she would be told later the duties she was to perform.

Gbadu is always in the tree. At night, when she sleeps, her eyes close, and since she cannot open them herself, Legba has been charged by his parent to climb the palm tree every morning to open the eyes of his sister. [2]

When Legba climbs the palm tree, he first asks Gbadu which eyes she wishes to have opened, whether those of the back or front, to the left or right. When he says this Gbadu, who watches over the kingdom of the Sea, the Earth and the Sky, does not want to speak, for others might overhear. In reply to Legba, she puts a palm kernel in his hand. If she places one kernel in his hand, it means she wishes him to open two of her eyes, and if she gives him two, one of a pair of eyes is to be opened. When Legba does this, he himself looks about to see what is happening in the sea, and on earth, and he has promised Gbadu, whom we also call Fa, he would also report on what happens in the domain of Mawu. And so that is the way it is.

After a time Gbadu began to bear children. The first child was Minona, a daughter, and the second was also a daughter. [3] The others, all sons, were named Aovi, Abi, Duwo, Kiti, Agbanukwè, and Zosẽ.

One day Gbadu confided to Legba that she was troubled because she had not as yet been told what her work was to be. Since Legba alone knew the alphabet of Mawu, he promised his sister Gbadu he would teach her that.

Some time after this, Legba said to Mawu that there was a great war on earth, a great war in the sea, and a great war in the sky, and that, were it not for Gbadu, all these three kingdoms would shortly be destroyed, since men did not know how to behave. The water of the sea did not know its place, and the rain did not know how to fall. This was because all those who had been given these kingdoms did not understand the language of their parent. Mawu asked, "What is to be done?" Legba said it would be best to send Gbadu on earth. But Mawu said, "No. Let Gbadu remain here, but let an understanding of my language be given to some men on earth. In that way men will know the future and will know how to behave."

Mawu said to Legba to go and find three men to send on earth. Legba went to find three sons of Gbadu to teach the "alphabet" of Mawu to men.

Now, before these children of Gbadu went down on earth, Mawu turned over the keys of the future to Gbadu. It is said that this is a house with sixteen doors, each one corresponding to the eyes of Gbadu. The palm tree on which Gbadu rested was called Fa. So, when Gbadu received the keys, Mawu said that since Legba is the "inspector" of the world, Mawu wishes that Gbadu be the intermediary between the three kingdoms and herself, the parent. When men wished to know their future in order to guide their actions, they should take palm kernels and "play" them at random, and this would open the eyes of Gbadu which correspond to the number that remained, and the order in which they fell. As the kernels opened an eye which corresponded to a door in the house of the future, the destiny of the one for whom the divining was done could be seen. That which each house of the future contained was taught to the three men who were sent on earth.

Now, Mawu assembled Gbadu and Legba and all Gbadu's children, and Duwo, Kiti, and Zosē were chosen to come to earth to teach Fa. They brought palm kernels with them, showing men how to use them. They did their teaching, and told each man what was his *sekpoli*. They said *sekpoli* is the soul which Mawu gave to all, but before calling this soul, it is Gbadu who opened the eyes to call it. It is always necessary to know the number of eyes Gbadu opened before calling this soul; so that if a man knows the number of lines that Fa has traced for him, he will know his *sekpoli*.[4] They said no shrines are necessary for the worship of the *sekpoli*, because the human body itself is its shrine. When the three had finished their teaching, they went back to the sky.

Later Mawu sent all the children of Gbadu on earth. They were led by Legba, who installed them. When they came, Zosē took the name of Faluwono, "Fa-secret-possessor-of," which Gbadu had given him. Minona became the goddess of women, and abides in the houses of women, where she spins cotton on her spindle. Duwo, who took the name Bokodaho, resides in the houses of Fa, while Kiti stays with Duwo to help Zosē, who is Faluwono, do his work.

Zosē plays the palm kernels. He has only one foot, and in the beginning, when he traced the lines by which he divined, people did not believe him. His brother, Aovi [Mishap], was charged with making people more respectful toward their cult. Today if Fa says something which you do not do, tomorrow he will tell his brother Aovi to punish you. Then at once you will respect Fa.

Fa made a small clay figure of Legba and put this in a little house to one side of the Fa house, called *agbanukwè*.

Abi was told to play for Minona the role which Aovi plays for Fa. Abi is ashes. He is the one who makes women respect Minona. When a woman cooks and Minona is angry with her, the fire burns her, or her house burns. And it is for this reason that the place where pottery is fired is called *abi*, because here the ashes are plentiful.

Little by little people began to understand the new "system," and since Aovi is very severe the cult came to be respected. So the cult of Fa has spread everywhere.

Meanwhile, when Legba was in the sky he slept with Gbadu, and when he came on earth, he did the same with Minona. That continued so. One day, he came on earth to visit the cult of Fa with Gbadu.[5] As was their habit, they shared the sleeping-mat together, but late that night he arose stealthily, disguised himself, and went to Minona. Gbadu awoke, however, and discovered that Legba had deceived her with her own daughter. They quarreled, and both went to the sky to bring the case before Mawu.

Legba did not want to acknowledge that he had slept with mother and daughter. Mawu ordered him to undress. As he stood naked, Mawu saw how his penis was erect and said, "You have lied to me, as you have deceived your sister. And since you have done this, I order that your penis shall always be erect, and that you may never be appeased." To show his indifference to this punishment, Legba began at once to play with Gbadu before their parent and, when reproached, pointed out that since his organ was always to remain erect, Mawu had herself decreed such conduct for him.

That is why, when Legba dances it is like this, and he tries to take any woman who is at hand.

[1] Cf. *Dahomey*, II, pp. 263-265.
[2] The narrator said, "ou bien son frère."
[3] The name was not given. No attempt was made by the narrator to reconcile Minona as the child of Gbadu with Minona as the mother of Mawu and Legba or (as in No. 10), as the sister of Legba and daughter of Agbanukwè.
[4] *I.e.*, it is, therefore, a predestined soul.
[5] In this portion of the tale, Fa ceases to be synonymous with Gbadu, but becomes a term for the children of Gbadu.

23

The coming of Fa [1]

After the world had been created, two men came down from the sky. The first was called Koda, the second Chada. It is said that in those days there was no medicine and nothing was worshipped. In all of Africa there were very few people. Now, these two men came down as prophets. They called the people together and told them that they had been sent by Mawu. They said it was necessary that every man have his Fa.

The people asked, "What is this thing you call Fa?"

The prophets said that Fa is the writing with which Mawu creates each person, and that this writing is given to Legba, the only one who assists Mawu in this work. They also said that Mawu herself is always seated, but that Legba is always before her. The orders given to Legba by means of this writing are called Fa, and that, therefore, all men who have been created have their Fa, which is in the house of Legba. They said, further, that the place where men were created is called by the name Fe. Legba, they said, possesses all the writing of each day and is sent by Mawu to bring to each individual his Fa, for it is necessary that a man should know the writing which Mawu has used to create him, so that, knowing his Fa, he knows what he may eat and what he may not eat, what he may do and what he may not do.

When they had said this, they also said that every man has a god whom he must worship, but that without Fa, without this writing, he can never know his god. It is therefore necessary that all inhabitants of the earth worship Legba, for if they fail to do so, Legba will refuse to reveal to a man the writing that is his destiny. If they do not address Legba first, he will not give to man the good things that are destined for him. Each day, they continued, Mawu gives the day's writing to Legba, telling who is to die, who is to be born, what dangers this one is to encounter, what good fortune that one is to meet. Legba, if he wishes, can change things about.

When Koda and Chada finished speaking, the people understood that Fa was necessary for them.

As time went on, though people remembered that Fa is the will of the gods, they forgot the importance of Legba. So three other men came to earth at a place called Gisi, near a river in Nigeria called Anya. The first was named Adjaka, the second Oku, and the third Ogbena. They came to tell that Mawu said that Legba was very important, that Legba is the son, the brother, and the assistant of Mawu herself. If people on earth are in need of anything, they must first of all address themselves to Legba, who has all power to do what he chooses on earth.

When they said this, the prophets showed a man named Alaundje how to make Fa. They had brought with them from the sky the fruit of the palm tree used for divining Fa, and now they showed Alaundje how, when a man wishes to know his destiny, he must enter a forest, take the kernels, himself throw them and trace eight lines on the earth. Now, these eight lines are the destiny of this man. He was told, further, how this same man must then gather the earth on which he has traced the lines of his destiny, put it into a small cloth, mix it with what is necessary,[2] so that it becomes his *kpoli*, and this he worships.

Now, this man who knows his destiny must give the writing to a

scholar to read it. The same prophets taught Alaundje the explanation of each line and, at the same time, the meaning of the lines
of the hand which correspond to the traceries of the *sekpoli*,
making it known that it is by the writing on the hand of man that
Mawu makes known his own writing. It is written like the lines
on the palm of the hand. They taught him it is necessary that
Legba have a shrine outside each compound facing the entrance,
because in the sky he is always so with Mawu. As the writing
which controls human destiny is in the house of Mawu, it is necessary that Legba, who is always before the door of this house, be
placed before the doors of the houses of men.

They said that before a man may eat, Legba must eat; that
when a person goes away from his home he must tell Legba so
that he may be led by a good road. When one is troubled, it is
also necessary to go to him. When one wishes anything at all in
life, one must tell him. Until a man had entered the forest to trace
the eight lines of his destiny, he must never erect a great Legba
in front of his house, since where Fa, the writing of Mawu, is
absent, Legba may not be present. When a boy approaches man-
hood, he is to be given his partial Fa, his destiny as a young man,
but until he has passed childhood and is a man, it is not permitted
for him to have a great Legba in front of his house.

Finally, they prophesied to Alaundje that after their departure
men and animals who were unlike ordinary beings would appear
on earth for the purpose of creating families, and that these beings
would give to men the gods they would in the future worship.
And they said the people should know that as all the rivers empty
into the sea, just so, even though men are called to worship many
different gods, they must recognize that Mawu and Legba have
given them their gods, and that if they desire their gods to be
powerful, they must make a Legba for all *vodun* and for all
tohwiyo.

When they finished saying all this, they left and went back to the
sky.

Alaundje spread the doctrine of Fa everywhere, and taught
what he had learned of the cult of Fa to Djisa. Djisa established
himself in Abomey and taught Fa and Legba to all the people of
Dahomey. And Djisa instructed the people that all those who

learned to know how to read this writing of Mawu were to be called *bokonon*, diviners, since in the sky Legba is called *bokonon*.

¹ This version was recounted by an elderly diviner.
² "What is necessary" is the characteristic Dahomean idiom for ingredients of a
    secret nature.

24

Introduction of the Fa cult ¹

Fa is a *vodun*. He came in Agadja's time, and originated with the Nago. When our ancestors died, it used to be necessary to go to a *gbokanton*, that is to say, a man who divines *gbo*. This system used a kind of pottery in which the pot has the bottom to the sky. The *gbokanton* holds ² a string of cowries, and these are forty-one times five. Now, when a man died and the burial was over, his family went to the *gbokanton* with two chickens and the two hundred forty-six cowries.³ These cowries are called *kaiza-aiza*, and the system of calling the dead, *degbodonu*. Now, when the family came to the *gbokanton*, he made this system. He rubbed his hand over the pottery, until a voice was heard. They say the voice is that of the dead. If the dead man left an inheritance, this voice told how it was to be divided. The voice told also the cause of his death—if he was killed by a woman, or by an enemy, or by an animal sent by an enemy. This sowed much hatred among people.

All this was what they used to do before Fa came.

They also went to the *gbokanton* when a child was born to know the soul of the dead who was the guardian spirit ⁴ of the child, the *djoto*.

This was like this until the time of Agadja. Some of the people did not have much faith in this, and a time came when the king, too, hated this *gbo*, because there were too many combinations of men.⁵ They plotted against the king. So the king looked for something which was truly of providence itself.

Sometime later, Gogo, a man of Zado, came to tell the king of the existence of Fa. Gogo said to the king that a Yoruba called

Mokobi told him about the system of Fa, and that there were in all four of these Yoruba in the kingdom who knew how to divine by the system of Fa.

Now, at first the people did not believe them. But this was during a great drought, when in all the kingdom no rain fell. Everything was done to make rain, but nothing happened. Then the king called on these men. They divined Fa and learned what sacrifices to make. The very day the sacrifices were made, rain fell abundantly in the region of Abomey. So people from other regions came to ask them to do the same, and wherever these men were called, they divined Fa, made the sacrifices, and the rain came.

This proved to the king that these men were true diviners, and they called them *djisa,* "men who sell rain."

One day, they were called on to explain their profession. They said first of all that all children, male and female, must be presented to the diviner three months after birth that he might divine the soul of the dead who is its guardian. They said, also, that there were sixteen Fa, or sixteen secretaries to God, Olorun, or Mawu.[6] The Great God, in order to do anything, uses these sixteen secretaries, who do all the errands and arrange the things of the Universe. And they said that each secretary had fifteen-hundred languages. When one of them came alone, he said one thing, and when he was accompanied by another, he said another thing. . . . Each Fa has its own language.

From Fa came all the stories of the world, for Fa brought them from the sky. Sacrifice also comes from Fa, and it has spread all over Africa. With Fa is associated *kpoli,* who "opens the door" of the sky to Fa, so that he may see the truth. Now, everything that happens on earth, has happened in the sky before. So Fa and Legba can advise human beings, because they themselves have discovered how to meet every possible situation in the sky.

[1] This is a secular version.
[2] At this point the narrator said, "They still exist, yes? But you go to them in secret."
[3] The actual number is 241.
[4] "Guardian angel" was the phrasing of the French interpreter.
[5] *I.e.,* alliances.
[6] Olorun is the Yoruba counterpart of Mawu.

25

How divination became the voice of the gods

Formerly there was only Fa. Good. The *vodun* had a boy called
Hunsu. Fa had a boy called Amusu. There were beads called
nana. One *nana* cost two thousand francs. That city was ruled
by the *vodun*. Every day they went about and found out what
was dear, and what was not dear.

The *vodun* told Fa their children would now go on a journey.
Fa sent for a basket full of *acasa* [1] for his child. He killed two cocks,
and prepared some *calalu* [2] for his child. *Vodun* took a papaya
and hid eighty *nana* inside it. So Hunsu became rich. His father
also gave him one *acasa*.

They left together, Amusu and Hunsu. On the road Hunsu was
hungry. Amusu also was hungry. Good. The two stopped under
a tree along the path and began to eat. Hunsu began first. Now
Hunsu said to Amusu, "Give me an *acasa*, and I'll give you a
nana." Now a *nana* costs two thousand francs. Hunsu gave him the
nana. Amusu gave him *acasa*.

A little later they continued on their way. As Hunsu eats too
much, after three kilometers he asked for food again. Amusu said,
"If you haven't a *nana*, I won't give you *acasa*." He gave six *nana*,
and took an *acasa* for them. That was twelve thousand francs!
They continued on their way. Amusu said, "Now if you ask me
again for food, I won't give you any. Here are ten *acasa* and give
me all the *nana* you have."

They reached the country of their destination. The next day a
man died. In that country if a man dies, one must find a *nana*
before burying him. Whether it cost ten thousand francs or forty
thousand francs, they must have a *nana*. Good. The king said,
"Go ask the strangers who just came; they might have it."

Amusu said to them, "I have many. If you want to give me two
thousand five hundred francs each, I'll sell you two."

The man said, "I have only four thousand."

He said, "All right, give me the four thousand." He gave him the two *nana*.

By that time, Hunsu had nothing to eat. Not a *sou*. He was poorer than an infant. Amusu asked for a place to build houses, since he had so much money. He had almost become king. He asked for women and one hundred workers. They began to work. Now this is the sixth day. He began to make the sacrifices. The chickens came, the sheep, the goats.

Hunsu was now his boy.[3] He was busy looking after the chickens, the pigs. Amusu gave him four francs to get food. At that time two-storey houses[4] were being built for Amusu. He had women. He had herds. He lacked nothing. All the people came and said, "We have a good diviner. He sells the *nana* for two thousand francs." When people came to him to divine, he always said they had to find a *nana*. He did this so he would sell his *nana*.

But all this time Hunsu was there to wait on Amusu. Amusu called Hunsu to come. He said to Hunsu, "You are the son of *vodun*. But the true things come from Fa. You do not seem to know it?" Hunsu did not even have a good cloth. "All this wealth comes from your father," he said, mocking Hunsu.

Hunsu said to him, "Yes. Now, I have nothing to say to you. You must feed me. That's all I ask."

They spent three years like this. The *vodun* at home was thinking that his son was the richest there, for he had *nana* to sell. He said to Fa, "Now, we'll go and see our children." They began their journey. They met a woman whom they asked, "Did you see two young men called Hunsu and Amusu?"

The woman said, "I, I know only Diviner Amusu."

They went on their way. They found Amusu seated on a stool, two women beside him, fanning him with fans.

Good. And the *vodun* Hunsu was the boy. *Vodun* and Fa, who stood at the door, said, "Good day, Messieurs."

Hunsu, when he saw his father, took a jar and covered his face with it. His father said to him, "Hunsu, Hunsu!" But he did not answer. He had changed into a *vodun*.[5]

Hunsu would not speak any more. He said, "If you have something to say, come and say it to me through Fa. If you have something to ask, come and ask through Fa."

Therefore, when we have something to ask of the *vodun*, we approach them through Fa.

¹ Corn-meal cake, wrapped in leaves and boiled.
² Stew of greens.
³ *I.e.*, his servant.
⁴ Symbol of greatest economic prestige.
⁵ The gods reside inside great ceremonial jars.

26

The good child and the bad: The magic gourds:
Punishment for revealing secret

There were two brothers who were traders. The elder left his home and went far away. He made a fire in the bush. In the bush of that country, it is Loko who is the diviner.

When Loko saw this trader in the bush, he said, "Come and see me. I will divine for you and you will have everything you want."

Good. He divined. He told the trader to find a dog, a jar of palm wine and pepper. He said, "Now do as the butchers do. Kill the animal and cook it. Then leave the cooked meat in the bush, and wait nearby." The place where the man stationed himself was the Segbo-Lisa road.

Segbo-Lisa was returning from the village and he ¹ was very hungry. When Segbo-Lisa saw the man, he asked, "Have you water? Have you something to eat?"

The man said, "Yes, I have palm wine here." But Lisa does not drink palm wine, nor does he eat dog. ²

Good. Segbo asked, "Is there anyone near?" The man said, "No, I'm alone."

He said, "All right. Give me some palm wine." The man gave it to him. He drank, and while he drank the man turned his back to Segbo-Lisa.

He asked again, "There is no one nearby?"

The man said, "No."

He said, "Give me a piece of meat and some pepper and turn away from me."

He ate. He said, "I was very hungry and your food was good. I will give you a present. I will give you three small gourds. Now, you will go far, where only the language of birds and animals is heard." Then he said, "You will go to sleep there, you alone. Tomorrow morning you will break a gourd."

[Next morning] the man broke one. The moment he broke it, a large field appeared with many, many men working there. He broke the second one and more men and women appeared. He broke the third and there were markets, animals, two-storied houses, money, cloths, everything. Nothing was lacking.

So he became king. They called him, "Dada!" [3] No sooner did he want to go out, than a hammock and hammock carriers were there. Everybody called out "Dada!"

So as he is there living like a king, his younger brother sets out to look for him. He looked for three years. The third year he found him.

Now, the name of the older brother was Alè. The younger brother said, "I came here to seek Alè."

The man at the door began to insult him, saying, "Who is this man called Alè? We don't know Alè here."

The boy said, "He is my older brother. I didn't know he had become king."

So they went to tell the king. The king said, "All right. Bring him here."

When the younger brother arrived, he gave him food and drink. The two ate together.[4] That night he gave him a house.

He said, "I don't want to sleep." It is the young brother who says this.

His brother said, "Why?"

He said, "Because we two were poor. We had nothing to eat. Now you have become rich, but I am still the same as before. You didn't tell me what you did to become rich. You only gave me some food."

The king said, "I beg you, go to sleep. Tomorrow morning we'll talk about this."

The next day he said, "It's Segbo-Lisa who gave me this gourd." He said, "That's what I did before he gave me this gourd. I got a dog and palm wine and I gave that to him."

When he said this, the younger brother said, "All right. I am going home."

So he returned home. There he got a dog, a jar of palm wine, and pepper and then stationed himself in the bush with these things. But he took along a bundle of switches. He killed the dog, cooked him well.

Again Lisa went by. The boy called him. Lisa came over.

The boy offered him palm wine. Lisa said, "I don't drink palm wine." He gave Lisa the meat with the pepper. Lisa did not ask for it. Lisa said, "Do you want to kill me? I am a *vodun*. I eat neither salt, nor pepper, nor dog's meat."

The young boy said, "Don't say that again. You must speak in a better voice to me than that."

When Lisa would not eat his food, he took a whip and began to whip Lisa.

As he struck Lisa, the god died. He said, "Ah, you are shamming. I have a whole bundle of switches for you, and you are already dead with but one. I will beat you with the others just the same."

So he pushed him with his foot to see if he were still living. He saw he was dead. When he was sure he was dead, he returned home. He left the meat, the palm wine, all, and went home.

That night Lisa awakened. He went to see the big brother whom he had helped. They said to him, "Lisa has come to see you."

The brother said, "I know. Let him come in, let him come in."

So now again Lisa gave him three gourds. He said, "At nightfall you are to break one gourd, at midnight another and at cockcrow you are to break the third. That way you will have double of what you have now."

Good. The man is sad. He did not do the thing to offend Lisa.

The next evening he broke a gourd. When he broke it, all was still. The birds, the people, no one spoke any more. He broke the second. His house became full of weeds and brush. Now there is left to him only one small house where he himself sleeps. The animals and the men are already gone.[5] When he broke the third, he was left alone. He found himself in the bush. No houses, nothing. He wore the same old cloth he had worn when he was still poor.

But he never went back home. He was lost in the bush.

That is why, when the *vodun* Dan has made you rich, you never tell anyone. The moment you tell, he will come and gather up all he had given.[6]

[1] Mawu (Segbo) is customarily regarded as female, while Lisa is held to be male. Cf. *Dahomey*, II, p. 103.
[2] This refers to the offerings given these gods.
[3] The salutation for royalty.
[4] This symbolizes recognition of equality of status.
[5] Note the change to the present tense.
[6] The example of Dan is used because this deity gives riches. Cf. *Dahomey*, II, pp. 251–252.

27

Flight up the tree: Diviner saves Hunter

The Azizā is found in the sea. It is a large animal, and it commands the sea. No hunter will ever kill it. It is also called Djehun. Now, all the hunters were told that there is an animal in the sea which no one ever kills. One hunter said to the king, however, "My king, I am the man who can kill this animal." He was chief of the hunters. So early one morning, he stationed himself near the sea.

First the wife of Azizā came out, then her husband, and they rested on the beach near the sea. They had something[1] in their mouths, which they buried near the sea so that they might not be killed by hunters.

But as the hunter was stronger[2] than they, he saw them clearly. He aimed at the man[3] and killed him. The Azizā fell into the water and came up again; fell into the water and came up. Three times this happened. The wife escaped into the water. To show to the king that he had actually killed the animal, he cut off its tail.

Good. He went now to show it to the king. He showed the tail and said to the king, "The animal which no one ever killed, I killed today. Here is its tail."

So the king told the people to go and divide the animal. The hunter took the skin, and he went home.

On the fifth day, a very beautiful Djehun girl came to the king. When the king saw her, he said he would marry her. Now the girl said to him, "It is not very difficult to marry me. You need only be a good marksman and break the calabash on my head."

The king said, "That is easy. I can do it myself." Good. So they told the girl to stand on a box, at a distance of ten meters. Good. Then the king himself took his gun, but he shot twenty cartridges without touching the calabash.

Now, the girl was doing this to find out the man who had killed her father. This calabash was a thing given her after divination, and it was magically treated to find the man.

The girl said, "I would like very much to marry you, but since you could not break the calabash, I am going away." The king begged and begged her to marry him, offering her two thousand francs. The girl shook her head and said, "No." She said she did not want money. What she wanted was a good hunter who could break the calabash.

So she left this king and went to another country, where there was a king called Dada Segbo. He, too, when he saw the girl, wanted her for a wife. The girl said, "My king, you cannot marry me, because I do not want money. I only want a man who can break the calabash on my head." So Dada Segbo took out his guns; he took six guns, five flint-locks, and one modern French gun. He took all. Again the girl asked for a box to stand on. She placed herself at a distance of fifteen meters from this king. And he shot, and shot, and shot, without touching the calabash.

The girl said, "I am not to blame. I told you what to do, but you could not break my calabash. I am not deceiving you."

Dada Segbo said to the girl, "If I can't break it myself, I have hunters here who can. You are not going to leave my kingdom. A hunter will be found among my men to break this and marry you."

The king now assembled the hunters of his kingdom. They all tried, but no one could break it. Now, there was the old hunter who had killed her father. He came. The others mocked him because he had no cloths, nothing. This hunter told her to move back, saying that she stood too close. She went a distance of one hundred meters. He aimed carefully and discharged his gun. The calabash broke.

When the calabash broke, the girl ran to him, embraced him, and said, "Here is my husband." Now, he took her to his house. At the house the girl prepared food for him.

Now, this hunter owned six dogs. They always accompanied him when he went hunting. During the night, the relatives of the Azizã, the Yehwe, came. The six dogs were asleep in front of the door, but they awoke and attacked the Yehwe. They tore their cloths, and put them to flight. The girl said to her husband, "Why do your dogs watch me so? If I want to go to relieve myself at night, they watch me."

Now, all this happened on the fourth day that the girl was at Hunter's house. On the fifth day, after they had gone to their sleeping mat, the girl asked him questions. If while hunting, he meets a dangerous animal, what does he do to escape? He said to the girl he could not tell her that before they had had intercourse. So she let him finish. Then he said, "If I aim at a leopard and miss him, and he attacks me, I change into a river. If I shoot at other wild animals, I may change into a tree. Then again, I can change into sand, or into a bottle."

Now, next to their sleeping place was the small room where the hunter's mother slept. When the man was telling his wife these things, his mother exclaimed, "Big mouth, why do you talk so much? Don't you know that a good hunter never tells women what he does on the hunt?"

So the boy fell silent. But the only thing his mother had stopped him from saying was that he could change into a horse.

The next day the girl asked him to go with her to the seaside to find leaves for *acasa*. They left together. The man found a tree and wanted to gather its leaves, but the girl said, "No, that's not what I want." He approached a banana tree, but the girl again said, "No." At last she showed him the leaves she wanted, on top of a tall tree. He left his gun on the ground near the tree and began to climb. The girl whistled to call her relatives, who already knew what was to happen. These were the Yehwe.

They came in great numbers and the girl exclaimed to them, "Here in the tree is the man who killed our father." So each asked, "What shall we do to this man?" Then they sang:

> *Both feet cut the tree*
> *With force, force;*
> *Both hands cut the tree*
> *With force, force;*
> *Our hairs cut the tree*
> *With force, force;*
> *Our teeth cut the tree*
> *With force, force.*[4]

When they finished their song, they began to chop at the trunk until the tree was about to fall.

Now, the hunter had seven small magical calabashes, called *glo*, in his sack, and when the tree was about to fall, he broke one of them. The tree stood firm again. Good. So they began once more to cut the tree down. When it was about to fall, he broke the second *glo*, and then, each time as they chopped, the third, the fourth, the fifth, the sixth. Now, he was left with only one. But at about this time, the dogs in his compound awakened and ran to save their master.

As the tree was again about to fall, he broke the seventh *glo*. The dogs have almost reached the tree. When they came, they attacked the Yehwe and drove them far away. They all escaped; the woman, too.

But she promised her relatives that this hunter would surely meet his death at her hands. And so she went back to the man's house.

When the hunter came home, he went to see a diviner and asked him to divine and tell him what he must do to be saved. The diviner told him he must make a ceremony. He ordered him to get twelve lengths of cloth, and seven chickens, four sheep, and a thousand francs. Then he would not be killed by the woman. The diviner also told him this girl was not one to marry, for she was the daughter of *djehun.*

When the hunter got home, he found the girl there. She told him she was going to pay a visit to her relatives, but she would be back the following day. After she left, the hunter performed the ceremony.

At about midnight, he took the sacrifice to the place near the sea where he had killed the animal. He took up the offering in his two hands, and, as the diviner had told him, he did not look behind him. He put his gun on his shoulder and began to sing:

> *Do not kill me,*
> *Child of* djehun,
> *With the white cloth.*
> *I myself have killed the wild buffalo,*
> *I have not been killed by him.*
> *I myself have killed the lion.*
> *I myself have killed the wild bull.*
> *I myself have killed the monkey.*[5]

When he had finished singing, he put the sacrifice beside the water. A great wind brought the family of *djehun* there and they thought the offering was the hunter. So they threw themselves at it and devoured the cloths and everything. But the hunter escaped.

When the hunter got home, he found his mother dead and his father, too. The girl had killed all his relations because she could not kill the hunter himself. Because in Dahomey, what others cannot do, one does not oneself do. And that is why one never kills the Yehwe.

[1] *I.e.,* a magic charm.
[2] Hunters are noted for the strength of their magic powers.
[3] *I.e.,* the male Azizã.
[4] Record No. 122–3.
[5] Record No. 126–1.

28

Tortoise as diviner for animals

All the animals and birds go at sunrise to the fields to eat. Tortoise, whose skin is like stone, also goes out. There was a bird called Awelè. When he saw Tortoise, he called together all the birds. None of them had ever seen an animal like that, an animal with a skin like stone. Awelè said to the other birds, "Here we go out at sunrise to eat, and today a stone also comes to eat with us."

Since Tortoise walks slowly, the birds flew down to see what was inside this thing Awelè said was a stone. But they saw nothing, for Tortoise stopped still.

Now the animals came too, and said to Awelè, "Repeat what you said."

Awelè said, "When the sun rises and you come to eat, here is a stone that comes to eat with you."

All the birds and animals went to see Mawu. They said, "Who gave permission to a stone to eat with us? Today we saw a stone come and eat with us."

Mawu said, "What you saw is not a stone." She fixed a time, three days later, and said, "On that day, when you go to eat, I too will be there."

The day came. All the animals and birds went to eat at sunrise. Mawu told the animals to place themselves on one side. She told the birds to go on the other side. Mawu said, "I will show you that what you thought was a stone is not a stone. For what you thought was a stone is older than all the animals, and is older than all the birds." And so she presented Tortoise to all the birds and all the animals.

Mawu said, "Tortoise is the diviner for the birds and animals." And on that day, Mawu forbade the sacrificing of Tortoise for the gods. One can kill Tortoise to make magic. But for the gods, never.

How Tortoise got his shell: Tortoise becomes diviner [1]

I

Formerly Tortoise was not a diviner. But today in the dry season when the grass begins to burn, it is Tortoise who consults Fa for the animals.

Formerly Tortoise had no shell. Now, when the grass began to burn, Tortoise tried to hide. But the fire burned him. He ran to Elephant and said, "It is I who consult Fa for you; here is my burnt back." Elephant answered, "You are not a large animal. I am a large animal. Who ordered you to consult Fa?" And Elephant drove him away.

Now Tortoise began to sing,

> *Fa asks for something,*
> *Fa said he would eat Tortoise;*
> *Tortoise put his head under Fa,*
> *And said, "Buy me back alive;*
> *Fa, buy me back alive."* [2]

Now Tortoise went to Dada Segbo and said to him, "It is I who consult Fa for the animals, and my back is burnt. I asked Elephant for something to cover my back, but he refused me."

So Dada Segbo gave him his shell. And that is why Tortoise has a shell.

In the bush there are Leopard, Lion, Elephant. But it is Tortoise who is the diviner.

II [3]

Tortoise is diviner because none of the other animals come near Dada Segbo. Now, Tortoise went to Dada Segbo. Dada Segbo said to him, "You have not much to eat, so you must become a diviner. You will always be a diviner, because you have suffered much."

Now during the dry season, Panther, Lion, and Elephant go to Tortoise. That is why Fa sings the song of Tortoise,

> *Fa asks for something,*
> *Fa said he would eat Tortoise;*
> *Tortoise put his head under Fa*
> *And said, "Buy me back alive;*
> *Fa, buy me back alive."*

[1] Cf. No. 17, above, for a related tale.
[2] Record No. 110-1.
[3] Another version of this tale.

30

Monkey's ingratitude: Why one does not deceive the diviner [1]

Monkey can climb, but Tortoise cannot. The two were not friends. Once, during a famine, Monkey found a cornfield where the harvest was fine. But he could not eat the corn, because people always chased monkeys away. So he went to the *bokonon* [2] to ask what to do. Tortoise said, "I am a great diviner, but I do not go out of my house. If you want something, you must come to my house. I am here for the poor, for all those who want to do something. If I were to go with you, you would not feed me, because you know how to climb trees, and I do not."

Tortoise did not want to go, but Monkey urged him and urged him until he finally went with him. He took the Fa sack along. [3]

When they reached the field, Monkey began to eat. He told Tortoise to wait a while for him. But he gave Tortoise nothing. So mid-day came and Tortoise had nothing to eat. Good. Then Leopard came to the same place where Tortoise was. He said to Tortoise "I have a sick child at home. I went to your house twice, but I did not find you."

Now, Monkey climbed up the tree and was watching them

from above. Tortoise told Leopard to come with him under the tree where Monkey was. "There I will divine for you." When they sat down, he began to divine. He said, "We must find a monkey in order to cure the child."

"Must I find one at once? And where shall I find one?" asked Leopard.

Tortoise said, "Oh, that is not hard. You are strong. What I need, you cannot fail to get. I know their ways. What present will you give me if I show you how to find what you need?" He asked for a thousand francs. Leopard gave him the thousand francs.

"Look up, above my head," said Tortoise, "and you will see a monkey."

Leopard called to Monkey, "Ah, you are quite close by! You didn't want to come down and hear what was said? You are mocking me, then? Are you bigger than my son? The divination points to you. I need your head and your tail. The rest you can have."

Hearing these words, Monkey fled. He said, "I am not here to give you my head and my tail."

Good. Monkey ran, and Leopard ran after him. At last Monkey was caught, and Leopard brought him to the diviner. The diviner said, "All right. Bind him." Leopard bound the monkey.

Then the diviner told Leopard to cut off Monkey's head and tail. Then he gave the rest to the diviner to eat. Good. The sick child was cured.

That is why, in Dahomey, a person does not deceive his diviner.

[1] The significance of this tale is explained in *Dahomey*, II, p. 217, where it has been given in abstract.

[2] Tortoise, as the previous tales show, is diviner for the animals.

[3] *I.e.*, the sack containing his divining instruments.

31

Why one does not displease the diviner

Dada Segbo had a field, which Lamb watched over. A road separated the field into two parts. Now it was the dry season. There was no rain.

This happened when the king of Oyo was a greater king than

Hwegbadja. When the time for rain came and there was no rain, one asked diviner Tortoise to come and divine, and Tortoise divined. Then if a person made the right sacrifices, the rain would fall.

The king of Oyo called Tortoise to come to his country and divine for him, for there was no rain in his country. In order to reach the king of Oyo, one had to go through Dada Segbo's field, where Lamb was on guard.

And so, as Tortoise went by there, he said to Lamb, "Give me a drink of water." But Lamb said to Tortoise, "I am not here to serve you."

Tortoise went on his way. There was a small market there. In that market Lamb's mother was selling gumbo and *acasa*, and she had some water. The diviner bought some *acasa* and cakes from her. When he had finished eating, he asked for some water, and the woman gave it to him.

He said, "Thank you very much. I saw a boy and asked him for water, but he would not give me any." He said this to Lamb's mother, but he did not know she was his mother.

Then he said to this woman, "What I am going to divine, I am going to divine against this boy. I will tell the king of Oyo that he must be killed before rain will fall."

The woman asked, "Where is this boy?" Tortoise said, "He watches over Dada Segbo's field. I am going to divine against him."

He left for the king's house. There he divined, and he said that in order for the rain to fall, they must sacrifice a lamb. The king of Oyo asked, "What kind of a lamb?"

Tortoise said, "The lamb that watches over Dada Segbo's field. It is he who has angered Hevioso."

When Lamb's mother heard this in the market-place, she went home at once and told her son to buy goats and chickens and bring them to Tortoise. She said Tortoise had told her he would see to it that he was killed. She said that since he had refused water to Tortoise, he would surely die if he did not obey her.

So the boy bought the goats and chickens, and brought those to Tortoise's wife, saying she was to tell Tortoise he had brought them.

Tortoise had said he would return in five days, and in the meantime he was to get Lamb. Now, everybody knew that Lamb must die. When Tortoise came home, he saw the gifts Lamb had brought. He said, "I told the king of Oyo that the boy must die in five days, and now here are all these presents from him." So he went to tell his Legba how he divined today, and that the boy had brought him all these presents.

Legba said, "That's nothing. Keep the presents. You will divine again."

Now, when the day came, Tortoise went to see the king of Oyo again. Since early morning, Lamb had been lying bound behind the king's house.

Tortoise said, "Bring what I asked for, and I will make the sacrifice." They brought chickens, pigeons, palm oil, white and red stew, everything. He said, "Where is the animal?" They brought Lamb. He said, "That's not what I asked for. I asked only for his hair, but you have tied him up. What will Dada Segbo say? You people understand nothing."

Then Lamb knew that Tortoise had received the gifts left at his house. Tortoise said, "Loosen this boy. I have not the power to kill a lamb which belongs to Dada Segbo. Find me the hair of another lamb."

So they untied Lamb, and he went home. They found the hair of another lamb and made the sacrifice. Legba took a small gourd, took out some powder from it and blew it into the sky. In a few moments rain began to fall.

And that is why today, when the diviner asks for something, they give it to him.

32

The dove that sacrificed and the one that failed to sacrifice

There were two doves, Kpanuhwelè and Hwelèagon. Once, in the dry season, they could not find water to drink. So Kpanuhwelè said, "Let us go to the diviner so that rain may fall."

Hwelèagon said, "If we go to divine, he will ask for chickens, goats, and money, and I have nothing to sell. I am poor."

Good. So Kpanuhwelè went to the diviner alone. The diviner told him to get a goat, chickens, a cock, pepper, and salt. When he brought these things, they performed the ceremony.

They killed the goat, and the chickens, and all the other animals, but they had no water with which to cook them. All at once, rain began to fall. So Kpanuhwelè found water for cooking his food.

Hwelèagon, who did not want to divine, also got much water. But after a few days, once more there was no water. In Kpanuhwelè's house, there was a small hole filled with water. Hwelèagon, who had no water hole at his house, was ashamed to ask for some of this. But he said, "I am going to drink from the hole; I am going to drink from the hole." Kpanuhwelè said, "If you haven't killed a goat, you must not drink from the hole."

The dove Hwelèagon stayed there a long time, but the other would not give him water. Every time he went away, he would come back. He went away; he came back. He did this until night. Finally Kpanuhwelè had to give him some to be rid of him.

That is why today doves talk as they do. One says, "*Nanu kodo, nanu kodo* . . . I want to drink from the hole, I want to drink from the hole."

And the other says, "*Awu gboa, gbo nanu kodoa* . . . If you haven't killed a goat, how can you drink from the hole?"

33

The boxing contest: Bird outwits Elephant:
Why Titagweti is honored at death

Titagweti [1] and Elephant challenged each other to a fight. Elephant promised to kill Titagweti with one stroke of his tusk. Titagweti promised to hit Elephant so hard that blood would come out of his eyes and his brains out of his head.

When Elephant returned home, he did not trouble himself. He

needed but to step on a little bird like that. But when Gweti went home, he sought out Fa.[2] Fa told Gweti to go to Legba. Titagweti went to Legba and knocked on his door. When he said, "*Atacho, atacho*," Legba opened and asked what he wanted. Gweti explained the challenge.

Legba told him it will be very easy to win over Elephant. He asked him for three small calabashes. When Titagweti brought them, Legba put plain water in the first calabash. In the second he put kaolin mixed with water. In the third he put a kind of red pepper called *zakpwakpwe*, which he also mixed with water. Then he told Titagweti to put all these in the tree under which they would fight the next day. Legba told him that the water was to represent tears, the kaolin brains, and the red-pepper blood.

The next morning when all the people had gathered, Elephant and Titagweti began to fight. When Elephant lashed out with his trunk, Gweti flew into the air and came down on Elephant's back. When Elephant turned his head, Gweti perched on his neck. When Elephant lowered his head, he flew onto his foot, and when he raised his foot, Gweti flew into the tree.

He took up the first calabash, and quickly threw the water in it over Elephant's head. Water covered Elephant's face, and Gweti flew down from the tree so as to fly about in front of Elephant. All the people shouted, "Elephant is crying, Elephant is crying!" Then Gweti took the calabash where the kaolin was, and overturned it on Elephant's head. The people shouted, "Elephant's brains are coming out!" Finally he threw the reddened water in the third calabash over Elephant's back. And now the people shouted, "Here's the blood!"

But when Elephant heard the people shout, he was so angry and ashamed that he fell down. And he was so heavy that he could not get up without help.

When Metonofi came and saw the elephant on the ground, he gave the order to all hunters that Titagweti should have the same rank as large animals. From that time onwards, when they kill Titagweti they must perform as great a ceremony as for the largest animals.

[1] A very small bird.
[2] *I.e.*, he went to his diviner to ask his Destiny what to do.

34

Goat's life saved by sacrifice: Why goats avoid rain

Goat had to go on a journey. So he went to the diviner, who told him what sacrifice he must make. He must take a leather bag with him and put two bottles of honey and a piece of meat in it. Goat got everything together and made his sacrifice. Dog, who was going with Goat, also went to the diviner, who told him the same things he told Goat. But Dog did nothing.

The next day, Goat and Dog started. Halfway to their destination, there was a tornado. But in the middle of a field they found a little rest house for travelers. It was a house with only one entrance. While they were there, Hyena came to get out of the rain. When he entered, they did not know what to do.

Goat said, "Good day, sir."

And Hyena said, "Where are you going?"

"On a journey, and I carry a very good thing."

"Let me see it."

Goat took the meat out of the bag that the diviner had told him to take, and dipped it in the honey. As he approached Hyena with the meat in his hand, he said, "Softly toward the mouth of the great one." As he said this, Hyena opened his mouth, and Goat let the meat and honey fall into it.

He ate and ate and ate, and though he found it sticky, he called out, "Goat, where did you find such a good thing?"

When the meat was finished, Goat became afraid that Hyena would go after him. He said, "Sire, I have still some honey, but with a leg of dog, it is still sweeter." Hyena ordered Dog to give him one of his legs. Bagba took the leg, divided it into two parts, put the first part in the honey for Hyena.

The rain had not yet stopped, and while Hyena was eating, Lion entered. Lion seated himself, and asked, "What are you doing here?"

The three all wanted to get out, but they did not know how. Goat said, "Ah, sire, I have a little thing here in my sack," and he took the part of Dog's leg that remained, put it in the honey, and said, "Softly toward the mouth of the great."

Lion found this to his taste, and said, "Goat, where did you find this thing? Is there some left?"

Goat said, "Sire, I have a bit more honey, but with the leg of a hyena, it is even sweeter."

So Lion told Hyena to give him a leg. But when it was eaten, Lion said that he had not had enough. Goat said, "I have what is needed to make meat sweet." And Lion told Hyena to give him his thigh.

Now the house was made of grass, and when he heard this, Hyena, who had worked his way through the wall, escaped. Lion ran after him, and Goat took the opportunity to run away, taking the dog with him.

He returned to his own house and gave a large gift to his diviner. The diviner told him never to go out while it rains. And that is why Goat stays out of the rain.

35

Outwitting creditors: The diviner's parable [1]

F~a~ owed money to a serpent, a leopard, and a hunter. The serpent was a poisonous one.[2] Each of the three lived in a different village and not knowing one another, had no means of finding out that Fa owed money to all of them. When the serpent came to ask for the repayment of his loan, Fa said, "Come tomorrow." When the leopard came, he was told to return the next day, and so was the hunter. As soon as the three left, Fa washed the head of *kpoli*. Then he divined, and the *du* was *gudamedji*,[3] which says that for a matter involving debt, the debtor must first find a raffia sack, and put small stones of the type called *gbadaken* inside it, and then close the sack. In those days, cowries were used for money, and these cowries were carried about in these raffia sacks. The *du* said that Fa should then put the sack against a wall of the house and give a chicken to Legba.

Fa did as he was ordered. The next morning the leopard was the first to come. Fa said, "I have your money here, but my son is away and will not be back for a short while. If you wait, though, he will help you carry away the money." The leopard agreed, and climbed a tree behind Fa's house to wait for Fa's son.

In a few moments the serpent came. Fa showed him the sack and said, "Here is your money, but if you wait a short time, my son, who will soon return, will help you carry it home." The serpent also agreed and went into the brush behind Fa's house to wait. Soon afterwards the hunter came and Fa showed him the same sack, saying, "My son has gone to the village with a friend, but he will be here in a moment, and will help you carry this money away." And having said this, he asked the hunter to wait in back of his house.

The three debtors had never seen each other before. Now, when the hunter went behind Fa's house, he saw a leopard crouched in the tree. At once he aimed his gun, shot, and killed him. He had taken no more than three steps toward his prey, however, when he was bitten by the serpent. As he felt the sting of the serpent, he threw his knife, which cut off the serpent's head. That moment the poison from the snake took effect, and the hunter died. Thus Fa rid himself of his debtors. He then gave another chicken to Legba.

[1] Cf. *Dahomey*, II, pp. 212–213.
[2] This is of significance, since it is only nonpoisonous snakes that are held to be sacred.
[3] One of the configurations in the Fa system of divination.

36

Outwitting creditors: Rabbit tricks Death

Rabbit was in debt. He owed money to Death. Death kept asking for his money. He asked all the time. Good. Rabbit went to a diviner to find out what he should do to get out of giving this money, ten thousand francs, back to Death, for he could not repay it.

The diviner said he must make a little ceremony, and get some long chains, six chickens, and two goats. After that he could tell Death to come in three days.

Good. Rabbit went to a friend and they worked out a plan together. Now, Rabbit lives in a square compound, which has a road in front of it. Rabbit told Death there was a slave to be sold, and that he should come before daybreak to get his money.

When Rabbit's friend came early in the morning he put the chains about Rabbit's neck so he might represent the slave. He put ashes everywhere, and clothed him in rags, and did all sorts of things to disguise him. They chained Rabbit to a stake and then the friend left.

Before daybreak Death came. He saw Rabbit there, but he did not know him. He asked, "Where is Rabbit?"

The slave said, "Rabbit went to look for the man who is coming to buy the slave." Then Rabbit asked Death, "Is it you who are coming to take the money from the sale?"

Death said, "Yes, it's me." Then Rabbit begged Death to take off his chains for a moment, so that he might go and urinate. He said he would come back again as soon as he had finished. Death said, "What, and let you run away? I am a stranger here!"

But Rabbit said, "No, no, I won't run away. I'll just go and urinate and come right back." So Death took off the chain, and Rabbit left.

He went to his friend's house. He bathed and dressed. Then he said to his friend, "Come with me." His friend went with him. They both carried umbrellas. His friend brought six thousand francs to buy the slave. Rabbit entered first. His friend came after him. Rabbit stretched out his hand to Death and greeted him. He said to him, "I see you came." He turned to his friend, "Are you going to buy the slave? Where is the money with which you are going to buy him from me?" His friend said, "You talked of ten thousand francs, but I brought six thousand."

Rabbit said, "All right. Come. We'll look at the slave." But they saw nothing. Rabbit asked Death, "Where is the man who was here? Where is my father's slave? Here is the chain I put about his neck, and he is gone."

Death said, "I released him."

Rabbit said, "You have taken off the chain without my permission? All right, I have nothing more to pay you. The slave cost me twenty-four thousand francs, but I'll sell him to you cheap. I'll give him to you for twelve thousand francs. You fear nothing, but we will go to the Residency." [1] So they had a trial at the Residency, and it was decided that Death had to pay twelve thousand francs before he could leave, since it was only out of consideration for him that Rabbit was willing to let the slave go for that.

Rabbit acted as though he was very angry, and Death had to pay Rabbit twelve thousand francs. "To show you how I am, I'll give you back two thousand," said Rabbit. But Death went home. He left the two thousand francs. He would not touch them.

Rabbit also went home, and he brought together all the diviners of his quarter for a ceremony, for his Fa was strong. And he sang,

> *Rabbit must settle with Death,*
> *He does not want to pay,*
> *He does not want to pay,*
> *Fa does not want to pay,*
> *Rabbit must settle his debt with Death no more.* [2]

If a person owes, and pays, he will be happy.

[1] The headquarters of the French local administrator, who would decide the case.
[2] Record No. 122-2.

37

Legba's wives reconciled: Why Rabbit is head of the animals and Leopard their king: Why Agbè is spotted

Legba had two wives, Nundè and Konikoni. Konikoni was the first wife, and Nundè the second. They did not get on very well together. Nundè went to Rabbit and told him that Konikoni and she did not get on well.

Rabbit went to consult Fa for Nundè. Fa said to make Legba love Nundè, she must get a goat and a cock, corn flour, palm oil, and salt and pepper. And she must have a covered calabash for water. They got everything together to make a sacrifice so that Legba should love Nundè.

Nundè said that Konikoni was the senior wife. Rabbit fixed the period of three days for them to become friends. Rabbit came on the day agreed upon and reconciled them. After that, when Konikoni cooked for Legba, Nundè added the condiments and ran errands.

Now, when Konikoni sends Nundè to market, she gives her one cowry, and that cowry buys there all sorts of condiments, and she returns home with the cowry.[1]

All the animals of the bush are the enemies of Rabbit. They always ask why Rabbit is a friend of Legba. The animals drove Rabbit from the bush, but he hid near Legba's house so that when the others came to kill him, he would have Legba's protection.

In those days, Leopard was the family chief.[2] He called all the animals together, Rabbit also, and said to them, "I want to make a ceremony." They told Antelope to go in the house first, because his skin resembled Leopard's. He would know the names of the members of this large family.

When Antelope came in the house, he said, "Let Deer come first." But Leopard was not satisfied with his choice, so he sprang at him, and caught him by the back of the neck, and strangled him.

Now Wild Goat was summoned. Wild Goat entered to make the ceremony, but when he called the name of Wildcat, Leopard seized him and strangled him.

Leopard called Porcupine to enter and perform the ceremony. Porcupine entered. He began to make the ceremony by calling the names of wild animals. But Leopard was angry, because he did not begin with the name of Leopard, and sprang at him and strangled him.

Now Rabbit said to Leopard, "The animals you killed are your brothers. Why did you kill them? The head of a family should not act like that."

Now Leopard called Agbè. And when Agbè called the names of the animals, he said, "Leopard, Lion, Hyena, Rabbit."

Leopard told him what he had done was good. "You are a little animal, and you know all my relatives. You will always remain my friend." Now Leopard asked him, "Who is the sib-chief over all the animals?"

Agbè said, "It is Rabbit, and Leopard is their king."

Leopard said, "You have spoken well. I will mark you, so that when people see you, they will recognize that you are my friend, and my brother."

So Leopard took the blood of the animals he had killed and sprinkled the body of Agbè. That is why the body of Agbè is always spotted.

---

[1] This seems to be the end of one tale and the beginning of a second, the two being connected in the teller's mind because Rabbit figures in both of them.

[2] The animals are envisaged as being organized into a sib, headed by a sib-chief. Cf. *Dahomey*, I, pp. 156 ff.

38

Why the king of the beasts, the king of the birds, and the king of the fish prey on their subjects

Now, Mawu created the animals, the birds, and the fish. Mawu said to them, "I want to give you a king, but I have not found one yet. I will send him to you later."

The animals said they preferred Lion. The fish wanted the Crocodile for their chief. The birds said they wanted Agbogbo, the largest bird of all.

So they were all told to leave for the world with their chiefs. When the animals came into the world, the moment one of them stepped on the lion's urine, it died. There was a road where all the animals passed, and lion would urinate there so that he might eat the animals. If a bird would not obey, Agbogbo seized it and ate it. If a fish did not obey, Crocodile ate it.

One day the birds, the animals and the fish met together to find out who among them would go and see Mawu and come back again. Good. All the birds began to call out. "I, I, I want to go. I will go." The animals, too, cried out they would go, and the fish said they wanted to go, too. But as one bird after another, one animal after another, one fish after another went up to where Mawu was, the moment they came in sight of Mawu, they were afraid and hid. They would not come close.

Now, when those who said they would go to Mawu, but had turned away afraid, came back, their chiefs ate them.

Then Vulture said, "I am going." They prepared food for him, and he flew away. It was three years before he came back. He called Lion, Agbogbo, and Crocodile and told them that Mawu had said that Lion should eat the animals, Crocodile must eat the fish, and Agbogbo should eat the birds. Lion told Hyena to be his sub-chief, and he also made Leopard a sub-chief. Crocodile took a fish called Sosoglosè as sub-chief, while Agbogbo took Crow.

Now that Lion had two sub-chiefs, no matter what animal he saw, he ate it. Since Crocodile made Sosoglosè his sub-chief, he no longer could eat him, but Sosoglosè gathered fish for his master and brought them to him. The moment Agbogbo and Crow saw the other birds, they ate them.

After a while Lion and his sub-chiefs, Crocodile and his sub-chief, Agbogbo and his sub-chief went to see Tortoise, their diviner. Lion said, "Since we live on the animals we get, how can we get more and more animals to eat?"

Tortoise told them they had to make a sacrifice. To Lion he said, "Find me a doe."

But Lion said, "I am quick and I have claws. Why should I make a sacrifice? If I make it I will eat the animals, but if I don't make it, I will eat them, too."

Crocodile, whom the diviner told to bring fish for a sacrifice, also went away. He said, "I cannot make this sacrifice, for Mawu commanded me to watch over the fish." And he said, "If I make the sacrifice I eat, but if I don't make it, I eat. Why should I make this sacrifice?"

When the diviner told Agbogbo to find birds for him, he, too, refused. "When Mawu has given me all, why should I go to the trouble of making this sacrifice?"

Now, the animals whom Lion was eating went to the diviner. "What shall we do so that Lion does not eat us?"

The diviner said to them, "You must make a sacrifice. Go and get a cock and bring some of the hair from your pelts." The animals went, and returned with the cock and made their sacrifice. The fish also went to the diviner. He told them to bring a cock, and some black earth from the bottom of the river. When the fish brought these, the sacrifice was made. The diviner told them, "Now that you have made your sacrifice, you can stay in the water safely." The birds, too, came to see the diviner. He told them to get a cock and to bring something of all that is eaten—manioc, yams, beans, maize. They found all this and made their sacrifice.

And when the animals had made their sacrifice, Lion could no longer eat them as he used to. Crocodile could no longer eat the fish, and, after the birds had made their sacrifice, Agbogbo did not eat them as before.

So Lion and Crocodile and Agbogbo had little to eat for a whole year. They did not have a good meal all that time. So they called a meeting. Lion and his sub-chiefs were there, Crocodile and his sub-chief, Agbogbo and his sub-chief. When the chiefs met, Leopard said to them, "I know the cause of this. The animals and the birds and the fish made the sacrifices which diviner Tortoise told them to make. That is why we chiefs find nothing to eat."

As the chiefs talked this over, Lion said, "Ah, yes, I remember. We went to Tortoise, the diviner, and he told us to make a sacrifice. Did you make it?"

The sub-chiefs said, "No, we did not make it." So they contributed a large sum and sent Crow to Tortoise with the money.

Tortoise said, "I told you before to make a sacrifice and you would not do it. Why do you now send me all this money? If you still want to make a sacrifice, we will divine again. The other is now useless."

The diviner divined a second time, and said to Leopard, "To make this sacrifice you must find a small antelope."

The other said, "We cannot find animals now, so how shall we get this animal?" But the diviner told him that the sacrifice the others made had expired, since a sacrifice is only good for a year. So he caught a small antelope. Good. He made the sacrifice and as the sacrifice of the other animals had expired, Lion again began to eat them.

The diviner told Sosoglosè to bring him a fish. Sosoglosè said, "Since we no longer can find fish, how shall I get a fish for you?" But he found a fish, and sacrificed it.

Diviner Tortoise told Crow to find a bird. "Bring me a bird with which to make a sacrifice, and you will find birds to eat as before, for the sacrifice which the birds gave is now expired." And after the sacrifice was made, the birds began to eat the smaller birds as before.

After this new sacrifice, when the animals saw Lion and his sub-chiefs, they ran away. Some were caught and eaten, but those who could escape got away. The same happened with the fish and with the birds.

So today, if a lion is in the bush, there are no animals nearby. They all run away. In the rivers, the fish do not come where there is a crocodile. And in the forest, no other birds perch on a tree where Agbogbo and Crow are found.

But among the animals, there are always those who go to Lion and tell him, "There in that place, if you come, you will find animals in hiding." The same thing happens among the fish; and the same among the birds. And as the animals can also do harm, the three chiefs no longer sleep on the ground. They sleep in the trees. From on high they spy on the animals. Crow and Agbogbo also make a hole in a tree and sleep inside. They no longer live in the open. When Crocodile finds nothing to eat, he comes out of the water and goes to the banks of a stream.

In her lair Lion gave birth to cubs, but when famine came and she had nothing to eat, she died of hunger. The children remained. The children said, "We haven't our teeth yet, and our mother is dead? What shall we do to get food to eat?" Crocodile also died of hunger, leaving her children, and Crow too, died, leaving her young.

As the lion cubs began to grow up, they spied on the other animals who left their children behind, while they went about their work. While the mothers were away, they took them, and ate them. But if the mothers saw them, they beat them. Crocodile's young did the same, and Crow's also fed on the young of others.

But in time the young lions, the young crocodiles, and the young crows became as strong as their fathers. The animals, the birds and the fish went to see the diviner. They said that the children of the chiefs were giving them much trouble.

Tortoise told them to make a sacrifice. They got all the things necessary, but when the sacrifice was ready, the diviner turned on them and said, "Mawu ordered that the animals should be eaten by Lion, the fish by Crocodile, and the birds by their chiefs. So it will always be."

> *Life's load does not rest on the head of a simple man,*
> *Agbogbolesu, to you Se has given it.*[1]
>
> *The animal Se has given us,*
> *Hyena sees Lion*
> *And says,*
> *This is the animal Se has given us.*[2]
>
> *It does not matter*
> *Whether life is good or not,*
> *Crocodile has become chief.*[3]

That is why Lion eats the animals, Crocodile the fish, and Crow the birds.

[1] Record No. 136–3.
[2] Record No. 136–4.
[3] Record No. 136–5.

39
Seeking poverty

The king of Adja, Adjahosu, had everything. One day when he went to see his diviner, he said, "You must divine something for me. I am too rich and do not know what it is to be poor. I want to know what it is to be poor."

The diviner told him, after he divined, to bring a drum, a gong, and rattles. "When you have them, tell your hunters to catch an animal called *la*." [1]

When he returned home, he ordered a drum, a gong and rattles to be made, and he commanded his hunters to catch a *la* for him. When they brought the animal, he gathered all the things the diviner had told him to get, and took them to him.

The diviner instructed them to tie the gong, drum, and rattles about the neck of *la*, and told the man to get on its back. Then they took a cloth and tied him in place, and the diviner gave him a little stick to strike the drum with. When he beat the drum, *la* ran away with him into the bush.

They passed through brush and thorny bushes until they were in the middle of the forest, when the cloth became so torn that the king fell off the animal. He did not know where his house was; he was completely lost.

As he could find no place to sleep, he climbed a tree and stayed there during the night. He was in the bush three months. The third month he came on an old woman looking for leaves of the indigo plant. Now the man had already lost an eye, so when the old woman looked at him, and she saw a man who looked to her as though he were blind, she led him to her house. And every five days, when the woman went to market to get cloths to dye and to sell those she had dyed, she put her load on the head of the man she had found, and led him to market.

This she did for three years.

In the meantime, the children of the king of Adja did not know what had happened to him. One fine day, however, the woman went to one of the king's fields to sell something to one of his sons. As usual, the man carried the cloths. When they reached the field of Adjahosu, his sons looked at the man who was with the old woman. He had only one eye, but he resembled their father, and each asked the other if this was not he.

He had put down his load, and while he was sitting there, someone called, "Adjahosu, come and sell me some wood."

When the sons came home, they said to the eldest brother, "Look, we were at a market in the field of Adjahosu, and we saw a black man whom they call Adjahosu. And an old woman commanded him to sell wood." The older brother said, "Good, we will go to the next market there.

So he went early to market and arrived before the woman came. He placed himself where his younger brothers had been, and after a time saw an old woman accompanied by a man, who was carrying her cloths. When the man put the cloths down, he took his bush knife and entered the forest nearby. In a short time, he saw the man returning with wood, which he put down beside his mistress. After this, the woman said, "You can eat," and gave him something to eat.

As he was eating, his son approached him. When he recognized his child, he began to cry, and the son did, too.

The son led his father to the old woman and asked her, "Where did you find this man?"

She answered, "I was looking for indigo leaves. One day I saw him alone in the bush."

The son took the man and said, "Now you will sell him to me."

She said, "If I sell him now, who will carry my load to my house?"

The son said, "I will buy him and give you the money, and you can buy another carrier with this money."

"Let me be! This old one here, what will you do with him?"

The son replied, "This is not an old one to me. He is my father. I beg you to sell him to me."

The old woman said, "Since he is your father, take him."

So his son took Adjahosu home, and bathed him and gave him fresh cloths. After that Adjahosu summoned all his people before him to speak to them. He said, "Because I myself am very very rich, I wanted to know what is poverty. Now I say to you, my sons and my family, never ask to be poor. Because poverty eats nothing, drinks nothing."

And so, a man must not seek poverty.

[1] Giraffe.

40

How Pig came to live with Man [1]

Once during the dry season, Dada Segbo gathered together all the animals of the bush and ordered them to work clay [2] for him. All the animals came.

They sent Antelope for water, and when Antelope reached the stream, he put the calabash in the water to fill it.

But a voice (it was Frog speaking) called out, "Who put that calabash in the water?"

Antelope replied, "I did."

Frog asked, "Who sent you for water?"

Antelope said, "Dada Segbo sent me."

Frog said, "I do not know Dada Segbo."

Now, when Antelope heard this he was frightened. He left the calabash and ran back to the animals who were mixing earth. They asked him, "Where is the water we sent you for?"

He said, "In the stream there is something which spoke to me and said I must not take the water. I ran away and left the calabash there."

When the other animals heard this, they scolded him. "You are stupid."

And Doe said, "I will go for the water." When Doe reached the stream, she put the calabash in the water to fill it.

But she heard a voice say, "Who put the calabash in the water?"

She said, "I did."

The voice said, "Who sent you?" No one knew it was Frog, for the voice came from under the water.

Doe said, "Dada Segbo sent me."

The voice said, "Dada Segbo does not command my water."

And when Doe heard this, she ran away. She went back to tell the animals.

Now, Leopard said he would go for water. He reached the stream, but the moment Frog heard his footsteps, he went under the water. Leopard put the calabash in the water.

The voice asked, "Where do you come from?"

Leopard said, "Dada Segbo sent me to get water."

The voice answered, "Get away from here. I don't know Dada Segbo."

So Leopard too left the calabash and ran away. He said to the other animals that there was a spirit in the river.

Elephant cried, "I am the biggest of all animals. I will go for water. I am afraid of nothing." He left, and when he reached the river he put the calabash in.

The voice said, "You, who are you?"

He said, "I am Elephant." The voice said, "What do you want here?"

Elephant said, "I want some water."

The voice said, "Who sent you?"

Elephant said, "Dada Segbo sent me here."

The voice said, "Get away from here." And then Elephant ran away.

Now Lion said he would go. Nothing, he said, could stop him from doing what he wanted. When Lion came to the river, he put the calabash in to fill it. Now, when the animals left their calabashes in the water and ran away, Frog threw them on the bank. Lion put his calabash in the water.

Frog cried, "Who are you?"

Lion said, "I am Lion. I came to get water."

The voice asked, "Who sent you?" Lion answered, "I was sent here by Dada Segbo." The voice said, "You annoy me too much, you animals. Stay at home! I do not know Dada Segbo."

Lion also ran, and when he came to where the other animals were working, he said they must not go to that stream any more. The spirit of the river was angry with them. He said, "Let us go for water elsewhere."

But Buffalo would not agree. "No. I am going there."

And when Buffalo went away, Pig knew that his turn was next. So he went to see a diviner who divined for him. The diviner told him to find a spear and put it in his sack, and with that he would get what he wanted.

Buffalo went to the river, and came running back like the others. So Pig said he would go.

But all the other animals insulted him. "Ah, you think you

will get water. When all of us tried and couldn't, you think you can get it? You haven't even claws."

Pig said, "All right. I can only try." Now, his calabash was made by the diviner. And the diviner told him that when he came there and the voice spoke, he had only to thrust his spear into the water. So when he got to the river, he put the calabash in the water to fill it.

The Thing said, "Who put this calabash in the water?"

He said, "It is Pig."

The Thing said, "Who are you, Pig?"

The Pig said, "I am Pig, who comes from Dada Segbo."

The Thing asked, "What are you looking for?"

Pig was now aiming his spear. He said, "I came to get water."

The voice said, "Go away . . ."

But before he could finish, Pig speared him, and then he saw that it was only Frog. So he threw Frog away and put his spear back. Then he filled his calabash. When he came back, the other animals would not believe that he got the water from the same river.

They said, "Ah, you lie. You found this water elsewhere."

He said, "All right. Follow me to the stream. You will see."

When they were all there, they said to him, "Now put the calabash in the water, and we will see." And when the animals heard nothing, they too began to dip up water. So they finished working the clay.

Dada Segbo called them all together. And to all the wild animals, Lion, Leopard, and the others, he said, "Pig is not an animal to be eaten by you. He will always be in the house with man." And that is why today the animals of the bush do not kill pigs. Pigs always stay at home.

---

[1] The teller of this tale belongs to a clan whose totem is the pig.

[2] English "swish," French "*terre de barre*." Cf. *Dahomey*, Plate 146, for a co-operative work-group engaged in labor of this kind.

III

Hunter stories

Hunter stories

HUNTER, under various names, or not named

AZIZÃ of the forest, the "little people"

HUNTER'S WIFE, sometimes named, sometimes not named

THE KING

AGBUI, bush rat

DASA, GBANLI, hunters

AFIANKU, type of antelope

AMUSU, a hunter

DEGAN, Chief of the Hunters

RABBIT, LION, CROW, DOG, ELEPHANT, HYENA, CAT, LAMB, SQUIRREL

AGBIGBI, a bird

AMANONU, a serpent

WOMAN FROM TOGODO

LUWÈ, small bush animal

YEHWE ZOGBANU, thirty-horned, fire-breathing monster of the forest

AIDO-HWEDO, rainbow serpent

AGBANLI, antelope

ADJAHÈ, Adja bird

AYOHÈ, Oyo bird

AGBO, buffalo

ADJAHOSU, King of Adja

SOKAME, his daughter

DÃ, serpent god

MINGÃ, Prime Minister and Executioner

KPADUNU, a hunter

HIS MOTHER

DADA SEGBO, a king

HIS DAUGHTER

NA ABIKU, bush spirit

AZIZÃ, a hunter

NA, mother of infants who die at birth

UWO, "resembles a squirrel"

41

Origin of medicine: Little folk of the forest give men their gods [1]

When people came into the world they had no medicine. No one knew that leaves could cure. When people fell ill, there was no knowledge of what to do to cure them.

Now, there were hunters in those days who hunted. They went into the deep, deep bush. One day a hunter came upon a mound of earth in the bush. When he was about to pass it, a voice spoke from inside it. Hunter's wife was a leper, and this voice said, "Hunter, I will show you a medicine to cure your wife. When you give it to her, she will become well again." Then the voice said, "Turn your back to me and wait." It was Azizā who was in the mound, and as Hunter's back was turned, Azizā put the leaves beside him. When Hunter looked again he saw the leaves. The voice said, "Take these leaves, crush them, and mix them with water. Then give some of this to your wife to drink, and use the rest to wash her sores."

When Hunter came home, he did what Azizā told him to do, and his wife was cured.

Now, Azizā had also told him, "When someone in your village is sick, come and tell me, and I will give you a cure." So Hunter showed the way to all who were sick, and these came to the mound of earth and told their troubles, and to each of them Azizā gave a medicine and explained its use. Those who followed Azizā's instructions were cured.

One day a hunter brought a sick stranger to Azizā, and this stranger went to the King of his country and told him that there was a kingdom where the sick only needed to tell of their ailments before a mound of earth, and they were cured.

The King said, "I will go there myself. I want to see." So the King went to the bush where the mound of earth was, and took with him a goat, a bottle of rum, and some palm oil. He killed the goat on the mound of earth, and said, "In my country we have no *vodun*. I want to take you to my country to be a *vodun*. If someone in my kingdom is ill, I will send him to you for medicine." And Azizã gave him magic and told him what *vodun* were to be worshipped that his country might prosper. Azizã gave to this King the deities Sagbata, Adjahuto, Tedo, Agasu, Agè, Dã and Dovo, and told the King to build a house for each of them. Azizã also said that if people wished to have any of these *vodun*, they had only to come for some earth from this mound.

So the *vodun*, you see, and the magic that is in the world were all given by Azizã. This is the way Azizã gave these things to man.

[1] For the significance of this tale, see *Dahomey*, II, pp. 261–262.

42

Hunters bring *vodun* from the forest

This happened during the dry season when they burn the bush. They had burned almost all the straw. But one part remained which had not yet been burned. The *agbui* met there. They played the drum there. Hunter came there, and he heard them sing,

> We are in the jar.
> The grass is not yet burnt,
> We are in the jar.
>
> I dance.
> The tail of Agbui is up, up;
> Agbui's tail is up.
> But it will fall.

Hunter went home. He went to see a friend whom he had seen the same day. He said, "The *awasagbè* are dancing." Both now went to see the dancing.

Formerly these animals were not called *awasagbè*. But the name was given them by the hunter. They were like the bush rats. They were called *adjaka*, or *gelesin*. *Adjaka* is the house rat and *gelesin* lives in a hole like an *agbui*. They are almost the same, but are not the same color. If these animals had not held their dance, one would not have known their names.

Agbui is a very small rat, but he is king of all animals. I do not know how it came about, but I know all the animals came from him.

First came the trees in the world, and of these the first was the palm tree which gives oil. After the palm tree came the trees called *akunkoti, deselesige*, a tree which has black leaves. To make Fa we use these leaves. After that came man. After man, the animals came. Agbui, the small rat; the lion, *kinikini*; the panther. After that the birds. The vulture, *aklasu; ohon*, the eagle, who is larger than vulture; *honsuhonsu*, a bird with large claws who eats animals. Mawu next sent the animals of the sea. The sea-monkey, *degbo*; the crocodile, *lo; nyigwinyigwi*, who never leaves the sea, and is as large as a room. After that the fish came, and after the fish Mawu sent crabs, and frogs. The Loko tree came by itself. It is a *vodun* given by Mawu.

Now, the earth already had people. Now, there were some hunters who always hunted. There were among these one called Dasa, and another called Gbanli. Every day they hunted. One day they found a place all cleared, so they camped there. There they saw a very small tree which had sprung up, and beside it a pot pierced in many places which is called *adjalala*. When the hunters saw that, then as they went to hunt they spoke to the tree and to *adjala*, they said, "If you give us luck on the hunt, we will bring you back the blood of the animals we get." After this the hunters had good luck at the hunt, and they brought back the blood to the tree and the jar.

Now, one day the hunters were ready to go home. They said, "Here we have two *vodun*, what shall we do with them?"

One said, "Let us divide." So Gbanli took the Loko, and Dasa took the pierced jar. Loko is now called Hevioso. Adjala is now called Sagbata.

43

Why some animals may not be killed without a sacrifice

There are animals a man may kill, and there are animals a man may not kill. And there are animals for whom you have to give a sacrifice when you kill.

There was a hunter who went to the bush to hunt. There was an animal called *afianku*. If you kill this animal, it says, "Give me something [1] so that I can fall to the ground [for you]. Give me your father or your mother, or your wife, or your child."

The hunter said, "I have nothing to give you."

The animal said, "If you give me nothing, I will not fall." The hunter's name was Amusu. The animal said, "Amusu, can't you give me a man?"

Amusu said, "No, I have nothing for you. You must fall down without any gift. When you do that, I will cut you up and eat you."

The animal said, "All right. I will fall. I know that you have no power to harm me. My heart tells me that you cannot eat me." Saying this, the animal fell.

Hunter began to cut up the animal. *Afianku* changed into a man. Hunter who was cutting up the animal did not know that the animal already had changed. This man took two pieces of the meat Hunter had cut off, and went home with these to Hunter's wife and said to her, "Here is meat which your husband sent. He asks you to cook it for him so it will be ready when he comes home."

The woman took the meat and cooked it. She thought the man was her husband's servant. But Hunter did not know anything about it, and when he finished cutting up the animal, he came home.

Hunter was very hungry. The woman greeted him and said, "I have food all cooked for you."

He asked, "What fish have you cooked for me?"

She said, "I did not cook fish, but the meat you sent me."

Now Hunter has already eaten the meat. [2] He says quickly,

"What kind of meat is this?" She says, "It is the *afianku* meat which you sent me."

The husband says, "Ah, I killed it myself."

The wife says, "Is that what it is? I did not know. I was here, and a man said you sent meat to cook for your homecoming."

Good. Hunter already has fever. He sent for the *dega* of his village and the other hunters. The *dega* asked him what he had done. The hunter told him.

The *dega* said, "All right. When you shot the animal, what did he say to you?"

Now this hunter was not old enough to kill such an animal. "He asked me for something when I shot him," said the sick hunter to the *dega*. "He said, 'Give me something so that I can fall to the ground.' When he said that, I had no powder to throw."

Hunters have magic powders to throw at the animals to calm them, yes? But this hunter was not big enough to know what to do with an animal like that.[3]

The *dega* said, "You are lost. Nothing can save you now. You ate the meat of this animal without doing anything. You should have gone to a diviner first, and had him divine to see if it is to be eaten." They sent for the diviner. But he was too late. He said there was no sacrifice for this. The hunter must die.

He said, "All right. When I die, bring the *sogbwe* drum."[4] And on the third day, at mid-day, the hunter died, and they began to wail.

So Afianku is not like other animals. If a person kills him, he must divine and find out the proper sacrifice to offer before cutting up the carcass. And no simple hunter must kill that animal. It is reserved for the *dega*.

[1] *I.e.*, make a sacrifice.
[2] Note the change of tense.
[3] The comments were interpolated by the story-teller.
[4] The hunter's drum.

44

False friendship: Hunter betrays Rabbit

In earlier days, hunters used to kill everything. They would kill any animal they found in the bush. Rabbit came to tell Hunter "Good day," and said, "I am your friend." He did this so he would not be killed by Hunter. "I come to be your friend, so that my daughters and my wives shall not be killed."

The next day Rabbit went to his house and told his relatives he had found a "good road" where they could pass without being killed by hunters, and where they could find plenty to eat. Later he went to tell Hunter he had set a day to show who were his relatives.

The day came. Hunter was in the bush. He went to Rabbit's house and they did all that was necessary to swear friendship.

• "First, a friend must not shoot another friend with a gun." This was what Rabbit said must be the first condition of their friendship. "In the second place," he said, "you must not hide to spy on me. When I pass you, I will say 'Good day,' and you must say 'Good day' when you pass me."

Hunter returned and called all his good dogs. He took them where Rabbit was to bring his relatives, and fed them there.

Along the road Rabbit took, Hunter placed his dogs in such a way that Rabbit could not see them. He told them, "I myself will shoot Rabbit, and you catch all his relatives."

When Rabbit came, he shot at him, and the hunter's dogs went after his wives and children. But when he shot at Rabbit, he did not kill him. The wives and children were taken by the dogs. Rabbit alone, the friend of Hunter, was saved.

> *One must not see people,*
> *And say of this one, of that*
> *"He is my friend."*
> *You will be killed for nothing.*
>
> *Now Rabbit and Hunter made a compact,*
> *Swearing by the vodun under the Koso tree.*

What Rabbit did not wish done,
He told all to Hunter;
What Hunter did not wish done,
He told Rabbit.

If a friend sees a friend,
And runs away,
It is not good.

A true friend seeing the other,
Who begins to aim,
I do not want that.

A true friend seeing the other,
Who sends his dog after him,
I do not want that.

After having sworn,
Rabbit said to his wives and children,
He told them, "This is what we must do,
Not to be killed by Hunter."

The eldest said,
"Father, I am content."
The second said,
"Father, I, too, am content."

The third said,
"Now that you have sworn by the vodun,
I do not sleep here today."

While Rabbit and his children
Were saying all this,
Hunter was there spying,
And aiming his gun.

The eldest said,
"Thanks to my father,
If it is a question of running,
I will get there first."

The youngest said,
"Thanks to you, I know
A man with a fine skin
Does not always have a fine heart." [1]

[1] Record No. 132. The singer could not recall all the verses.

45

False friendship: Why lions kill hunters

In the beginning of the world—in those days all living things were equals—Lion went to marry Lioness, and Lioness became pregnant. Now Lioness had a friend, a bird called Agbigbi, who was also a friend of Crow. Agbigbi went to see Crow and said that his friend Lioness was about to give birth.

When Lioness gave birth, she called Agbigbi and Crow and said to them, "Now I have nothing to eat."

Agbigbi sent word to Hunter to come and take out a speck of dirt from his eye. When Hunter came, he asked him to kill an animal for him, so he could give it to his friend, Lioness. Hunter went to kill a *demoje*.[1] Now when Hunter brought the *demoje*, Agbigbi carried it quickly to Lioness.

Lioness ate for three days. Then she said to Agbigbi, "I finished this meat. Can you kill another animal for me?" Agbigbi went to ask Hunter to kill another animal. Hunter killed an elephant and Agbigbi carried it directly to Lioness.

Lioness ate the elephant nine days. When there was no more meat, Lioness asked for more. But now Agbigbi said, "Now your children are grown, you can go out to hunt."

Now, at the place where Lioness gave birth to her children, there was a fruit tree where Agbigbi came every day to eat fruit. During the absence of their mother, the Lion cubs walked about near the tree, and they too ate its fruit. One day they caught Agbigbi. They ate him until there was only a little left.

When their mother returned, they gave her the meat. The mother said, "What meat is this?"

One of the children answered, "It is Agbigbi's meat."

The mother said, "I did everything I could to trap Agbigbi and I never could, and you, my children, did it. Agbigbi was my friend, but all the same I am going to eat this meat."

After several days, Hunter came to see Lioness. Now, the place where Agbigbi was killed was the place where Hunter came to spy on the antelope. He saw Lioness. He said, "Is it here you stay?"

Lioness said, "Yes, this is my home."

When the children came to eat, Hunter shot at them and he killed two lions. Good.

When Lioness returned, she looked for the children. She looked for them till she came to the tree, and there she saw the blood and skins of the baby lions. She went and hid behind the tree. Now, Hunter did not know that Lioness was there. So when he climbed down from the tree, Lioness seized him and killed him.

That is why, today, when a lion sees a hunter he eats him.

[1] An unidentified feline.

46

Serpent gives riches: Why women are not told secrets

There was a hunter who had a dog and a cat. When he hunted, if he saw a lion, he killed him. If he saw a buffalo, he killed him. Now Hunter came on a serpent called Amanonu, and he wanted to shoot the serpent. The serpent said to him, "Do not shoot me."

Hunter said, "I must shoot you, because I eat only meat."

The serpent said to him, "Turn your back to me." When Hunter turned around again, the serpent gave him a ring. He said, "This ring will bring you good luck." The serpent also gave him a small jar full of medicine, and he told him to put it where he lived. When he came home, he was also to dip the hand which had the ring into the medicine and throw the medicine away.

Hunter did this. He put his hand in the medicine, and then he sprinkled the rest of it all about him in the bush. All at once two-storey houses sprang up everywhere. He became rich.

The serpent also told him that a fat woman would come a little later to marry him. But he was never to tell her his secret. When the woman came, she was fat, fat. The man began to talk to her and he told her, "It is because of this ring that I am a rich man now."

The girl asked him to tell her the story of how he became rich. She was a girl who came from Togodo. "It is the serpent Ama-nonu who gave me the ring."

That night when they went to sleep, the man fell asleep first. Then the woman took off his ring softly, softly. As soon as she had taken off the ring, she got up softly and went back to Togodo.

When the woman got home, she took steps to become rich. She put the ring on her finger and dipped it in medicine. When she did this, Hunter's houses, everything vanished. He was a poor man again.

The cat and the dog came to Hunter and said, "All right, the ring is lost. But we will go out and look for it everywhere, and we will surely find it for you." So the cat and the dog went away to the village where the woman lived. As soon as the woman saw them, she recognized them. She gave them food to eat. When she fell asleep the cat tiptoed over softly and took away the ring.

Now, cats cannot swim, but dogs can. When they came to the river, the dog asked the cat to show him the ring. No sooner did the cat take out the ring to show it to the dog, than the ring fell into the water.

They went home and told their master that the ring had fallen into the water. Then they said they would go to see Mawu about it.

When they came to Mawu, they told her what had happened. Mawu said to them, "Go to that river, and there you will see a man fishing. Buy the first fish which he catches, and inside that fish you will find the ring."

They went to the river and bought the fish. Once home, they cut open the fish, and there inside its belly was the ring. So they gave the ring to their master. Hunter now put on the ring, dipped his hand in the medicine and sprinkled the grass all about him with medicine. At once the woman's houses disappeared, and his again sprang up all about him.

Now, Hunter was a rich man once more. He was richer than before. He called together the dog, the cat, his children, his wives, all his relatives. He said, "If you are rich and you marry, never tell your wives what you did to become rich."

The dog is greedy because Mawu has given him that character, but the cat is more serious than the dog. And that, too, is because Mawu has given her that character. The cat can come and sit down on the mat beside her master, but the dog cannot. That is why the cat always lives in the house. If a person goes out, he leaves the cat at home. But if he wants to go away, he never leaves a dog behind. He takes him along.

The words I told which you now heard, tomorrow you will hear a bird tell them to you.

47

Hunter's magic powers: The password: *Luwe* and Serpent give riches: Why one never tells women the truth

In olden days Hunter hunted everywhere. One day he reached the country where Adjasivi Luwe is found. Hunter left early in the morning. He climbed a tree and waited until mid-morning. Toward mid-day animals called *luwe* came out in great numbers. Those who made indigo began to prepare indigo, and those who dye the cloths began to dye the cloths. While the *luwe* were dyeing with indigo, some among them changed into young girls and went to market to sell the cloths they dyed. They brought the money back, and hid it in the bush where they lived.

Now Hunter saw all this. When he had seen this much, he was astonished. He asked, "Are there animals like this in the bush that are as rich as men?"

That day was market day. So all the cloths they had dyed they took to market, and those who took them changed into young women. When the *luwe* left for market, Hunter climbed down from his tree. But before the *luwe* had left for market, they locked the door. To close the door they cried, "*Abilahun!*"[1]

Thus Hunter learned the word, and when they left, he went to the house and said this "*Abilahun!*" to the door. The door opened. And Hunter took all, all the money that was there. If a person wanted to leave, he had to say "*Azagada gakunkun.*"[2] When Hunter had gathered up all the money, he said these words, and the door closed.

When Hunter's wife saw the money, she was very astonished. She said, "You did not bring any game, but what you brought is better than animals." So the woman began to ask him how he came to get all this. Hunter said, "Adjagbwe[3] gave this to me." He said, "A man does not only go hunting to kill animals. One goes hunting for all sorts of things."

After six days Hunter again went out to hunt. He went to the same place, climbed up a tree, and watched again. The *luwe* began to work their indigo, and as they worked they sang a song:

> *Cut the field, cut the field*
> *I have seen the king,*
> *I have seen the Son of the Leopard.*[4]
> *Where is your wife's hoe-handle?*
> *Is it a club to strike with?*
> *Is it a club to strike with?*[5]

That day was also a market day. The *luwe* finished dyeing their cloths, and left for market again. Again the hunter climbed down,

walked to the door, and said the same thing. He said, "*Abilahun!*"
So the door opened, and he gathered up all the money that was
there.

When he came home, his wife said, "Ah, you no longer go to
hunt for animals, you hunt for money now." She said, "The next
time you go, I will go with you."

Egbwlo moyo! [6] On the fifth day Hunter took his wife with him
into the bush. They both watched the *luwe* working, and when the
animals left for market, they went to the door, spoke the words,
entered, and gathered up all the money.

Hunter said to his wife, "This is a dangerous place. You must
never come here without me."

The two carried away the load and brought it to their house.

One day, when the husband was away, the wife took the road
which led to the house where the *luwe* lived. She walked from
morning till night, until she reached the tree which her husband
had showed her. So the woman slept there that night. The next
morning the *luwe* left for market. The woman walked over to the
door and spoke the word. The door opened. She gathered up all
the money that was there. Now she was ready to leave, but she
did not know what to say to the door.

There were many sacks of money there, so the woman lay
down between these sacks, so that the *luwe* should not see her.
At night, when the *luwe* came home from market, one of them
said, "There is a living being here."

That day Hunter also went out. He went on a journey. When
he came home, he found that his wife was gone. He looked for
her everywhere, but he did not find her. He took his gun and
went to the place where the *luwe* lived. When he arrived, and
from the tree spied on the *luwe*, all these animals were hunting for
the living being they smelled.

Hunter watched them looking for his wife. They looked and
looked for her, but they did not find her. So the next day the
luwe dyed their cloths, put them out to dry, and went away to
sell those they had already finished. Hunter approached the door
and said what was to be said. The door opened. He entered. From
on high he had seen where his wife was. When he came to his

wife, he struck her, and asked her what she was doing there. But the two of them took up the money and went home.

The next time when Hunter wanted to go and take money, he came on the Yehwe Zogbanu. He said, "Ah, I'm too astonished. I come to take money, and here I see the Yehwe Zogbanu."

The Yehwe were dancing. One danced to the right, another to the left. But all hunters have a [magically treated] cord. When they see large animals, or the Yehwe, they put the cord in the mouth. When Hunter put his cord in his mouth, the Yehwe continued dancing, and he passed right by them.

So Hunter came to the place of the *luwe* when they were away. Among the *luwe* there was a woman who had not before had a child. She was there alone, having just given birth to her first child. Hunter was astonished to see her. He said to the woman, "Give me something, or I will kill you."

Egbwlo moyo! The girl began to cry. "It is the first time I bore a child. I have nothing to give you. What do you want? Do you want something to eat?"

Hunter said, "No, I want nothing to eat. I want nothing. I am going to kill you."

So Hunter shot her and her child. He cut off her head, and began gathering up the money as always. When he finished, he took up his load and went home. On his way home, he saw the Yehwe again. They were still dancing. They danced from Adja to Ayo, and from Ayo back to Adja again.[7]

He again put the cord in his mouth. He passed them and came home. Again he found his wife was not there. He said, "Now, if my wife went there, she will surely be killed."

So he called together all of his family and all his wife's family, too. He told them how he had found the house of the *luwe*, and how he had brought back the money. When his wife saw the money, she asked him how he got it, and he told her. He told them everything. He said, "I told her never to go there alone, but all the same she went." He said, "That day, if I had not come, they would have eaten her up."

Egbwlo moyo! The family forbade the woman to go there.[8] Hunter said, "Since there is still much money there, I am going

to take away all. It is not necessary that the animals of the bush
be so rich.

Now there was a place called *Gbodu-mahu-gbode*,[9] where there
were two Aido-Hwedo.[10] One Aido-Hwedo was married, but
the other took his wife away. So the Aido-Hwedo who was a
little old changed into a man. He called to Hunter as he was passing
by, "Don't be afraid. Come here, I want to talk to you. I am
married to a woman, and a young Aido-Hwedo took my wife
from me. I want you to help me."

So Aido-Hwedo gave a powder to Hunter which he told him
to put in his hair. There was a place where the other Aido-Hwedo
and his wife passed. They went by there in order to go to market.
This older Aido-Hwedo took Hunter home with him and gave
him many things. He told him to come back the next day in the
morning, because it was market day.

Hunter came there early, and the older Aido-Hwedo hid him so
that the others could not see him. So the other two Aido-Hwedo
were going to market. The woman was in front.

Now the older Aido-Hwedo said, "You must never shoot at
the blue spots. If you shoot at them, you will die. You must shoot
at the black spots." The older Aido-Hwedo was there himself beside the hunter, and he said, "I will tell you when to shoot."

Egbwlo moyo! So as the two were going to market, the older
Aido-Hwedo said, "Now I'm going to tell you the place where
you must shoot." When those others passed, there was a wind
which accompanied them. As they were passing, the older Aido-
Hwedo said, "Here's my wife passing. Do not shoot." So the
woman passed. He said, "Now is the time to watch for the color."

As Aido-Hwedo [11] has many colors, Hunter asked, "Isn't it that
color there?"

Aido-Hwedo, who was beside him said, "Wait a moment yet."
Then suddenly he said, "Shoot now at this color." The hunter shot.
As he discharged his gun, the wind stopped. So he killed the other
boy.

So Hunter went and cut off the head of the serpent. The older
serpent took his wife, and told Hunter to come and see him on a
certain day. Before the hunter went away, he gave him much

money and told him he would never in his life be poor. He gave him many wives, many cloths, all that could be given.

That is why one never tells the truth to women.

1 Lit., "as fast as lightning."
2 Lit., "hat, on high, close."
3 A diety of the hunt.
4 The leopard is the totem of the royal family.
5 Record No. 145–1.
6 This is a phrase repeated from time to time in telling a tale. Usually the interpreter employed the French word "*Bon.*"
7 This hyperbole indicates great distance, Ayo (Oyo) in Nigeria being some 300 miles from Adja.
8 There would seem to be an ellipsis here, in which Hunter apparently went to the place of the *luwo*, found his wife, and brought her back to the family council.
9 Lit., "No-goat-is-as-big-as-our-goat."
10 Here the narrator joins two stories which have in common only the fact that Hunter is the protagonist.
11 A reference to the fact that Aido-Hwedo is the rainbow.

48

Revealing secret identity: Animal ancestry taunted: Understanding bird language: Why one never tells a woman the truth

Hunter saw Agbanli as he was hunting. As Hunter spied on her, she changed into a young girl. She took off her skin and put it into a hole. When she changed into a young girl, she took her gumbo to sell in the market. Formerly, it was Deer who sold gumbo. After she left, Hunter took her skin. But she went on her way, not knowing that her skin had been taken away by Hunter.

At night Hunter came there before she herself returned. As she came back from market, she went to the place where she had hidden her skin, but the skin was not there. She looked everywhere.

Now Hunter came toward her. He said, "My girl, what are you looking for?"

Agbanli said, "If I tell you, you must never tell anyone."

Hunter said, "No. I will never tell it."

The girl said, "I lost my skin."

Hunter said, "If I bring it to you, what will you give me as a reward?"

The girl said, "If you will tell no one about it, I will become your wife."

Hunter promised her. He said, "If you will surely become my wife, I will tell no one, and you shall have your skin."

Agbanli said, "All right."

Hunter had this skin at his house. He took Agbanli with him as his wife. Coming home, the hunter went to his first wife, and said, "Now you must be careful with this new wife I brought. She is not a girl, she is really *agbanli;* and you must not quarrel with an animal."

After the fourth day, while Hunter was away, the two wives began to quarrel. The first woman said, "What airs you put on. You are only an antelope."

The girl began to cry. She thought, "Hunter promised he would tell it to no one, all the same he told."

Hunter came back home. The young girl said to him, "Did I not forbid you to tell anyone?"

Hunter said, "What did you hear?"

She said, "Today, while quarreling with your wife, she told me I am only an antelope.

> *O my skin, my skin,*
> *How are things with me,*
> *Now that Hunter has taken my skin?"* [1]

Hunter said to her, "Say nothing."

The next day Hunter left again for the bush. After the fifth day, the women began to quarrel again.

The senior wife of the hunter said, "You had better find your skin again. It is buried in back of my house. I do not want to be annoyed by *agbanli* in my own house."

But when she went to look for the skin, it was not there. As she did not find her skin, she went to tell her husband's other wife,

"You will never again see an antelope change into a woman for your husband. You will remain alone here."

Hunter came home. The girl told him what happened. He told her again not to be angry. On the third day the husband returned to the bush. He spent ten days on his hunt. The women began to quarrel for the third time. As they quarreled, the other woman went and found the other's skin and threw it at her.

"Take your skin and get out of my house! You are not a girl to marry!"

She took her skin, and, turning her back, changed back into an antelope. At once she ran away. On the way she met her husband. He took his gun and aimed it at the antelope. He did not know it was his wife. She raised herself on her hind legs and made a sign to him with her paws not to shoot. She gestured to him to come to her.

Hunter refused. She motioned again. Again he refused. "I, I have never before been called by an animal."

She said, "I beg you. Come to me first. You must not shoot before you come."

Hunter approached the animal.

She said, "It is I who changed into a young girl for you. I came back here, but it is not my fault. You told your wife to return my skin to me."

Hunter said, "I beg you to change again into a woman, and to come home with me once more. We will talk this over at home. I want to judge which of you was at fault."

She said, "I do not want to go home with you again. If I go now, she will say again to me what I had forbidden you to tell. You, too, cannot keep a secret."

When she said this, there were two birds up a tree. The two birds were called Adjahè and Ayohè. The two birds did not know that these were a hunter and an antelope talking together. The Adja bird said to the Ayo bird, "People are too foolish. If they would take our excrement and would put with it a leaf of this tree and a little water and then would put that on the head of an animal, that animal would change into a woman." The Ayo bird said the same thing. Hunter heard these words. Then the two birds flew away.

Hunter gathered the things the birds had talked about and approached the antelope. He put the mixture on her head, and she changed into a young woman again. The skin fell off. The two now returned home.

Seeing them come, the wife said, "Is that Agbanli you are bringing again?"

> *The Adja-bird has seen the Ayo bird,*
> *They said, "It is hard to understand things;*
> *Men who eat with five fingers,*
> *It is hard to understand their ways."* [2]

When they came home, Hunter forbade his wife to quarrel with this new wife.

That is why one never tells the truth to women.

[1] Record No. 136–1.
[2] Record No. 136–2.

49

Revealing secret identity: Why animals no longer change into women

There was a hunter who hunted for king Sinmegba.[1] This hunter killed all the animals of the bush. In those days, all the animals were also human beings. Now, the hunter was hunting in the bush. He went to see Agbo. Agbo did not know a hunter was there. Agbo took off her skin, hid it inside a mound of earth and changed into a young girl.

She took up her calabash and went off to market. The moment she left for market, the hunter went over to the mound where the skin was hidden, took it home and buried it there. Then he went back to the bush and hid there where Agbo had put her skin.

So the girl came back from market and looked for her skin, but the skin was not there. She began to look for it everywhere.

The hunter came to her and asked, "What did you lose?"

She said, "I lost something."

The hunter said, "I did not find what you lost, but will you marry me?" The girl began to weep. The hunter embraced her. "Why do you cry? Tell me what you lost. I was here before you took off your skin, and I will never tell it to anyone."

So the girl stopped crying. She said, "All right. I'll marry you, but never tell anyone that I am called Agbo." So the hunter took her home.

At home his first wife asked him, "Where did you find this young girl?"

The hunter said to her, "She is an *agbo* whom I found in the bush, but you must never tell this to anyone."

The hunter dug up the skin and put it on a roof pole.

One day the hunter went to hunt and the two wives began to quarrel. The first wife said, "You have no right to insult me, you are only a buffalo, there's your skin on the ceiling."

When the girl heard these words, she went quickly to find a ladder so as to climb up and get her skin. She put it on and changed back into a buffalo with horns. When she did this, she charged the woman. She said, "All right. I'm Agbo, and so I've become Agbo." She killed the wife and her children.

Then she went out to follow the road her husband took. Now, the hunter was in the bush spying on another animal. All at once he saw the buffalo under the tree, striking the tree with its horns in order to kill him.

The hunter began to shout from on high. He had a hunter's charm. If he put this about his neck, he could not be seen any more. When the hunter saw that he was in danger of being eaten by this animal, he put the cord about his neck. When he did this, the animal could no longer see him.

So the hunter escaped and came home. Instead of seeing his wives and children there, he saw only the dead bodies of his first wife and her children.

That is why animals no longer change into women. Before, all the animals and the dog, too, used to change into men and women.

¹ An early king of Dahomey.

50

Why human beings are no longer sacrificed to bring rain

I

This happened in the time of Agadja. There was no rain. To have the rain fall, they had to give a man or a woman to the god Dã before rain fell.

Adjahosu had a very beautiful daughter. Now it is the turn of Adjahosu to furnish a sacrifice for Dã.

One day a hunter came to the king of Adja and asked him for his daughter. The king said, "Here is my daughter. She is beautiful, true. But she is for Dã."

The hunter asked the girl, "When are you going?"

The girl said, "In two weeks."

When the day arrived, the hunter went away. He left early, early in the morning. He took with him his gun and his knife. He hid in a treetop so that no one saw him.

Now, they gave the girl to the *vodun* at a river where the serpent came to take his sacrifice. The girl who was to be taken to Dã was called Sokame. In order to give a being to Dã, all the people of the country came together to hold a ceremony, and they took the girl to the river.

When they came to the river, they bound the hands of the girl, and put her on her knees beside the water. Beside her they placed oil, beans, everything. The people did not know that the hunter was there, but he was, and from the treetop where he was hidden he saw everything. The girl herself did not know that the hunter was there.

Now, in the river there were two Dã, one male and the other female. After they placed the sacrifice like that, the people went home. When they turned to go home, the two serpents came out of the river to claim their sacrifice. But as soon as the hunter saw the two heads coming out of the water, he aimed his gun at them, and shot them both. He climbed down from the tree, and cut off their heads.

When the girl heard the shots, she trembled with fear. She did not know who did the shooting.

Now, beside the girl they had left a closed calabash. The hunter cut off both heads and put them inside this calabash. He unbound the girl, put the calabash on the girl's head and began to sing,

> *The Dangbwe wish to eat Sokame;*
> *Cut off their heads,*
> *Put them in the calabash;*
> *It is on the hunter's knife we rely.*[1]

Then the rain began to fall in torrents. The people all believed that Dã had received the offering and had sent rain.

Now a boy came down the road, and from a distance saw the girl walking with the calabash on her head, and behind her a man with a gun, who was singing. He went home and told this to the father.

The king said, "No." He sent the Prime Minister to see if it was true. The Mingã said it was true. So the king called together all the people, and the men and women came to hear what the king wanted of them.

As soon as the people came together, the girl and the hunter appeared. They went down on their knees before the king. The king said, "This man came to ask me for my daughter, and I told him that my daughter belonged to Dã." He said, "This man told me that there is no *vodun* Dã. He said that he wanted to marry my daughter."

Now, there were so many people that only a few could see the girl. Each one said, "I want to see her, I want to see her." They pressed forward where the man and girl were kneeling.

At last the king quieted them. He ordered them to be seated, announcing that he would speak. He said, "Now, before this, there was no rain. If rain was to fall, we had each to give a son or a daughter to the serpent Dã. From today on, we shall no longer give things to Dã. Here are the two heads of the dead Dã. And you see the rain is falling."

That is why to this day, we no longer give a human being to Dã.

II

In olden days if it did not rain they gave a girl to Dā in order that rain might fall. Good. Now there was a girl called Sokame. And there was Hunter, who came and asked her father to marry her. But the father said the girl was reserved for the serpent.

When Hunter heard this, he said, "I, I'm going to marry her without fail."

He went to see the girl. The girl said, "I am here for the serpent." Hunter asked her the day she would be given to the serpent. When Hunter learned the day that had been fixed, he climbed into a tree-top beside the river.

The people brought the girl to the river. They said, "We want rain. Dā, here is a girl for you." They bound the girl, and left her on the bank.

Good. So Hunter is there. He spies on them. The moment a serpent's head appeared from out of the water and reached toward the girl, Hunter shot him. He climbed down and cut off the heads of both serpents.[2] He put both heads inside a calabash and closed it. Good. He put the calabash on the girl's head, and put the knife on the closed calabash. Then he told the girl to take it to her father's house.

As the two started on the way to the girl's house, rain began to fall.

Hunter began to sing,

> *The Dangbwe wish to eat Sokame;*
> *Cut off their heads,*
> *Put them in the calabash;*
> *It is on the hunter's knife we rely.*[3]

On the way a boy met them. He ran to tell the king that he saw the girl on her way to the village, and behind her a man singing.

But they said that the boy who came to tell the king that he saw Sokame and Hunter was lying. They said he was mocking the king, and killed him. For as the rain was falling, everybody believed that the serpent had taken his wife already, and that was why rain was falling.

The second man who came to tell this to the king was also killed. As for the third one, they said, "All right. Now we will kill no more. Mingã, go and see for yourself."

Mingã went to see and he came back and said, "Dada Segbo, it is true."

At this moment Sokame and Hunter entered. They called together all the people and they said, "From today on you need not give a man or a woman to the serpent to have rain fall."

This was forbidden by Hunter. If he had not done this, then in the dry season we would still be giving men and women to Dã to make the rain come. Dada Segbo said to Hunter that he could take the girl, and he asked nothing of him in return. He also gave him cloths and money.

[1] Record No. 160–2.
[2] The serpent-spirits are often worshipped in pairs; here it is apparently taken for granted that it was such a pair that came to take the offering.
[3] Record No. 160–2.

51

The flight up the tree

There was a hunter called Kpadunu. He had medicine. To make the dogs eat one put *acasa* into this water. Good. Before going hunting, he said to his mother, "I leave early in the morning every day to go hunting. If I am not back by mid-morning, go and see if the medicine had not changed into blood. If it is red, put in the *acasa* and call the dogs. If it is not red, do not trouble, for I am not in danger."

One day, the son went away early in the morning. At about mid-morning his mother was asleep.

The hunter climbed a tree in order to spy on the animals from there. This was a tree of the Yehwe, but he did not know it. The Yehwe were not there when he climbed up the tree. The Yehwe

..me back at about mid-morning. There were twelve of them. The man had three small magic gourds in his sack.

When the Yehwe came, one said, "I smell the smell of a living man." The second said the same thing, the third the same, and so on.

The youngest of them said, "Look up, I think I see a man. Let us be quiet, for he has a gun in his hand." Among the Yehwe was a pregnant woman, who was resting on a mound of earth. She was tired.

The Yehwe now said to the hunter, "Why don't you stay at home? We want no hunters here. We are going to kill you." They began to cut down the tree. Good. When the tree was about to fall, the hunter broke the first gourd. The tree at once became whole. They began to cut the tree down again, and again he broke a gourd.

His mother is still asleep, yes?

They began to cut the tree for the third time and the hunter has already begun to weep. When the tree had almost fallen, he dropped the third. When he dropped the third, his mother awakened, and she went to see the medicine. It was all red. The mother at once put in the *acasa* and called the dogs to eat. She said to them, "Go look for your master. I do not know where he is." The dogs ate and ran away.

At last they reached the tree, just as the tree was about to fall. They fell on the Yehwe and began to devour them. They killed twelve, but the thirteenth was pregnant. The dogs wanted to devour also this pregnant one, but Kpadunu called to them and told them to let her go. "If it were not for this woman, I would have been eaten by the others, because when they were cutting down the tree, this woman said, 'Let the man live. He is not after you.'"

Now among these dogs, there were those who ate only blood; there were those who ate nothing but bones; there were those who ate nothing but flesh. One ate nothing but skin, one took what fell. One goes only for the rescue, and one eats only the eyes of animals.

The hunter is in the tree. He came down after they had eaten the dead Yehwe, and he took the pregnant one home with him.

In ancient times,[1] to hunt well, one had to be on good terms with the *azizā* and have many charms from them. Finished.

[1] The storyteller interposed, "It isn't in our days, yes?"

52

Why Dog must be fed

Mawu created men, the animals, and birds. All people talked the same language. Men and animals understood each other. In those days men did not give presents to each other. Those who had things kept them for themselves.

There was a man who had a wife. This woman was pregnant. Now this man never stayed at home. He was always away hunting. While the husband was away, the wife was in labor. Now there was a dog beside the woman. The woman had a hemorrhage as she was about to bear her child. She said, "If I only had someone here I could send to call my husband."

The dog was there and he got up without saying a word and took the road in search of the husband. When he found the man, he beat against the man's legs with his tail. The man did not get up. He came back and did the same thing again and again. The hunter thought he had trapped an animal, and so he followed him. Because in those days dogs trapped animals when their masters were away, and later came to find the master, and beat against his legs with the tail to let him know.

After the man had walked a bit, he stopped to look about. The dog, who was running ahead, ran back to his master and beat against his legs again. The man stopped again, and the dog ran back to call him. He did this until he brought the man back home.

The man got back just in time to help his wife, as she gave birth to the child.

Now in order to give birth, there was a medicine. The man gave the medicine to the woman. Then the woman gave birth to a son. He was called Hunsu.

The woman told her husband if it had not been for the dog, she would have died. To thank the dog, the woman's husband killed a cock and made a stew of chicken, meal and palm oil for him to eat.

That is why today when one eats one never forgets the dog. In those days, man never gave presents to dogs, but dogs gave presents to man.

Now, this man has a junior wife, too. She is also pregnant. Now this wife is stingy, and never wants to give anything to anyone. When she ate, she never gave anything to the dog. Now her time to give birth came. Now the dog is beside her. The girl is in pain, and she cries, "If someone were only here, I'd send him to my husband."

The dog said, "You have only to tell it to the stew you like so well that you never share it. It will go and bring your husband."

The woman said to the dog, "Ah, you know how to talk? And you don't want to call my husband? I beg you, go for him."

As the woman pleaded with the dog, the dog went to call the husband. But when he found the husband and brought him home, it was already too late. The woman had given birth to a dead child.

The husband was angry with his first wife. He said, "Why didn't you tell the dog to come for me?"

Then the husband told the woman who bore the dead child to feed the dogs.

53

The chosen suitor

There was a very beautiful woman. She was the oldest daughter of Dada Segbo. Whenever her father found a husband for her, she refused him. Her father offered her many, many husbands. She did not want them. Her father said to her, "All right. Now you yourself find a man who pleases you."

On market days, the girl went to all the markets and looked at every man there. She did not find one she liked. Every market day she went. Everywhere she went she looked. No man pleased her. But she went to market every market day. Every five days she went to market. She had nothing to sell, but she went. She bought nothing, but she went. She went to find a man who pleased her, so she might marry him.

There was one man who came to market. The moment the girl saw him, she said, "Here is the man I want to marry."

She approached the man and they talked, until they arranged to meet in nine days. The girl came home and said, "I found what I have been looking for, father. I found the man I want to marry."

But the man was not a man. When he wanted to go to market, he changed into a man. He borrowed a cloth, trousers, hat, even a stick.

Dada Segbo said, "All right. Bring your man here, so that I may know him."

When the day came, the girl went to the same market and found the man there. She asked him to go home with her, so that her father might meet him.

Dada Segbo saw him, and said to his daughter, "Does the man please you?"

She said, "Yes."

He said, "All right. Marry him."

So when market was over, the girl went with the man to his house, as his wife. Now they went on their way until they came to the place where the man had borrowed the trousers.

The man who loaned him the trousers said, "Since you took my trousers, I have not left my house. Give them back to me." He returned the trousers.

They went a little farther and came to the place where he had borrowed the cloth. The man who had loaned him the cloth said, "Since morning I haven't gone out. You took my cloth, and I had to stay home." He gave him back his cloth.

The girl seeing this began to tremble. For the man was naked.

They came to the place where he had taken the hat. The owner at once asked him for his hat. He returned it.

Now, the only thing left him was his stick. They walked farther, and they came to the house of the one who had loaned him the stick. The man said to him, "Since morning I have been here. You know very well I cannot go out without a stick." He was an old man, that one.

When he returned all that he had borrowed, the man had nothing at all. He told the woman to walk ahead. Now, his house was in a hole. He had another wife there and their children. These were the same kind of animals as himself.

Now, to change into a man he had also borrowed two feet and two arms. He returned the two feet and the two hands, and he is now round like a serpent, but more round.

The girl began to cry. The husband called his wife and his children, and they began to bite the woman.

There was a hunter up a tree. When they began to bite the girl, he shot at them. He killed those who were attacking her, and so the others escaped. The hunter climbed down, and led the girl back to the house of Dada Segbo.

He said, "I saw animals who wanted to eat your daughter, and I shot at them." He said, "Those animals had neither feet nor hands."

Dada Segbo called together all the people. He said, "I offered my daughter all the men of my kingdom, but she refused them all. She went out to find a man for herself, and this is what has happened to her."

So a daughter must not disobey her father, and do what she likes.

Her father said, "Now you have made your journey, and you came back unharmed. Whom will you choose to marry from among these men?"

She said, "I will marry no other man than the hunter who saved my life and brought me back here."

Her father said, "All right. I will let you marry this hunter. But when you are his wife, and you want to go somewhere, and he does not agree, you must not go there."

That is why from that day to this day, one listens to the advice of one's father and mother. It is because of this that a woman takes the husband her father chooses for her.

54

Hunter's magic brings to life Girl-born-to-die

There was a woman who the moment she gave birth to a child, the child died. And there was a woman in the bush called Na Abiku. When the poor woman gave birth, Na Abiku came and took the child away.

One day the hunter Azizā was hunting. He went to see the woman called Na, who is found in a large calabash called *akpakpo*. The hunter Azizā hunted from Hwegbo, *ka, ka, ka, ka*[1] . . . [till] here. Now this hunter Azizā climbed up a tree. To this tree came the children who wanted to come into the wombs of women. Na asked each, "How long do you want to stay in the world?"

The first said, "The day I am born, I will die."

The second said, "I will bear a son and I will return."

The third said, "When I am twenty, you will see me back here."

The last one said, "All right. I'll stay in the world till I marry. When I am with my husband, the first time I take my bath in his house, I will go away. You will see me again here then."

Na asked, "What womb do you want to come out of?"

So they all said, "We want to be born in the Sokame family, from the womb of the Boko woman, who is called Na."

So as Azizā learned this, he changed into a man and went to see the woman. This woman was now pregnant. Azizā said, "I will marry the girl you are going to give birth to."

The woman said, "I never give birth to a live child. They all come still-born." Egbwlo moyo! The first one she gave birth to was a girl. The woman said, "Ah, she will not live. She will die, as the others died." When this same woman had given birth to other infants, the others all died. She had only this girl.

Now, Na Abiku had told that girl there was a staff, and if you touched anyone who was to die with this staff, that person did not die on the day set. Azizā learned about all this.

So tomorrow is the day for them to get married.[2] Hunter placed himself along the path which the girl must pass to go to Na. He had the staff in his hand. When the time came for the marriage,

Hunter was not there. No one knew where he was. But he was there on the path.

Now they said to the girl, "Our older brother is not yet here, but you had better bathe." The women came over where the girl was bathing, to ask her if she needed to have her back dried. When they came near, they saw she was lying on the ground. She was dead.

There was a man at the home of Na Abiku who was impatient for this girl. He kept asking, "Na, isn't the girl here yet? Na, where is my wife?"

But Hunter is there on the path. The girl[3] goes by, now, with cloths, with a calabash on her head, with everything. The moment she came beside Hunter, he began to beat her with the staff. He said, "Go home! Go home!" As he beat the woman, the woman at home awakened.[4]

So now Hunter took the path that led to the girl's house. When he came home, everybody cried out, "Look! Your wife is dead! Your wife is dead! What shall we do?" But as soon as he came into the house, he saw the girl, who was dead a little while ago, seated on the bed. Now all the people were astonished.

Then the mother said, "I have something to say to all of you. Whenever I gave birth to a child, it died at once. When Hunter came and asked me for my unborn daughter, I did not know that he told the truth. But this daughter lived. Now on her wedding day she died, and she understood that that was what was to happen." She said, "Now I see my daughter alive again, and I am very happy."

She gave the girl to Hunter, and she asked him for nothing. She said, "Look after the girl, whether she is alive or dead."

It is for this reason that the wives of hunters do not talk very much.

[1] Onomatopoeic expression indicating duration or intensity of action.
[2] The action shifts in time to a period when the infant is grown and ready for marriage.
[3] *I.e.,* the spirt of the dead girl.
[4] *I.e.,* the corpse came to life.

55

When animals were men: Hunter is entitled to his kill

In the beginning of the world, a hunter hunted every day. There were only elephants in the bush, so Hunter killed nothing but elephants. Whenever hunters went to hunt, they killed nothing but elephants.

Once when Hunter was hunting, he saw an elephant and he shot at him. Elephant was wounded, but escaped. Hunter recharged his gun and went after the escaped animal. Elephant ran until he came to a river and fell into it. Now, this was a man who had come from the water and had changed into an elephant. He had his house in the water.

Hunter looked, looked, until he came to the river, and there he saw blood in the stream. He said, "My animal is here," and plunged into the water with his gun. He must surely find his animal here.

Suddenly he fell into a compound where there were several houses. He saw many people, many women, well dressed. Everyone asked, "Where do you come from with your gun?"

But Hunter said, "Where is your king? Show me his house."

A child took him to the king. And to the king he said, "Now, I shot at an animal. It is an elephant that I shot at. But he escaped and has come here to your house. [I know this] because his tracks have led me here."

The king summoned everyone, and said that several times he had forbidden them to leave the country. Then he told Hunter to look and see if his elephant was here, for all had left their doors open.

Hunter saw someone, who had been shot, lying down near the fire. He went to tell the king that he had found his animal. The king sent for the animal. When the wounded elephant came to the king, he had changed into a man. The king said to him, "I told you many times not to go out." He gave the animal to Hunter.

Hunter took him away. Later he came to a stream where four

calabashes were afloat. The man who was shot took his legs and put them in one calabash, his arms into another, his head in another, until he had changed back into an elephant. Hunter again shot at him, and this time he killed him.

Long ago all the animals were men. Each had his own house.

56

Hunter cures boastfulness

There was Agbo. Every morning when he got up he wagged his tail and said, "No one is bigger than I. I am sure I am the strongest, too."

His wife said, "You should not say that. There are people in the bush who are bigger and stronger than you."

He said, "All right. Do you know one? Show me."

That happened every morning. He said this and his wife answered him. Every morning, every morning the same thing.

Now his wife went to plot with Hunter. She said, "Every morning my husband says this. You must come and shame him."

She told Hunter to be there before dawn, because Agbo got up at sunrise. She said, "But you must not shoot him. I only want you to frighten him."

So Hunter is there before dawn. Agbo got up and he went out, and said the usual thing. His wife stood at his side. He said, "I am stronger then all those in the bush." When he finished saying this, Hunter shot a shot.

When Agbo went out he closed his door after him. So now, when he heard the shot, he broke the door down with his horns, and rushed inside to hide.

His wife said, "You've been telling me every day that you are strong. Why are you running away? I see better than you. The strong never go about saying they are strong."

That is why when a person is strong, or brave, or rich, he never talks about it. That finished the day this happened to Agbo.

57

Hyena into suitor: Why women do not travel great distances alone

Good! It happened that there was a woman of Abomey who had married in Whydah. At that time there was no train. Everyone had to walk. Each day she went from Whydah to Abomey on foot.[1]

One day at noon as the woman was on her way from Abomey with her food, Hyena, who had changed into human form, greeted her as a man. The two went on together. They continued on their way without meeting anyone on the road. When they came to a certain tree, the man changed a little into an animal, and spoke through his nose.

He said, "You are very beautiful. Haven't you noticed the young Abomey men? Don't you want to marry one of them? Why have you left them to marry a man from Whydah? I am going to eat you. As you are so beautiful,[2] you must be good to eat."

Just then a hunter was trapping an antelope nearby. The two did not know that Hunter was there. He had been trying to catch the antelope since early that morning. The woman started to cry, and Hyena said, "Why do you weep?"

Now, Hunter, hidden in the tree above them, heard them, but he did not say anything.

Hyena first said, "Sit down, give me what you have, and then I will eat you." Then Hyena said, "Now put me on your two knees and feed me, for I have no hands with which to eat. Your fingers will serve me as forks."

Hunter listened to everything. The woman thought she was surely lost this day, but Hunter knew in his heart that she would not die. He loaded his gun, put bullets in it.

Hyena finished eating. He said, "Now that I have finished eating, and I am still not satisfied, I am going to eat you."

At this, the woman stood up, dropping Hyena.

Hyena said, "Now it is almost over." But Hunter was always looking on. Now Hyena began to take off her cloths. He took off the first cloth, and as he reached for the second, Hunter fired at him. Hyena cried out, "He who wishes to take the life of another, it is his life that will be lost now. If I had known that my life would be so unlucky, I would have left the woman alone."

Now, Hunter came down from the tree and took the woman to her husband's house in Whydah. She told him what had happened, and her husband said, "After this, we shall go together to Abomey. Now I cannot marry you any more,[3] so I will give you to the hunter as a reward for having saved you." So he gave her to Hunter.

The man said to those who asked him why he had given his wife to the hunter, "If I do not tell you, you will not know. If it had not been for Mawu, you would say that my wife was with me in Whydah. But as I was absent, the hunter was there in my place. The hunter replaced me, and did what I should have done. I have no daughter to give him for a wife, so I have given him the woman he saved."

It was for this reason that in olden times, it was forbidden for a woman to go from Abomey to Whydah without taking the train.[4]

[1] Since the distance between these two places is about eighty-five miles, the exaggeration is patent.
[2] *I.e.*, "beautiful, too much."
[3] *I.e.*, "remain married to you."
[4] At the end, the following dialogue took place: "In olden times a train?"—"No, without being accompanied by a man."

58

Tell-tale grease: Why Cat goes on all fours

There were two hunters. One came from Atogon and one came from Allada. The Allada hunter always took water with him when he went to hunt, and this time he had a bottle of water. The hunter from Atogon had no water.

In the bush these two hunters met, and the Atogon hunter asked the man from Allada for a drink. The Allada hunter said, "No."

Now, the Atogon hunter became more and more thirsty. He picked some corn and began to eat that. When he finished eating the corn, his thirst was satisfied for the moment, so he continued with his hunt. On his way he met Cat, who was eating a cock. He stopped and asked Cat for some water.

Good. Now this hunter was lost in the bush, and did not know that he was quite close to his own compound. Cat had stolen a cock from a house nearby, the hunter's own house. When Hunter asked Cat for water, Cat took him to his compound.

Beside his mat, Hunter kept a bottle full of palm oil. When he entered his house, he saw that the bottle of oil was broken. He turned to Lamb who watched his house, and asked who had broken the bottle? Now Lamb cannot talk. Hunter asked her, "Who broke the bottle? Who broke the bottle?" Lamb kept looking at Hunter, but said nothing.

Now Cat stood by and said, "Look inside the mouth of Lamb and you will know." Cat had already poured palm oil over Lamb's mouth, for it was he who had broken the bottle and eaten the oil. When he said this, and showed Lamb's mouth, Lamb said, *"Mewe? Mewe?*—Who? Who?"

Hunter came over to Lamb and saw the oil all over her mouth. He was very angry. He took up his gun, but Lamb ran away.

Lamb went straight to Dada Segbo's house. He said, "I watched Hunter's house. Cat came and stole a cock, and broke the bottle of palm oil, and ate it all himself, and put a little over my mouth. Then he told Hunter I broke the bottle and ate the oil."

Dada Segbo sent a messenger to find Cat, his friend Uwo and Hunter. Now, before everybody, Lamb told what the cat had done. Cat had stolen a cock, broken the bottle, eaten the oil, and blamed it on her.

Lamb said, "Hunter has two feet and Cat has two feet, and I have four."

Dada Segbo asked Uwo if he had ever seen a lamb eat oil. Uwo said, "No."

Dada Segbo said to Cat, "After today you will never agein walk on two feet. You will go on all fours."

That is why, to this day, cats go on all fours.

59
Mock funeral: Hyena plays dead

In earlier times, the animals had a king. They had as their king a man named Hyena. One day the animals were told Hyena died. He was not really dead, he was alive. He pretended to be dead to get food, because when he was alive the other animals did not come near him. He wanted them to come within reach, so that he could eat them.

He had a sub-chief named Squirrel, and he was the one who assembled all the animals of the bush when their king had something to tell them. So now he brought all the animals together. They made a grave, and Squirrel named the animals who were to take care of the burial.

When Squirrel went to look at the body, he saw that the hyena's eyes were open. They had bought cloth to cover him, and since Squirrel was cunning, he had one of his friends, Rabbit, who is as cunning as he, come. He said to Rabbit, "Now that man is not dead. He wants to eat us. I have seen his two eyelids move."

When Rabbit heard these words, he said, "We need only sing to tell the other animals. This will let the others know quickly that Hyena is going to get up and eat them."

> *Is it the way of a man lying dead,*
> *To get up and strike us dead?*
> *A blow from a stick will not kill me,*
> *I dance far off;*
> *Lightly, lightly,*
> *Far away will I dance.*[1]

After hearing the song, the animals ran away.

Hunter was in a nearby tree, and he saw and heard everything that happened. As the other animals ran away, Hyena ran after them. Hunter fired at him.

And this is why, if there is something secret that happens in the bush, it is the hunter who sees it.

[1] Record No. 135-1.

IV

Enfant terrible tales

twins, orphans, and the abnormally born

Enfant terrible tales

DRAMATIS PERSONÆ

NESUHWE, deified abnormal births of royal descent

ZUMADUNU, TOKPA, KPELU, BOKO, ADOMU, SEWA and SEMASU; members of the Nesuhwe cult, and their wives

DODOGBODÈ, wife of Tokpa

YO, mythological figure, hero of the humorous tale

DADA SEGBO, a king; and his wife

TOHOSU, a precocious, abnormally born child

ZINSU, ZINSI, DOSI, twins

AIDO-HWEDO, rainbow serpent

HUNSI, a mother of a Tohosu

SAGBO, a twin; worker of magic

HUNTER

YEHWE (Yehwe Zogbanu), thirty-horned, fire-breathing monster of the Dahomean forest. May be male or female.

HESA, HESU, twins
Their father

DJELUBA, tree of the forest transformed into woman

First wife of Zinsu

Mother of Zinsu

KOFLE DJOMBI ALAHWEKPÈ, best friend of Zinsu

DOSU, first male child born after twins

AZIZĀ, forest spirit

DOSI, first female child born after twins

KU, Death

HWESE, Hwevi, twins
Their step-mother
Their dead mother

ORPHAN (Nochiovi, lit. "mother-dead-child")
Her step-mother and step-brother

NA, an orphan

AKABA, Agadja, Tegbesu, Kings of Dahomey

HOMENUVO, a prince

GLELE, a Dahomean king

60

Strife amongst royal abnormally born: Royal seducer must not be named: Why Tohosu have separate houses [1]

In very ancient times, the Nesuhwe sat in the doorway and played a card game called *ako*. They did this every day. One day when they were playing, three young girls passed by. They were on their way to market.

In the Nesuhwe, the first is Zumadunu; the second is Tokpa; the third Kpelu; the fourth Boko; the fifth Adomu; the sixth Sewa; seventh, Semasu. These were the men who were playing the game. As they played, they saw the girls passing. Zumadunu said, "I won [2] the card which fell just now."

When the girls heard this, one of them said, "I must marry you. You are so fine a card player."

Tokpa said, "I killed the card which followed."

The second said, "I will have intercourse with you."

Kpelu said, "I killed the third card which followed."

The last girl said, "I am going to marry you."

So the three girls did not go to market. They married and stayed there.

The girls now did not want to leave for market. Zumadunu told his wife, "Go to market and buy something which will please your hand." [3]

Tokpa told his wife the same thing. And Kpelu, too.

Zumadunu's wife bought *kelekele*.[4] Tokpa's wife bought a calabash, tobacco, a pipe, sugar, and also *kelekele* and a package of chewing sticks for cleaning the teeth. She put all these in the calabash and closed the calabash. Keplu's wife bought cassava and some cakes.

At night when the three girls came home, they found the men there still playing their game.

Zumadunu's wife gave what she had bought to him. Tokpa's wife gave what she had bought to Tokpa. Kpelu's wife also gave her husband what she had bought.

So Tokpa opened the calabash in front of everyone, and he saw what his wife had bought. When the others saw that, they called out, "Your wife is clever. Among these girls, you got the handsomest and the trickiest." [5]

Zumadunu was angry when he saw this. When the game was over and they all went home, Zumadunu became sick. He was so sick that no medicine could help him. There was a leaf on a tree between Adjabenu and Ayogbenu. Zumadunu asked Tokpa to go find this medicine for him.

Now, Zumadunu was really not sick at all. He was deceiving Tokpa, because he envied him. When Tokpa left that night, Zumadunu went to see Tokpa's wife. He knocked on her door.

The woman called out behind the closed door, "Tokpa is away. Who knocks here?"

This woman was called Dodogbodè. Zumadunu began to call her, "Dodogbodè, Dodogbodè."

The girl said, "I know you. Mawu! My husband is not here, and you call me?"

So Zumadunu went home. At midnight he went back and knocked on the door again. Now he changed his voice, so that he sounded like Tokpa. As the girl thought it was her husband, she went and opened the door. When the girl saw instead of her husband Zumadunu stand before her with his knife, she was very upset. Zumadunu said to her. "Go into your room."

She said, "My husband is not here, and you tell me to go in."

Zumadunu said to her, "Your mother is Anagonu,[6] your father is Anagonu, if you don't go in, I'll kill you with this knife." The two entered. The girl was crying. Zumadunu said to her, "Give me some water. I want to bathe."

The girl said, "My husband forbade me to give water to anyone but himself."

Zumadunu said, "Your mother is Anagonu, your father is Anagonu, if you don't do this, I'll kill you with this knife." When Zumadunu had washed, he asked her to come and dry his back.

She said, "My husband is not here, and you ask me to come and dry you."

Zumadunu said, "If you refuse, I'll kill you with this knife." The girl went and dried his back. Zumadunu asked for the cloth to dry himself which her husband used. The girl refused. But again he threatened to kill her, and the girl gave it to him. Zumadunu asked her to make the bed.

She cried out, "My husband is not here!" He threatened her again, and she made the bed.

Zumadunu lay down on the bed and asked her to come. The girl cried out, "My husband is not here, and you ask me to come?" Again he threatened her, and she went. So they slept together. He asked her to have relationship with him. The girl refused. She said her husband forbade her to have anything to do with another man. The girl was now crying very hard. Zumadunu again threatened to kill her. So the girl had to submit.

The next day Tokpa came home. The girl wept from midnight till mid-day of the next day.

In those days if a king's son had relationship with another woman, the girl had no right to speak his name, for she would be killed. Now, Tokpa asked her who was there in his absence. The girl cried and said nothing. He asked her again and again, but the girl could say nothing. Tokpa beat her *ka, ka, ka, ka!* till all her black skin came off. Now, he had a medicine, and when he put the woman in it, the skin came back in its place.

There was a tree in back of the house called *lise*. There Zumadunu hid and watched Tokpa and his wife. So from on high Zumadunu began to sing,

> Say it is I, so that you may not die,
> Name me, so that you may not die.

The father of this girl was called *Nyamasukudokon*, If-death-comes-to-kill-anyone-a-man-coming-from-far-cannot-see-death. Zumadunu said, "Tell him it was I, so that he lets you go."

Now Tokpa was beating his wife, beating her. Dodogbodè also began to sing, "Why do you ask me to name you? Did you and I do anything which deserves my naming you?"

Zumadunu's father was called Yemehwesu. She sang, "Son of Yemehwesu, did we do anything which deserves naming you? I do not recall it." [7]

Zumadunu said, "Don't you remember what we did last night? You turned to the right and left." [8]

So now Tokpa unbound the girl, put medicine on her, and the skin again came back, and she was beautiful.

By this time Tokpa already knew that she had had intercourse with Zumadunu. So Tokpa fell ill. Now, he told Zumadunu to go and find leaves for him in the same place. When Zumadunu went away, Tokpa took his horse and went to Zumadunu's house. Now, since Zumadunu's wife was not the least clever, once he knocked on the door, she opened the door. So here Tokpa had not much pleading to do. She did what he asked of her, and they had intercourse.

Now, Tokpa did not go to Zumadunu's house alone. He was accompanied by many men, and when he came out and mounted his horse, he asked them whether they had gongs. Then he sang that the wife of Azuwa, another name for Zumadunu, had had relationship with him today. Now all his followers sang this, till he reached his house.

Now Zumadunu was returning. He had bought cassava and cakes and was eating them on the way. When he saw Tokpa and his men, he said to himself, "Ah, here comes Tokpa from my house." At home, he asked his wife, "What man was here?" He held his knife in his hand and threatened with it. The wife was afraid.

She said, "Tokpa was here, and we had intercourse together."

The moment she said this, Zumadunu cut off his wife's head. For a woman must never mention the name of a king's son as seducer.

After this Zumadunu and Tokpa were enemies. Now since they were enemies, the little Kpelu had them come together and he asked for the reason. Good. Tokpa said Zumadunu deceived him. "He said he was sick and sent me for leaves to cure him. When I left, he slept with my wife." And he said, "I too fell ill and sent him for leaves, and when he was away, I went and slept with his wife."

Kpelu said they need be enemies no longer. After the war, they would find fine wives among the slaves. Good. Tokpa was willing to forgive, but Zumadunu said they must remain enemies forever.

Kpelu said, "Two brothers must never be enemies. If we cannot be friends, let us all go and throw ourselves into the river." The little one said, "All right. We will go then."

So the three threw themselves into the river. Their father missed his sons, and he could not find them anywhere. He went to see a diviner. The diviner said he must find a drum for Yo, who would beat it in the middle of the river, and there he would find his sons.

As Yo was beating the drum, the sons came out of the river and began to dance. They asked Yo where he found this fine drum. Yo said to them that the drum came from that doorway, over there. Yo beat the drum, beat the drum, and the children danced till he led them to the house of their father.

Their father asked them, "Why did you throw yourselves into the river?" They told what had happened. The father said, "All right. Before you lived in separate houses. Now go and live all in one house."

The three slept on the same mat. At night there were quarrels. Each told the other to move to one side, to give him more room, give him more room.

But Zumadunu said nothing. Their father asked them, "Why do you quarrel?" Adomu asked for a separate place. So the father gave each a separate house again.

So now if you go to Abomey, you will see that each one of these princes has his own house. You see the house of Zumadunu, the house of Tokpa, of Kpelu, of all, in different quarters.

It is finished. *Ewo.*

[1] Cf. *Dahomey*, I, p. 211.

[2] The idiom is "killed."

[3] Narrator's aside: "This is an expression for what will please her."

[4] "It is something prepared from corn, and is dipped in oil, and cooked with sugar."

[5] Narrator's aside: "We use the word *malin* in two ways. If one deceives you, he is *malin*. But if we say *femme malin*, we mean no one gets the best of her. If you deceive a woman who is like that, it is no joke. She will leave. It will be costly later. But it is good to have a clever wife. She gives good advice."

[6] A Yoruba group.

[7] Narrator's interpolation: "Ah, one must beat wives. European wives, too, for they are the same *race*."

[8] NARRATOR: "Those were good days. If it had been me. . . ." He sang a song here, which he would not repeat for recording.

61

Contest between Tohosu and twins: Substitute victim: Changing into stone

Dada Segbo had a wife who had been pregnant for ten years. Everyone was amazed, and the king himself did not know what to do. One day as this woman was chopping some firewood with an axe, the axe cut her leg and the child came out of this wound. With him a gun came out, too.

Now, no sooner was he born than he began to speak.[1] So he said to his mother to name a day for their family to come together, and to say that the child wished to talk to them. At this, the woman named the day for all the family to come together.

When they were all assembled, he said, "Do you know my name?" The others all said, "No, no, no."

He said, "I am a child who has come into the world out of my mother's leg, and that is my name. What I have come to do in life is not to cultivate the land and not to suffer. I have come to hunt. When I kill a bird, or an animal, I will give it to my mother to sell in the market. When my mother was pregnant so long, you were very surprised. But I, I prepared myself to come into the world with everything that is necessary. That is why I have come with my gun and all things needed for the hunt." He saluted them and said. "There, that is what I have to say to you."

The people were astounded and returned to their homes.

So the next day the boy went to hunt. The first day he hunted, he killed an antelope. This he gave to his mother to take to the market. She took it to the market.

At the market, there was a pair of twins,[2] who asked, "What do you sell the antelope for?"

In those days, they had cowries and not money. When she said "Two cowries," they said "One." As the woman did not want to sell it for their price, they said, "All right, we are the ones who command the bush," and they told the animal to run away. So the antelope came to life and ran away.

The boy said, "All right. It makes no difference."

The next day he killed a deer and a buffalo, and his mother took them to market.

Again the twins came and asked the cost of the animals. For the deer, she asked three cowries, for the buffalo, four. They replied, "For the buffalo we will give one cowrie, and for the deer one-half." And when she did not accept this, they commanded the animals to escape.

The child said, "It is nothing." And the next day, he came back with many animals. He said, "Today, you will take me with you to market. But you must carry me on your back with my head down and my feet up."

On the road, those who saw them would say "Ah!" And when they said this, their mouths would remain open.³ So half the people had their mouths open.

When they got to the market, the child said, "Now put me under your calabash, and sit down."

When the twins came, they did the same thing they had done before. The mother refused their offer. So they said, "All right." And again the animals ran away.

When all the animals had left, the child said, "All right, mother. Let me out." So the mother let him out.

When the twins saw the child, they were very astonished to see a baby standing before them. The child shook hands with them, and said, "Thank you very much. I have received all your messages at home, and I come to thank you."

He said, "Now, I have nothing to say to you. But all the animals you have caused to run away must come back here, and be sold. I want all the animals you have ordered to leave to come back quickly, so that my mother may sell them. After that, I will talk to you." At these words, all the animals returned, and were dead. The mother sold them.

When the others saw this, they thought, "Ah, but he is as terrible as we."

One of the twins now made a mat and caused it to rest in mid-air.⁴ On top of it appeared two bottles of drink, and all three drank this there on the mat. The second twin made a needle rise in the air, and the three went and sat on it and ate there.

The child had a very large pipe. He lit it, and the smoke rose into the air. The three of them climbed up on the smoke and rested there, and did all they wished.

Now, as they were about to take leave of each other, the twins said, "Let us set five days as the time when you are to come to see us."

When the fifth day arrived, the child started on his way. He walked until he came to a crossroad, and he did not know the way. So he separated himself into two parts. The head followed one road, and the feet the other.

Someone who knew the road came along, and he said, "Who is it who had put his head on the road to Zinsu [5] and his feet on the path where people pass to get water?" When this person had gone, the child got up and brought his two parts together. Then he followed the right road, until he got to the house of the twins.

When he was there, the twins gave him a house to rest in. And they gave him food. But they had put poison in it. He said to the poison, "Get out of the stew, I want to eat." And the poison came together and separated itself from the food. He ate it. In the evening, he looked in his pipe, and asked, "Who will watch my sleeping room this evening?"

The serpent Aido-Hwedo said, "I will take care of it."

The next day, they also put poison in the stew. And the child again ordered the poison to gather itself together and get out of the stew. In the evening he said, "Tonight, I myself will watch my sleeping room."

When the twins came at night to kill the child, they saw nothing outside. So they entered the room. Then they cut the child into pieces and put the pieces in a pot. They cooked it and cooked it from morning till night, but it would not get cooked. When their father saw this, he sent them to get more wood. He was angry, and he said they did not know how to prepare food.

No sooner did they leave to look for wood, than the child came out of the pot and killed their father. He took the skin of the dead man and put it over himself. When the twins returned, they thought it was their father who was there. He now told them how to prepare the food in the pot. For, he had cut up their father, and put him in the pot in his own place.

So they ate until they came to the head. This they gave to the child [6] who they thought was their father. He said, "Now I have eaten your father." As he said this, he took off the skin and escaped.

Instantly, the others were after him, to catch him. Now, a river separated the child's country from the country of the twins. When the child was well ahead of them, so that they could not see him, he changed himself into a stone.

The twins came to the river. One of them said, as he picked up the stone, "If I saw that boy now on the other side, I'd kill him with this stone." And he threw the stone.

When the stone hit the other side, the boy stood up. He said, "I ate your father, and you have kept me company." And he said, "Thank you very much for your company. I am going." And he went.

At this, he returned to his house. His mother said to him, "I did not think you would come home. I thought you were dead."

He said, "To celebrate, I will kill some game."

From that day on, if he wished to take a journey and asked his mother for permission, she would say, "Good. I have confidence in you."

[1] This marks the child as a Tohosu. Cf. *Dahomey*, II, p. 262.

[2] Twins are held to have special powers derived from the spirits of the Forest.

[3] A common theme of punishment for not being discreet when seeing the unexpected.

[4] Here begin a series of contests of supernatural skills.

[5] This is a generic name of a male twin.

[6] A mark of respect, and in ritual apportioning of a kill, always must go to a ranking member of the group.

62

Contest between Tohosu and twins: Substitute victim: Changing into stone

There was a woman whose name was Hunsi. She was pregnant. She had been pregnant for three years without giving birth. When finally the boy came into the world, he had a gun, a machete, and a hoe. Good. The day he was born the child went to hunt. Everybody was astonished that a child should go hunting as soon as he is born.

The first time he went hunting he killed a deer. He brought it home, and they divided it among the old people. The second day, he killed guinea hens, partridges, turtledoves. He told his mother to go and sell these in the market. He told her to sell the guinea hens at twenty-five francs apiece; the partridges at twenty, and the turtledoves at fifteen. Now there were many, many guinea hens and partridges and turtledoves, yes?

There were a pair of twins who were very powerful and mischievous. The birds came to market. The twins came to ask the price of each bird. The boy's mother told them the price. But, as the twins were mischievous, they told her they would give her only a franc for each bird. As the woman did not wish to sell for a franc, the twins took some powder they had and threw this at the birds. So the birds changed into live birds, and flew away.

The woman went back home. She told her son that a pair of twins came to buy the birds, that they offered one franc apiece, and when she would not sell them, they ordered the birds to come to life and fly away.

Her child said, "It is all right." Again he went to hunt. He killed six deer. He said each deer was to sell for one hundred francs.

She took them to market. Now, again the twins came. They asked the price of each. They said, "Seventy-five francs, seventy-five francs." She refused. They said, "If you insist, then the deer will leave." So now the deer left. The woman returned home.

On the third day, he killed a boar. And he said to his mother, "Now we will both go to market. I want to see the savages who annoy me. When I go with you, you put me under your basket. Then sit down on it, so that no one sees me."

They left for the market. They brought with them all they had to sell. The two came again. They did not know the child was there. They asked the price of the boar. The mother said, "One hundred fifty francs." They offered her fifty francs, yes? They said, "You have no gun. You must have found this on the road."

Now the woman said, "You come every day to annoy me. Today you will see what will happen."

The two boys said, "All right. If that is so, then the boar will leave." Instantly, the boar went away.

The child said, "Mother, get up. I want to come out." The twins wanted to go away, but he called them back. "Come here," he called. He said, "Good day. I heard all that you have been doing in the market. That is why I am here today. I am here to show you that there is someone stronger here." [1] And the hunter asked the twins, "What are your names?"

The first twin said, "I am called Sagbo." The other said, "I am Zinsu."

The boy said, "My name is Child-who-does-not-look-for-any-thing-to-eat, has-come-forth-from-his-mother's-shoulders." He said, "I came today for you. Here is money. Go and find a mat."

He gave them twenty-five francs for a bottle of gin. When the drink came, he had the mat rise twenty meters above the ground, and it rested in the air with the bottle on top of it. He told the twins to climb up. All that there was to eat was already on the mat. They ate too much. They drank.

The twins bought three needles. He showed them things, and they, too, had things to show him. For they were endowed with magic powers, just as he was. They threw the needles up in the air, and in the air the three came together. With their magic charms, they accomplished this. The three of them went to sit down on the needles. There they ate and drank. The twins bought this food. It was now their turn. For the hunter had treated them first.

They finished eating. The hunter said to them, "Good. Now wait, and we will see if I am not stronger than you. I am going to sell all the animals you had caused to disappear." Now, the twins are already amazed at what the child can do. The boy said, "The animals that disappeared—the birds, the boar, all—I want them to come back at once." Instantly, the animals, the birds appeared. The twins were most astonished to see the birds and animals appear.

The boy began to sell the meat, as the twins stood by. He told them to wait a little, until he sold all the meat, and then he would fix a day to decide who was the more powerful. The twins waited until he sold the meat, and then they arranged to meet again in five days at their place. The twins said, "We'll come for you to show you the way. You do not know the road that leads to our house."

He said, "If it is far, it is nothing. If it is Abomey, or Porto Novo, you wait for me, and I'll come there."

Good. On the fifth day he started on his way. He saw one path, two paths. He divided himself into two before leaving. He put the two feet on one path and the two arms on the other. An old woman went by. She said, "Who killed a man, and put two feet on the road to Zinsu and two arms on the way to the well?" The old woman passed on, and the child awakened. Now he knew that this was the way to Zinsu's house.

When the old woman was out of sight, he gathered up his arms and feet and went on his way. He walked right to the door of the twins' house. There was a drum before the door. There, at that time, the twins were on high, above the houses. The boy put his hands on the drum. The twins said, "He who did this, let his hands stick." The two hands stuck.

The child said, "Those who said this, let them be bound by a cord, and let them be flogged." At once they were bound, and they began to beat the twins.

The twins said, "All right, let your hands come loose." The child, too, ordered that the flogging stop. They were loosened.

The three met and the twins welcomed him. They gave him a stool, and water to drink. They said to him, "Since you have a hard head, you will be eaten today without fail." They shook hands.

The little one said, "As strong as I am, I hardly think you'll be able to eat me."

Zinsu said, "How many days do you expect to stay here?"

He said, "I am staying here five days. What do you expect to do to me before the five days are up? Have you no wives? Is it your mother who cooks for you? Tell her I have come."

They gave him *acasa*. They put powder in to kill him. The boy said, "Why did you put powder inside?" He said to the powder, "Powder, put yourself to one side. I'm going to eat." And he ate.

At night they gave him porridge to eat. They again put in some poison. He knew it at once. He said, "Poison, go to one side." And he said, "Zinsu, Sagbo, go and plan some other things. I am too much for you."

Zinsu said, "Fear nothing. You'll sleep here."

They told him to go to sleep in a room near theirs. The boy had the animals come. "Among you," he said, "who can be my watchman?" Six hyenas said they would serve him. That night the twins came to kill the child. But the hyenas drove them away.

The next day, the boy said to the twins, "Why do you disturb me at night? Is that how you do here? I could not sleep at all. I, I like to sleep at night." He said, "And you who run about all night, you slept well?" On the third day, he had the animals come again, and he asked them, "Who will be my watchman?"

Panther said, "I will." At night the twins came back. The panther drove them away. The child told the panther not to kill them, so he saved their lives. The panther said, "All right, I'll only annoy them."

The next day he asked the twins again, "Who is coming tonight? You are not men, you are women."

The day came. The twins said, "All right. We'll put you in a mortar." They put him in.

He told them, "All right. Put me in." He himself went in. Now the twins began to pound him in the mortar. They pounded him, and put him on the fire to cook him. The following day, at midday, the water that had been on the fire since the day before was colder than that in the hand. They burned almost three bundles of wood.

Their old father said, "You don't know how to cook." He said, "You haven't yet been able to cook the child? You don't know how to build a fire. Go find wood. A big² man would know how to cook."

The twins went to the bush for wood. When they had walked six kilometers, the child in the pot awakened. He got out and killed their father. He took off their father's skin and he covered himself with it. He took his hair, everything, and he changed himself into an old man. When the children came back, he had already cooked their father. He now scolded them, "You don't know

anything. Here's the child all cooked." He said, "Bring me flour
and I'll make red dumplings." They ate. The old man [that is, the
child] said, "I am the oldest here, I'm going to eat the head."
They finished eating. He said, "Now you go to sleep. I am not
going to sleep yet."

Zinsu said, "That child was tough. One cannot finish eating
him, and go to sleep right after." He said he was tired, he would
wait. Now, the old man was there. He said nothing. They said,
"Father, are you going to sleep?"

He said, "No, Zinsu told the truth. One shouldn't eat, and then
go to sleep right after." They sat about for an hour, and then they
went to sleep.

After an hour, he said, "My children, what shall I do for you?
Shall I thank you? What would you like? And this is why I say
this to you. I myself, Djegbingbin-djegbinta, I am here. I came to
see you, and you killed your father for me. And you even went
so far as to give me his head to honor me. You did this to show
your true friendship. In your heart you will know that there are
things stronger than twins. Don't you believe it?"

Zinsu was too foolish.[3] He said, "Father, what are you saying?"
But Sagbo was already trembling. Zinsu said again, "What are you
telling us?"

"I want you to know that you really killed your father. Here
is his skin." He dropped the skin and escaped. They saw he was
the boy. They began to run after him. They ran after him, but
when they were almost within reach of him, he said, "Let your
hands and feet stick to the ground." The hands and feet stuck.
Four kilometers from there, he said, "Stand up. You are good for
nothing."

They ran after him again, and had almost caught him near a
river. The child changed into a stone. The twins were there. They
did not see him. The child could not cross the river. Zinsu said,
"If the child had been there, I'd throw this at him so." He picked
up the stone and threw it across the river.

The boy stood up on the other side and said, "Goodbye, my
friends. Here I am."

The twins began to quarrel. One said, "It's your fault."

The other said, "It's your fault."
The *tohosu* who belong to the rivers, are stronger than twins.

[1] Story-teller: "He meant someone more powerful, more terrible."
[2] *I.e.*, an experienced, important man.
[3] *I.e.*, very foolish.

63

Flight up the tree: Why hunters do not tell what they see in the forest

There were twins, one was called Zinsu and the other Sagbo. Sagbo was a worker of magic. He hunted all the time. Now he found Yehwe. When a *yehwe* ate, his nostrils, ears, all parts of his body ate separately. At once Zinsu composed a song. He played on his flute, and sang,

> *Zinsu, brother of Zinsa,*
> *I see he rolls,*
> *I have fixed a year.*[1]

When he sang this, Azizā drove him away. Zinsu changed himself into sand.

Now, one day Zinsu took his gun and went to hunt. His medicine was kept in his out-house. If there was danger, the medicine turned the color of blood. Before going to hunt, he said to his mother, "Buy three balls of *acasa*." Now he had three dogs, and he said, "If you find blood in the medicine, you must put the *acasa* in it and call the dogs, and let them eat. When they have eaten, they will go in search of me."

When Zinsu was in the forest, he again came on the Yehwe. A *yehwe* was again eating. Zinsu said to Yehwe, "Do you eat like this?" Yehwe drove him away, and Zinsu climbed a tree. He had seven small calabashes in which he had magic powder. The Yehwe sang and chopped at the tree.

> *The calf of the leg cuts the tree,*
> *The nose cuts the tree.*[2]

As he sang, Zinsu broke one calabash filled with powder, and the tree, which was about to fall, swelled in size, and became large again. Again the *yehwe* began to sing, and once more the tree was about to fall, when Zinsu broke the second calabash and the tree swelled, and grew large again.

Now there was a pregnant *yehwe*. She sat with her legs spread out. While the other *yehwe* were striking at the tree, the pregnant one said to them, "Leave Zinsu alone; let him be."

Now Zinsu's mother went to the out-house and found that the medicine had turned to blood. So she put three balls of *acasa* into the medicine, and called the dogs to eat. At once the dogs ran to look for Zinsu. They jumped at the *yehwe*, and ate them all except the pregnant one. For Zinsu told them not to touch the pregnant *yehwe* who had spoken for him. Good. The *yehwe* who was pregnant gave birth to many *yehwe*.

If a man is not brave, he does not hunt. But Zinsu was very brave. If one goes to hunt, one must not tell all that one sees. That is why hunters do not tell what they see in the forest.

[1] Record No. 109-1. The reference is to Zinsu's magic power; that is, if he said a person would die within a year, this always happened.

[2] Record No. 109-2.

64

Twins seek riches: Why fathers must be obeyed [1]

There was a man who had twins, Hesa and Hesu. One day these two boys went to see their father and asked him what they must do to become rich. "To be rich, you must obey and do everything that is asked of you."

Hesa, the older, said, "I, I can never do this." But Hesu, the younger, obeyed his father and did all that his father asked of him. After a time, the father fell ill. Now, Hesa did not come any more to say good-day, for he was always away. If he saw anyone, he asked whether his father was dead. Hesu was there all the time, and when his father asked him for something, he gave it to him.

One day, while the father was still ill, Hesu was given the key that opened some chests in his father's room. His father told him to open the first one and he saw it contained gold. The second was full of silver. The third was full of palm kernels. He told Hesu that when he became rich, he should not show too much pride, and that if he wished to eat [2] this gold and wealth, he must put it in a canoe and hide it under water.

His house was near a river, so during the night, about midnight, Hesu took the three chests, put them in a canoe, and paddled with his father until they reached a place where there was a dead Loko tree near the river. When they reached this place, the father put a large stone in each chest, so that it would stay at the bottom, and told Hesu to put the chests in the water.

When they returned, the father summoned all his children, but Hesa did not come. He kept on going about the village, asking if his father was dead or not. Since he did not come, the father sent one of his children to find him.

Hesa said, "Why do you call me? Is my father dead?" But since the child told him that he must come without fail, he went to his father.

> *Hesa, if you are to be a good man,*
> *You will have to learn things;*
> *Hesa, brother of Hesu,*
> *If you are to be good,*
> *You will have to learn much.* [3]

When the father had given the keys to the chests to Hesu, he had told him not to say anything to anyone. Now that all his children were gathered, he gave the key of the house to Hesa, who, because he was the oldest, had waited for him to die. And he had a small house built nearby for Hesu, and told him that after his death he should live there with his family. He also told him, "You must wait for four years after my death before you take the money in the river."

After the father's death, Hesa took the key to the house and would not allow anyone to go in it. The younger brothers said nothing, but only wept. The money that Hesa found in the house he did not divide among the children of the dead man. He only gave them a little, and the rest he kept for himself.

At the end of the fourth year, Hesu told his brother that he was no longer going to stay in the father's house, but was going to his own.

Hesa said, "You can go."

So Hesu went to his own house, but he was very poor, for when they had divided the palm groves, they had only given Hesu a small portion.

After a time, Hesu got into a canoe at night, and brought the chests to his house. He began to sell palm oil and palm kernels. He never rested, but worked all the time. Little by little he began to employ workmen. And before long Hesu became rich.

Soon his brothers began to say that Hesu had taken all the inheritance of their father. They said they were going to kill him. When Hesu found out what they were saying, he hid all his money. To show that he was really poor, he would take only a little money at a time. He would buy forty francs' worth of goods and then sell this for a hundred francs. And everyone wondered why this man who had been rich had become poor.

Hesa went before the king to tell him that Hesu had taken their father's inheritance. But when Hesu bought for forty francs and sold for one hundred, he marked down everything in a book. So when the king told him to come before him, he brought the book. And when the king looked in the book and saw the account of what he bought and what he sold, he called all Hesu's brothers to see how hard he had worked. He told them to go and work as Hesu had been working.

That is why, if you want to become rich, you must obey and serve your father.

[1] This tale has motifs strongly reminiscent of the "Good Child and the Bad" type, but differs enough so that it might be misleading to title it with that particular catch-phrase.

[2] *I.e.*, to consume, to use, and, in a secondary sense, to own.

[3] Record No. 114-3.

65

Flight up the tree: Why the Abiku are worshipped in the bush

There was once a pair of twins whose father and mother had died. They had no one to give them food, so every day they themselves went to hunt. The diviner told them never to cut their hair when they went hunting. Since they respected the diviner, they did as he told them.

One day, as they went to hunt, the rain drenched them. Night fell. They shivered with cold; they had nothing to eat. They fell asleep hungry. The next day, when they awoke, they saw smoke rising to the sky far away in the bush. Zinsu said to his brother Sagbo that a man must be near that fire. They went to find the fire, but though they walked through the entire bush, they could not find where the smoke was coming from.

After some time, however, Zinsu succeeded in reaching the place. There he saw a thirty-horned giant called Yehwe Zogbano. And as Zinsu approached the place, he saw the head, the feet, the arms, the ears, the nose, and the eyes separate from each other. Each organ ate by itself. The moment they saw Zinsu, however, they reunited, and made a man. The man asked Zinsu what he wanted. He said he had come to find the fire. The man said, "All right, take the fire." Zinsu took it, and went away.

Now when Zinsu left for the hunt, he had put a small flute in his hair. So as he left, he took out his flute and began to sing,

> Zinse,[1] my eyes have seen a strange thing:
> The head which carries loads,
> Does it eat by itself?
> The hand that works,
> Does it eat by itself?
> The feet that walk,
> Do they eat by themselves?
> Zinsu's brother Sagbo,
> My eyes have seen a strange thing.[2]

When the Yehwe Zogbanu heard this, he ran to Zinsu and asked
him who was whistling. Zinsu said he did not know, and the giant
ran everywhere without finding the whistler. When the giant returned to his place, Zinsu extinguished the fire which he had gone
to find, and came back to the place where the giant was. He saw
what he had seen before. This time the giant asked him if he had
seen anything, but he said, "No," and took the fire. On the way
he played his flute again, and again when the giant asked him who
was whistling, he said he did not know. He returned a third time
and everything happened once more as before.

When Zinsu came back to his brother, he told him what had
happened. Zinse said, "Very well. We will go and see the diviner
about it when we get home." But when they got home, Zinsu said
it was not necessary to go to a diviner, because there was nothing
evil in the Yehwe Zogbanu.

While they were there, a very, very, very beautiful girl came
to their village. All the men wanted to marry her. But she refused
all her suitors. One day, she said to Dada Segbo that she wanted
to marry the best hunter in his country. He asked her, "How will
you know him?" She said she would hold a calabash with a single
pea in it on her head, and the one who shot at the calabash
and pierced the pea in it would become her husband.

Dada Segbo called together all the hunters of his country and
told them the news. As each hunter brought a closed calabash in
which was a pea, the beautiful woman would put it on her head.
All the hunters, except Zinsu, shot without succeeding in piercing
the pea. But when Zinsu, who had not even cared to shoot, shot
his gun, he split the pea in two without breaking the calabash.

At once the woman ran to him, embraced him, and said he was
her husband.

> If you hear the voice of Zinsu trembling,
> Sagbo, you must know what has happened to me;
> The hyena of Adja, who carried off the body of Hwegbo,
> Fell asleep under a tree and was killed.[3]

Dada Segbo told Zinsu to take his wife home, where Zinsu kept
his forty-one dogs. But when he slept, the wife changed herself
into a giant and tried to swallow him. The barking of the dogs

stopped her. When Zinsu awakened and asked her what this was, she said the dogs were keeping her from falling asleep.

It was like this until Zinsu went hunting. He traveled for eight days through the forest but found nothing. One day he sat down under a tall, slender, beautiful tree which pleased him very much. Zinsu said to himself, "I am very unhappy in my own house. If this tree could change into a woman for me, I would become happy. I would not sleep any more with that creature who lives with me."

When he said this, the tree spoke and answered him, "I would like to come to you. But I am afraid that when I am with you, you will tell me sometimes I am just a tree from the bush." But Zinsu said he would not do this, and the tree said to him, "Close your eyes." And when he opened them, before him stood a beautiful girl. He said he would call her Djeluba.

Now Djeluba was very jealous. And she did not cook for Zinsu. One day, when Zinsu came from the hunt and asked her for something to eat, she had nothing to give him. So he went to the house of his first wife to eat. When he finished, his first wife asked him where he got his second wife. Because Zinsu was angry with Djeluba, he said, "Don't tell anyone, but she is only an ordinary tree from the bush." ·

When he said this he left, and the next day he went hunting. After a while the wives began to quarrel, and the first wife said, "Get out of here. You are an ordinary tree from the bush." When she heard this, the other ran straight to the bush where Zinsu had found her, and changed back into a tree.

And when he returned home and asked for his wife, his mother told him that the first wife had called her some name, and she had run away to the bush. After this the first wife left him, too, and went to the bush where her relatives were waiting for her. They had looked for Zinsu everywhere.

One day Zinsu went hunting. He hunted without finding anything. So he went to his mother's family, and they gave him a drum to play, which they told him never to play in the forest. On his way home, while passing a great forest, he saw a man, who told Zinsu that if he played his drum, his wife, who was very beautiful, would dance. Zinsu began to play the drum, singing,

My mother gave me a drum
Asi ko do,[4]
My grandmother gave me a drum
Asi ko do.
They told me not to play it,
But I play a new song on it,
Kege kege ke
Kugu kugu ku.[5]

But the sound of the drum brought all the Yehwe Zogbanu to this place. When he saw them, Zinsu climbed a tree. They chopped down the tree. Zinsu changed into a partridge, and flew home.

When he got there, he told his adventure to all his family.[6] It was at night. Now, his mother's hut in the compound was not far away from that of Zinsu, so she overheard Zinsu tell his wife how the *yehwe* had tried to kill him. His wife asked him what he did to escape. He told her he had changed into a partridge. The woman asked him what he would have done if one of them had caught the partridge? He said he would have changed into an ant.

Then the woman asked, "Suppose they tried to crush the ant?"

He said he would have become a leaf. What if they cut the leaf? He would change into a small river. But if they drank up the water in the river? He would change into sand. If they removed the sand?

Zinsu began to answer, but his mother [possibly father's sister] cried out, "You gossip too much! To a woman whose relatives one does not know, one never tells [all] the truth." So he kept quiet.

In Zinsu's hair were seven magic gourds, which he always kept with him. One fine morning, his wife asked him to come with her to the bush to find leaves to make *acasa* balls. Now behind Zinsu's compound was some medicine,[7] which gave warning when he was in danger. So before leaving, Zinsu told his mother that she should look at the medicine from time to time. If she should see the water troubled and spilling over on the ground, red like blood, she should take this water, mix it with corn flour and give that to his dogs to eat, telling them to go find their master.

Then Zinsu led his wife into the bush. She pointed to a large tree and told him those were the leaves she wanted. When Zinsu was up the tree, the woman cried out,

> *Zode, Zogban, Mito, mi Yehwe,*
> *Let your thirty horns appear before me.*

As she called, more than a hundred monsters appeared and began to cut down the tree which Zinsu had climbed. At this moment, the water in the medicine became troubled, but no one was there to give the dogs food, for Zinsu's mother was not at home. But Zinsu's best friend,[8] Kofle Djombi Alahwekpe, was hunting in the same bush. When Zinsu, from on high, saw his friend, he began to sing, so that he would know his danger, and come to his rescue.

> *Kofle Djombi Alahwekpe,*
> *Come quickly;*
> *Djombi Alahwe,*
> *It is a lion who is attacking me,*
> *It is a leopard, attacking me,*
> *It is war;*
> *My life will be ended*
> *Djombi Alahwe.*[9]

The friend came, and with his gun saved Zinsu. When Zinsu climbed down from the tree, his wife said the monsters came without her knowledge. So Zinsu was obliged to take his wife back home with him.

Several days later, very early in the morning, while Zinsu was away, Djombi Alahwe came to Zinsu's compound. When he asked for Zinsu, the wife told him that Zinsu had been dead for two days.

Djombi Alahwe returned to his home and, without saying anything to anyone, hanged himself in the bush. They were very great friends, and when they swore friendship, they promised that one would not survive the other.

When Zinsu returned, his wife told him that in three days she would want him to go back again to the bush with her to hunt for *acasa* leaves. Since there was always danger in that bush, Zinsu went to the compound of his friend to consult with him. But Djombi Alahwe's wife told Zinsu that her husband had not returned since he left two days ago. She said he was looking for Zinsu's body, and that Zinsu's wife had told Djombi Alahwe that Zinsu had died while hunting.

So Zinsu went to the bush to hunt for Djombi Alahwe. He had not gone far before he saw the body of his friend hanging from a tree. He took the corpse, brought it to his own compound quietly, without saying anything to anyone. But Zinsu's wife knew that Djombi Alahwe was dead, and she was happy. Now she would be able to undo Zinsu. For his friend Djombi Alahwe would not be there to come to his rescue.

One night, Zinsu told his wife that he was going to hunt. His wife said, "All right. I will go with you to look for leaves." In the bush, the woman showed Zinsu a great baobab tree, saying that she wanted the leaves of this tree. When Zinsu had climbed the tree, the woman told him to give her the fruit. Zinsu threw down the fruit, but instead of catching them in her hands, they struck her on the head. And at once she began to cry out as before.

Immediately the monsters appeared and began to cut down the tree. When there were no more than a few strokes needed to fell the tree, Zinsu broke one of the calabashes in his hair, and the tree became whole again. This continued until all the seven *glo* which Zinsu had were exhausted.

Sagbo was waiting for his brother's return. When he did not return, he entered the forest with Dosu to hunt for their brother. They sang,

Quickly, na-na-na-na-na-na-na,
Someone is lost,
Here Zinsu passed,
But Sagbo can see nothing more.
We are here.
The yehwe *are coming from their home in the forest.*
The twins have been separated;

If it were our mother, she who bore twins, she would cry out.
Zinsu, catch them, Zinsu, catch them!
Quickly, na-na-na-na-na-na-na,
Sagbo has not found Zinsu,
And we are troubled.[10]

They spent two days in the bush looking for Zinsu, but they did not find him.

Now the seven *glo* were exhausted, and the tree came down. But as it fell, Zinsu changed into an ant. The monsters tried to crush the ant, so Zinsu changed himself into a small mound of earth. When the monsters tried to destroy that, Zinsu changed into a partridge. But one of the *yehwe* changed into an eagle, so as to hunt him down. So he changed into a river, while the *yehwe* changed into animals and came to drink up all the water. Then Zinsu changed himself into sand, while the monsters changed into people to take up the sand. Finally Zinsu changed back into a human being, and began to run. The *yehwe* ran after him, and it was a race between them.

After Zinsu had run some distance in the bush, and the monsters were almost at his heels, he came to a tree which cried, "Wahadjiye! Wahadjiye!" Zinsu immediately climbed the tree, for it was the one which had changed into a woman and had been his wife. It had returned to the bush in anger to change back into a tree after the quarrel with Zinsu's other wife.

When the Yehwe tried to cut down this tree, it did not allow itself to be cut. For with each stroke, the tree closed up; with each stroke, the tree closed up. The tree was angry at the woman who had sent her away from her husband.

All this time Zinsu's old mother was sleeping. But towards midday she awakened. She said, "I am going to look at my son's medicine." When she looked at it, the medicine was so troubled, it spread like blood all over the ground. Without losing a moment, she got some corn flour, and fed it to Zinsu's forty-one dogs, calling to them to go and look for their master. Seven of these forty-one dogs are chiefs. The first, who was strongest, was called Loka, the second, Loke, the third, Loki, the fourth, Wesi, the fifth, Wesa, the sixth, Gbwlo, the seventh, Gbwloke. The dogs divided themselves into seven groups to find their master. Zinsu from on high in the tree which protected him, sang,

O my dog named Loka, my dog named Loka
If Loka comes, the yehwe will not rest in their forest-home, e-e-e!
And Zinsu will not end his days in the forest.[11]

     *   *   *

If Gbwloke Gbwlosa, my dog, is not dead.
Zinsu will not die in the forest,
Gbwloke, Gbwloke, cry out my name everywhere;
Zinsu is not dead,
But it is finished.[12]

When he had sung this, he called the seven names of his dogs. After a moment, he saw Loka, and when he saw the dog, he called out, ". . . One . . ." This is to say his forty-one dogs had been given magic charms, and the language he used was magic language. When Loka heard the song, he became enraged, but Zinsu told him to go to one side with his group [of dogs]. Next Loke arrived with his company. Zinsu said to him, ". . . Two . . ." This was the language of the magic he had given Loke to eat. Next Loki came with his group, and Zinsu said, ". . . Three . . ." Then Wesi came, and Zinsu called out, ". . . Four . . ." Wesa arrived, and Zinsu cried out to him and his dogs, ". . . Five . . ." When they heard this, they became enraged, but all waited. Now Gbwlo came up, and Zinsu said, ". . . Six . . ." Finally Gbwloke arrived, and was told ". . . Seven . . ." Then Zinsu sang his song again,

O my dog named Loka, my dog named Loka
If Loka comes, the yehwe will not rest in their forest-home, e-e-e!
And Zinsu will not end his days in the forest.

     *   *   *

If Gbwloke Gbwlosa, my dog is not dead.
Zinsu will not die in the forest,
Gbwloke, Gbwloke, cry out my name everywhere;
Zinsu is not dead,
But it is finished.

When all the forty-one dogs were in a rage, he ordered them to attack the monsters. When the *yehwe* struck at the dogs, they changed into stones, but when the dogs caught the monsters, they tore them in two, and swallowed them.

When the dogs had eaten up all the *yehwe*, Zinsu came down from the tree and he asked the tree if she wanted to come again with him to his house. The tree told him she now had four children. They were the small trees near the big tree. The tree was called Adiku, and when Zinsu arrived home at his compound, he found that he now had four children. The tree said she would not go with him to his house, but if he wanted to send food by his children, they could come and place it before her.

When Zinsu got home, he went to Dada Segbo and told him all that had happened. And Dada Segbo ordered that dogs should be the inseparable friends of man, and that one should not eat their flesh like that of pigs and goats, because they rendered service to men.

Then Zinsu now went to the place where he had left the body of his friend, Kofle Djombi Alahwekpe. He began to sing,

> *O my friend, the time has come*
> *When I must bury you,*
> *When I must bury you.*
> *Shall I bury you in the house?*
> *Shall I bury you at the bank of a river?*
> *Shall I bury you in the bush?*
> *In what country must you be buried?*
> *Death has troubled you,*
> *And I must find a place to bury you.*[13]

Then the dead body answered,

> *Zinsu-e I call o!*
> *Bury me under the* adikun *tree*
> *Zinsu-e, bury me under the* adikun *tree,*
> *Sagbo, brother of Zinsu, bury me under the* adikun *tree,*
> *Life never ends its troubling the living*
> *Gbwlo gbwlo zeye,*[14] *bury me under the* adikun *tree.*[15]

So Zinsu carried the dead body there, and buried it. And as he buried his friend, he said that in life there were only two things which were dear to him. The first was Djombi Alahwekpe and the second his dogs. As he had lost the first, he was also going to sacrifice the second. To show his friendship for the dead, he called his dogs, and buried them with his friend.

Kofle Djombi Alahwekpe became god of the hunt. He does not take the name of Agè, but of Djombi. The story also says that the name of this tree, which is sacred to Adikun, was later changed to Abiku. And this is why the ceremonies for the Abiku are held in the bush, and why their right name should be Adikun.

[1] The twin of Zinsu.
[2] Record No. 116-1.
[3] Record No. 116-2. The last two lines are an old proverb which preaches prudence when in a difficult situation.
[4] The sound of the drum.
[5] Record No. 116-3.
[6] The disguised wife had apparently returned in the meantime.
[7] *I.e.,* magic.
[8] Each Dahomean has a best friend. For the institutionalized friendship of this culture, cf. *Dahomey*, I, pp. 239-242.
[9] Record No. 116-4.
[10] Record No. 117-1.
[11] This is repeated, naming each of the next six dogs in place of Loka. Record No. 117-2.
[12] *I.e.,* the adventure.
[13] Record No. 118-1.
[14] Lit., "little monkey of the forest"—another name for twins.
[15] Record No. 118-2.

66

Flight up the tree: Why there are *yehwe*

Once there were twins. They worked till mid-day in the field, but they had no fire to cook their food. They were very hungry. Sagbo looked for fire everywhere, but he found nothing. He climbed up a tall tree to see where smoke could be seen. Forty kilometers from there, through the bush, he saw smoke. He took to the road. When he had walked half his way, he lost his road and came back without having found anything. Again he climbed the tree, and again he saw the smoke.

This time Zinsu started. He came to the place where the fire was, and there under a baobab tree he saw the Azizā. He saw the head separate from the body, and stomach. The ears lay on the earth, and so did the nose, the two eyes, the two limbs, and the two hands. Each part of his body was busy eating.

When Zinsu saw this, he was afraid to ask for fire. He was frightened too much.

First the mouth asked him, "Where do you come from?" Zinsu said, "I came to find fire."

The mouth asked him, "What did you see?" He said, "I saw nothing."

Zinsu sang,

> *Sagbo, I am here;*
> *I have returned;*
> *I have seen a head about to eat,*
> *I have seen hands about to eat,*
> *I have seen feet about to eat.*
> *Well, well like this.*[1]

Zinsu joined his brother Sagbo again, and they went home. At night, when it came time to eat, one of the *yehwe* changed into a young girl, and came to the village where the twins lived. On her head she carried a closed calabash in which was one kernel of corn, and she told the king to make a mound of earth, for her to stand on. Anyone who wanted to marry her must break the calabash and split the grain of corn in two.

All the men shot at the calabash, but no one could hit it. At last it was Zinsu's turn. He took his gun, and broke the calabash and the grain inside in two. So the girl embraced him, and took him for her husband.

One day she asked Zinsu to get wood for her. Zinsu said to his mother he had medicine. "When you find blood, here is some meal to put inside for my dogs." [2]

They left together for the bush and went on and on. Zinsu

said, "Here's some wood," but the girl led him farther into the bush.

He showed her all the trees of the forest, but she kept saying, "No. That's not what I am looking for." The woman brought Zinsu to the place where he had seen the Yehwe eating, and she led him to a tree. Then she told him to climb this tree, for the wood she wanted was there.

When he had climbed up, the girl began to shout, "All the *yehwe* with thirty horns who are about, come quickly!" Many *yehwe* began to come out of the earth. They began to cut down the tree.

> *All feet cut the tree,*
> *Hard, hard!*
> *All teeth cut the tree,*
> *Hard, hard!*
> *All heads cut the tree,*
> *Hard, hard!* [3]

Now, Zinsu had two magic gourds with him. As the *yehwe* cut away at the baobab, and the tree was ready to fall, Zinsu broke the first one. At once the tree closed up and stood erect again. They began to chop at the tree again. Now, Zinsu's mother was not yet awake.

Now, there was a bird called *alè*. The bird flew to where the mother was sleeping and called out, "The *yehwe* are going to kill your son!" Again and again the bird sang out the same words, but the mother did not hear it. At last the bird flew down to where the old woman was sleeping.

In the bush, the baobab is ready to fall.

Now, the bird sang into the old woman's ear, and she awoke. She went to look at the medicine and found it had turned to blood. She put the meal inside, and called the dogs to come and eat. At once the dogs ran to the bush in search of their master. The bird went with them to show them the way.

When the dogs arrived, the tree had almost fallen. Zinsu called out to his dogs to eat up all the *yehwe*. The dogs also wanted to devour a pregnant *yehwe*, but Zinsu called out to them to stop, for when the *yehwe* began to cut down the tree, this woman had asked them not to cut it down. So the dogs let her go.

That is why there are always *azizā* and *yehwe*. If the dogs had killed the pregnant woman that day, there would today be no *yehwe*. It is from that woman that all the *yehwe* we have today are descended.

[1] Record No. 135–2.
[2] A developmental motif, well known to the audience, and given in the preceding version of this tale, is here omitted.
[3] Record No. 135–3.

67
Market of the dead: Why those who die do not return to life

Dosi [1] had twins. She looked after them well, but one died. It was the boy who died. The girl remained. Now Dosi, who has this daughter, never goes out of her house. The little girl does everything for her. She goes to market; she does all. When the girl is in the market and sees cooked meat, she buys it.

Now, one day in this market she saw a hunter with smoked meat for sale. Though the hunter had much meat, the girl said, "I'll buy all of it." So he sold her all his meat at a very good price.

When the girl bought all this meat, a woman said to her, "Take this meat to that other market. They have no meat there at all. You can sell it dear." So the girl went there, and she sold the meat at a high price.

At night she came home and told her mother how she found the meat in the market, and how she sold it. She earned much money. Her mother said, "Good. Next market-day, do the same thing."

The hunter always came to this market. Three times the girl bought meat from him. For the third time she bought the meat and sold it dear in the other market. But when she came home with the money for her mother, her mother was dead.

By this time the girl had some money. So she called together many people and said, "I am my mother's only child. I have no brothers, I have no sisters. I must, therefore, see to it that my mother has a proper burial." So she bought much to drink, and called together many people for the funeral.

When all the funeral rites for her mother were finished, she again began to trade in the market. She went back to the same market, and saw the same hunter who came there with his smoked meat. The girl said to him, "Now I am alone at home. I had only my mother, and now she is dead."

Egbwlo moyo. The hunter said, "The next time you come to market, I will go home with you." The next market day, the hunter had all his belongings with him. He said, "I am ready. Take me to your house." When the hunter found himself alone with the girl, he made her his wife. And when he hunted, he brought the meat home to her, and she sold it in the market dear.

One day the girl went to the market of Ku.[2] There she saw a woman who looked like her dead grandmother. The old woman knew her at once, but when the girl greeted her, the old woman vanished. When she went home, she told her husband about the woman she saw in the market. "I am sure she was my grandmother. When I greeted her, she vanished."

Good. When she said this her husband said, "That market must be the market of the dead. But go again and make sure."

When market day came around again,[3] the girl went there once more. This time she saw her brother Zinsu, who had died years ago. But when she came near to him to say "Good day," he vanished. The girl started for home to tell the hunter about this. On the way she saw her dead mother. Now, she still had a piece of meat in her calabash. So when she saw her mother, she called to her to give her the food. But her mother did not answer her, and she, too, vanished.

This time the girl said nothing at home, but went back again the next market day. When she got there, she looked for the three she had seen—her grandmother, her brother, and her mother. When she found them, she said to her grandmother, "I knew you at once. Why did you vanish? It frightened me." She gave some of her meat to the grandmother; and to her mother and brother she gave some as well.

They told her, "When you go home, you must not tell anyone that you saw us here, or that we talked together." So the girl said nothing to anyone.

Now this girl had a friend, her best friend. So she went to her, and told her how she had seen her grandmother, her mother, and her brother in the market. Her friend said to her, "You are lying. No one sees the dead. I'll go to the market with you."

But the girl refused to take her. She said, "No one must go with me." Good. The friend pleaded with her until she agreed to take her. In the market, she saw only Zinsu, her brother. The others were not there.

Zinsu said, "We forbade you to bring anyone here. You brought your friend. Very well. She stays here. You can go." But the friend did not want to stay. She followed the girl down the road. So Zinsu cut off her head.

Then the girl said to her brother, "It is my fault that my friend had her head cut off. I brought her here to this market. Since you killed her, kill me, too." So she, too, died.

Now in those days, when anyone died, if you whistled a whistle, you found out where they were. When the friend did not come home, her family and the husband of the girl whistled and whistled. But they heard nothing. That is how it happens that, to this day, when one is once dead, he is never seen again. Before that, if you whistled, you saw them. It is the girl who did that by going to the market of the dead.

---

[1] This name, given to a female twin, indicates that the mother herself belonged to this category.

[2] Death; *i.e.*, she went to the market of the dead.

[3] Dahomean markets operate on a four-day cycle.

68

Orphaned twins visit dead mother: Market of the
dead: Mistreatment avenged

There were two co-wives. The first wife gave birth to twins, but
herself died in childbirth. So the second wife took care of them.
The elder twin was called Hwese, the other Hwevi. When the
stepmother pounded grain, she took away the fine flour on top,
and gave them what was not fit to eat.

One day the stepmother gave them each a small gourd, and
told them to go for water. They went to the stream, but on the
way back Hwese slipped and broke his gourd. The other said, "If
we go home now, she will beat Hwese, and let me go free. So
I'll break mine, too." He threw it down and broke it.

When the stepmother saw what had happened, she got a whip
and whipped them.

Hwevi said, "I am going to buy a bead." Hwese said, "Yes,
let us each buy a bead for Ku. We will go there and visit the one
who watches Death's door. Perhaps he will let us see our mother."

> The grave is deep,
> Deep, deep,
> Stepmother [1] bought some gourds,
> But Hwese broke his gourd,
> And Hwevi broke his, too.
> When we told our stepmother,
> She flogged us with a whip,
> So Hwese bought a bead,
> And Hwevi bought one, too.

Good. So they went to see the guardian of Death's door. He
asked them, "What do you want?"

Hwesi said, "Yesterday, when we went to get water, my brother
Hwese broke his gourd. So I broke mine, too. Our stepmother
beat us, and did not give us anything to eat all day. So we have
come to beg you to let us enter here. We want to see our mother."

When the guardian heard this, he opened the door.

> *The grave is deep,*
> *Deep, deep.*
> *Stepmother bought some gourds,*
> *But Hwese broke his gourd,*
> *And Hwevi broke his, too.*
> *When we told our stepmother,*
> *She flogged us with a whip,*
> *So Hwese bought a bead,*
> *And Hwevi bought one, too.*
> *We gave these to the door's guardian*
> *And the door opened.*

Inside there were two markets, the market of the living, and the market of the dead.

Good. Everybody asked them, "Where do you come from, where do you come from?" The living asked this, and the dead asked it, too. The children said, "This is what happened. Yesterday we broke the little gourds our stepmother gave us. She beat us and gave us nothing to eat. We begged the man who watches at the door to let us come in to see our mother, so she might buy two other gourds for us."

Good. Then their mother came and bought some *acasa* in the market of the living for them. Then she turned her back, and gave money to a living man to buy two gourds in the market of the living for them, and gave these to her children. Then she herself went to the market of the dead, and bought palm nuts to send to her husband's other wife. For she knew that the other liked these nuts very much. Now, once the woman ate the palm nuts, she would surely die.

Good. Then the mother said to the children, "All right. Go home now, and tell your stepmother good-day. Thank her for looking after you so well."

> *The grave is deep,*
> *Deep, deep.*
> *Stepmother bought some gourds,*

But Hwese broke his gourd,
And Hwevi broke his, too.
When we told our stepmother,
She flogged us with a whip,
So Hwese bought a bead,
And Hwevi bought one, too.
We gave these to the door's guardian
And the door opened.
Our mother, hearing our story,
Bought us two gourds,
For our stepmother.

The stepmother looked for the two boys. She looked for them everywhere, but she could not find out where they had gone. When they came back, she asked them, "Where were you?"

They said, "We went to see our mother."

But their stepmother scolded them. She said, "No, you lie. Nobody can visit the dead."

Good. The children gave her the palm nuts. They said, "Here, our mother sent these to you."

The other woman laughed at them. "So you found a dead one to send me palm nuts?"

But when the stepmother ate these palm nuts, she died.

The grave is deep,
Deep, deep.
Stepmother bought some gourds,
But Hwese broke his gourd,
And Hwevi broke his, too.
When we told our stepmother,
She flogged us with a whip,
So Hwese bought a bead,
And Hwevi bought one, too.
We gave these to the door's guardian
And the door opened.
Our mother, hearing our story,
Bought us two gourds,
For our stepmother.

At home our stepmother wanted to buy life,
But we gave her the fruit
In abundance, abundance.[2]

In Dahomey, when a person dies, the family goes to a diviner and he makes the dead talk so that you hear his voice.[3] So when they called the dead stepmother she said, "Tell all the other women that my death came from the orphans. Tell them also that Mawu says that when there are several wives, and one dies and leaves children, the others must care for the children of the dead woman."

This is why, if a man has two wives, and one dies leaving a child, you give that child to the second wife, and the second wife must look after the dead woman's child better than after her own children. And this is why one never mistreats orphans. For once you mistreat them, you die. You die the same day. You are not even sick. I know that myself. I am an orphan. My father never lets me go out alone at night. Whenever I ask him for something, he gives it to me.

[1] Lit., "second of our mother."
[2] Record No. 147–1.
[3] This interpolation is explanatory of the transition to the moralizing end.

69

The good child and the bad

There was a girl whose mother died, and whose father gave her to his second wife to look after. One day the girl broke a water jar that belonged to this woman. Now, there was a stream some forty kilometers from where they lived. The girl was sent to fetch water from that stream and she knew she would surely be eaten by the animals. For there where the stream was were wild animals who ate nothing but human beings.

This woman had a son who was almost a man. She forced the orphan to go for the water. She thought, "When the girl goes, she will not come back. She will be eaten by the animals, and all the possessions of the father will go to my own son."

The girl went on her way until she came upon two stones fighting. The stream from which she was to get water was called Azili. The girl asked of the stones, "Which is the road to the Azili?" The stones said to her, "One does not go there for water. It is forbidden. You cannot go there." The girl begged them, and she said, "My mother is dead. My stepmother mistreats me. I broke her water jar, and she sent me to get water from the Azili."

The stones asked her, "Did you see anything just now?"

The girl said, "No, I saw nothing."

They said, "All right, come between us, and we will keep you from falling." She placed her feet between the two stones, and they immediately began to roll against them. They crushed the girl's feet until blood ran. The stones asked, "Do you see anything? Are you hurt?"

The girl said, "No, I see nothing. I am not hurt."

So the two stones showed her the road and she continued on her way. Then she met an old woman who took off her head, and began to delouse it. The girl greeted the old woman.

The old woman asked her, "Where do you come from?"

The girl said, "My stepmother sent me to get water from the Azili."

The old woman asked her, "Did you see anything?" The girl said, "No."

The old woman said, "Go. There is your road."

She walked on, until she came to a crossroad. At this crossroad sat a woman whose body was covered with running sores. The girl asked her the way to the Azili. The woman said to her, "Come and clean my wounds with your tongue. When you have done this, I will show you the way." She did this and the woman showed her the road.

She went on her way until she came upon two buffalos who were attacking each other. They said to the girl to come between them and they would attack her. The girl came between them, and then the buffalos showed her the way. They said, "Here is the stream. The *tohosu* are there."

The girl came to the banks of the stream and saw the *tohosu*.

One of them was bathing. He said to the girl, "Dry my back." Now the back of the Tohosu was covered with knives, broken bottles, thorns and the claws of wildcats. The girl began to dry his back with her hand. When she did this, her hands were badly cut. The *tohosu* asked her, "Is there anything the matter with you?"

The girl said, "Nothing."

He gave her some water to wash her hands and when she washed them, her wounds disappeared. The *tohosu* said to her, "You are not leaving today. You are to sleep here." At the house, he gave her a grain of millet and he told her to grind it. This one grain gave much flour. He had her cook it, and everybody at the house ate some of it.

Then she went to sleep. They put her with the animals, and at night the goats urinated on the girl. The next day the *tohosu* asked her, "What happened to you during the night?"

The girl said, "I slept. I know nothing."

The *tohosu* said to her to go to the stream, and he said, "Now there are little gourds there, and among those little gourds, the ones that say 'Gather me' you must not gather. But from among those that are silent, take seven. Then go and get water from the river." Then they told her, "When you are on your way, if you come on something that obstructs your path, break a little gourd. After five kilometers break the second."

She walked on until she came to a closed road. She broke a little gourd, and at once the road opened. She broke the second and she saw many people appear. These at once began to cultivate fields. She broke the third, and more people appeared who began to put up houses. She broke the fourth, and many women came, and animals. She broke the fifth and she saw large animals, like cattle and horses. When she broke the sixth, she came into possession of much money and gold. With the seventh, she saw appear many-storied houses everywhere, and hammocks and everything needed for a king. The water is no longer on her head. The jar was taken away by another. She is carried away by two hammock-bearers. Forty men accompany her to her stepmother, to bring the water for which she was sent.

Good. The stepmother greeted the girl, and was greatly aston-

ished to see her arrive in this fashion, accompanied by so many
men. She gave her water to drink and spoke to her nicely. The
girl refused the water. She said, "Why are you angry with me, my
girl?"

The girl said, "No, I do not live here any longer. I have my
house. I live now on the road to Azili."

The mother said, "All right."

After having given the water to the stepmother, the girl went
back to her own house. When the girl went away, the mother was
very angry and she began to beat her own child. She said to him,
"Here, now an orphan became rich. You, too, must go for this
water so that you, too, may become rich."

The boy did not want to go. To force him, she went and brought
some water, and placed it in front of him, so that he would be
sure to break the jar and spill the water when he got up. He was
asleep, and he did not know that the water was there. He rose
and as he did so, the jar broke and the water was spilled. The next
day the mother was very angry. She said, "You must go for the
water today. If you do not go, I will give you nothing to eat. You
will go hungry till you go."

The boy went. On the road he came on two stones fighting
together, just as had happened to the girl. All that the girl came
across on the road, the boy too encountered.

The two stones asked, "What do you see?"

As the boy was not discreet, he told them, "I saw two stones
fighting together." Now, he said what should not have been
spoken. "Ah, I never saw that before. But it's terrible all the same
for two stones to be fighting."

He continued on his way. He went along and saw an old woman
take off her head, and busy herself delousing it.

The old woman asked him, "Where do you come from?"

As the boy was tired, not having eaten all day, he said, "I am
on my way to look for water, the water from the Azili."

The old woman asked him, "Did you see something?"

The boy said, "I am not blind. I saw an old head put down, and
lice searched in it." Now, he should not have said that.

The old woman said to him, "So you are like that. All right."
She showed him the road.

He next came on two buffalos fighting. The two said, "Place yourself between us."

The boy asked, "But what for? I am not strong enough to fight against two buffalos."

They said to him, "All right, go ahead. Here is your road."

The boy said, "I must pass on. I did not ask you the way. I know my way."

He went on and met a girl who had the plague. The boy asked her about the road to the Azili. The girl called to him to come and clean her wounds first, but the boy exclaimed, "What do you take me for? I am not a fool. I am a stranger, and you ask me to clean your wounds."

The girl said to him, "All right, go on your way. Here is your road. You will see the chief of the Azili." [1] The boy reached the stream. There was the *tohosu* bathing. The *tohosu* asked him, "What do you see?"

The boy said, "It is terrible. You have knives, needles, broken glass, and thorns in your back. And now you ask me to dry your back, so that I should cut my hands. I did not come here to cut my hands."

The *tohosu* said, "All right. You will see what you are looking for." He showed him the road to the house. He said, "All right, you will leave tomorrow morning."

The boy said in anger, "If you do not want to give the water, let me go back. Why should I stay here overnight?" He gave him a grain of corn. The boy said, "What am I to do with one grain of corn?"

The *tohosu* said, "You are to pound it."

The boy said, "At my house, one gives this to chickens."

The *tohosu* said to him, "All right."

At night, he put him in a room with the goats. The boy protested, "Do you want me to sleep here? The goats defecated everywhere. Where am I going to lie down?" The boy went to sleep. During the night he began to cry out that the goats were urinating on him. He said to the *tohosu*, "It seems that you never gave birth to a child."

The *tohosu* said, "Why do you say this?"

The boy said, "Because you told me to sleep with the goats, and you yourself took a clean place. I could not sleep. And I believe that you all slept well."

The *tohosu* said to him, "You are a bad boy. You are good for nothing. You will see the reward of a bad boy before you leave. Misfortune always has friends."

The next morning, he was sent to see the little gourds. Now, one should never gather the little gourds that ask to be gathered. One should take those that are silent. Now, the *tohosu* asked him to take seven of those that spoke. The boy went to take them. The *tohosu* also told him to go and get the water. After six kilometers he broke a little gourd. When he broke it, the road closed and the boy could not pass. He wandered about in the bush like a blind man and did not know where to go. The boy began to cry and cry. He broke the second little gourd. The road opened a little. He was on the road. After ten kilometers he broke the third one. When he broke that, he found himself facing a river. At the stream he broke the fourth, and when he broke this he found his road. He went on again. He broke the fifth, the road closed again. And there many animals appeared. Panther, Lion, Elephant. There, there was a hunter in a tree. The panther asked the boy to tell him what he had been about. The hunter was watching them. The boy was seized by the animals, before he could even break the seventh gourd.

And that is why one should not mistreat and annoy orphans. Now the hunter who saw the animals devour the boy, went home to the boy's mother and told her his fate.

[1] NARRATOR: "That is, the *tohosu*."

70

Orphan outwits trickster: Why orphans are not mistreated

It was a time of famine when there was nothing to eat. But there was a tree full of turtledove nests. There were nails on the tree so that people might climb it. Yo went there. He climbed the tree, and as he climbed he began to gather up the small birds. Good.

Now there were two of them who climbed up, Orphan and Yo. Those that Orphan took he put in his pocket, but those Yo took he ate at once. But because Orphan put his birds in his pocket, Yo was very angry. He climbed down, and as he climbed he removed each nail as he stepped on it, leaving Orphan up the tree. He took the nails out one by one, until all were taken out. When Orphan had plenty of birds and wanted to climb down, he could not, because there were no nails.

There was a hunter, and there was a stream there where the goats went to drink. Hunter saw a he-goat there and he aimed at him. The animal ran until he fell down dead under the tree. When Nochiovi saw the animal, he called out, "Mr. Hunter, here is the animal. It fell down right here." Hunter had not heard well. He looked about him. Nochiovi said again, "Come here. Your animal lies here." Hunter came and saw Nochiovi. Nochiovi was very hungry. Good. Nochiovi said to him, "Since you have no nails, put sticks in where the nails should be, and I'll come down and show you where the animal lies."

Now Nochiovi came down, and he went and showed the hunter where the animal was. Hunter took the animal. Hunter said, "Now, I will divide the animal between us." Orphan refused. Nochiovi did not want the meat, he only wanted the intestines. Hunter gave him all the intestines. And now Nochiovi left for home.

Yo came to him to see him, and asked him, "My friend, where did you find this?" He complimented him, "My friend, how cunning you are! Where did you get the intestines?"

Nochiovi said, "The place where I found them is where we went to find the little birds. Beside the stream there is much meat. If you want intestines, you have only to leave early in the morning and stay till exactly mid-day, and you will have them. There is much meat there at mid-day. Buffalo comes there at mid-day. Go there and wait till he defecates, and then you pull them out."

As Buffalo was about to defecate, Yo put in his hand to pull out the intestines. The animal closed. As he closed, he began to run, and Yo was behind him. He began to cry, "Mr. Buffalo, let me go! It is not my fault. It is Nochiovi who told me to take out your intestines. Go look for him. I do not know him!" As the animal would not listen and continued to race, he cut Yo's arm. Yo was left with one arm.

That is why one does not vex a child who has lost his mother.

71

Slandering co-wives: Death befriends victim: Public contest: Abiku avenged

There was a woman, and when she bore a child, the child died. One day the woman went to the river to get water. Now, this woman was not yet pregnant again, but there was the spirit of a girl who wanted to enter her womb. That girl was called Abiku.[1]

A hunter who went to hunt was there near the river and he saw a girl standing nearby. This girl said to herself, "I am going to enter this woman's womb." The hunter heard this. There was a baobab tree nearby. This girl wore a bracelet, but she took it off and buried it under the baobab tree. She said to the baobab, "I am giving you my bracelet, because I am going into the womb of this woman. When I leave her, I'll come back for it."

This is how it is with Abiku. When a child is born, and later comes back to the baobab tree and finds the bracelet, she dies. But if she cannot find the bracelet, then she lives.

After the hunter saw the girl hide the bracelet, he went and took it away. The girl entered the womb of the woman who was dipping up water at the lagoon. This woman had just finished menstruating and was washing her clothes at the river bank. The hunter approached her and spoke to her. "Mother-in-law," he called her.

The woman said, "Ah, you tease me. Let me be. Have you ever heard that I bore a living child?" The woman went home, and after this she did not menstruate. The next month came, and the next month. She knew she was pregnant again. And when her time came, she gave birth to a girl.

The hunter came to see her. He said, "I told you you would bear a girl for me. I want you to give her to me to marry when she grows up." He gave the mother the bracelet, and told her to put it on the child, so that the child should not die.

The little girl is there, and she is beginning to walk. Now, there were other little girls her age who came to play with her. When they played, they took off their bracelets, and put them on again, took them off, and put them back on. But the bracelet of the Abiku would not come off.

One of the little girls said, "All right. You can't take yours off yourself, so I'll take it off for you. But when you grow up, you are to marry my father." Good. One day the parents of the little girl were away, so the playmate said, "All right. Your bracelet doesn't come off. So I'll cut off your hand to make it come off." The little girl cut off the Abiku's hand.

When the mother came home, she said to the little girl, "Come help me with the load on my head."

The girl said, "I cannot get up. I have fever." There was blood everywhere.

Now, the hunter was the greatest hunter of all. He had become king. The father of the Abiku came to tell the king what his daughter's playmate had done. The king said to let her go.

Little by little the girl grew up, with her hand missing, until she was a young woman. Now, the king had four daughters. As this girl was ready to marry, he brought her home with him. The girl never took out her stump of an arm. She always hid it under her cloth.

The king's wives were asked to thresh millet to separate the grain from the chaff. They fixed a certain day to do this work. To take out the grain, it must first be threshed. So the other women said to the king, "Ah, that woman there, she has always a cloth about her neck. What is the matter with her?"

The king had a wall built in such a way that no one could see the girl when she bathed. There she undressed. One day, the king's other wives hid and watched her, and saw that the girl had one hand missing. The other girls went to tell Dada Segbo[2] that the girl was without a hand. Dada Segbo fixed several days when the women were to go and thresh millet in the field. Now the place

where this girl lived had three doors and three dogs. Each door
had a dog.

Now, there were only four days left before threshing time. The
other women came to Dada Segbo and said, "You fixed the day
for threshing the millet. What will the other do?" The new wife
heard this. Dada Segbo thought long about what he could do with
this new wife.

Only three days remained before going to the field. The new
wife cooked a stew of corn meal and palm oil. She went out and
took the stew with her. At the first door she gave a little of the
stew to the dog. The dog said nothing. At the second door she
did the same thing. At the third door, the same. When she had fed
the dogs, she left the house. Good. She thought, "There are only
three days left. They will bring together Mingā, Meu, everybody.
They will thresh millet, and I have no hand." The girl walked and
walked and walked. She said, "Ah, there are so many women in
the house. When they see my hand they will laugh at me. It is
better that I go and find Death, that he may eat me." [3]

Good. So she followed the road and entered the grove belonging to Death. Death sat on a stool. He was drowsing. Monkeys were
there working at a forge. Ku awoke and asked her, "What do you
want here?"

The girl said, "All my life the thing I have disliked most is
shame. One of my hands is cut off, and my husband says I must
come and thresh millet." She said, "That is why I have come. That
is why I followed the road which led to your house."

Death said, "I, I do not eat people. I send sickness to go and fetch
them for me." Good. Ku said, "I do not want you to be shamed
before the others. I will give you my anus and you push your
stump in there." When she took out her hand, she saw it come
back with gold and everything. He told her to put in the second
hand. The second also came out full of everything, like the first.
He told her, "Put your hands in again, and ask for anything you
wish." The woman did this, and when she took out her hands,
there were precious stones in her hands, and gold, and everything.

Ku said, "Is that what you want?"

The woman said, "Yes."

Death said, "All right, then go."

But when the woman had taken two steps, she found herself in front of her husband's compound. Now, Na had a servant. When she opened the three doors and came in, the slave asked her, "You are back?"

The woman said, "Yes," and she showed her both hands. The slave was very happy. No one knew the woman had been away. Her husband, too, had been thinking very hard.

Now, there is a woman there and she is a gossip. She is the first wife of Dada Segbo. It is she who first saw that the other had no hand, and it is she who told the others. So this woman who was such a gossip said to Dada Segbo, "If, on the day of threshing the millet, that new wife threshes with both hands, take a large knife and kill me, and take my head and put it at the door of this woman, and the other part of me where the woman bathes."

So when the day came, they swept the yard. Everybody is there. Dada Segbo is seated on his stool and he is thinking. His new wife does not have two hands. Will she be able to beat the millet with the others? The other wives said, "All right, Dada Segbo. We are ready. But where is your new wife?" Now, the new wife has not yet come. The others began to work, and they kept saying to the king, "But where is your new wife? Order her to come and work."

Meantime the other wife bathed, powdered, and put on fine cloths. She arranged the hand which had been cut as she had always carried it. She put it inside her cloth. Only the other arm was outside.

The calabash filled with gold she gave to two of her slaves to watch, and she ordered them to cover it well. The slaves followed her with it.

They gave her the stick with which to beat the millet. Everybody is there. As the girl takes it up with one hand, the others murmured, "With one hand? What can you beat with one hand?" Good. As the others were annoying her too much, the woman Na dropped her stick and fixed the cloth which had come loose about her breasts. But she did this with her other hand, and the arm was covered with gold. Everybody was astonished. Dada Segbo was very happy. He rose and came over to his wife. He was so pleased that he himself took up a stick and began to thresh the millet. So glad was he.

When the girl saw Dada Segbo himself thresh the millet, she sang,

> *At our house,*
> *A bracelet alone*
> *Will thresh the millet until the grain is free.*
> *In my country*
> *A bracelet alone*
> *Will thresh the millet until the grain is free.*[4]

Now, since the other woman had said, "If the woman can beat the millet, you can do this or that to me," Dada Segbo called Mingā and all the people to him. He asked, "If someone wants to do evil, and asks for evil, can we refuse to give it?" He said to Mingā, "This one asked me to cut off her head. This one asked me to kill her."

Mingā answered, "She who asked to be killed, she who asked to have her head cut off, since it was she herself who asked it, it must be done."

When he said that, they killed the woman.

That is why today when there is a king and the king says, "Do not do this," one must not do it.

[1] A child destined to die in infancy.
[2] It would seem that Dada Segbo is the hunter.
[3] *I.e.*, kill me.
[4] Record No. 145-3 and 4. This is a "song of allusion" against the co-wives of Na.

72

Identity revealed: Outwitting the Abiku

There was a woman who lived in Golo. She always gave birth to Abiku. But if you bear such children, they never live long. She gave birth to a daughter. This daughter was very sick. Her father went to divine and the diviner said he should find a black goat.

So her mother did not wash any more. She was always with the child. She was even sadder than the father. Now, when the father left to buy the goat, the mother left the child alone for a little while to go and do some washing. While she was washing, a woman came by selling mustard greens. Now, the mother was behind the house washing.

As soon as her mother went out, the little one, who was so seriously ill, who couldn't lift her head, went and stood in the doorway. She was no longer ill. When the woman, who came with the mustard, saw the girl, she said, "Old woman, you are here? We haven't seen you for some time."

So the woman, who was washing, stopped pouring out the water and listened to her daughter's voice.

She said, "Now I am here waiting for a goat. My father went to buy it. When my father comes with the goat, I will take the sacrifice, and you will see me back there." [1]

The woman said, "All right. I will go on ahead."

When the woman went away, the girl changed back into an infant who was seriously ill. Her mother came back and saw the child asleep. The mother said nothing. When she saw her husband with the goat, she said, "Let the goat go. I now know my daughter's name. She is called 'Old Woman.' " So the girl's mother told the father that the daughter was waiting for the goat in order to leave, for those in the forest had fixed her day of return from the human world. The mother said, "Don't make the ceremony."

He said, "All right. I'm not going to make the ceremony." And to the child he said, "If you die, I will bury you and I will go back to my field." [2]

So the child began to cry. The child had not taken her mother's breast for some days. But as it cried, and it was ignored, it cried all day. At night her mother gave her the breast and she took it. She became a real child.

If the woman who sold the mustard had not come that day, the little girl would have died. It is because she had called the girl's name that she did not die. If they had not known to call her name, she could not have lived.

---

[1] *I.e.*, to the forest, the home of the Abiku spirits.

[2] Feigned indifference and neglect are used to pique the spirit, who impersonates a child, to turn into a normal, human child. Derisive names are often given children born after several births of short-lived infants.

73
How the Tohosu cult was established [1]

As far back as Akaba's reign the little people, the *tohosu*, were known. Akaba neglected to do anything to placate them because he was afraid. He knew how difficult it would be to appease them, for even in his time, it was known that the *tohosu* were ancestors who wanted a cult started for them.

After him came Agadja, and he, too, was afraid. Once when he went out with his soldiers to fight an enemy, the little people came and killed all the soldiers. But still he was afraid to do anything. When he died, Tegbesu came to the throne, and he, too, delayed and delayed, doing nothing for the little people.

One day a bat appeared with a burning leaf under its wing, and set all Abomey on fire. Tegbesu left Abomey and established the capital in Kana, to save himself from the spirits of these little people. They came to Kana to torment him. He said, "They are here, too. I might as well go back to Abomey." [2]

One year about a million of these little creatures, all with beards, and whips in their hands, came to Abomey and drove out all the people. They wanted to catch the king, but he left his hammock, and, hiding, escaped on foot. Abomey was deserted. The king stayed away three months at Hlanwa. From there he went to Zado, fifty kilometers from Abomey. [3] There was hunger. People planted maize, and they reaped stones.

In Abomey, a Prince by the name of Homenuvo, who suffered from guinea worm, was left in his house. One day, the little people who were more than two million, came and broke down the door of his house and caught him, and brought him to their chief. This chief, and the other chiefs had their camp where now stands the temple of Zumadunu. This chief had six eyes, two in his forehead, two where human eyes are, and two in the chin. They brought Homenuvo and tied him.

Zumadunu said that he, son of Akaba, would destroy all Abomey, if a cult for himself and other ancestors like himself were not started.

Zumadunu left all the songs you [4] heard at the Mawu-Lisa ceremony. It was he who told how to make the ceremony for the ancestors, and how to call the *dokpwegan,* and what the *dokpwegan*
was to do. All in all, he left seven hundred sixty-six songs.[5]

He told how to kill the goats; he told how to bury people. He
talked of Hevioso, and of Mawu, and of Sagbata, the Earth. He
also told where he wished his house built, and he predicted everything that has since happened. "Eleven *tohosu* will come to the
family," he had said.

Homenuvo's illness was cured. He went to see Tegbesu, and
Tegbesu believed him. He came to the place Zumadunu had designated, and there heard the rattles, and he heard the singing of a
chorus of singers that was heard more than a hundred kilometers
away.

Zumadunu gave Tegbesu seven rattles, and they still exist. He
instructed what each was for. Then he gave Tegbesu eleven times
three cowries.

Tegbesu's mother was an Adja woman, and she was a priestess
for Mawu, Agè, and Lisa. Tegbesu put his mother in charge of
these *vodun,* building the temples for Lisa, Mawu, and Agè, just
in front of his mother's house, and the temple for Zumadunu in
back of his mother's house.

The army came again. This time they said each dead person
must have someone to represent him, and this was done.

[1] Cf. *Dahomey,* I, pp. 229 ff., for discussion of the *tohosu.*
[2] The narrator laughed as he finished this comment.
[3] This is a generous estimate of the distance.
[4] *I.e.,* the ethnographers.
[5] In story telling, the Dahomeans use numbers with an exuberant disregard for
accuracy.

74

The Tohosu appear on the battlefield and win a bloodless victory

In Glele's time, the king was about to open war on the Meko people. This was a large Nago kingdom. Zumadunu was asked to prosper the expedition. That night he appeared to Glele in his sleep, and said not to go to war against this people this year, but to wait for the next.

The following year Glele again saw Zumadunu in his sleep. Zumadunu said the time had come. Zumadunu also said that Glele had no need to arm the warriors, for the "little people" would fight for them.

Glele did not have sufficient confidence in the dream. He asked himself, "How is it possible to fight a war without arms?" So he called the diviners and they said Zumadunu was right.

When the first shot was fired, a million "little people" appeared on the battlefield. To each Dahomean soldier they brought six Nago captives. They said, "Go to Glele and deliver these slaves to him."

The battle lasted only one day—this was the entire war. On his return to Abomey, Glele enlarged the house of Zumadunu in gratitude, and to the *vodun* and the *vodun* priests, he gave many handsome gifts of cloths, and money, and sacrificial animals.

V

Yo stories

Yo stories

YO, a glutton, with supernatural
  endowment; protagonist of the
  humorous tale.
DADA SEGBO, also called Dada Se and
  Asegbo, an early king
Old women, fishermen, smiths,
  farmers
GIRL, symbol of Hunger
TREE, which changes into a woman
LOMO, the Lizard
DOG
AKLASU, the Vulture
TOKÈ, the Bat
LEOPARD
CHILD

HEVIOSO, the god of Thunder
SOSI and SOSU, children of Hevioso
KU, Death
NOCHIOVI, Orphan
HYENA
BOATMAN
PIG
RABBIT
ANTELOPE
MOLE
GOAT
SHEEP
Yo's mother-in-law
HWENO, Yo's wife

75
Profitable amends: A wife for one cowry

When people first came into the world, Dada Segbo had no wife. He called all the people together. He took out a cowry. He told his people to take that cowry and find a wife for him.

The people said, "What does the king mean? Can one get a wife with only one cowry? It is impossible." Everybody said, "No, we cannot do it." They said, "A man can never find a wife for one cowry."

Now Yo came, and he said he could get a girl for one cowry. Dada Segbo said, "All right." He gave him the cowry.

Yo sent to buy flint and bamboo tinder. Then he went and found dry straw. With these he set the straw on fire. The grasshoppers began to jump. Yo had a sack beside him, and he collected them inside the sack.

So now he went on his way with this sack of grasshoppers, until he came to the house of an old woman. Now, this woman was drying beans in front of her house, but the chickens came and ate them.

Yo said, "Haven't you corn to give your chickens?" Now, this was the time of famine. There was nothing to eat. Yo said, "All right. I have grasshoppers here. If I throw these to your chickens, they will let your beans alone."

The woman said, "Yes." So he gave the grasshoppers to the chickens, and when the chickens finished eating them, he took the beans.

The old woman cried out, "But, Yo, why are you taking away my beans?"

He said, "Didn't you tell me to throw my grasshoppers to your chickens? I bought them with a cowry."

> The grasshoppers came from the straw;
> The money for the straw came from Dada Segbo.

So Yo went on. Now he came to a river where fishermen were fishing. He saw that the people from the village of Tofi were try-

ing to fish, but that the fish had nothing to eat. So he said, "If
you like, I will throw my beans in the river. The fish will come to
eat, and you will have a good catch."

The people said, "True, true . . . ," and they told him to throw
in the beans. So the fishermen caught many, many fish.

Yo picked out the largest fish for himself. The fishermen cried
out after him, "Yo, why are you taking away our fish?"

Yo said, "Did you forget that you took my beans?"

> *The beans came from the old woman,*
> *The old woman took my grasshoppers;*
> *The grasshoppers came from the straw;*
> *The money for the straw came from Dada Segbo.*

"I do nothing without getting my reward."

Yo continued on his way. He came to a place where blacksmiths
were working. There were many hoes on the ground. When he
saw the blacksmiths, they were tired.

Yo said, "Why are you tired, blacksmiths? Have you had nothing to eat? You cannot even lift your hammers. If you like, I will
leave you my fish, so you can eat."

The blacksmiths said, "True, true. . . ."

They took the fish and ate. When they had finished eating the
fish, Yo took hoes and knives [1] and filled up his sack with them.

The blacksmiths cried out, "Where are you going, Yo? Where
are you going with our hoes and knives?"

But Yo said to the blacksmiths, "Didn't you know, before you
took my fish?"

> *The fish came from the fishermen,*
> *The fishermen took my beans;*
> *The beans came from an old woman,*
> *The old woman took my grasshoppers;*
> *The grasshoppers came from the straw,*
> *The straw came from the money I got from Dada Segbo.*

Then Yo came to a field where men were working. Now,
these men had neither knives nor hoes. They worked with their

hands. He asked them, "Don't you want knives and hoes to work with?"

The men said, "Yes." He gave them the tools, and when the men had the knives and hoes they worked fast.

Yo stood and watched them. Now the men had with them a dish of beans and cassava flour called *abla*. Yo went and gathered it all up.

They cried out, "Yo, Yo, what are you doing with our food?"

Yo said, "Don't you know?"

> *The hoes and knives came from the blacksmiths,*
> *The blacksmiths took my fish;*
> *The fish came from the river,*
> *The fishermen took my beans;*
> *The beans came from an old woman,*
> *The old woman took my grasshoppers;*
> *The grasshoppers came from the straw,*
> *The straw took my cowry;*
> *The cowry came from Dada Segbo,*

"I do nothing without getting my reward."

So again he went on his way. He walked for a long time, until he came to a house beside the road. In this house there was a dead girl. All the people were wailing. They had nothing to eat.

Yo went inside and said, "I see you have nothing to eat. I have *abla* with me. Divide it among you and drink water with it. Then you will be refreshed, and you will find a way to bury your dead."

So they made Yo sit down next to the dead. Yo was a stranger. At night, while the others were digging the grave, he took the body.

The people ran after him and cried, "Yo, Yo, why are you taking the body?"

Yo answered, "Don't you know?"

> *Abla came from the farmers,*
> *The farmers took my hoes;*
> *The hoes came from the blacksmiths,*
> *The blacksmiths ate my fish;*

The fish came from the river,
The fishermen took my beans;
The beans came from an old woman,
The old woman took my grasshoppers;
The grasshoppers came from the straw;
The straw came from one cowry;
And the cowry came from Dada Segbo.

So he left with the dead body. That day Yo traveled from early morning till night. He went to see the king of the country, and said to him that Dada Segbo had told him to go and look for a wife for him. And now, as he had found her, he wanted a place to spend the night with this girl who belonged to Dada Segbo.

Now, he put the dead body in the house which they gave him, and himself went inside with it. At cockcrow he left the body there and went away. When he returned at six o'clock, he came back to the house and began to wail.

"The people here killed Dada Segbo's wife! They killed here Dada Segbo's wife! What shall I do? What am I going to tell Dada Segbo?"

The head of the family now called together all the people. The people said, "Yo is lying. This woman was dead when she came here. No one saw her. No one went near her. Yo is deceiving us."

Yo said, "I dare not take this dead body to Dada Segbo. I must have another girl, as fine looking as she."

So all the old people came together and talked this over. They said, "We cannot anger Dada Segbo. Yo says he brought this woman here alive. Now she is dead. She died in our country.[2] We must find another woman." And since the king of that country had a fine young daughter, they said he must give that one to Yo for Dada Segbo.

Yo began to wail again. "What shall I do? What will I tell Dada Segbo?"

But they gave him the girl, and he went on his way. They came to a village called Bodenu-Mawu-Bode. From there Yo sent a message to Dada Segbo that with one cowry he found a wife for him.

The girl began to sing,

Hunger comes from afar,
Hunger has followed the road here;
The intestines come from afar
The intestines have followed the road here.[3]

Now Dada Segbo had had many, many dishes cooked. He sent many men to meet Yo on the way. So the girl and Yo had much food.

When the food came, the girl said, "Swallow it fast." And when the girl said this, the food disappeared. Yo was astonished.

So the girl and Yo arrived at a place called Todogba. Yo sent another message to Dada Segbo asking for food. Dada Segbo sent him much food, more than before. There were six hundred and forty calabashes of food. There was water. There were bottles of strong drink. When the girl saw the food coming, she began to sing the same song again. And when the men and women came near with all the food, the girl called out, "Swallow fast." The food vanished.

Yo said to Dada Segbo's people, "This woman astonishes me. She never eats with her hand, but when she says 'Swallow fast!' the food disappears." He sent a message to Dada Segbo saying he wanted forty guns, and powder, and eight hundred calabashes of food.

When the girl saw this new food approaching, she began to sing the same song. The people went back to tell Dada Segbo that the girl was too much for them. The moment she saw food come, she had but to exclaim, "Swallow fast!" and everything vanished.

But Yo sent still another message to Dada Segbo, that he wanted food. This time he asked for three thousand calabashes. This food came. Now, the girl did the same thing, and when she had made the food disappear, she began to eat the men. The moment she saw a man approaching, she called out "Swallow fast!" and the man was not to be seen.

A man hurried to tell Dada Segbo that the girl was too evil. She had finished the three thousand calabashes, and now was doing away with the men. Dada Segbo called all his elders. They said, "It is terrible to have a beautiful woman like this, who eats people. It is very strange."

They brought the girl to Dada Segbo. All the people of the country were gathered before the king's door to see her. But the moment this girl fixed a man with her eyes and said, "Swallow fast!" the man disappeared.

Dada Segbo asked the Mingã, "What shall we do now? Here is a girl who eats much, and is not satisfied unless she eats men, too. What shall we do?"

The Prime Minister said, "This woman knows only to kill. Let us kill her. Yo has no family, so he is no man to send to find a wife."

In former times one needed only to have a cowry to marry, but with that one cowry a man often got a woman who was a sorceress. That is why today, in order to marry, a man must have much money.

¹ From the context, it is the large "bush-knives," variously termed cutlasses or machetes, that are meant.
² That is, "in our village."
³ Record No. 145-2.

76

Profitable amends: A wife for one cowry

Yo asked Dada Segbo to give him a cowry that he might go forth to find a woman to marry. With this cowry he bought a bamboo, and with the bamboo he lit a fire. He put the fire down in a certain bush, and when the bush caught fire, he caught some small insects. Then he went away.

He went now to an old woman who had put her corn in the sun to dry. This woman was being troubled by chickens. She held a stick in her hand, and she chased them. Yo said to her, "Poor woman, if you wish, I will give my insects to your chickens. When they eat them, they will leave your corn alone."

The good woman said, "All right." When the good woman said "Yes," Yo gave the insects to the chickens, and the chickens ate and went away.

Then Yo was ready to leave, and he took a portion of the corn and escaped.

The old woman called after Yo, she said, "Do not take, do not take!"

When Yo left that place, he went to the river. The river had small fish, and the water was ruffled by the fish. Yo said, "River, if you like, I will give my corn to your fish and you will have peace."

The River said, "If you please." So Yo gave his corn to the river. But when he left, he took the fish. The River called out, "Do not go, do not go, do not go!" But he went.

He continued on his way until he saw a blacksmith. The blacksmith was very hungry. Yo said to him, "Blacksmith, if you like, I will give you my fish to eat, so that you will have the strength to forge the axe you are making."

The blacksmith said, "Yes." He gave him the fish, and when he went away, he took an axe. The blacksmith shouted, "Do not take it away, do not take it away!"

When he left there, he met a man who had climbed a palm tree. He was cutting the palm kernels with his teeth. He had blood all over his mouth. Yo cried to him, "Young man, you have bled too much. If you like, I will throw you my axe, and with that you will get your fruit."

The man said, "Gladly," and took the axe, and gathered his fruit. But when the fruit of the palm tree fell, Yo took it and went away. The other cried out, "Do not take, do not take, do not take!"

After this, Yo met a woman on the way who was selling corn bread. Now, in order to eat this, one must have a great deal of oil. But the woman could not find even one drop of oil. Yo said to her, "Good woman, if you like, I will give you these palm kernels. You can make oil, and use it to prepare your bread.

The woman said, "Gladly." So Yo gave her the fruit. The woman put the oil on the bread, but Yo took all and ran away. The woman cried, "Do not carry away, do not carry away!"

When he left, he came on a large *dopkwe* [1] cultivating a field. He said, clapping his hands, "I salute the Dokpwegan. I salute the Dokpwegan."

All the members replied, "Yo, come to work, come to work."

Yo replied, "You are hungry. I must first give you something to eat." He gave them corn bread and they ate. Since he had to show respect for the *dokpwe*, he took a hoe and went to work. When he finished two rows, he ran away with the hoe.

Everybody cried, "Yo, do not go, do not go, do not go away!"

After this he saw a grave-digger with a corpse beside him. He was using his hands to dig the grave. Yo said, "Grave-digger, if you like, I will give you my hoe, and you can dig the grave with it."

The grave-digger said, "With pleasure." He took the hoe and dug the grave. The moment he finished it, Yo took the corpse and ran away with it. The grave-digger cried out, "Do not take it away, do not take it away!"

Yo met the owner of a large compound. He told him that on the way he saw a queen who was gravely ill, and that he had brought her here. They all hastened to prepare something to eat for her. Yo put the body inside a dark house. They brought food. Yo had them bring it in. He ate all of it himself.

The people outside asked Yo, "Was the sick one able to eat a little?"

Yo said, "Yes, she ate, but she hasn't had enough." They brought other dishes. Yo ate it all in the dark, and then he said that the sick one was full. He called the compound head. He said, "You see, the sick one is sure to get well. I am going out, and I will leave her in your care. But be very careful. She must not die in your care, for she is a queen. You must not touch her."

The head of the compound obeyed. He remained there. Yo went out and spent half a day away. When he returned, he said to the compound head, "Did you give the sick woman anything to eat?"

The compound head said, "No."

Yo began to wail: "Oh, you killed the wife of Asegbo!" Yo took off the cloth that covered the corpse, and called the compound head to come and see whether or not the woman was dead.

Then he asked the head of the compound what he could tell Asegbo, now that his wife was dead. The compound head said he did not know, but Yo must advise him. Yo said, "If I go before Asegbo now, I will be killed."

The other said, "I will go and hang myself, and die."

But Yo said it was not necessary. All he need do is to give a handsome girl to replace the dead one. At once the head of the compound brought six girls, and asked Yo to choose the one he liked best. Yo chose the most beautiful, and left with her.

When he arrived at his house, he gave the girl to Asegbo, telling him that he had bought her for one cowry. He told Asegbo the history of his journey. He told all, and Asegbo forbade anyone in his country to complain against Yo.[2]

---

[1] A cooperative work-group.
[2] At the end of this tale, the narrator volunteered the information: "The story tells that it is after this that Yo became the great hero of humorous tales."

77
Tie me: Elephant no scapegoat

Dada Segbo wanted to buy an animal so he could perform a ceremony for the dead. They looked everywhere for an animal for him, but could not find one. Now Yo came to Dada Segbo and said he heard he was looking for something he could not find. Dada Segbo said, "I want to make a ceremony for the dead, and I need an animal." Yo said, "All right. I'll find you an animal. It is nothing."

They gave him a carrying basket for animals and a rope, and Yo left for the bush. First he sought out Elephant and said to him, "Let us amuse ourselves. You tie me in the carrying basket, and when I tell you that the rope hurts, you untie me. And when I tie you, and you tell me the rope hurts, I, too, will untie you."

The first one to be tied was Yo. Yo called out, "The rope hurts now." The elephant untied him. When Yo was free, he put the elephant inside the basket and bound him tight, tight.

The elephant cried, "The rope hurts me."

Yo said, "But I promised Dada Segbo that I would find him an animal. Now, since I've found you, I'll take you to Dada Segbo." Yo brought the elephant to Dada Segbo and said, "I brought you something to eat." Then he went away.

When the time came to kill the elephant, the family head said, "Since the animal is so big, we will kill it without freeing it."

There was an old woman there who said, "To kill an animal for the dead, you must untie it first." For when an animal is killed for the dead, the cord is taken off. The family is all assembled. Then the cord is cut into small, small pieces, and each member of the family crosses his hands as though he were bound. The one who officiates goes from one to the other, and as he makes the gesture of cutting their cords, says, "Here I have cut the cords of the living and of the dead."

But when they untied the elephant, he escaped.

78

Tie me: How kings keep promises

Dada Segbo had a daughter. He said he wanted a very reliable man to marry his daughter.

Yo came to Dada Segbo and said, "I want to marry your daughter."

The king said, "Since you are the first one who has asked me for her, if you can catch a live hyena which I need to make a ceremony, you can marry my daughter."

When he said that, Yo said, "All right. If it is only that, I will marry your daughter."

He took a rope and left. Then he walked, and walked, and walked until he came on a hyena. Yo said, "Now let's play a game. I will bind you and unbind you. Then you bind me and unbind me."

So Yo tied up Hyena first, and when Hyena said, "The rope is hurting me," Yo unbound him. Then Hyena bound Yo.

Yo said, "The rope is hurting me." Good. Hyena unbound him.

Now it was the turn of Yo to tie Hyena. He bound him, saying, "The root in the bush which is not thick is foolish."

Now Hyena said, "What kind of a game is this, binding and unbinding, binding and unbinding?" Then Yo sang,

> *A tree which does not have a large root,*
> *Is not important in the forest;*
> *We amuse ourselves with a cord*
> *I, Yo, pull you,*
> *I will pull you to the house of Dada Segbo.*

Now, Yo again unbound Hyena, and Hyena bound and unbound Yo. The third time, Yo went and found a carrying basket. Yo said, "All right. Now we'll play the game this way. Each of us will lie down in this carrying basket, and we'll tie each other in it." So Yo let himself be tied first. When he said the cord was hurting him, Hyena unbound him.

Now Hyena went into the carrying basket, and for the third time Yo bound him. This time again Hyena called out, "The rope is hurting me."

Yo said, "Whether the rope hurts, I do not know."

Hyena cried out, "Untie me, Yo."

Yo said, "I am not the one who wants you. Come and ask Dada Segbo to untie you."

So Yo took Hyena to Dada Segbo. Dada Segbo was astonished to see Yo come with the living hyena. He sent word to all his people, to all his children to come. He said, "Here is the hyena I've been looking for for a long time to make my ceremony."

Everybody said, "Who found him? Where is the man who found him?"

Dada Segbo said, "Here is the young man who did it. He asks to marry my daughter."

Now, the day of the ceremony approached. Dada Segbo asked his people, "Shall we untie Hyena, or shall we leave him bound?" There were those who said it was necessary to free him before sacrificing him.

But an old woman said, "No, leave him bound."

They unbound him all the same, and the moment they loosened the cords, Hyena escaped.

So as Dada Segbo had promised Yo that after the ceremony he would have the daughter, he said, "I promised Yo my daughter. I will give her to him, because he brought a hyena. I cannot hold him for our losing Hyena later. It is we who unbound him." So Dada Segbo gave the girl to Yo, and gave him a place to live near his own house. So Yo lived there and became rich.

Whenever a king makes you a promise, and you do what he asks, if it is good or bad, he will keep his promise. So kings do.

79

Tree into woman: The king must not take the wife of a poor man

In earlier times, the animals and the trees used to change into women in order to marry. There were no mothers-in-law or fathers-in-law. This was in the time of Dada Segbo. Yo had no wife. One day when he went to look for firewood, he came on a tree with thorns. He asked the tree to change into a girl.

It said, "Yes. But if I change into a girl, are you going to throw it up to me later? Are you going to say, 'You are not a woman, you are only a tree'?"

Yo said, "I will never do this."

The tree said, "If I become a woman, what name will you give me?" He said, "I will call you Yawo."

The tree said, "Turn your back." When he turned around again, the tree was changed into a very beautiful girl. They went home together.

Dada Segbo saw Yo and his wife. He said, "The girl is very beautiful. Yo should not marry so fine a girl. He eats too much. The girl will only suffer with him."

So the king wanted to take the girl. Yo would not give her to him. Good. One day, Yo went to the field. While he was away, the king sent to find the girl. Good. Yo came home at night, and his wife was not there.

Yo asked his children, "Where is my wife?"

The children said, "The woman was led away by a man who carried the king's staff." [1]

Then Yo went to the king. He said to the king, "I would like to give a dance [2] before your door, in order to thank you. You did well. I want to thank you with my drum." He said, "I have only one wife. You have many wives. Your wives do not please you. And mine is the only one who pleases you."

The king said, "All right. Bring your drum."

Yo agreed to come in three days. Now Yo's wife was already with the king. She cooked for the king, slept in his room. She was no longer Yo's wife. The king asked the girl, "Who are you? Where are you from? Where is your village?" But the girl said nothing.

To all that he asked, she answered, "I come from Yo's house."

The day came. Yo collected all his friends. There were many of them who came to the king's door. They began to beat the drum. The girl was seated beside the king. The king himself danced first. His first wife danced next. And now it was the turn of the new wife.

As she began to dance, Yo sang in a loud voice, so she could hear, speaking her name.

> *O white, white egg,*
> *You cannot carry away the thorn tree;*
> *I, Yo, went to the bush to marry the thorn tree.*
> *The hands I put behind me,*[3]
> *And went to marry the thorn tree of the bush;*
> *Good! Stay as wife of Dada Segbo,*
> *Or change into a thorn tree!*
> *Change into a thorn tree!*
> *Change into a thorn tree!* [4]

The girl danced and danced. When she heard her name, her clothes fell off and she ran away from everyone. Everybody ran after her. Dada Segbo cried after them, "Catch her for me. Get her for me. Do not let her get away."

Yo had spoiled the magic. When the king's officer almost touched her, and tried to hold her, then instantly the woman changed into a thorn tree. So they went back home and told the people that the girl had changed into a tree.

The next day Dada Segbo called together all the people of his village, and said that a king must not take away the wife of a poor man.

Yo began to tell everybody that if a person wants to marry, he has only to go into the forest and address himself to the thorn tree. So the thorn tree became tired of this. Yo spoiled many things discovered by our forefathers. Nowadays when we want to marry, we cannot get a wife by going into the bush. Yo did that.

[1] In preconquest Dahomey, the king's messengers and other functionaries carried a carved wand of office.
[2] In native idiom, "I have a drum to play."
[3] This refers to the episode of turning the back during the tree's transformation.
[4] Record No. 133–1.

80

False friendship: The killing fire: Why Lizard does not talk

There were two animals, Lomo [1] and Yo. These two were friends. They always went about together. When anything happened Lomo always told Yo.

One day Yo said to Lomo, "Tomorrow we are going to have a good time." Lomo made a hole. Yo went to look for sticks. Now Yo said to Lomo, "Each of us will go into that hole. Now we will light the wood, and if one of us says '*Zole, zole*, the fire burns me, the fire burns me!' the other must put out the fire."

The first to go in was Lomo. Yo put the wood over him.

Good! Yo lit the fire. Now when the fire began to burn, Lomo called out, "*Zole, zole-o!*" But Yo did nothing, and the more Lomo called, the more wood Yo put on the fire.

Now, Lomo began to burrow underneath, and he came out through that hole. But Yo did not see him. From where he stood, he watched Yo adding and adding to the fire, believing that Lomo was already dead. When Yo finished with the fire, and there were only ashes on top, he looked inside to see whether Lomo was well cooked. But he saw nothing.

Lomo approached him, and said to him, "You are a fine friend! You wanted to kill me!"

Yo said, "I am sorry. I did not know what I was doing. I drank too much. When the fire was burning, I had dozed off and did not hear you cry out." He said, "Now we'll do something else to amuse ourselves. This game we'll play in a hole which is near a tree. This is called *atinsome*."

The two began to play this new game. This time Yo was the first to go in the hole. Lomo lit a fire.

In a few moments Yo cried, "*Zole, zole!*" Lomo put out the fire. Now Lomo went inside the hole. Yo made the fire.

Lomo cried out, "*Zole, zole-o!*"

Yo said to him, "It's your father's fire."

When Lomo cried again, "*Zole, zole-o!*"

Yo said, "It's your mother's fire." And so Yo killed Lomo.

He cut up Lomo and ate him.

Now, Lomo was the hammock-bearer of Dada Segbo. Yo ate Lomo, ate him all, and now he did not know what to do with Lomo's head. Then he saw Lizard. Now, Lizard is the man who whistles for Dada Segbo.

Yo said to Lizard, "Open your mouth, and let me see your tongue."

Lizard knew that Yo had already eaten Lomo. Lizard showed him his tongue, and Yo cut it out. When he cut out Lizard's tongue, he asked if he could talk now. Lizard shook his head. Yo pierced Lomo's head, put a cord through it, and hung it about Lizard's neck.

Then he said, "He who ate Lomo has Lomo's head about his neck."

Now Dada Segbo called all his people to come together. He said to them that he lost his hammock-bearer. Yo went to one side, off by himself. Lizard had not yet come, he was late. When he came, Lomo's head was about his neck.

Dada Segbo asked, "Who saw my hammock-bearer, Lomo?"

When none of the animals answered, Yo said, "It is better to look at people's necks than to ask them. He who killed Lomo carries his head about his neck." And he said, "If you see someone with the head of Lomo about his neck, you can be sure it is he who ate him."

Now Lizard was there, and Lomo's head was about his neck. Dada Segbo gave forty-one sticks [2] to flog Lizard, saying it was he who ate Lomo. In former days, Lizard knew how to talk. But as Yo had cut out his tongue, he no longer can speak. When they flogged him, he looked at Yo, and Yo got uneasy.

Yo said, "I am going away from here. Why does he look at me so?"

Now all at once Lizard escaped, and hid himself inside a hole in the king's wall. It is because of Yo that to this day lizards do not talk. If a lizard today wants to say something, he beats his head on the ground. That is how he talks. He has no tongue.

[1] Lizard. Both syllables of this name are nasalized.
[2] *I.e.*, he ordered Lomo to be beaten until forty-one sticks had been broken over his back. This was a customary Dahomean form of chastisement.

81

False friendship: Tar drum: Guessing names: Why dogs are killed

Yo and Dog were good friends. They always hunted together. As Yo did not know how to hunt, Dog killed the animals and brought them to him. The two always ate together.

One day Dog left for the bush before Yo. Yo saw Dog from a distance, and began to insult him. "You are my friend, yet you went away without me. You are my friend, yet when you went, you left me at home. Now I think you eat up all the meat [1] you kill. After today I no longer trust you. I am no longer your friend."

One day Yo went to see Vulture and he said he wanted to kill Dog. He asked Vulture to kill Dog for him. So the two plotted together to kill Dog.

Vulture was a friend of Dog. But Yo did not know that. When Yo went home, Vulture went to Dog's house and told him what Yo asked him to do. "Yo asked me to help him kill you." Now, when Dog heard this, he in turn plotted with Vulture to kill Yo. Dog brought together many of his friends, and caught Yo and bound him. They flogged him with a whip.

Dada Segbo told Dog to bring Yo to him, that Yo was a good-for-nothing. Dada Segbo punished Yo. He kept him with him for six months, and told him to stay at the house of one of his wives and lay the fire for her.

One day, as Yo was laying the fire for the woman, a boat and a boatman came by. Yo went to plot with the boatman. Yo said, "Today I have many things to carry away. I have stolen many things here, and I have a big load."

Good. As he began to get the load ready, a child of Dada Segbo saw him. The child caught Yo and bound him. Now, there was a place where they were building a wall for Dada Segbo. They carried Yo there. There were many men at work where they put Yo, and Dada Segbo told Yo to watch over these workmen. As Yo had nothing to eat, one day he took one of the workers; he sold him to a stranger, and took the money and bought food. When Dada Segbo found this out, he forbade Yo to do this again. He said there was a place where no animals are ever thrown, but that if Yo kept up his tricks, he would surely throw him there.

Good. Now the walls of Dada Segbo's compound are made of food prepared from beans, like balls of corn meal which are prepared with oil. Since this wall was made of a mixture of this bean paste and oil, Yo ate of it at night.

Dada Segbo heard of this, but he did not know who did it. He sent a man to set a trap for the animal who ate his walls at night. "If I do nothing, all my walls will be eaten up by this animal."

There was a drum there, and on this drum they put a sticky thing. Dada Segbo ordered them to place the drum so that anyone who came to eat the wall would have to move it to one side.

Now, Dog came to see Yo every afternoon. Dog and Yo had become friends again, because Yo had shown Dog where to get food. Each night, Yo told Dog to come. They both began to eat at the wall right beside the drum. Now, that night, as Dog did not see Yo, he went first, and began to eat the wall. When Dog saw the drum, he put his paws on it to beat it. He struck it with his right hand. His hand stuck. He called Yo to come and loosen his hand.

Yo said, "It is you who come every day to eat Dada Segbo's wall, but I command this drum. If I told the drum to let you go, it would let you go." Dog begged him to tell the drum to free him.

Yo told the drum to let Dog go. But the drum held him. Now Yo approached the drum, and struck it with his hand. And his hand stuck. He said, "Let go." The drum would not let go. He struck with his left hand. Now his left hand stuck. Yo said, "I am angry! I won't be played with! Let me go!" The drum held him. He kicked it with his foot. His foot stuck. He struck with his other foot, and both feet stuck. He struck it with his head, his head stuck.

Now when the workers came, they saw Yo and Dog stuck to the drum. At once they went to tell Dada Segbo that Yo and Dog were there. Dada Segbo sent one of his chiefs to see if it was true. Good. Now when the chief saw it was true, he came back and said to Dada Segbo that Dog and Yo were there. Dada Segbo ordered his hammock brought. Dada Segbo put his hand on Dog and said, "Lift up your hand." Dog's hand became unfastened. He said the same thing to Yo, and Yo came loose. Dada Segbo said, "Yo, I see that it is you who ate my wall."

Yo said, "It is not I, it is Dog. I tried to get him loose, and I myself stuck."

Dada Segbo said, "Now that I have caught you, and you both deny your guilt, I will find out the guilty one in this way. I have two wives here, whose names no one knows. You will have to guess their names."

Now, behind Dada Segbo's house there was a tree. This tree

was a fruit tree. Good. These two women always went to this tree at night to gather the fruit. When night came, Yo climbed up on top of this tree. Dog hid under the tree. By the time the women came, Yo had gathered all the fruit. There was no fruit left. When the two were right under the tree, Yo threw down a fruit. One of the women said, "Hwedame, I found one." Now Yo threw down another. The other said, "Bodjo, did you find one, too?" So Yo threw down all the fruit he had gathered, and the women picked them up.

Good. Yo remained up the tree until the women went into the compound. Then Yo climbed down and went home.

Good. The next day Yo went to see Dada Segbo. Dada Segbo said to Dog and Yo, "Thieves must be punished. The punishment for thieves is death. If you do not guess the names of my two wives, I will have you killed."

Good. Now, Yo did not tell the names of the wives at once. He said he did not know them. So Dada Segbo called together all the people of his country. When the people were all there, they bound Yo and Dog. Dada Segbo said, "Now, since you do not know the names of my wives, I will give the order to have you killed."

Yo said, "Ask Dog, perhaps he knows."

But Dog said he did not know. So Dada Segbo told Mingã to kill Dog. They cut off Dog's head.

Now, only Yo remained. They said, "Now, Yo, it is your turn to die."

Mingã came toward Yo to cut off his head, but Yo called out, "Wait! I will tell you their names." He said, "The oldest is called Hwedamè, and the second Bodjo." So they had to free Yo. They sent Yo out of the country, and said thieves must not live among people in cities. They must stay in the bush.

Formerly they did not kill dogs, for Dog was a man. It is because of Yo that they began to kill dogs. But today, when a dog does something bad to anyone, he is killed.

[1] *I.e.*, animals.

82

False friendship: Killing Leopard and his children

It was a time of hunger. There was a tree called *vo*. This tree stood in back of an old man's house, and Tokè, bat, came and ate its fruit. Now at this time Yo found he had nothing to eat. He told Tokè to take him to eat *vo* with him. Before they came to the tree, they passed another fruit tree along the path, called *asolo*. Tokè did not eat the fruit of this tree.

Tokè took Yo to the *vo* tree and there they ate. But the moment Yo noticed the *asolo* tree, he left the *vo* tree and went to eat the other fruit. After Yo ate all that he wanted, he put the rest of the fruit in his sack. In order to let the owner of the tree know that he had eaten his fruit, he threw one into the house of the owner.

Good. But the sack was very heavy, and Yo could not climb down with it. He would have to throw the sack down.

The moment the fruit fell into the old man's house, he said, "Something is eating my fruit. I'll go and see." He went out.

Now Yo's sack reached from on high right down to the ground. The old man, seeing the sack, went over to it and touched it. He tried to take the sack, but Yo would not let go. The old man pulled at the sack, and Yo pulled at the sack. Yo said nothing, and the old man, too, said nothing. So they did from early morning till mid-day.

A young boy passed. He said to the old man, "What are you doing here?"

The old man said, "I want to take my fruit, but the tree won't let go."

The small boy came close, and saw Yo hiding in the branches. He told this to the old man, and brought many men together there. Then they made Yo climb down, and they bound him, and they flogged him, and they left him underneath the tree.

They left the fruit beside Yo. As Yo was hungry, he crawled over to the fruit and began to eat it. When the people came to take away the fruit, there was no fruit left. They said, "Where is the fruit we left here? Where is the fruit?"

But Yo said, "You left me bound. I know nothing."

The old man's children went home. A goat passed, and Yo said, "Come and untie me. I stole some fruit, and they bound me."

The goat refused. He said, "I don't know what you did. I can't unbind you."

Now Leopard had borne her young and had nothing to feed them. She went to ask Yo to help her and found him bound under the tree. Yo said, "Untie me, and I will help you find food for your family." Good.

Leopard said, "Before I loosen you, you must tell me what I must do to get food for my young."

Yo said, "Hide here. They are coming to flog me again." The old man now came back to see whether Yo was still there. Leopard caught him and killed him. Having done this, she unbound Yo. She told Yo to bring the old man to her house.

When Yo and Leopard finished eating the body, Yo went out. He told a hunter that there was a leopard nearby who had given birth to young, and since she had nothing to eat, she had caught an old man and killed him. "If you do not kill the leopard, you yourself will be caught by her. If I did not know tricks, I myself would have been killed and eaten by the leopard." And Yo said, "If you like, I will show you the way. I know where her lair is."

Now Yo went to Leopard and told her that there was a hunter who wanted to kill her. There were two paths leading to Leopard's house. Yo had the hunter lie in wait on one path. He told Leopard that when she wanted to go out, she should take this road. He told Leopard that the hunter lay in wait on the other road.

Now, when Leopard goes out, he runs fast. But Yo told her that to save herself she should walk softly, softly. They left the house together, walking quietly, softly, Leopard first, then Yo. When they had taken several steps, the hunter shot Leopard and killed her.

Now, Leopard's children did not know that their mother was dead. Yo came to see them and he said he would take them to his house. He was giving a dance.

The oldest said, "Where is my mother? I have not seen her since early morning."

Yo said, "Keep quiet. No one can kill your mother. I am her friend. If your mother were dead, I would not dance. But I am going to dance."

Good. Now the children were dancing. Yo said to them, "I am going to see if your mother has caught an animal yet." He went into the bush, cut up Leopard's body, brought the meat back, and put the meat on the fire to cook.

When Yo and the hunter had finished eating the leopard, Yo said to the hunter, "Leopard was a bad animal. Now that the mother is finished, the turn of the children has come. First you must kill the oldest son."

He brought Leopard's oldest son to the hunter. When they came there, the hunter killed him. Yo went back to the children and said that their mother had kept their brother with her. When the hunter and Yo finished eating the first son, it was the turn of the second. Yo brought him to the hunter. He said to him, "I will take you to your mother and your brother." They did the same with the second.

But the third, who was the youngest, followed Yo and his brother softly, softly. No one saw him. When the hunter shot at his brother, he saw it. The youngest now ran back to Yo's compound and began to dance.

When Yo came home, he found him dancing and he suspected nothing. He said, "Now you must go to join your mother and your brothers."

The boy said, "Go tell my mother I do not want to go. I like to stay here."

Yo said, "I cannot take this message. When a mother calls a son, the son must come." And Yo said, "All right. I will go and bring your mother here."

He went to get the hunter. But the child ran away and saved himself. When Yo came back he could not find him anywhere.

That is why we have leopards today. If Yo had killed the last one, there would have been no leopards left to make other ones.

83

The young are more cunning

Yo wanted to climb a tree. He had a bottle full of water. There was a child under the tree. He said, "You cannot climb with a bottle of water hanging in front."

As Yo did not understand the language of the child, he thought the child wanted to annoy him. So he took the bottle and threw it at the child, and the child, in turn, caught the bottle and threw it back at him.

Yo, then, hung the bottle over his chest and began to climb again. But he could not.

The child said to him, "If you did not understand me, I will tell you again. Put the bottle on your back, and you will climb up easily."

As Yo was already very tired, he put the bottle on his back, and climbed up the tree. Then he said to the child, "The young are more cunning than the old."

84

Yo visits Thunder-god: Why axe strokes make echoes

Aklasu, the vulture, and Yo were good friends. In order to eat, Aklasu flies high, high up, until he reaches Hevioso. Now Yo's oldest sister was married to Hevioso in the sky. As Aklasu always went high, high up, he became a hired man for Hevioso. On high there, they make walls by mixing *acasa* and cakes. Aklasu did this for Hevioso. After a day's work he would go to sleep, and the next day he would go to work again. He did this day after day.

One day after finishing his work with Hevioso, he went down to visit the earth. He had with him *acasa, kandji* and many cakes. Now up on high, the children of Hevioso, instead of using oranges to roll as the children do here, use *kandji* and cakes. Aklasu brought three of these for Yo.

Yo welcomed him. "Good day," he said. He ate what Aklasu gave him. Yo said to Aklasu, "Tomorrow, when you go by, you will see a parcel in my compound. Take it with you. I will leave it there for my sister."

Aklasu said, "Yes."

The next day Yo found old clothes, and he himself went inside them and rolled himself up into a parcel. Aklasu, believing it was for Yo's sister, took up the parcel and climbed, climbed, climbed up high. A strong wind began to blow. Aklasu tried and tried to hold on to the parcel, but the wind was too strong. At last he had to let it go. Now, he did not know that Yo was inside.

That day he worked as always. At night, Aklasu came to see Yo again and brought him three more cakes.

Yo asked him, "Did you give the parcel to my sister?" Aklasu said, "Yo, I'm sorry, but the wind was too strong. It was blown away while I was flying."

Yo said, "That's nothing. You are my friend, and I believe you. Tomorrow I will give you another."

Aklasu said to him, "Good. But tell me, Yo, why are you so bruised everywhere?"

Yo said, "I had a quarrel with a friend, and we fought."

Aklasu said, "Now today when you make the parcel, make a good one, so that I do not lose it on the way."

Yo said, "I sent eggs yesterday. What you broke yesterday were all my eggs."

The next day Yo took a great deal of trouble with the parcel. He rolled himself up in the cloth, then he tied himself carefully inside it. And so Aklasu took him up. This time he reached the sky without accident, and gave the package to Yo's sister.

Yo's sister took the parcel. When she opened the parcel inside her house, Yo came out. His sister asked, "Where do you come from?"

He said, "Since you left me, I have had nothing to eat. I came here to get food."

There were walls everywhere, all made of *acasa* and cakes. So she gave Yo to eat. The children now began to play their game, rolling the balls of *acasa* and cakes. Hevioso had a daughter named Sosi who said to Yo, "Come and play with us."

Yo said, "I play this game well. It is my favorite game." Yo began to play. If the children on the other side threw ten balls, instead of sending back ten, he ate four and sent back six. After a while the children began to miss the balls.

Everyone looked for the missing balls, everyone asked, "Where are the playthings? Where are the playthings?" But as Yo was a stranger they did not ask him.

But he himself said, "Just now I saw so many balls here. Where are the playthings? Where are the playthings?"

Sosi sent Yo away and her brother Sosu asked him to join his group. When he joined Sosu's group, he did the same thing. The children brought their balls together and Yo watched them. They left them there and went home. When they were gone, Yo ate all the balls.

His sister cooked for him at noon, but Yo did not come. Instead he began to eat the walls of the quarter. The people went to tell Hevioso that a stranger came to their village who eats nothing but walls. If he wanted him, he could find him beside the market. He was eating the wall there now.

Yo's sister came to Hevioso to tell him that she did not know how to make Yo leave the sky and go down on earth.

Now, there is a place in the sky where no person ever puts his foot. That part is not very solid. If a person were to put his foot there, he would fall through space clear down to the earth.

Hevioso asked his wife to cook for him a dish called *adovolo*. It was Yo's favorite dish. Then they closed all the roads, and only left open the road to that place. Behind this place they heaped up a great deal of *adovolo*. Hevioso came to Yo and said, "Your sister is in the market. I am afraid you have nothing to eat at home."

Yo said, "Yes, I have had nothing to eat. I am hungry." So they showed him the *adovolo* all heaped up in the distance. As Yo went for the *adovolo*, he stepped into the space which was not very solid and fell. He fell into a river. In that river he found a house inhabited by an old woman.

The old woman said to him, "So you are the man they call Yo? I have heard a great deal about you. I am going to ask you to do something for me." She gave him an axe. Yo began to chop at a silk-cotton tree.

For food the old woman prepared corn mixed with palm-kernel shells. Yo worked at the tree till noon. The tree was almost ready to fall when the woman called him to eat. Now in order to eat, Yo had to pick out the shells. It took him so long to pick out the shells, that in the meantime the tree grew back in place, and stood as firm as before he had begun to cut it down.

Today if you strike hard, you will hear another also striking. That is Yo chopping at the tree. He always chops at the same tree. He has not yet finished cutting down the silk-cotton.

85

Take my place: False friendship

Good! It was a time of hunger. There was a market created by Ku, Death. Nochiovi [Orphan] was always seated at the side of this market. When it was full of people, he would throw a stone. The people were afraid of stones, so they left their wares and escaped. Nochiovi would then gather up everything. Fish, pepper, *acasa*, everything, he put in his sack and took them. It was a daily market.

One day his friend Yo came to see him. He asked him, "Where do you always find food? During a famine, when even chiefs have nothing to eat, you people eat. You are poor, you don't work, but you always eat."

Nochiovi said, "Great Mawu does this. I who have neither father nor mother, Mawu shows me a way."

Yo said, "All right. I will come and see you again."

He came back with his knife, and said, "If you do not tell me where you get your food, I will kill you."

Nochiovi said, "All right. Come tomorrow early in the morning and I will show you. I get it in the market."

At night he went to sleep. In a few minutes Yo comes and asks, "Isn't it time to go to market?" Nochiovi told him to go home. It was not time yet. Yo went to sleep and slept a little, and then came back again.

Nochiovi said, "All right, if you come again, I won't show you the way."

Now Nochiovi's sack was hanging there at the side, and Yo cut it open and put ashes in. Then he went back to sleep. At five o'clock Nochiovi took his sack without looking at it. He did not know it had holes in it. Yo went to Nochiovi's house and found he had gone. But the ashes spilled as Nochiovi walked, and Yo followed the line made by the ashes. Nochiovi was very astonished to see him. He asked, "Where do you come from?" Yo said nothing.

Now, cereal cakes were being brought to market, then cooked pork. Yo said, "I am going to throw the stones." Then came the sellers of fowls. Yo liked cocks more than anything. Nochiovi said the market was not full. They must wait. Then *acasa* was brought. An old man brought fried fish.

Yo could not wait any longer. He began to throw stones. The market women, who were the dead, came from holes. So they disappeared into their holes when Yo threw his stones. Now, as the woman who had brought pork meat was disappearing, he stuck his hand into the hole she went into. The woman held on to his hand. She would not let his hand go. "If you cry out again, I won't release you."

The market became full once more, and Nochiovi threw his stones. The people left without taking their wares away, and Nochiovi began to collect them. "I am not in a hurry, so I collect the food, and then I go. I do not suffer."

But Yo is still there with his arm in the hole. Nochiovi went home. But at midnight the woman had not yet let go of Yo's arm.

Now, Yo is the friend of Hyena. On market days, after market, Hyena comes to pick up the bones and other things that had been left. When he saw Hyena, Yo said, "My friend, I have a large pig here which I cannot get out. He is too heavy. Come and help me get him out."

Hyena said, "Is there such luck? I am looking for that kind of meat. I like it better than anything else." He said, "We'll eat this today." Now Yo's arm is almost cut off. At that moment Hyena put his arm into the hole, and the old woman took his arm and let go Yo's arm. Hyena began to pull at what he thought was a pig.

Yo went away, saying, "I am saved." He took his knife with him. He went to Hyena's house to sleep, instead of to his own house. Yo said, "This animal can never hear you talk about pork without wanting to get some."

Now, Hyena struggled and struggled. He broke his arm, but he saved himself from the dead woman's grip. He went home. He put his broken arm in a hole to protect it from the wind. Now, Yo was sleeping in this hole, but Hyena did not know it. Yo had a pin, and stuck him in the wound. He did this again and again.

Hyena said, "Who is doing this to me?" He thought it was an insect. "I am going to see Yo tomorrow morning. He is a friend one can never trust. I'll teach him what it means to trick a friend."

When he said that, Yo was in the hole and he gave him a stab with his knife in the wounded arm. As he did this, he tried to escape, but Hyena caught him.

Yo said, "Let go, and I will find your arm for you. I know where to find it."

Hyena said to Yo, "Are you telling me the truth? If I let you go, will you bring me back my arm?"

Yo came back after a few hours with a goat's leg. "Here is what I found. You have only to put it where your arm was."

Hyena called together his friends, and said to them, "I am going to give you some advice about friends. I want especially to tell you about Yo. Yo is a bad friend. One must never follow Yo. If you have a friend who tells you to come and see something, you had better know what he will show you before you go to him."

86

Yo as cicatrizer: Killing boatman's children:
Why Yo does not live with the gods

Yo and Vulture were great friends. Good. There was a palm tree which gave oil, and this tree was ripe. Vulture went there every day to eat. This palm tree was in the middle of the sea.

Now, this was the time of hunger. No one could find anything to eat. Yo went to see his friend Vulture, and Vulture gave him a nut. Yo asked Vulture, "Where did you find this, my friend?" Vulture told him he would take him to the place.

Vulture said, "We will go together. But you have no wings, how are you going to get to the middle of the sea?"

Yo said, "All right. I'll go and find wings." He went and stole the wings of a cock. He brought the wings to Vulture. Vulture went to look for clay. He pasted the wings on Yo with this clay, so that Yo might fly. He put Yo in the sun for a whole day for the clay to dry.

The next day they left together. Yo flew very nicely, and they both reached the palm tree in mid-ocean. When Yo picked a nut, he put it in his mouth. When Vulture picked a nut, he put it in his sack. Yo had come there with a large, large sack. It reached from Allada to Atogon.[1] He expected to fill it all.

Now Vulture said, "The rain is coming. Let us go."

But Yo said, "Wait. I still have to fill my sack."

Three times Vulture asked him to leave. Each time he said, "We must go, the rain is coming." When the rain came in small drops, Vulture flew away. Yo would not leave. Then the rain came down harder and harder. With the rain, Yo's wings got wet and the clay softened. He could no longer fly. So he broke off a branch and made careful marks on it, and dropped it into the sea.

Now a boat passed and the boatman picked up the stick. He said, "Ah, who made these careful marks?"

Yo said, "It is I who made them. These are the marks I make for the girls. I do it to amuse myself."

The boatman said, "Come with me, and do it for my girls, too."

Yo said, "In order to make these marks, I must have eight girls, and then a house must be built which has no doors. I must also have all that is necessary—flour, salt, pepper, palm oil."

They gave him all that. They gave him eight girls. Then they made a house without doors. To go inside one had to use a ladder, and enter from the top. Yo said, "No one must come here for thirty days." At the end of that time, he told them, they could bring the ladder again, and he would show them the girls. So they had him enter there with the eight girls, and all the food.

The next day Yo began to eat the girls. He ate until he had finished all eight. On the fifteenth day, he called them to bring the ladder. He said, "I must go to find medicine on the other shore to clean the cuts." In the house only bones were left. Yo had eaten all.

Now, he said, to help him find the leaves,[2] they should give him a deaf man to row him to the other shore. They gave him a deaf man, and Yo climbed out of the house and into the boat.

Now, one man who was curious climbed up the ladder and looked in the house. He saw the bones. He cried out, "Ah, Yo ate them all!" When the others heard this, they wanted to stop Yo. They shouted, shouted, shouted. But the man was deaf. He heard nothing. They cried, they did everything, but it was no use.

> *Row me softly,*
> *So that my two feet may stand*
> *On the other side;*
> *He who finds himself in a boat,*
> *Does not quarrel with the boatman.*[3]

Yo made signs to him to go faster and faster. Another one was following him. Yo showed the deaf man money, and made signs again. He brought Yo to the [other] shore.

When he reached the shore, he saw a child of Dada Segbo. He said to Dada Segbo's child that he would tell him something if he would go with him. Yo said to this boy he was charged with making cicatrizations on girls. "If you have girls here who have no marks, I am the man to make them. Have you girls like that here?"

The boy said, "Yes, we have some."

Yo said, "This is never done at home. It has to be done in the field where crops are ripening."

The boy said, "What do you need to do it?"

Yo said, "I want flour, salt, pepper, palm oil." Dada Segbo's son took him to the field.

On the way to the field they saw a very small bird called Gbesavè. Dada Segbo's son caught the bird and put it in his sack, without letting Yo know. When they reached the field, Yo said, "Now I will make you two marks, and you go home and show them what I do."

The boy said, "No, I have a bird here. Do it to the bird." So he gave the bird to Yo, and Yo told him to come back in six days. Dada Segbo's son hid nearby. Yo did not know he was there. He saw how Yo killed the bird and put it on the fire. On the sixth day the boy came back. He said, "Where is Gbesavè?"

Yo said, "He just left to get some leaves." Now, when Yo killed the bird, he plucked its feathers and put them to one side.

The boy had seen all that, and he now said, "What is that there which looks like the feathers of Gbesavè?"

Yo ran to close up the hole. He asked, "What are you saying? What are you saying?"

The boy caught Yo and brought him home. There he was beaten until they thought he was dead. He no longer could talk. They threw him away in the bush, for everybody believed he was dead. But that night, when they went to look, Yo was already gone. And that is why Yo is never found in the city of Dada Segbo. This is true until today.[4]

[1] A distance of about 25 miles.

[2] Since most medicines (and many magical remedies) are made from infusions of various kinds of leaves, the two words are used interchangeably.

[3] Record No. 138–3.

[4] NARRATOR: "Yo is an animal. He's always the same. He never dies. He is found in Paris, in Dakar, everywhere. Mawu created him for no useful purpose. You cannot kill him, you cannot eat him. He is alone. One is enough for the world. He has no child. He eats what should not be eaten, kills what should not be killed."

Bargain with Death: Substitute victims: Boxing contest: Rabbit as king of the bush

There was a great famine. Death alone cultivated a great field of yams. There was a man who ate more than all other men, who was called Yo. Yo came to Death one day to ask him for yams. Yo agreed that Death could come every morning and give him two blows.

Death said, "Well, if I hit anyone, it is his death." Yo said that was all right, and returned home.

On the way he saw Pig. He said to Pig, "You suffer for want of food. Come home with me, bring all your children, and you will eat." Pig followed him home.

When he came home, he gave Pig much food and made him sleep next to him. At cockcrow Death was there. He knocked on the door. Yo awoke, but Pig was fast asleep. Yo took him up gently and held him to the door. Death struck the pig with his fist "Pa!" But Yo threw the pig back inside the hut, and called out, "Ah! You are not so strong."

That afternoon he went for more yams. On his way he saw Antelope. He said the same thing to him.

Now, Antelope was a friend of Rabbit. While Antelope was at Yo's house, Rabbit went to her house to find her. He asked Antelope's children, "Where is your mother?" They said that since yesterday their mother was at Yo's house. So Rabbit went there and asked for Antelope. Yo said she was not there. But as Rabbit left, he saw Antelope's head. Yo had thrown it on the ground.

Rabbit went at once to the house of Death and told Death that Yo was plotting to eat all his yams during the night. He told Death he should gather all the yams quickly and bring them to his compound. At once, Death collected all his yams and took them to Rabbit's compound, putting them in a small house. Rabbit told Death to come and sleep there near his yams.

When night came, Rabbit went to Yo's compound and told Yo

that Death had sworn to burn down his house that very night. He told Yo to come and sleep at his house.

The house where Death was asleep had no light. When Rabbit brought Yo, he put him in the same house, but on a different side. One was behind the yams and one was in front of them. Then Rabbit went to his own house, and spoke to Yo at the top of his voice, "How does it happen that you, who have received a blow of Death's fist, aren't dead?"

Yo answered, "Ph! Death is stupid. The first time I put Pig in my place, and the second time Antelope." All this Death heard. Then Rabbit asked whether he would stake all the yams in his house against a blow of Death's fist. Yo, not knowing that Death was hidden there, said that two blows of the fist were nothing.

That instant Rabbit went out and locked the door. Then he cried out, "Yo! Death is with you in the house!"

Death stood up ready to fight with Yo. But Yo had a magic *gbo* which allowed him to change himself into an animal or an insect. Death struck at him, but Yo changed himself into a spider. Death looked all about for the corpse, but he could not find it. So he asked Rabbit to open the door, but Rabbit did not want to. He asked, asked, begged, begged, and finally Rabbit did open it. Death said that Rabbit had tricked him. Yo was not there, and he was going to kill Rabbit.

But Rabbit said, "No, I am stronger than Yo." And he said that if Death ever came to his house to give him a blow, Death would never leave.

Because Rabbit said that, the two went to Asegbo and made a compact. Death said that if, when he went to Rabbit's house, Rabbit did not fall dead at his first blow, they could drive him from the country. Rabbit said that if ever Death came to his house and he did not succeed in escaping Death, they could burn him alive. Asegbo fixed a time two days away for Death to go to Rabbit's house.

When Rabbit left, he came on Mole. He told Mole that tomorrow Death would come to Mole to kill him. He brought Mole and all his family to his house. Now, his house is here. The only road to his house is there. He said to the moles to dig big holes and to hide in them. The moles dug a hole six meters deep, but Rabbit said it was not deep enough. So they dug ten or eight bamboo lengths more, and then Rabbit told them to come out. Rabbit went to find small twigs. He put them all across the holes. He put leaves on top of the twigs, and on top of that he put sand. When the work was finished, he went immediately to Segbo and said that he wanted Death to come and fight him during the day, and not during the night.

Then Segbo sent a message to Death to go at once to Rabbit. Rabbit placed himself behind the hole, and Death is there in front. When Death came, Rabbit doubled his fists and said, "Come on!" But Death did not want to come. Death told him to come there. Since Rabbit is little, he leaped over the hole and made as if he were boxing with Death. But when Death followed him, he jumped back. The third time Death followed him, he fell into the trap.

Rabbit began to laugh. Everybody who stood about began to laugh. That shamed Death very much. They told Death to come out, but Death said, "No." It was a disgrace for him. Dada Se himself went to the hole, and asked him to come out and eat. But Death said, "No." He would not leave his hole any more. There he would stay. He did not want to see the face of men again. And that is why, when a person dies, he is buried in a hole.

Now Rabbit returned home. He found spider webs over all the trees. When he saw that, he stopped at once. Yo was waiting for him. But instead of throwing himself at Rabbit, Yo took hold of him by his two ears. Rabbit struggled, and ran away.

He went before Segbo to tell how he had won over Death. Segbo assembled all the animals and said to them, "From today, Rabbit is to be recognized as King of the bush, and all the world must respect him."

And from that day also, Segbo designated an animal called Hyena to place Rabbit's body when he dies in a hole in a tree. That is why today, when a rabbit dies, he is placed inside a hole in a tree, and his body is not buried.

88

The greed test: Dog's head in the path

There was Goat and there was Yo. So the king sent them to visit another country. They spent several days there. Then one day Yo said to Goat, "All right, tomorrow we leave."

In the village where they were there were houses all about them. Now, there was one house which was all closed, and inside that house were the animals. In the walls of this house were holes through which ropes which held the animals were pulled and tied to stakes. Now, the large animals had thin ropes, and the small animals had thick, thick ropes about their necks.

So the next morning they said to Yo and Goat, "Good. Now, you cannot go away with empty hands." So they brought them to this house where the animals were kept, and told Yo and Goat to choose among all those ropes one for each of them.

When they said this, Yo ran and took a thick rope. So Goat took a thin rope.

Now they said, "Good. We will bring out the animals you chose." The first one led out was the animal for Yo, and what came out was a little goat. Then they brought out the one which Goat had picked. That one was a big steer.

So they told them, "Good-by."

On the way Yo said to Goat, "Let's kill our animals."

Goat said, "No, I won't kill mine. I will take it to show it to the king. It is the king who sent us here."

So Yo killed his goat and he gave a piece to Goat to eat. But Goat did not eat it. He put it under his tongue. Now Yo finished eating all the meat. So Yo asked Goat, he said, "Give me the piece of meat I gave you."

Goat said, "You thought I ate it, well, here it is."

Yo said, "Can't you take a joke? I'm only joking. But I gave it to you to eat, not to keep."

So Goat hid it again under his tongue. After they walked a piece, Yo asked again for the meat. Goat took it out and gave it to him. So Yo was annoyed. Now, to get back to their own village they must cross a river. When they came to the river, Goat dropped the meat in the river. So when they reached the other shore and had walked a piece, Yo said, "Give me my meat. I know you did not eat it."

This time Goat had no meat to give him. He said, "I don't know how it happened, but I don't have it."

Yo said, "Good. I want my piece of meat, or else kill your steer, and give me a piece."

Goat killed the steer. Then he gave a piece to Yo and kept the rest. When Yo finished his piece, he began to bother Goat to give him more. Goat refused and refused, but Yo annoyed him so much that he gave him a joint. So they walked a piece more and Yo began to ask again, and then again, until he took all the meat away from him. When Yo had taken all, Goat went off ahead of Yo. Yo had not eaten all the meat. He was bringing it home.

So Goat now found the head of a dog, and he placed it on the road where Yo must pass. He made a hole there, too, for himself. Now he attached a cord to the dog's head, and the other end he took with him inside the hole. When he heard Yo's steps, he began to move the dog's head.

Yo saw this and was afraid. He stopped before the head. He began to ask it, "What do you want?" The head moved all the time. He said, "Do you want a joint?"

The head made the sign "Yes."

He threw it down. But when he wanted to pass, the head would not let him. He said, "Do you want the forelegs?"

The head said, "Yes."

When he wanted to pass, the head signaled he could not pass. Yo said, "Yes, yes, I know you want all the meat."

The head said, "Yes."

So he threw down all the meat. Now, all that was left was the basket. But the head still did not let him pass. Yo said, "Ah, I forgot. You are asking for the basket in which to put the meat."

The head said, "Yes."

He threw down the basket. So he wanted to pass now, but the head would not let him. He said, "What are you asking for now?" The head continued to move. He said, "You want Yo himself?"

The head said, "Yes."
Then he began to run. He ran . . . !

89

The greed test: Why Yo is an unwelcome companion

Yo and Goat were sent on a journey. When they arrived at their destination, their hosts put a steer and a goat together to find out which of these two was the trickier. They put a thick, thick rope around the goat's neck and a thin cord around the steer's neck.

Good. People said to them, "Now, take a rope." So Yo took the thick rope. Good. So the Goat took the thin rope. Then they told them to pull at the ropes. As Goat pulled, he saw a steer. When Yo pulled his rope, he saw a small, small goat that was worth nothing.

So they went on their way. As they walked, Yo killed his goat. He gave the tongue of his goat to Goat. Yo ate all the rest of his animal. After they had taken a few more steps, he asked for his goat's tongue. When he said this, Goat gave it to him. Yo said, "I am joking. Eat it." When he said this, he thought Goat would eat it. But Goat hid it under his tongue.

After a few steps, Yo asked him for it again. So Goat said again, "Here."

Yo said, "Ah, I'm joking. Eat it. I gave it to you to eat."

After a while they came to a river. They began to drink, both of them. Now without wanting to do it, Goat swallowed the tongue. When they finished drinking, Yo asked him again for it. He said, "Give me the tongue." Goat said he had swallowed it. Yo said, "All right. But I must have my goat's tongue, or you will have to kill your steer and give me his tongue."

So Goat had to kill his steer. When he killed it, he gave Yo the tongue. Yo ate it. But as they walked, he began to ask Goat for some meat. So after a while, Goat gave Yo a joint. He ate it until he finished it.

That is why one never goes anywhere with Yo.

90

Tables turned: Diviner saves goat from Yo's greed

Yo married a girl [1] and took her with him to her father's compound. Yo told Sheep to find water for them. When Sheep left, Yo ate everything there, so that nothing was left for Sheep to eat. At noon, they gave them beans to cook for their next meal. Yo sent Sheep to the market for oil. While she was away, Yo once more ate everything.

That evening they gave them food again. This time it was cooked meal. Yo sent Sheep to look for salt. Before she returned, Yo had eaten all the meal. Since morning the other had had nothing to eat.

Next morning they gave them cooked corn. Yo sent Sheep for coconuts to eat with it, but before her return he had eaten all. At noon they also gave them cooked yams, and Yo told Sheep to go and get peppers. But before she returned he had eaten everything. In the evening they gave him a live chicken, and he sent Sheep to get wood; but when she returned, Yo had already cooked the chicken and eaten it.

The next day they prepared to leave. They arrived at a stream and Yo drank all the water. Since Sheep had had no food, she died. He left the body and told the relatives that this good-for-nothing woman had died.

Sheep's relatives were very, very angry, but when they arrived, they found only her skin, for Yo had devoured the body.

The next time Yo asked Goat. But as he was a good-for-nothing, who had no manners, Goat went to a diviner. The diviner told him to get a sack, two bottles full of water, some palm nuts, and some stones. He also told him to take a closed calabash, pepper, salt and a cock. Goat put all of this in his sack, tightly wrapped, and left with Yo early in the morning.

When they left, they gave them corn cakes to eat. Yo sent Goat to look for water, but since Goat was cunning, he said to Yo, "Here is water."

Yo was so angry that he said, "Eat everything, I don't want it. Who told you to get water?" Yo ate nothing.

At noon, they gave them cooked beans. Yo told Goat to get oil, but Goat said, "Look, here is oil."

Yo was angry again, and said, "Who told you to go and look for oil? You are no good." And Yo wanted to take Goat's sack to see what was in it.

At night, they were given some cooked meal, and Yo told him to go for salt. Goat said, "I think I have some salt."

And Yo said, "Don't bother. Here is money; go to the market and buy it."

Goat said, "No, here is salt." Yo was so furious that he would not talk to Goat any more. It was Goat alone who ate, yes?

Yo went to see his mother-in-law and said, "Since I came here, I have eaten nothing. The stranger is stronger than I am." Now, they were preparing beans for him. Yo said, "When I go to bed, you bring it to me at night." Goat was hiding and heard this, but Yo thought Goat was away. Goat was in a corner. Yo said, "Look, I will sleep on the outside of the bed, and my cloth is white. The other has a black cloth. You mustn't say anything more about it. See, my mouth will be open. You mustn't say anything, but you must put the food in my mouth. If you talk, you will wake the other."

During the night, Yo slept too much. So Goat gave his own cloth to Yo and took Yo's place. He opened his mouth and put the cloth over Yo's mouth, so that the mother-in-law would know nothing. When the mother-in-law came, she pushed the food into Goat's mouth, instead of into that of Yo. Goat ate all.

The next day he hid himself in the same place and Yo came once more. He said to his mother-in-law, "You are no good. You knew very well that I had eaten nothing yesterday, and now I shall have colic. I do not even have strength to raise my voice." His mother-in-law said, "You will not die. I myself brought the beans last night, and put them into your mouth. You said you would sleep on the outside; I gave the food I prepared to the one who was lying there. You said you would lie there with your mouth open."

Yo answered, "It was not I who got the food."

She said, "No, you are fooling me. I gave what I cooked to the one who had the mouth open."

Yo said, "You must not be angry. Prepare the same things, and bring them to the house. With my stranger, I must eat in the house. He annoys me too much. If I do not watch out, he will take my wife."

She prepared the things for him, but Goat had heard everything. Goat went away first and climbed a tree that hung over the path along which Yo would have to pass. When Yo came there, he sat down to rest, and Goat entered the basket where the prepared food was. Yo did not know that Goat was in the tree. Goat began to eat, and Yo got up, and walked with him. Goat finally ate it all, but Yo kept on, for he did not know this. Finally Goat put his sack in the basket, with the empty bottles and the other things that had been in it.

Yo kept on walking until he got under a tree. He began to relieve himself. Goat climbed the tree very quietly. Yo lifted the basket, to see if it was still heavy with the things in it. He went into the house, into the room, and closed and locked the door. At once Goat came. He knocked on the door. Yo said, "My friend, I come, I come." Yo thought that the food was still there, and so he asked Goat to wait by the door. Yo thought that Goat was waiting for him, but he left, because he knew very well that there was nothing there.

When Yo saw there was nothing to eat, he said, "Ah, my mother-in-law has prepared nothing for me." He took a trap, and put it on the road where Goat had to pass. Then Yo went to look for palm nuts. But when Yo got the nuts and put them down in front of his door to prepare them for himself, Goat came and took them. He put some of them in the trap, and began to cry, "Ba-a-a, ba-a-a, ba-a-a." Yo thought that Goat was caught and came with a large stick in his hand to kill Goat. It was night, so he could see nothing. He began to strike the trap; but Goat was hidden at the side of it. He took the palm nuts, thinking it was Goat, but when he got home and lit the light, he saw what he had and said, "Ah, Goat has got the best of me again."

This is the reason why, in Dahomey, when you are going to do something, you must first divine.

[1] The girl, from context, is obviously Sheep; but the incidents with Goat show a telescoping of two tales.

91

Mock sunrise: Tables turned

Yo was the friend of Hyena. Every evening Hyena took him to his house, and he would come back from the hunt to give food to Yo. He never failed. One evening, Yo arrived when Hyena had been gathering boa eggs. He gave one to Yo. Yo ate it and asked for another.

He said, "Ah, Ahonugbedje! Where did you find these things that are so sweet?"

Hyena said to him, "My wife is pregnant and every evening I go to her stomach to get these eggs."

At once Yo said, "Softly, softly! My wife is pregnant! To-morrow morning early you come to my house, and we will take out her eggs."

He returned home at once. His wife's name was Hweno. When he came, he did not want to go and say good-night to his wife. He went to sleep in his own house.[1] About midnight, he went to Hyena's house. He raised his arms as though he were a crowing cock lifting its wings, and crowed. At once he tapped on Hyena's door and called him to get up and come to his house. He said that his wife was asleep, but that it was morning and the cock had crowed. Hyena told Yo he was too early, and went back to sleep.

When Hyena came it was daylight, and Yo's wife had gone to market a moment before. When Hyena came, Yo took him into his house. He asked Hyena how he got eggs from his wife. Hyena said that he used a knife, and so Yo went to look for a knife, which he put near him. But as he talked with Hyena, his oldest son, who was behind the wall, heard everything.

Yo came out of the house and sent this son to find his mother. When the boy got to the market, he said to her, "My father has put Hyena in your house to take out the eggs."

Hweno said, "Yes, I know, I know, he is a greedy fellow, that husband of mine." Hyena had gone to sleep in the woman's house while waiting for her.

Hweno took a flat calabash and bought honey to fill it. Then she went home, carrying the honey on her head. Yo always held his mouth open, and when Hweno came to the house, she called, "Yo, come and take down the calabash I have on my head." She was much taller than he, so when, with mouth open, he held up his arms to take the calabash, she lifted it in such a way that the honey fell right into Yo's mouth.

When this happened, he said, "M-m-m-m, Hweno! Where have you found this good thing?"

She replied, "Don't you know? All your friends have killed hyenas, and this is hyena-fat which I bought."

Yo said, "Keep quiet! I have a hyena here now, and I'll take his fat right away!"

Hweno said, "Where is the hyena?"

"Keep quiet! There!"

Now, the house where Hyena was sleeping had five entrances. Yo put one of his boys at one with a knife, and other boys at the others. He himself took a large piece of wood with which to strike Hyena. But instead of hitting Hyena on the head, he hit the wall of the house. Hyena started up, and ran, but when the children chased him, he turned. Yo called, "My children, don't let him get away!" But Hyena leaped over the head of one of the children and escaped.

When Yo came back, he threw the child who had guarded that entrance into the air, and it became a butterfly. And the story says that the butterfly called Adjambla-gudo is Yo's child.

---

[1] In a polygynous Dahomean compound, each wife has her own hut, while the common husband likewise has a house apart.

VI

"Historical" tales

exploits of the Aladahonu dynasty

"Historical" tales

ADJAHUTO, a ruler of Adja
KOZOË, his friend
TEDO, brother of Adjahuto; or his
  friend
AGASU, a hunter, brother of Adjahuto
  and Tedo
TE AGBANLI, brother of Tedo and
  Agasu
HWEGBADJA, king of Dahomey,
  reigned 1650–1680
DAKO AHOKAKA, brother of Te
  Agbanli; in Tale 96, son of
  Adjahuto
GBAGIDI, man of Kana
AGILI, resident of Abomey
DĂ, autochthonous ruler of Dahomey
AYO MAN
DJUGU MAN
AKABA, king of Dahomey, reigned
  1680–1708

DADA SEGBO, mythical king
Daughter of Akaba
AYAHASÈ MAN, maker of charms
KING OF AYAHASÈ, also Yahasè, and
  Ahasè
KING OF AYO
AGADJA, king of Dahomey, reigned
  1708–1728
Son of Agadja
GLELE, king of Dahomey, reigned
  1858–1889
KONDO, his son, later called Behanzin
KPONUWE, daughter of Agadja
Nago worker of magic
TOFA, king of Porto Novo at time of
  French conquest
BEHANZIN, king of Dahomey, reigned
  1889–1894; exiled by the French to
  Martinique

92

Origin of the royal sib: Magic flight [1]

A long time ago Adjahuto lived in Adjatado. In those days animals and men lived together. There were two women who were married to a man. The two women always quarreled. When one of them became pregnant, the other, the senior one, said, "You have become pregnant by an animal." This was said to the mother of Adjahuto.

So when the woman gave birth, they began to say that this child was fathered by a leopard. So they quarreled until they fought.

Adjahuto became angry. He left Adja and came to Allada. So when the Adja people pursued Adjahuto, there was a war between them. The war was fought from Adja to Adjadji.

When Adjahuto saw that those pursuing him were stronger, he called on a friend, and asked him to remain stationed at a certain place. When he saw the pursuers approaching, he was to come and warn him. But this friend of Adjahuto, he went and talked with the people who were making war against Adjahuto, and then he went back to Adjahuto. He was plotting to bring Adjahuto into the hands of the enemy.

Adjahuto knew what he did. So he killed his friend. This friend was called Kozoè. Adjahuto took a new name.[2] He said, "I am called now Adjanukozoè-hunton," which means a man of Adja who killed Kozoè. Now that he had killed a man of Adja, he refused to drink from the calabash of an Adja.[3]

So when Adjahuto warred against his enemies, Tedo helped him. Agasu was their hunter. These were the three *vodun* who came here. But it is Agasu who came to rank first, because he had the gun, and he found the road.[4]

So when the three came to Allada—these three all came from Adja—Tedo said, "I am tired." He said he wanted to rest. He took a side path and sat down to rest, and that is where the temple of Tedo is today.[5]

So now Agasu and Adjahuto are left. The Adja people continued their pursuit to Allada. Adjahuto went deeper and deeper into the bush. The people came after him. He put his cloth on the ground and said, "I want a river to spring up here so that I might be separated from my pursuers." So a river sprang up. He had many magic charms. Now he had a spear. He took the spear and said,

"Now, I'm going to throw you, and you must fall at a place where I can come and stay without being killed by the enemy." When he said that, he threw it. So he had people with him. He sent them to look and see where the spear had fallen. "When you see it, don't touch it," he told them.

So the people came and told Adjahuto they found his spear. He went with them, and he said, "Good. It is here I am going to stay." This is called to this day Adjahutohwe, the house of Adjahuto. There are many houses there. When we make a ceremony for Adjahuto, we go there.

The place we call Togodo got this name because he had a river spring up there.

So Adjahuto is there. He begins to have children, and his children are called people born of the leopard; and the wives are called wives of the leopard. His children began to become kings.[6] When people saw their wives, they called them *kposi*, wives of the leopard; and when they saw their children, they called them *kpovi*, leopard children.

As everybody feared the children of Adjahuto, the moment people saw them, they called them Dada Kpodjito, Kings, descendants of the leopard. So, in olden days, when the wives of these men went to market, no one ever met them.[7] They were called the wives of the leopard, and their faces were covered with beads.[8] If you ever met them, you were killed. This was so until the time of Behanzin, the last king of Dahomey.

Now in Allada, Adjahuto and Tedo are more important; but in Abomey it is Agasu.

[1] This version is from Allada.

[2] Deeds of valor, or wisdom, or acts that benefit the group are rewarded by the public bestowal of a praise name.

[3] Drinking from the same calabash is a symbol of friendship.

[4] Here used figuratively to express the idea of finding refuge, but also a way to conquest. The symbolic meaning of weapons and tools as "opening the road" occurs as an idiom in religious and secular connotation.

[5] An elliptical way of saying Tedo lost heart, and the appetite for further adventure.

[6] The word *king* is here used, as in all of West Africa, to designate a village head, as well as the head of a more ambitious territorial grouping.

[7] Those who heard the tinkling of the bells, fled from the paths, and prostrated themselves so as not to see them.

[8] *I.e.*, hanging from a head-dress.

93

Origin of the royal sib [1]

In the early days, a male leopard came out of a river, and lay with a wife of the King of Adja. The King alone knew this secret. He told it to his principal wife. This wife was childless.

Now this wife spread the news, and the people did not want these leopard children to be kings of Adja. So the three brothers born to the "wife of the leopard" killed their enemies and escaped to Allada. Here they became rulers over the Aizonu, who lived there.

The three brothers could not live together without quarrelling. The blood of their animal father brought about their separation. The hunter, Agasu and his followers went north. Adjahuto stayed in Allada. And Te Agbanli, the third brother, went south. His descendants came to rule over the land of Porto Novo. The leopard favored Agasu more than the other two, because, as we see, it was his descendants who came to rule ancient Dahomey, Adja, Allada, and many other kingdoms.

Now the father of Adjahuto, Agasu, and Te Agbanli was a warrior and a lover of human blood. But their mother wanted peace and had taught them peaceful ways. So to carry out their mother's wishes, they conquered an enemy kingdom southwest of Allada. Here they commanded the people to live forever at peace, and in this way to act for them.[2]

[1] Told by an Abomey diviner.
[2] That is, symbolically complying with their mother's wishes.

94

Origin of the royal sib [1]

There was a female leopard. She changed into a woman and became a wife to the King of Adja. She bore him a son named Adjahuto. The King knew of her identity, and he had promised her that he would never reveal to anybody that she was not a woman at all, but a leopard. But the King told his other wives.

Now, the King had no other sons. So when he died, Adjahuto was named to take his father's place. The other wives were angry. They said, "Should the son of a leopard rule over us?"

Now before her death, the mother of Adjahuto, who had taken the name of Agasu, told the secret of her origin to her children. She said that if anyone called them children of an animal, they must leave the country. She said, if ever they must leave their native Adja, they should dig up her bones and take them with them. She would then become a *vodun* for them, and watch over them, and help them.

So when the wives of the King disputed Adjahuto's succession, Adjahuto killed those who had insulted him. He escaped to Allada, and he did as his mother had told him. He took her bones to Allada with him.

There he met a man named Tedo. They swore friendship. Tedo promised to help him against the men of Adja, who were pursuing him. The Adja people wanted to kill him. Tedo lost courage at the last moment because there were so many pursuers. He gave Adjahuto no help. But with his mother's protection, Adjahuto was successful in his fight against the Adja men.

When Tedo heard of this, he was ashamed. He disappeared into a large pottery jar, and died. Adjahuto said that none of his descendents was ever to look at the remains of Tedo. To this day, no member of the Aladahonu family in Allada enters the temple of Tedo or takes part in his festivals.

[1] Cf. *Dahomey*, I, pp. 167–168. The narrator was a native of Zagnanado, resident in Whydah. This tale runs counter to the pattern of Dahomean worship. The essence of the Tohwiyo concept is that the spirit must be male. Here, however, Agasu is designated as merely a *vodun*, a diety, and is given a plausible role. The narrator was young, in his thirties, not especially friendly to the Abomey chiefs, and he thought of himself as a French functionary. The distortion may therefore have been conscious.

95

How the Aladahonu dynasty came to rule
the Plateau of Abomey

This happened in ancient times before our people came to this
country [the Plateau of Abomey]. In the days of our forefathers,
if a man died, the custom was not to bury him. They took the body
and put it in the hollow of a tree. Then the dead man's enemies
removed the head, and sang and danced. In those days there was
no cloth. To cover the body, they took bark and beat it.

At that time there were many kings who ruled the country, not
one. Each one had his district. Awisu was a big king. He took the
throne for a year, and the following year another village took the
throne. So it was. When one king ruled, he made a law. The following year another king made another law.

Our ancestors were kings in Allada before they came here. Then
in the days of our ancestors, when Hwegbadja lived, the family
had many men. So people said he should become king. They liked
him very much. In those days, when anyone was to become king,
he had to go to Awisu's gate to be confirmed. If you were to become king anywhere, they would call a council meeting. That
was all. Nobody gave them food.

When Hwegbadja called the first meeting, he ordered much food
to be cooked. But the carriers who were bringing the food were a
little late. The people were so impatient for the food that the food
was spilled. Now the people said to Hwegbadja, "If you want to
call a meeting, call it at your house. This way food goes to waste.
You do not have to go to Awisu's gate."

Then, when Hwegbadja was king, he called the second meeting
at his own house. Everybody came to his gate, not Awisu's gate.
Then he showed them how to spin cotton. He did it first, and then
gave it to the women. They began to make cotton thread. Then
they made cloth. But it was too white. They did not know how to
make colors. Everything was white.

Hwegbadja commanded one of his servant's to make a white

cloth. Then, this servant's father died. The father's name was Kakpokpolekese. So when the father died, Hwegbadja ordered him to take the cloth he wove for his father's burial.

The man said, "I will make another one for you. I will start on it today." So he took the cloth and wrapped his father's body in it. Then they went to prepare the earth. They dug the grave.

Then, the people to whom the country belonged [the autochthonous people], told Hwegbadja, "All right. We never did this before. But if you want to bury a person in the earth, you must pay. You must buy the land from us." They said, how much would they pay them? They said they wanted two hundred francs in cowries. The man who received this money was a very rich man. Hwegbadja paid before they dug the grave, and buried him.

Several days after the man's father died, his mother died. The people of the country began to denounce him. They said, "We did not bury people. No sooner do you begin to bury people, than they begin to die off." Then the people began to quarrel about it.

Hwegbadja assembled all the other kings, and said, "Now I tell you people, during my command here, nobody must throw away the dead; nobody must put them inside trees. All must bury the dead. If this is not done, I will kill him who disobeys."

He gave them another law, and said, "If a man puts fire to another man's house; or, if someone who does not like me burns my house, then he who catches him in the act should kill him, and bring his head to show me, saying, 'That man burned your house. I saw him do it, and I killed him.'"

Then he told them, "If a man has an enemy and cuts off the head of an innocent man, and brings it, then if I find out that the man is lying, I will kill him."

Then he said, "If someone deflowers a young girl, not yet of age, I will kill him." He said, "Let no one seize people who pass by with loads on their heads and sell them. If someone does this, and I find out, I will kill him."

He said, "If there is a minor chief who persecutes a poor man, let the poor man come to me, and I will summon the chief and investigate, and tell him not to trouble the poor man." He said, "If any man takes a load and escapes with it to another country, if I catch him, I will kill him." He said he wished all men to remain [not to flee the country].

He said, no one is knowingly to poison another. If there is a dispute and quarreling, they must inform the chief, and it must be settled. Whoever is to be put in prison will be put in prison. But no one is to poison another man. Whoever is to be flogged, will be flogged. But no one is to poison another man.

Everybody liked these laws against bad people.

Then the minor chiefs, whom he told about these laws, would not agree [to obey them]. When there was a death in the districts ruled over by the other kings, the people hurried to Hwegbadja, and said, "When my father dies, you will bury him for me. It is not good to put the dead inside trees." When people died, each one of the other kings would say, "All right, you must pay. If you pay, they can bury them." So people from another country came to Hwegbadja, and said, "Our father died. Pay the money, and let us go bury him." But that king, if he did not like the man [who appealed to Hwegbadja for the burial fee], would flog the man, and dig up the grave, and cut off the head. So the man came to tell Hwegbadja.

Hwegbadja said, "Ah, I went and paid the money, and you did this! I will kill you." He went and made war, and he killed the king.

So he began making war on all the kings. If a man came to say that his king did this, he [Hwegbadja] would say, "All right. I will go and make war on him. I will kill the king. I will catch him."

The people liked this very much. They said, "All right. We like you. We will make you king for all time."

For that reason, he told the whole country. He said, "Now, I will die. When I am dead, my son will succeed me. After I am dead, and before my son becomes king, he must pay that money." For that reason, before a king is enthroned, he distributes much money among the people, because he must buy the land. Everybody gets money. A woman gets some. A man gets [some].

Everybody says, "I am Hwegbadja's slave. Hwegbadja paid for me."

The king pays, and says, "I buy from the son to the son to the son." The kings bought [the land] until our father's [Behanzin's] day.

When the son succeeded, he changed the laws he did not like. The next one who succeeded made his laws. So the laws grew to be plentiful. Then the important law was against selling guns; against selling powder. Then when somebody died, they said [as part of the ritual], "Hwegbadja gave us the land to bury our father, our mother." When anybody died, then they called Hwegbadja's name.[1]

In earlier days, every king had to war against another king, Yoruba, or Mahi. But it was not done this way. We did not go and make war on them [without a pretext]. It happened this way. There were two men, each of whom wanted to become king. One of them ran away to Dahomey and told lies, saying the other king insulted Dahomey. So they made war.

[1] This was by edict, *i.e.*, another of the laws. This is still observed.

96

Early days of the Aladahonu dynasty

There are three lives. Now we are living our third life. First, Mawu gave life to a people who were called Ado.[1] As the Ado people did not know how to value life, Mawu took life from them. Mawu next gave life to the Ayonu.[2]

There was a man who came from Adja who was called Adjahuto, because he had killed some men of Adja. As he had killed men of Adja, he no longer drank from their calabashes.[3] So he left Adja and came to Allada.

There were two brothers. The first was called Te Agbanli, the second was called Dako Ahokaka. Ahokaka was very evil. As the younger was so very evil, the elder, Te Agbanli, said, "We'll throw him into the water."[4] At night, when the boy was sleeping, his brother, Te Agbanli, took him and threw him into the river. A boatman saw the child, and saved him, and brought him home with him.

The child Dako Ahokaka was there, and he began to make friends. His first friend was called Ahwango, the second Dodome, then came Adohun, Ayu, and Azowe. He had friends in Tori, in Adjara, and a friend in Donu. When the boy grew older, he went to his friends and said, "Now you will take me to my father in Allada."

The boy had been living near the lagoon, in a house where boatmen lived. One day they all met and took him to his father.

The son had been away from his father for six years. They had looked for him everywhere, but could not find him. So the son returned to his father. He told one of his father's guards to go and tell his father that his son Dako was looking for him. The guard was astonished, astonished that the child who had disappeared so long ago, was there at the door. He ran to tell Adjahuto that his son Dako was there.

Adjahuto came. He was old now. Dako asked his father to have his brother Te Agbanli bring together all their brothers and all the women. When Te Agbanli came, he saw the young man, but he did not know it was Dako. Now, Dako told his father that it was Te Agbanli who had thrown him into the water one night, and that a boatman had saved him, and had taken him home with him.

Dako said to Te Agbanli, "The house which you built for the fish, the fish refused to enter." From this came Dako's other name, Hwegbadja.

Adjahuto said, "Ah, I have but few children, and you threw my son in the water."

Now, Hwedgbadja was very angry. He said to his father, "I and Te Agbanli cannot remain here. Te Agbanli must leave."

Te Agbanli took a horse and he mounted it. The horse faced towards Calavi, and his back was to Allada. On mounting the horse, he faced about with his tail to Calavi and the head to Allada, and he said, "Allada-e, today is the last day I behold you. But all places can be called Allada." He left for Calavi.

Now, Hwegbadja Dako left for the north toward Agbomè. The two separated. Te Agbanli was in Calavi, the other in Agbomè.

One day Te Agbanli asked of another, "Where is that wicked brother of mine now?"

The man said, "Your brother is in Agbomè." The name Calavi means, "I am now a child, with arms folded."

In ancient times, there was no Lake Nohwe. Now, Te Agbanli had a wife. While on his way to Hogbonu [5] with his wife, he met a man who was a Hala man. That man took his wife. These were the people of Akono who were the first inhabitants at Hogbonu. Te Agbanli went to see the people of Akono to ask for a place to settle, and they said, "In order to stay here you must go see Hala."

Now a Hala subject had taken his wife. He went to Hala. He said to Hala, "Your man took my wife on the road."

Hala said, "No one shall take your wife." Hala now went out to find the man who had taken the wife of Te Agbanli. When they came there, the man was bathing. Hala told his spies to bring the man to him. When the man was called, he refused to come. So Hala took his knife and himself went to see the man. Arriving there, he cut off the man's head and gave it to Te Agbanli's wife, who was living with this man.

Then Hala brought the woman to Te Agbanli. Te Agbanli took the head of the dead man from his wife. [6]

In those days there was no money. If you wanted to buy something, and you had salt and another man had corn, you gave him some salt and he gave you some corn. If you wanted fish and I had pepper, I would give you pepper and you would give me fish. In those days there was only exchange. No money. Each gave what he had to the other, and got from him what he needed.

Now, as Te Agbanli was a stranger, he said to the people of Akono, "I see you have no market here. I want to invent a market for you."

There was an Akono man there, who said, "Why should one give everything to a stranger? We gave him a place to live, and now he is asking for land for a market."

Te Agbanli did not forget this. After several days, he had the man who had said this come to him. He said he wanted to be friends with him. And the two set a day for beginning work on the market. That day the Akono man, who was his friend, came dressed as an important man, in wide shirt, and trousers, and hat.

Now, Te Agbanli ordered them to dig a hole, and where this was dug he had all the people of Hogbonu gather. He said, "With us, when we make a market, we first of all put in a living man." As the other had annoyed Te Agbanli, and he had kept this on his heart, Te Agbanli said, "Now you take this man and put him inside." The man protested. But they pushed him in and closed the hole.

The man who was put inside, could talk Anago.[7] He cried out, "Take me, my chief." This is the market Gagbamio, meaning, "Take me, my chief. Save me." This is the name of the market to this day in Porto Novo.

Now Hwegbadja went to Kana. He went to see Gbagidi-zamu-do-hwawe. There was a Loko tree before the house of Gbagidi. There Gbagidi and Hwegbadja played *adji*[8] together.

Hwedgbadja had come from Adja where there were no cloths in those days. The Adja people wore only a bit of cloth about the loins. No large cloths. They were almost naked, the Adja people, and Hwegbadja, too. Gbagidi had large cloths, as large as the funeral cloth on the table here.[9] Gbagidi's people insulted Hwegbadja's followers, saying, "Here are people without cloths. They hide only the organs."

Hwegbadja was angry. He forbade them to call his people Kati—"without cloths"—but they were to say softly of themselves, "We have cloths."

There was a quarrel about this, and Gbagidi ran away to Savalou. There was a river there called Adjuluhwe. As there was no water there, but only a hole, they called it Gbafo-Dogudo. Hwegbadja said, "I can come and trouble you where you are, but as we ate from the same dish, and drank from the same calabash, I will forgive you." He said, "Of two friends they say, 'Friends forgive.' Because of that I will leave you in peace."

There was a man called Agili. Hwegbadja went to see him in Abomey and asked him for a place to build a house. He gave him a piece of land. Later Hwegbadja asked again for land. There were no guns in those days. There were only spears. Now, Hwegbadja came a third time to ask for more land.

Agili said, "Do you want to build on my spear?"

No sooner did he say this, than Hwegbadja took Agili and killed

him. Then he put Agili on the ground, and he built his house there.
In Abomey there is the Agiligome quarter. This is what was built
on Agili, and his spear.

Good. Hwegbadja went to see Dã. He asked Dã for a place to
build a house. Dã gave him a place. He came the second time to
ask for more space.

The third time he came to ask, Dã said to him, "Do you want
to build inside my belly?"

He took Dã, split him in two, and built on him. That is why
now the name is Dãhome.[10] This means, "Inside the belly of Dã."

There was a man called Agwa-Gedè. He came from the sea.
These are the people who command the earth. We call them Aïno.
As Hwegbadja was related to those who came from the sea, and as
Agbomè belonged to Hwegbadja then, he said I am now called
Agwa-Gedevi. Now, this was the name of the people who repre-
sented the earth.[11] So he said that in order that he might take their
place.

Then Hwegbadja said, "Since you gave me the name, you must
leave." But the people did not want to leave. They began to quarrel. The rains stopped falling. So they brought together all the
people of the village. The people said, "If it does not rain, we cannot find food to eat."

Agwa-Gedè said to all, "The earth belonged to my father. If
you deny that the earth still belongs to my father, rain will not
fall. But if you acknowledge that the earth belongs to my father,
then I will order rain at once."

They told him to order rain, and rain fell from morning till
night.

There was an herb called *tengbwe*. It sprang up at the moment.
He said again, "If the earth is truly my father's, then when I pull
up this weed, a peanut will be pulled up with it." He pulled up the
weed, and a peanut was there.

The people cried out. They put their hands over their mouths
and acclaimed him.

He said again, "If the earth truly belongs to my father, if I
pull up an herb, I shall see cowries." He did this, and there were
cowries.

People now found food to eat, and no longer exchanged articles. They had money.

Then he invented a magic charm, called *kelè* or *nwe*, [locusts]. Not all the people were willing to recognize Agwa-Gedè as king. They began to quarrel. So Agwa-Gedè told his magic charm "locusts" to eat all the corn of that region. They began to eat all the corn, the calabashes, all.

The people hurried to Agwa-Gedè, and declared, "You are our king. We have no other."

He told them, "To stop the locusts from eating your crops, you must give me much money, and cotton, and cocks, and many goats." Then in order to stop the locusts from eating, he took a male and female locust and killed them. These he embedded in earth in the shape of an image. Then he spoke to this image and ordered it to summon all the other locusts. The locusts stopped eating the crops.

And so the people refused to recognize Hwegbadja, and it was only after the death of Agwa-Gedè that Hwegbadja began to reign.[12]

[1] The people of Benin.
[2] The Yoruba.
[3] Drinking from the same vessel is a mark of trust, and therefore, friendship.
[4] This rivalry among royal brothers is a recurrent theme in these "historical" tales, and historical records actually corroborate many of the incidents recounted.
[5] Porto Novo.
[6] This story is incomplete. Tale No. 145 tells of Te Agbanli's revenge on this woman, and how, to escape her tormenter, she changed into Lake Nohwe.
[7] *I.e.*, Nago, or Yoruba.
[8] A game of counters, played with seeds.
[9] A large cloth that the narrator observed in the house where the tale was recounted.
[10] That is, Dahomey. This incident has been recorded many times, and is in the literature as far back as Norris' work, published in 1759. Cf. *Dahomey*, I, pp. 15-16.
[11] *I.e.*, because they were the autochthonous inhabitants of the region.
[12] These "histories" were given in Allada. It is interesting to observe that emphasis is here laid on the treachery of these royal brothers. In Abomey, Hwegbadja is credited with bringing cloths to the plateau peoples, but here he and his followers are taunted with being unclothed. The struggle with the Gedevi is also not heard in Abomey.

97

War by ruse: Why women must not be

told secrets

There were two Nago[1] men, one from Ayo,[2] and one from Djugu.[3] This second place is very far away, near Pila-pila, where people live who go about naked and do not use cloths. The two came to see Dada Segbo. One of them played *adji*, and the other, from Djugu, always caught crocodiles.

In those days they did not know *adji* here, and the man from Ayo taught it to Dada Segbo. The other, from Djugu, was always looking for crocodiles so that he might give the meat to Dada Segbo, who had no meat.

As the man from Djugu was always going to the same place to catch crocodiles, the crocodiles went away, and there remained no more for him to catch. So he went to the Yahasè country, which was some distance farther.

There was a Yahasè child who observed the Djugu man searching for crocodiles[4] in the holes. He said to this hunter, "As my father is away, do not come here again to catch crocodiles, for this is not your country. You do not command here. Go to Whydah, or some other countries. But do not come here."

When the man from Djugu returned to Dada Segbo, he told him that he went to the Kingdom of Yahasè, and as he was about to catch a crocodile, a boy annoyed him, and told him not to come there any more to catch crocodiles.

Now, in the house of Dada Segbo there was a man named Akaba who was greater than Dada Segbo. If there was anything Dada Segbo had to do, he always asked the advice of Akaba. Whether a man was to be set free, or killed, or sold—whatever there was to do—he went to Akaba. And what Akaba told him, he did.

So when Dada Segbo heard this, he told the man from Djugu to bring a crocodile to Akaba, and to tell him that a boy in the Kingdom of Yahasè forbade him to kill any more crocodiles.

Akaba said, "Now, it is my turn to send this man to look for crocodiles." And Akaba told the man to go to the Kingdom of Yahasè to look for crocodiles. And Akaba said, "When you go there, and kill a crocodile, if you do not see that man, take the crocodile's head and put it before his door. And we shall see what he will say."

When he arrived there, he was met by the chief of Ayahasè and many of his people, who asked him, "What are you doing here?" The Djugu man replied that Akaba had sent him to catch crocodiles. To this the chief said, "My son forbade you to catch them here. Anyone who does this is killed. So today you will be killed." So he had the man killed, and they buried him with the crocodile.

And he told to all his people, "If I am away, and a man sent by Akaba comes here, you must kill him."

Eight days went by, and still Akaba did not see his hunter. He sent a child to Dada Segbo to ask him if the man from Djugu had returned. Dada Segbo replied, "Was it not you who sent him to look for crocodiles?"

So Akaba sent a man to the Ayahasè country to search and inquire for the man from Djugu. When he inquired of the people there, they asked him, "Where do you come from?"

He replied, "I come from Akaba."

The chief answered, "Though I have forbidden Akaba's people to come here, I will not kill you, because you only brought a message. But return to Akaba and tell him that I killed the man. And here is his head. Take it to Akaba."

And so he sent the head to Akaba. Now Akaba's mother was always there, and before he did anything, he always asked her permission. She said, "I have only you, and so you must not make war with the Ahasè people. He has too many men."

Now, Akaba had two daughters. So he said, "To make war with Ayahasè, I will give one of my daughters to the king of Ayahasè, and I will give the other to his maker of *gbo* [magic charms]. They will beg their pardon, and will say that the man from Djugu never obeyed anybody."

But Akaba knew very well that he was going to make war on those people.

When the Ayahasè maker of magic charms saw the girl, he

said to the King of Ayahasè, "I will go to Akaba to thank him for having given me his daughter."

Now, the daughters of Akaba were leaving for the country of Ayahasè, and their father said to the one who was going to the king, "There, if your husband asks about me, you must explain nothing. Only watch, and see what goes on there." And to the one who was going to the king's maker of magic charms, he said, "You must ask the worker of magic what kind of war charms he makes for his king."

When the maker of magic charms came to Akaba, he asked him, "Sir, what kind of charms do you make to make war?"

The other asked, "Why do you ask me?"

He replied, "Oh, I want to make war somewhere." And so the other told him about the magic, and made several *gbo* for Akaba.[5]

Before the maker of charms left his house, he explained to his wife, the daughter of Akaba, "This charm does not eat pepper. This one does not eat salt. This one never eats palm oil. And, if you are menstruating, you must not come here."

When the maker of charms was away, the daughter put pepper on the *gbo* that must not eat pepper, and salt on the one that must not eat salt. She put palm oil on the one that never ate palm oil. And when she did this, she was menstruating. And so she went to all the places where she was told she must not go when she menstruated.

She had told her father, "You must await my message before you come to make war on the Ahayasè people." So when she did all this, she sent word to her father that all was ready.

When the father heard this, he sent a message to Ayahasè that in eight days there would be war.

Now, Akaba had a *gbo* called *adjaka*, which could change into a rat. He called this *gbo*, and he ordered it to go to his daughters and tell them that they should be at his house before cockcrow the next day. So the rat went there during the night. And as the daughters knew well that their father had such a charm, when the rat passed in front of them, the daughters recognized it, and followed it, shouting, "There is a rat, we must kill it!" And so they went after it. When they were outside the town, the rat gave them the message that they must be at their father's house before cock-crow. Then the rat left.

That same evening, both of the daughters asked permission of their husbands to go and visit their father. The husbands said, "Yes, you may go." And they returned to their father's house.

Now, the King of Ahasè had said to his wife sometime before, "I have two ox tails, one white and one black. It is with these two tails that I make war." He explained that he had a medicine, and when he put the white tail in it, and sprinkled the opposing army, all would die. When he put the black tail in the medicine, and sprinkled those who had been killed, they would come to life again.

When the daughter who was married to the king heard these words, she bought two new tails, one black, one white. And when the king was out one day, she exchanged the ones she bought for those the king had. She made an exchange, and took the good ones. She divided the medicine into two parts, taking one part, and adding water to the King's portion, until it was as much as before. All this she took to her father. The two girls told their father everything.

The day fixed for the war arrived. Akaba said to all his people to start for the Ayahasè country to make war.

Ayahasè said to all his people to start for the war. But he did not really believe that Akaba would make war on him. He took the two tails and the medicine, so that if it were really a war, he could win. So they began the war. Ayahasè, thinking that his charms were in good condition, put the white tail in the medicine and threw the water at the enemy. But nothing happened.

Now Akaba took his tail, the good one, dipped it in the medicine, sprinkled all the enemy, and everyone fell down dead. Only Ahasè, being king—the king is never in front—remained alive. And so Akaba told his men to tie Ahasè. And so he broke [6] the Kingdom of Ayahasè.

At the place where Akaba camped during the war, they planted a silk-cotton tree. When Akaba took Ahasè to that tree to kill him, there was a wife of Ahasè who had been caught as a slave. The woman embraced Ahasè. When the king wanted to shoot at

Ahasè, the girl turned and with her body protected him. The girl did not want to see him die before her eyes.

A man was sent to tear away the woman from Ahasè, and when they took her away, they shot at Ahasè. When they shot at Ahasè, he did not fall, but dropped to his knees. But all the same he was dead.

Akaba said, "One can die in many ways. One can die while standing, while on one's knees, while lying down. If you do not wish to fall, all the worse for you. All the same you are dead."

Akaba now ordered all that was needed for the burial of a man. They made a grave, and they buried him on his knees.

That is why one should never tell secrets to a woman, for a woman never keeps a secret.

[1] Yoruba.
[2] Oyo, in Nigeria.
[3] Djugu, northern Dahomey.
[4] Many west African peoples do not kill the crocodile, but hold it sacred.
[5] A son-in-law owes respect to a father-in-law. Here he was especially indebted because Akaba gave him a wife, without bride-price, and without exacting any gifts.
[6] *I.e.*, "conquered."

98

How tribute to the King of Ayo was ended

In earlier times, they used to give forty-one women and forty-one men to the King of Ayo. It was the time of Agadja. Each year they had to send them. They were given by the people, not by the family of the king.

One day, the King of Ayo said that for the coming year he wanted a child of the king. If this were not done, he would break Dahomey. When the King of Abomey learned this, he sent his own child, and about the neck of his child he placed a magic cord.

When the boy went down there he did not eat or drink. With this cord he wore about his neck he ate and drank, because attached to the cord was a small magic gourd. The boy stayed with the King of Ayo for five years without either eating or drinking, but he worked all the same.

So the King of Ayo sent a message to the King of Abomey that he wanted another boy to replace the one who did not eat. But the King of Abomey said he only had this one son. When the message came back to the King of Ayo, he sent back the boy to his father.

When the boy returned to his father, he said to him, "Now I have found a way for you to become King of Ayo, and to command the people of Ayo. When I was there I saw everything, and I know what you have to do." He said that the following year when the men of the King of Ayo came to demand the annual tribute of men and women, the King of Abomey must kill them, and declare war.

The next year when the *marabout* [1] came looking for the men and women, the King of Abomey commanded that all but one were to be killed. To the one alive he gave a gun to take to his king and show him that he is offering him a gun. [2]

Now, the child of the King of Abomey was more terrible [3] than his father. He knew the roads that one must follow to kill the people of Ayo. Now, he had something, and he said to his father, "I have something that you must put in the great river that they have in Ayo. If you put it in the water and someone drinks it, he will die." And he did this. His father asked why he did this, and he answered, "So that the Ayo people may become somewhat less in number."

So, now that he put the thing in the water, the people of Ayo began to die. Once they drank the water they would die instantly.

When the son told his father that men and women were dying, the King of Abomey sent a message to the King of Ayo that in fifteen days there would be war. Before they were more numerous than the people of Abomey, but as they drank the poisoned water they died off, men, women, children, so that there were only a few left in each compound. Instead of finding six thousand men, there were only three thousand.

So the people of Abomey entered the town and killed many, and brought the rest back as slaves. They did not have to use their guns. They killed them with sticks, they were so few.

So in the days of the other kings, they were forced to give each year forty-one men and forty-one women. It was this king that forbade this. If he had not done this, we should be today for the King of Ayo,[4] as we are today for France.

[1] That is, a Moslem Yoruba.
[2] Narrator's aside: "He couldn't send any message, because the people of Ayo and the people of Dahomey didn't understand each other's language."
[3] *I.e.,* "more audacious."
[4] *I.e.,* his subjects.

99

Death as raider of the king's sons:

The wilful heir-apparent

This history is of the time of the death of Glele's mother. To announce her death, they said that it was night.[1] In olden days, to bury the mother of a king, they buried her with living people. So when the mother was dead, King Glele went to see the people of Onowini and commanded them to give him one of their sons to accompany his mother. He said he would choose one who was fit to go. But if there was none fit, he would take one away and sell him.

They brought all the people of this village together. When they were all there, they were seized and sold, as the King did not want any more of that race around.

After this he went to Agbafodugudo, and brought all the people of this country together. Among these people, he killed half and sold the others.

The following year, he went to the village called Sokologbo, and here he again called together all the people. Whenever he called together a people, he would kill half of them, and sell the rest.

After this he went to Meko, and thought he would do there as he had done with the other countries. But the people of Meko made war against him. And so he did not succeed in capturing all the people of Meko. He only got a few.

The King had planned to return to his country when he had conquered the people of Meko. But as he had only been able to get a few of them, he said he would stay until he had got them all.[2] After Meko, he went back to Keèlei, and made war there. After that, he returned home.

Now, when Glele went away to make war on these kingdoms, he left behind him several grown sons. But when he returned, the eldest son was dead. The second was also dead. The third as well. And the fourth. He said, "Now, I do not desire any more children. I wish that after these, my dead sons, my family bury me next."

Now, there was a chief who said that the King must have an eldest son. As most of the surviving children were too young, he chose his son Kondo, and took him for his eldest son. It was a chief who had counseled him to take Kondo for his heir. After his death, the King said, all his domain was to go to his son Kondo. And Glele forbade Kondo to make any more war.

But Kondo said that a good child must follow in the path of his father. Kondo said, "If there is to be no war here, there is a town called Kana, and I shall go and make war from there."

Once his father said to him, "All right, you are to buy a carrying basket, a calabash, and a hoe." Then his father gave him five francs and said to him, "With these five francs, buy what you like." The child took the five francs and he went to buy gunpowder. After five days his father again gave him five francs to buy what he liked. The child went and bought a *machete*. So after another five days, they once again gave him five francs to buy what he liked. The boy went and bought a hoe, and ordered the blacksmiths to make him cartridges.

Very well. When he brought all these things to his father, his father said to him, "I told you there is to be no war, why do you bring me cartridges?" His father said to him, "As I have forbidden you to make war, and still you bring me cartridge shells, I will take half away from you, and you may keep half of them only." And his father said, "See what an eldest son I have! I believe he does not wish to obey me."

Kondo began to build many houses in Abomey and in all the

districts. There is no quarter of Abomey that does not have a house belonging to Kondo.

His father, the old King, had all the people of the kingdom come to him, and he gave them much money. He said, "Now, I am performing burial rites for myself during my own life time. As I have no child to do this for me, I do this for myself, while I am alive." He was angry at Kondo because Kondo prepared to make war, and he had forbidden this. But he did not disinherit Kondo. He hid this thought in his heart.

Belonging to Glele, in Abomey, there was a house made of branches[3] that was called *ato*. Glele himself had built this. There were two of these together, the one under the other. Glele made a staff for it, and put this on the roof. He ordered a sack, and hung this from the roof. Glele had all his chiefs come, and the people, and he said to them, "You see where my sack is up there? See where my arms have reached to put it? See, all I have done in my lifetime? Now, this is where I stay. I cannot prolong it more."

Glele said, "It was during the time of Dosu Agadja that *ato* was invented. He had made one of them. I, I have not invented them, but I have made thirty. I have made two that are very large." Glele himself, who had made thirty, made forty more before he died.

So Glele said to Kondo, "After my death, take the chief who advised me to choose you, and make him Yovogan[4] in Whydah." And after the death of his father, Kondo put the other in Whydah, and he himself became king.

Sometime later, the whites wanted to make war on Kondo[5] but the chief in Whydah said that he must not war against them, for it was the whites who made the guns.

---

[1] This is the traditional manner of proclaiming a royal death.
[2] The narrator sang a song at this point in the story, but no amount of urging could induce him to give the words, or sing the song into the phonograph. The fact that a grandson of Glele was present from time to time during the telling of this tale, may be the explanation.
[3] *I.e.*, with walls of palm fronds, not of mud.
[4] *I.e.*, chief in charge of relations with Europeans.
[5] The narrator commented, "As king he was called 'Behanzin.'"

100

Royal exiles: Royal daughter as trickster

In Agadja's reign, his sister's husband was a chief. Agadja liked him very much. But some chiefs caused trouble between him and Agadja. He knew he was about to die, so he escaped to the land of the Mina.[1] His wife loved him very much, so she escaped with him. They had a son and several daughters there.

When the man died, his wife died shortly after. Her daughters brought the mother's body home to be buried here in Abomey. The son they sold to Portugal. The man's name whose son was sold was Sinyegba. . . . Agadja's brother Agbosasi went off to the Mahi[2] country. He was not exiled. He went away on his own account.

In Agadja's reign, they sent a princess away as a slave, and brought her back again. . . . This princess was very quarrelsome. If she married a man today, the next day she left him. She made everybody suffer. She vexed her father very much. So he sold her, and sent her away. He could not kill his own daughter, so he sold her away.

When he no longer saw his daughter, he grieved. He said, "If anyone finds my daughter, I will give him many gifts. I will give everything." So they brought her back.

Now, she began to make trouble again. Her father said, "You are my own blood. I like you when you are quiet." But she made too much trouble. He sold her again to the Portuguese. The white man took her away.

They were in Whydah. They had not gone to sea yet. She asked the white man for *keke* [a spindle]. But the white man did not know what *keke* was. She began to cry. She said, "Give me *keke* with which to make thread, or I will die." The white man brought her back to her father.

This princess was very proud. She was beautiful. She was the most beautiful of all women. Her name was Kponuwè. There was a pit in Allada where no one was allowed to go. The princess went and stole her father's sandals at night. The following day, an old

377

woman noticing that someone had entered the pit, came to tell the king. Everybody went to look, and they saw the king's feet.

The king was vexed. He said he did not go there. The princess laughed. She said, "Who then went there? Look, here are your footprints."

The king said, "I did not even waken."

She said, "Look, here are your footprints." Now she said, "I stole your sandals myself, and I went there, and I am not going to die. If I had not stolen your sandals, then one day they would have taken another woman and killed her."

Once there was a big rain. Water filled this pit. The princess did this. She looked about and saw that nobody was there. So she took off the gold ring her father gave her, and she threw it into the pit. She began to cry now, she must have her ring. If not she would go in the water and die.

Her father called for people to dip up the water. They took two nights and two days to empty the water. They found the ring.

"Here is your ring."

She said she threw it in to cause people to go into the pit, where the king had said nobody was to go. If her father commanded, "Nobody is to go there," before three days were up, she went there.

[1] The present Togoland.
[2] The Mahi live north of Abomey, and are at present a part of the larger political division called Dahomey.

101

King as spurned suitor: Poor stranger as king's conscience: King above morality

There was once a king. And there was a young girl. A wall separated the king's houses from the outside, and the girl lived outside this wall. The king asked to have intercourse with the girl. The girl refused. He offered her a thousand francs. He promised if he could have her once, she would then be free. The girl refused.

On the third day, he had the girl brought to him, and he made her the same offer. He begged to have relationship with her. The girl again refused. The king said, "Good."

The king went to find an *azondato,* a man who makes evil charms. He began to use such a charm against the girl. On the seventh day the girl died. The dead body of the girl lay there. That night, the chief in charge of burial was behind the house. Two men were digging the grave. The king came and had intercourse with the dead girl, and went away.

Now a Nago [1] man saw the king do this. The king ran away. The Nago said, "All right. Why do you run away? Come here."

The king said, "I beg you, do not tell any one."

The Nago said, "If I tell no one, what will you give me?"

The king said, "I will make you a present of six girls, whom you can marry, and I will add four thousand francs."

The Nago said, "Good. I drank too much today. I will come and see you tomorrow at four o'clock." The next day the Nago went to the king, and said, "I want nothing from you. I ask only to command you."

The king said, "No, you cannot live here. If people come to me to pass judgment, what will I do?"

The Nago said, "All the worse for you. That does not trouble me. All I know is that I desire to command you." The king pleaded with the Nago. The Nago would not listen. To all the king's entreaties, he said, "No."

The day of the King's court, the Nago came and stood behind the king. They judged, and the sub-chiefs came and said, "We have finished judging. Speak. Give us the verdicts."

The king wished to speak. The king said, "I say. . . ."

But the Nago rose and said, "Enough, my chief." The king fell silent. The king ordered the sub-chiefs to leave. They were all astonished.

The people went out talking. They said, "What does it mean, the king cannot speak? A worker of magic commands here? That cannot be."

Arrived at the house, the king said to the Nago, "Please, I beg you, I will give you ten thousand francs. I will give you a village."

The Nago said, "No, I do not want that. I will remain here,

wearing my old cloths, and I will command you. If they say in the city, 'Here's a poor man who commands a king,' it is enough for me."

Again the day came when the king was to hold court. They went to the court-house. The Nago sat down behind the king. They judged. The chiefs brought the verdicts to the king. The king wanted to speak. He said, "I say . . ."

The Nago said, "Enough, my patron."

The king said again, "Go back to your houses." All the chiefs of the district went to see the king at his house.

The chiefs asked, "What have you done, that you cannot confess, so that a poor magician can command you so? Have you killed?"

One chief said to him, "If a man wishes to be king, he steals, he kills, he has intercourse with the dead, he sells slaves. All that is forbidden to do, he does, before becoming king." Good. After he said this, he asked again, "Why does a poor man annoy the king in his own kingdom? If the king gives a command in court, the others will throw themselves at the Nago."

The king said to them, "Yes. It is true." He gave four thousand francs to this chief for his advice. He gave them drinks, and they drank till they were drunk.

The Nago did not know that they had made a conspiracy. The Nago came and sat down in the same place. They finished hearing the cases, and then the chiefs came to the king to learn his decisions. The king said, "I say . . ."

The Nago arose, and said, "Enough."

The king said, "Silence, my people. I wish to speak. Listen to me." He followed the advice of the chief. He said, "Why does this Nago disturb me every day? This is the third time he has annoyed me in this council. I am not in his district here." The king said, "If one wishes to be king here, one steals, one kills, one sells slaves, one has intercourse with the dead, one does all the evil. I did all before becoming king.[2] This Nago troubles me. Take him and kill him."

The Nago escaped. They ran after him, ran after him till they caught him. There were two very tall trees. There was a small wheel. A long, sharp nail was put into the tree, with a very sharp head. Everybody was there. They put the rope about the neck of the Nago. The king commanded them to have the Nago lifted up to the nail. The nail was placed so that it would enter his head. They raised up the man till the nail entered his head. The Nago died.

The king said, "All right. I'll make him climb up to the flag."

This tells that here in Dahomey a Nago must not command a king.

¹ Yoruba; here, again, the specific reference is to a Moslem Yoruba.
² This is a reference to certain symbolic rites of accession which give immunity against transgressions of the moral code, which a King either by caprice or political necessity might be guilty of.

102

How Behanzin fought against the whites ¹

There is a village called Wefi which is found behind Porto Novo. Wefi belonged to King Tofa. Tofa had his wife there, his mother and father-in-law, his children. But the people of Wefi did not want to obey Tofa.

Tofa and Glele were brothers. Tofa sent a "commission" to Glele to say that there was a village in his province that did not obey him. Glele sent back a reply asking what he wanted him to do to these people. And Tofa replied that he wanted him to make war against them.

At this, Glele came with the people of Abomey, and made war there. He killed, and caught slaves there, and took the slaves to Abomey. At this, Tofa sent a message that among those people he had taken, were his own children, his father-in-law, his mother-in-law, his wife. He asked for those people.

But these people were already with Prince Behanzin—Degeno was his name then—for his father had given them to him, when he returned to Abomey. So Tofa called on Behanzin to bring back the slaves that were of his house.

Behanzin said to Tofa's messengers he was wrong to ask this, for it was not he who had bought the powder that Glele had used in capturing these slaves. He said he would never return the slaves that his father had caught. He [Tofa] had no right to ask to share the slaves. And he said if Tofa was not careful, he would one day make war against him.

When Glele died and Behanzin became king, he sent a message to Tofa to say that he was now ready to make war; that war was near. Behanzin brought together all the people of Abomey and gave each a gun with which to make war against Tofa. In this war, Hevioso could not quite kill Tofa, but he took an arm and part of one side. But Tofa is not yet dead. He escaped from Porto Novo, and stayed at Agosa, where his uncle was.

When Behanzin arrived in Porto Novo, he killed all the people he found there, and cut down all oil palms. At this, Tofa sent a message by Hazoume to the French. Because in France Tofa had a friend. He told Hazoume to speak to his friend in France, and tell him the king of Abomey had come to break Porto Novo. He begged the French to come and make war, so that Dahomey might belong to him.

Behanzin did not know that the messenger had been sent to France.

Soon after, the whites, many whites with their guns, landed in Cotonou. They had all sorts of weapons with them, and they sent a message to Behanzin, who was in Abomey, that they were going to amuse themselves.

Behanzin sent a message back that he was ready for everything.[2] And that very evening, Behanzin brought together all the people of Abomey and told them he had received a message from the whites, and that they must leave the following morning at cock-crow.

When they left for Cotonou, the war began. They killed all the whites, and the few who remained fled, leaving their guns. These whites did not return to France. They were on the sea, in their vessels, and from there they sent a message to France.

Much later, many, many landed. Now, the whites sent another message to Behanzin saying that they had come once more, and that they were going to take their coffee in three days, with the sugar that was in his house. So Behanzin started toward Cotonou to make war. But the whites had separated their army into two parts. One remained in Cotonou. The other was already in Abomey. But Behanzin did not know it.

As Behanzin continued his travels to the coast, the other whites followed him. They began the war at Cotonou. They did nothing but kill. They killed the whites; they killed the blacks. But as the whites were stronger than Behanzin, the Dahomeans retreated. But they did not know that there was a white army behind them.

As Behanzin marched toward Abomey, one of his children who had been in Abomey, and had seen the whites, came to warn him. He came to say to Behanzin that the whites were in Abomey now. Behanzin was not yet in Kana when he received this message. Behanzin sent the same child back with the message that all houses were to be burned, that none should be left for the whites.

With this news, his wives and children escaped to Agbadogudo, and Behanzin changed his route, not passing by Kana.

So the whites, who were in Abomey, believed that the whites in Cotonou had killed all the Dahomeans. And those in Abomey descended to Cotonou and said that all were dead.

But the whites in Cotonou said that when you break a country you must get the king, and that they wanted Behanzin. So they returned to Abomey to catch Behanzin. They searched for him for three months. If the whites, who were looking for Behanzin, thought they had him in a certain house, he would change into a cat. Once he changed into a vulture. He changed into a lion, into a panther. But the whites bothered his family in Abomey so much that Behanzin finally said, "Well, I will go and give myself up."

When he arrived, he went before the door of his dead father, and asked for all the whites to come, saying he wanted to speak to the commander and his aide. He shook the hand of the general and his next in command, and said, "If you go, you will die, since I have shaken hands with you." And so, when the two of them arrived in Cotonou, they died.

He said, "I myself [of my own free will] want to go to France. If I did not wish to go, you could go on looking for me for many years without ever finding me. If I did not wish to be caught, not one of you could catch me." So he said, "Go on." He had the whites go before him, and he walked behind, as he wished.

He told one of his brothers, Agoliagbo, that he should stay in Abomey while he was in France. He entrusted his wives to Agoliagbo, and he said that if one of his wives wished to find another husband, Agoliagbo should look for one for her. He forbade his brother to marry his wives.

He said it was Tofa who had brought the whites, and that he would go to Porto Novo and greet Tofa before he embarked for France. Tofa sent a message that he did not want him to come to Porto Novo, that he should depart for France from Cotonou, because, if Behanzin had come there, Tofa would have been killed.

So the whites came here because Glele broke Wefi.

[1] This title was given by narrator.
[2] Narrator's interpolation: "Ah, but he was strong!"

VII

Tales of women

love, intrigue, and betrayal

Tales of women

103

Woman tempts cult initiate: Lover makes supreme sacrifice: Initiation period reduced

Long ago, if a child was "named" by a *vodun* [1] he went at the age of twenty to live with the priest for eight years. After eight years they gave him a wife. Formerly a man was married at twenty-eight. If a woman, she waited till twenty-eight years, too, for at the age of twenty, both men and women entered these cult-centers for eight years. In those days, no one saw them. The priest used to provide food for them.

Good. There was a woman, a young girl, who sold *acasa* and cakes. Now, no one might enter where the young man was, for he was with the god. But the woman, while walking, saw the man. The woman said, "You are a fine fellow, I like you." And the young woman entered where the young man was, and she said, "I never saw you before. Yet the moment I see you, I want to lie with you."

The man said, "The priest forbade me to touch a woman."

The girl went away. Turning her back, she threw off her cloths, and she remained in beads alone. Now she went back into the house to tempt the man. The girl said, "Today we will have intercourse, whether you wish it, or you do not wish it." [2]

The boy begged her to leave. "Here they do not do such things."

The girl said, "You are not a man. A real man, seeing a young girl naked, would take off his clothes and would be naked with the girl." And she sang a song tempting him. [3]

The boy now approached the girl. They had intercourse. When this was over, the boy died.

The *vodun* priest came and gave orders that the girl should be bound.

The girl said, "Do not trouble to bind me. I am here." When she said this, she did not rise. She remained there seated. She sat beside the dead body, keeping off the flies.

The *vodun* came to the head of another male worshipper[4] and said, "If you wish the boy to come back to life, bring three bundles of firewood, and three jars of palm oil." They brought the things he asked for. They dug a hole before the door leading to the temple of the *vodun*. There they put in three bundles of firewood, and they poured three jars of oil on top of that, and they lit it. This made a great fire. The dead boy was called Hundjo. They went to take his body, and put it in the fire. . . . Now all the people of the village and all the worshippers of the *vodun* were gathered there.

They said to them, "Those among you who have courage to enter the fire with Hundjo, will come out from the fire with Hundjo." Not a man was willing to go into the fire. Not a woman among these.

Hunjo's mother rose and said, "If it is true that my son will come back to life, I will go into the fire. He is the only son I have." She went close to the fire, but as she smelled the fire, she said, "No, I cannot enter. If I do not die, I will bear another son."

His brother rose and he went to the fire. He said, "I am going to take my brother." He approached the fire, but he, too, lost heart. "If I am not dead, I will have another brother."

His first friend came. "I am going to find my friend." He approached the fire. But he lost heart. He went back. "If I am not dead, I will have another friend, better than this one."

Now, there was no one else willing to go into the fire. The girl Ahwala who caused his death now rose. She took out from her sack two pipes, a small calabash, two sticks for cleaning the teeth, tobacco and matches.

Now, if the fire subsided, they added oil; they added wood.

The girl put her calabash on her head, her pipe in her mouth, the other pipe, tobacco and matches in the hand. They poured so much oil on the fire that it was now a great flame. She began to walk round and round the fire. She said, "Now, if I did not enter the fire, I would be ashamed."

Then she sang a song,

> *If I do not go into the fire*
> *I will not be able to live with my soul.*

After having sung her song, she threw herself on the fire. In a few minutes, the two came out of the fire alive.

All the villagers began to beat the drums, to dance.

Metonofi ordered all the people of the village to assemble. When the people came, Metonofi said to them, "If a child comes into the world and is named by the *vodun*, he must not be kept secluded for eight years. From this day on, the ceremony of the *vodun* initiation must be concluded in three years."

When he said this, the man and woman were there. They now took the girl and gave her to Hundjo to marry.

Long ago, a child named by the *vodun* was held for eight years without seeing the sun, or playing with women. As Hundjo disobeyed, they changed it. Now they keep them for three years instead of eight. The disobedience came from Hundjo.

Metonofi is king of all the world. He rules the *vodun* and Destiny, the animals and all men. He rules not only in Dahomey, but everywhere—in France, as well. He is like the sun. But he is not the sun. No one ever saw him. He lives in the air, and he eats with all the gods.

Metonofi was born before Destiny. Destiny does his bidding. He is Mystery. We say that about all things that exist, and that we do not see. Metonofi, Yehwe,[5] Yo, are Mystery.

[1] *I.e.*, either vowed to a deity, a *vodun*, by the parents before its birth, or as determined by divination, after some illness.
[2] Interpolation by the narrator: "She is strong, that woman!"
[3] It was not possible to record this song.
[4] *I.e.*, the man became possessed, and thus what he said was interpreted as the utterance of the god.
[5] In this sense, a synonym for *vodun*.

104

The faithless wife: Love knows no fear:
Creator moved to pity [1]

There was a man called Degeno. In olden days, a son never went out to get one of his father's wives. But there was among his father's wives one who loved Degeno. The two spent day and night together.

Now, a brother of Degeno's went to tell their father that this wife of his had been sleeping with Degeno. The father said, "No. Degeno cannot [2] have relationship with my wife. It is impossible."

Now this woman, and her name was Sewezo, always slept with Degeno. Degeno had intercourse with her all the time. When this was discovered, the people of the house [3] were called together and they were told that Degeno had taken his father's wife as his wife. The father called on his sons and said, "What should be done to him among you, who took a wife of mine and made her his wife?"

Now, the woman Sewezo always came to Degeno. If Degeno hesitated, she urged him on, and said, "Death is nothing." She was the one who tempted him. She said, "Ah, you are not a man. If a real man sees a woman as beautiful as I am, he takes off his cloth." Degeno took off his cloth. The girl said, "When a man takes off his cloth, and sees a girl like myself ready for him, he takes [4] the woman." But Degeno did not want to do it. The woman taunted him, and urged him, until he had intercourse with her. She sang,

> *Why not sleep on the road?* [5]
> *It is not death to sleep on the road;*
> *If on awakening,*
> *One does not see the mother's house,*
> *It is nothing.* [6]

The father called all the people together. He told them, "What should be done to a man who sought out his father's wife, and made her his wife?"

The people said, "A son who took his father's wife, should be killed and thrown to the vultures." They killed Degeno and threw him away.[7]

Now, there was an old woman who said, "Kill the woman, too." But another old woman said, "The woman must not be killed."

The woman, Sewezo, let it be known everywhere that this thing happened, and that they killed her lover. She wanted a medicine to bring him back to life. Now, at the place where they threw the boy, the vultures came to eat the body. But the woman sat beside him, and drove away the vultures. Day after day she sat beside him, keeping the vultures away, and weeping.

One day Mawu sent her two ox tails, one white and one black. And Mawu said that in order to resuscitate the young man, the woman must sit there for seven days and seven nights, without sleeping. On the seventh day, she must take the white tail and strike the dead man with it, and he would awaken.

Now this happened, and as she did this, Degeno awakened.

[1] Cf. No. 105.
[2] This is one of the strongest incest taboos, even though this woman was not his mother, but her co-wife.
[3] In this usage, "house" refers to the extended family.
[4] The native idiom is "touches."
[5] This is an image for a clandestine meeting; not one inside a house.
[6] Record No. 142-3.
[7] To deprive a man of a ritual burial is a punishment far greater than death itself.

105

The faithless wife: Death as moralist [1]

It is said here that a son must never sleep with one of his father's wives. It is a *su* [taboo] for us.

*   *   *

Now Metonofi had a very, very beautiful wife. If they had searched far and wide, they could not have found a woman to rival her beauty. So Metonofi shut his wife up in his house, saying that no man but himself should see her.

Now, his eldest son, who was called Degeno, climbed the wall and lay with the woman. One day Metonofi surprised his own son with his wife. He was so enraged that he renounced this son and killed his wife. They threw the body of the dead woman outside.

The story says that in ancient times when a person died, the vultures came from the sky to eat the body, for the vulture is the bird of Death. Now that night, Degeno armed himself with two good sticks, and sat down beside the dead body of his loved one. When Death sent the vultures to eat the dead woman, he threatened them with the sticks. So the vultures returned to tell Death that there was a man beside the dead body who kept them from eating it.

Death said it was not true. Death now sent the great vulture called, Akun. But when Akun arrived and was no higher than a house top from the body, Degeno threw a large piece of wood at it, and wounded it in its wing. The bird returned to Death and said it was not possible to eat the dead body.

Now, Death called his first servant, Headache, and he ordered Migraine to measure his eyebrows. It is said that Death's eyebrows reach to the earth. He next called Diarrhea and he called Measles, Influenza, and Yellow Fever, and said, "Go bring my hammock." They brought the hammock, and Death himself went to the dead body. He sang,

> *Death is going to appear,*
> *Agbla is going to appear.*[2]

He set out to see the dead body.

When he came within a height of several feet, Degeno called out, "Stop. If you do not stop at once all the little children will know him who is called Death." He took his stick and threw it at Death.

Death came softly towards Degeno, and he asked him why he did this. Degeno told him his story, and he said he would rather die beside the body of the woman he loved so much, than to let her be devoured by the vultures.

Death said to him that he had decided to revive this woman, but that sooner or later this very woman would cause Degeno's death. Degeno accepted Death's proposal, and Death brought her back to life. She became beautiful as before.

Now, Death gave Degeno two horses's tails, one black and one white. He said if a war came to Degeno he should take the black tail and wave it before the attackers, and all would instantly die. If he waved the white, he would revive them. Then Death gave him seven small calabashes, and Death said to him to go off into the bush and break these calabashes wherever he desired.

Degeno went to the bush and broke all the seven. Instantly, he beheld a great palace with many people about, herds, and riches of all kinds. There was a house where he was to stay with his wife, and it had two stories. He lived there for several months.

One day his wife asked his permission to go to market in Adja. Degeno agreed. The woman left for the Adja market. That day the King of Adja went to market. When he saw the woman, he said he would give two thousand women to have one like her. He said she pleased him very much. And the king said all that could be said to win the woman. Now, the woman could not resist the King, and she did not return to Degeno.

When Degeno did not see her, he did not eat for three days.

But the woman said to the King of Adja that if he started a war against Degeno, one day Degeno would be captured. Before going to market, the woman had taken the two tails belonging to Degeno, to amuse herself on the way.

Now, Adjahosu sent at once a war against Degeno. Degeno looked for his two horses' tails to make the soldiers die, but he could not find them. So he was killed by the King of Adja.

His wife, the one the King of Adja kept, ordered that Degeno's head be cut off and brought to her. Now, as the woman saw that the King of Adja was a great king, and rich, she spoke ill of Degeno to please him. She ordered that the head of Degeno be placed at the foot of a tree, in the middle of the compound.

Every morning the children of Adjahosu showed the two tails to the head of Degeno, and said, "Degeno, here are the two tails."

Then the woman sang to the head of Degeno,

> *See if Degeno still breathes?*
> *Does he see?*
> *Does he hear?*
> *No, I do not believe it.*

And she sang,

> *Gather up for me his fat,*
> *With which to light my lamp;*
> *Give me his bones,*
> *To use as firewood.*

She said it to please the King of Adja. He found it strange. When he heard it, he was displeased. He too began to sing,

> *Women are strange;*
> *Do you remember the watch Degeno kept over your*
> *   dead body?*
> *Do you recall how he watched those days?*

Death from on high sent two strong vultures to take the head of Degeno. The birds came when the children were showing the two horses' tails to Degeno's head. One bird struck with its wings the small child, and took the two tails. The second took the head, and they flew away.

They brought all this to Death. Death revived Degeno and gave him the two horses' tails, and the birds were commanded to bring him down on earth. Degeno arrived with a great army, and sent a war to bring back as slaves the King of Adja and his wife.

Now, when they came, Degeno had these two brought before his tribunal. The King of Adja said before Degeno's tribunal that it was the woman who had wooed him, and the woman said it was the King of Adja who had wooed her. Degeno then gave great gifts to the King of Adja, and said he could return to his Kingdom. He had done no wrong. He said, "I, Degeno, would do the same for a woman as beautiful as she."

Now, he went to his house. He dug a hole and he covered it with a mat. On top of this he put down his pipe. Now, he told his women that when he sent for his pipe, it should not be one of them who is to bring it to him, but the woman whom the King of Adja had taken away. Now, when the moment arrived, he asked for his pipe. The wife the King of Adja took from him hurried to bring it. At once she fell into the hole. Now Degeno began to throw stones at her. Then he threw cloths, and cowries, as he sang,

All that we have said, I shall never forget;
We have talked of the pieces of cloth, here they are.

He threw them into the hole. He did the same with beads and oil, and corn. Everything that must be given the dead, he gave. Now, when he had done this, he closed the hole. Then he made a figure of a woman out of earth, there on the grave, and he made a roof over it, and he called it *hweli*.[3] This is the *vodun* of the women of a household. She watches over women. Where there is a *hweli* in a house, she will keep the women who live there from committing acts like these. And it is forbidden till today to take an oath on *hweli*.

[1] Cf. No. 104.
[2] Record No. 143–1.
[3] This is the woman's shrine found in every compound.

106

Fate of a faithless royal wife

There was a young girl who had never seen the sun. She was the wife of Dada Segbo, and she was more beautiful than the beautiful. If one is Dada Segbo's wife, one never has anything to do with another man. This woman had everything. Fine cloths, money. Nothing was lacking.

Now, this woman went one day to find firewood for cooking. Now, there in the bush she met a man. This man flattered her. He talked to her, talked to her until . . . she let him seduce her.

When the woman came home, she said nothing to Dada Segbo. Now, there was one of Dada Segbo's sons who was a hunter. He was there when this happened between the man in the bush and his father's wife. They did not know he was there, but he saw all. This boy went to his father and told him that Nyunyomamohwe, Good-one-who-had-never-seen-the-sun, went to find a man in the bush. Another of Dada Segbo's wives overheard this. She took her corn, and ground it on the grinding stone, and as she worked this woman began to sing,

> *If Segbo wishes to drink water,*
> *And does not see her,*
> *Good-one-who-had-never-seen-the-sun,*
> *He does not drink;*
> *If Segbo thirsts for a drink,*
> *And does not see her,*
> *Good-one-who-had-never-seen-the-sun,*
> *He goes without drinking.*[1]

When Dada Segbo heard this, he sent word for all those who were in authority at the house to meet. He said he had something to tell about that song.

Now, they all came together, and Nyunyomamohwe was among them. An old woman said to the king, "Dada Segbo, a thing like this must not happen in your house. You must cut off her head." So they cut off the head of Nyunyomamohwe.

One of the women said, "Now, we must bury her."

But the old woman cried out, "No. A woman like this must not be buried. We must put her outside for the vultures."

They threw her in the bush, and the vultures came to eat her. When they finished eating her, Dada Segbo sent to get her cranium, and he called together all the women of the house. He showed them the head. He said, "Now, any woman who lives with me must never lie with another man. Nyunyomamohwe did this, and here is her head."

That is why the wives of the kings of Agbomè never must have anything to do with other men.

[1] Record No. 142–1.

107

Slandering co-wife: Why there are several attendants at childbirth

There was a girl whose father was called King Abiliba Numa-yago. The girl was called Agenu, and another name for her was Tohwesi. So this girl married a king, and she was pregnant. Now, as she was pregnant, she lived among the other wives.

When this young woman was in labor, another wife was beside her. She said to her, "It is the custom here to close the eyes when in labor." Now, there was an old woman in the room, and she spied on them. The woman in labor gave birth to a boy. But this second wife took the child, threw it into a calabash, closed it quickly, and laid a stone beside the mother. Then she took the calabash to her own house. The old woman went into this woman's house, and took the child away.

The woman, who helped deliver the child, went back to the mother, and said, "Ah, women here give birth to children, not stones. You gave birth to a stone. We will tell your husband. You will surely be killed."

So, the old woman went away with the child, and she took care of it secretly.

When the king came, his other wives told him that this wife gave birth to a stone. They beat the woman, who had just been de-livered, with the intention of killing her. But she did not die. The king called all the people together, all the wives, everybody. He told them, "In this house, a woman gave birth to a stone. What should be done to that woman?"

Some called out, "She must be killed."

Some called out, "Sell her."

Some said, "Bind her and expose her in the bush so the vultures may take her."

Some cried, "Strangle her with a rope."

The king said, "Go sell this woman. But if on the way she says one word, you must come back with her."

The old woman was there with the boy, but she said nothing.

There was a place called Kome. It was a place where there was clay for making pottery. They arrived at that place. Now, the king had said she must be sold beyond Kome, so that she might never return to Abomey.

Very well. So, while the woman was on the way, she fell down. She cried out, "By Beu's hair!" Beu was the name of her husband. So they returned home with her and told the king that the woman fell at the place called Ko, and that she cried out, "By Beu's hair!"

So the king commanded that she be shut up in a house. So the woman was there. No one gave her anything to eat. She was poorer than the poor. Meanwhile the old woman was taking care of the child, taking care of him until he should be grown.

The other wives continued to insult the woman, who they believed had given birth to a stone. They said, "We women, when we give birth, we give birth to boys or to girls. You came here to spoil the name of our husband!"

So, one day the old woman came to see the king, and she said she had something to tell him. She said, "But you must call together all the people." She said he must call all his wives, too.

Very well. The king was very astonished. He asked, "What could this woman have to say?" This old woman was one of his father's wives, and she was very old now.

Fine. The old woman said, "I want to talk, but the king does not wish to allow me. I demand permission to speak from the Mingã, the prime minister, and the second minister, the Meu."

Now the day arrived. The old woman dressed the boy nicely. She brought the boy where all the people were gathered. She had taken her stick and had led him there. She came and she called out, "Silence! I have something to say." The old woman spoke to the Mingã, the Meu, and to the king, also. She said, "Do you know this child?"

Now, the mother of this boy was the dirtiest among all the other women. Her hair was dirty. Her cloth was dirty and torn. And the old woman said, "Now, the boy is going to find his mother." The boy looked everywhere. He looked and looked. Then far away in a corner, he saw this dirty woman. He recognized her. He went straight to her and greeted her. Then he came back to the old woman.

Everybody was astonished. The old woman said, "I lived in the same house when I was young. Among us, in our days, there was never a woman who gave birth to a stone. Yet we were many." Fine. "The day this woman bore this boy, that woman there said, 'Here to give birth, we women close our eyes.' She said, 'If they tell us to open our eyes, we open them. If not, we keep them closed.' And when this woman had given birth to this boy, that one put it into a calabash, closed the calabash and then brought it to her own house. Then in place of the child, she put down the stone beside the mother." She said, "I took the boy away, as he was the king's son. I fed him and brought him up. Ask, then, this boy, who is his mother? and who is his father? He will show you himself."

So the boy went again to his mother. He went to the king, also. When the boy approached his mother and called to her, "Mother," they shot a cannon salute for joy. Everybody was astonished. But, everybody was happy.

The old woman said to the boy, "You found your mother. And now, where is your father?"

The boy went and knelt before the king. And he called him "Father."

The king could not believe the story. He looked at the boy, and he asked, "Is that my own son?" He told the Mingā to look well. He told the people to look well.

They said, "All right. Bring the woman here who had put the infant into the calabash. Let us hear her talk."

The king gave orders to take the boy's mother, to wash her, to shave her head, and to give her fine cloths. They brought her back. The woman was crying.

Now, they placed the guilty woman right in the center of the courtyard. Everybody could see the woman who had thrown away a child fathered by the king. The Mingā asked what should be done to a woman like that?

One said, "She should be burned."

One said, "She must be killed."

One said, "She should be thrown to the hyenas."

One said, "She must be killed and thrown to the vultures."

One said, "She should be sold."

Then they asked the old woman. They said, "You are the one who watched over the boy. What is your wish that we do with this woman?"

She said, "To teach other women that this should never be done, she must be killed. Her head must be cut off."

The king said, "We must follow the advice of the woman." He gave the command that they make a mound of earth, and bury the woman in it. And the Mingā was told to cut off her head. The king also commanded them to split the woman's body and hammer pickets inside her belly.[1]

Very well. So the king gave the old woman hammock-carriers, and many women, and many men [2] as a reward for what she had done. And to his wife who had borne him this son, he gave girls and boys, and many cloths, and much money. He commanded that she be freed of the task of going for her own firewood. She was never to crush corn, never to go for water, never to go to market. She had nothing to do but eat.

That is why now when a woman is about to give birth, she gives birth in the presence of many women. She is never alone with but one. If she were to give birth in the presence of only one of her husband's wives, the co-wife would harm her.

[1] This is done so that in some later reincarnation, she may not bear a child.
[2] *I.e.*, slaves.

108

Wives cure boastfulness

This happened long ago. When the family head let out his pigeons[1] in the morning, he mixed beans and corn and threw this to them. When the pigeons finished eating, there was a jar of water for them.

No sooner were they satisfied, than the pigeons began to annoy the girls with their boasting. They kept saying, "If I had someone, I would fight him. If I had someone, I would fight him." The pigeons always said that.

The women got together and said, "After they eat, our husbands always say, 'If I had someone I would fight him. If I had someone I would fight him.' Are they really so strong?"

The women went to see Aklasu, the vulture, and said to him that their husbands were always looking for a fight. They said, "Tomorrow you come, and when they are finished eating, you fight them. But you must not kill them. You can give them a good scare, though." They repeated, "But you must not kill them."

When vulture came, he settled on a tree nearby. The male pigeons knew nothing about his being there. But the women knew. Now, as usual, the master had them all come out to eat. At sunrise, they had corn and beans thrown to them, and when they finished with that, they drank the water.

Each began again. "If I had someone, I'd fight him. If I had someone I'd fight him." When they said this, the vulture threw himself at them, tearing at them, pulling at their feathers.

Now, the women were at the side and watched.

The pigeons cried, "Let us go. We do not want to fight. We said that only to frighten the women. Let us go." Vulture plucked all their feathers and then he flew away.

Now, the women came to their husbands. The pigeons were all without feathers. The women repeated mockingly, "If our husbands saw something, they'd fight. If our husbands had someone, they'd fight him."

The battered pigeons pushed their wives away and said, "What are you saying? What are you saying?"

Today Pigeon keeps saying, "I don't want to fight. I am not here for a fight."

[1] The family head is here mentioned specifically, because pigeons are given in sacrifice at certain rites which he performs, and he is thus expected to keep a large number of them.

109

Guessing a hair-tying conundrum:
Wife as informer

There was a man. One year, he parted his hair in three parts. One in front, one at the right, and one at the left. And he tied these with thread.

When he did this, he went to see the king. He showed him, "There." He asked the king to name the name of this tying. But the king did not know, so they gave him money.

So now the king wanted to know the name of this tying. But he did not know what to do. Then he sent for the man's wife. He plotted with her. He gave her much money. Now the king said, "All the money I gave is not just a present. It is to pay you for telling me the names of the three designs of hair tying."

Now, this man tied his hair like that to earn money. He went from one king to the other and asked him to guess, and when the king could not guess, he had to give money. Now, it was also agreed that if someone learned the name of this tying, the man would be killed.

So the woman said, "The one in front is called Another's-child-is-not-my-child. She said, "The one to the right is called Sleep-does-not-know-death." The third was called Wives-never-keep-their-husband's-secrets.

The following year the man did the same thing. He tied his hair in three sections. But he did not know that his wife had told the king their names.

There was another man's child in his house. The child hung up his coat on the wall. This man took the child's coat and went out.

So now this man went to the king, and he lowered his head and showed him. The king said, "This time I know the names." He said, "The design in front is called Another-man's-child-is-not-my-child." He said, "The one on your left is called Sleep-does-not-know-death." He said, "That to the right is called Wives-never-keep-their-husband's-secrets."

So there was a flag pole. They bound the man to that flag pole. Now, the man was there from early morning till mid-day. He became drowsy and fell asleep. So the king had all the people come together and all the sub-chiefs. They talked about what should be done to him. But he heard nothing. He was asleep. When he awoke, the king said, "All right. Now we will kill you. We will have you climb to the top of the flag-pole."

So the young boy, whose coat was taken away, came there. As they said they would kill him by making him climb the flag-pole, the boy cried out, "You mustn't kill the man who wears my coat. You mustn't kill him in my coat."

The king said, "Listen to the child's voice." He told them to bring the child to him.

The boy said, "I say it is my coat. You mustn't kill the man in my coat."

The king said, "All right. Undress the man and give the coat to this child." So the child was very pleased. He laughed.

The king said, "Now wait. Don't kill the man yet." The king said, "I forgot to tell you something. This man came to me each year with three kinds of hair tying, whose names I could not guess. If I hadn't been more cunning than he, I should never have known them."

So they brought the man to the king. He said again, "Here, the hair in front is called Another-man's-child-is-not-my-child. That to the left is called Sleep-does-not-know-death. That to the right is called Wives-never-keep-their-husband's-secrets."

A sub-chief said, "As we know the names of the tying, let us not kill the man. Let us free him." He said, "You saw the child who came for his coat. If it had been his child, he would not have laughed after taking his coat." He said, "If it had been his own son, he would have wept. So let us free the man."

The king said, "There, Sleep-does-not-know-death. Here we met to decide his fate, whether to kill him, but he fell asleep." So the king said, "Since we know the names of your tying, and that is what you do to earn your food, now that we know it, we will let you go on with it. But when you come each year, come to my sub-chief, and he will give you food."

That is why they did not kill him.

And the king said it was his wife who had disclosed the names. So it is true that women never keep their husband's secrets. So they brought the wife before everybody, and they told the people that it was she who had told.

VIII

Explanatory and moralizing tales

Explanatory and moralizing tales

DRAMATIS PERSONÆ

NYA, GODUWÈ and AFI, three brothers
AJAMBLATA, their father
KING OF AYO
AZIHÃ, a large bird
DADA SEGBO
VULTURE
KING OF FETOMÈ
His three sons
BULL
ADO, the egret
HETABLÈ and AMIFUNHÈ, two birds
AJINAKU, the elephant
WUTUTU, a bird
AGAMA, the chameleon
TURTLEDOVE
PARAKEET
HEVIOSO, god of Thunder
SOFISOFI, a bird, daughter of Dada
   Segbo
PIG
ELEPHANT, LION, MONKEY
HEN
CHICKEN, HAWK
MAWU, Sky deity
RABBIT, BUFFALO
FROG
PIGEON, DUCK, COCK
DONU, a seller of okra
ANTELOPE
TORTOISE, Diviner for the animals
ZINHO, GHA, and KLA, three monkeys
NANA LOLWÈ (Kupa Ajasivi Nana
   Lolwè), a woman with seven,
   (forty-one) children
ASOGBWA (Kitikli Asogbwa), her
   youngest child
LEOPARD

SAMEZO, Kitikli's horse
MOLE
HYENA
GOAT
BAT
METONOFI, King of the Universe
LÃ, an animal with a red skin
AGBUI, the wild rat
SERPENT, living in the river Halã
Son of Dada Segbo
CAT
Mahi man
His son
His friend
BOSU AGUDANKOTIN, a sweet potato
   turned man
An old farm woman
HUNTER, his best friend, his diviner,
   and his father-in-law
KAKPO, a farmer
AMUSU, his brother, a thief
DOSU, their brother, a merchant
KAKPOVI, lover of a wife of Dada
   Segbo
An informer
A woman
Her children
HUNSU, a wealthy man
His dog
A dead relative
DEATH
FIRE, FIREFLY, two brothers
HORSE
AGON, KPANUHWELÈ, two birds
AGBIGBI, king of the birds
ZOMADJALI, a subject of Dada Segbo

110

Human ingratitude: Why the races of man differ in color

There were once three brothers. The first was called Nya, the second Goduwè, the third Afi, and their father was called Ajamblata. Well, they were hunters, and they hunted everywhere.

One day the brothers went to hunt in a country called Adja. While they were there, a daughter of the King of Adja fell ill. Now, they did not wish that people should know their individual names, so they all called themselves Ajamblata. Now, when they heard that the King's daughter was sick, they sent a message to the king saying they could cure the daughter. They asked for forty-one sacks of cowries and forty-one cloths, and they took all that.

At night they took the money and the girl, and escaped. While on their way they sold the girl to the oldest son of the King of Ayo, who was looking for a princess to marry. The Ayo prince was very pleased, and he divided his kingdom in two. He gave one part to King Ajamblata, and kept the other for himself. The girl enjoyed his full confidence.

Now the eldest of the Ajamblata brothers, who was Nya, lived in a house which was next to the house of the Ayo Prince. At night whenever the prince was away, Nya went into his house. He made the woman pregnant, and she gave birth to triplets, all boys.

But later the Ayo prince found out that the three children were not his, for they were like Nya in every way. The Prince then called together all the people, and announced that the three strangers and the three children were to be killed.

Now in ancient times, there was a bird which today does not exist, called Azihā. It was the largest of all birds. Strong! Now, when the three brothers learned that the next day they were going to be killed, they took the three boys and escaped to the bush. The prince followed in pursuit.

History tells us that at that time the birds talked. Now, in the country where the Ajamblatas and the three children had run away was a great, great mountain called Feso. The three brothers went to seek refuge at the foot of this mountain. Azihā had built her nest on top of this mountain. It was more than one hundred kilometers high. One day, the bird came down on earth in search of prey. Azihā saw the three children and wanted to take them and eat them. But the Ajamblatas begged her not to eat the three children. They said they were not ordinary [1] children, and explained to Azihā their adventure.

Just as they were telling this to the bird something happened. Their pursuers were coming towards them. The bird picked up one brother and held him against one thigh, she picked up the second and held him against the other, the three children against one wing, the other brother against the other wing. Then she flew away, and she put them down high on the mountain where her nest was. When she did this, they were out of danger.

Every morning now, the bird went down on earth to find food for the three men and the three boys. The bird also had three children. Morning, noon, and night she brought food. But a day came when the great bird went away and did not come back at night. The following day the bird did not return. In the morning the bird still did not return. At mid-day the Ajamblatas are hungry.

The first says, "Ajamblata." The second says, "Ajamblata." The third says, "Ajamblata, what is to be done?"

The first says, "Let us eat the bird's children." So they took a small bird and killed it, and ate it. The great bird had not yet returned. So the next day they did the same thing. They killed the second small bird. And the third day the same thing happened. And they ate all the three children.

On the fourth day the mother bird came back, bringing many, many animals for them and the children. When she came, she did not go at once to her nest, but stopped first to give her human friends food. When she approached the nest, she saw the three heads of her little ones and nothing else. In a great rage, she took one of the boys under a wing and flew away toward the sky. When she was up high, she threw him to the ground. That one fell on the Coast of Africa. And when he fell he changed into clay. The bird flew back to the mountain, took up the second twin and threw him toward Europe. That one changed to chalk. She went back and took up the third, and threw him in North Africa to the Moors. That one was changed into a river called the Nile.

She now went back to the mountain and seized Nya whom she threw down here in Africa. Nya fell on a palm tree. As he struck the tree the palm kernels fell to the ground. In the morning, a girl came to pick them. From on high in the tree, Nya begged the girl to bring him a ladder. The girl brought him a ladder, and Nya came down. There, in that country, it is said there is a river called Duwaya, or the Niger. At that time the Niger was all black. Now, every morning this small girl and the man Nya went to the Niger to wash. So they became black. Then they peopled all of Africa. The first child born to them was called Nyavi, Nya's child.

The bird returned again to the mountain, and now seized the second brother, Goduwè, and flew away, and threw him toward the European Coast. This one fell on an orange tree. On this tree there was a large worm. It was half human, and it had one foot. The worm was all white, and it was a woman. Goduwè was on the tree for three months. He lived on oranges, and he finished by making the worm pregnant. They had a son whom they called Yovo, the white man.

The bird returned to the mountains and she took up the third brother, who was Afi. She took him and flew away. This one she threw toward the coast of Arabia, the land of the Mohammedans. In that country a woman was frying cakes. The bird from on high threw down the man, and he fell into the oil in which the cakes were cooking. He became yellow. The woman kept Afi with her, and later he made the woman pregnant. Their first child was called Ime, the Arab.

Now the mother grieved so much for the three children that she threw herself into the river and became Damballa Hwedo, the rainbow, and when the rainbow is seen in the sky, they say the mother is looking for the three Ajamblatas.

This is why, it is said, that the blacks love palm oil, and the Europeans love fruit.

[1] As triplets they were sacred to the Goddess of Twins and the Creator.

Why there are liars, adulterers, and thieves

In the days of Dada Segbo there were no courts. If the chiefs happened to be at the place where they held court they said nothing. They remained there till mid-day, and went home.

A bird called *gangan* went to a place called Fetomè.[1] It is where Death lives. This bird said to Dada Segbo that there at Fetomè they knew how to speak. So Dada Segbo called Vulture. Dada Segbo said, "You are always at Fetomè. Have you found there a thing called speech?" And he said, "When you go there again, then tell the others to send me speech without delay."

So Vulture went to tell the king of Fetomè that so the king, Dada Segbo, had said. Vulture said, "He asks you to send him speech." The king of Fetomè said, if Dada Segbo wished to look after his children, they would come and teach Dada Segbo speech. Vulture returned and said to the king, "The king of Fetomè agreed to send you some of his children, and they will teach you to speak."

Dada Segbo said, "Good."

When Vulture left Fetomè, they gave him three rolled-up mats. He took them up with his claws, and he brought the three to Dada Segbo. When the king unrolled the mats, he saw three small boys.

These boys grew up. Now, the eldest went after other men's wives. But, in the king's house, there must not be a man who goes after other men's wives. The second began to rob. But in the king's house there cannot be thieves. The third was on good terms with the king's senior wife.

Now, the king had a long beard. The third said to the king's senior wife, "You must get some hair from the king's beard, and I will make you a charm that will cause you to be loved."

Next, he went to the king. He said, "Tonight your senior wife will try to kill you." So when they went to sleep, the king did not fall asleep. The senior wife came with a knife to cut off some hair from the king's beard. The king caught her by her wrists, and he began to call. They bound the woman.

Now, as the woman had a grown son working in the field, the young man from Fetomè went to tell him that the king had bound his mother and would kill her. He said, "If you are prepared to save her, you must bring your gun and your knife. For your father is ready for war."

Then, he went to see the king, and he said, "As you bound this woman, her son has gone with the news to all his brothers, and they are coming with guns to kill you."

When the king heard this, he called together all his people, and he told them that his son was about to make war on him. Now, all these people were before the king's doorway awaiting the arrival of the son.

When the young man and his friends approached the king's house and saw so many people gathered there, he began to shoot, for he thought his father was ready for war. So they began to fight.

The liar climbed up a tree and he called out, "Silence! Those who come from the fields, stop firing! Those who are here at the house, stop firing!" He asked, "Where is the king?"

But the king had already run away to hide. So, they went to find the king.

The liar said, "The king asked for three children to care for. But it is a child, and only one, who conquered his kingdom." [2] He said, "The king had asked for three liars,[3] but I alone showed myself able to break his kingdom. One can never watch over [4] the people of Fetomè."

So the king had Vulture come, and he said, "Now, since you were the one who brought these people from Fetomè, you must be the one to return them." So Vulture took them back to Fetomè.

Now, the three already had wives, and their wives were pregnant. No one knew that these women were their wives. But that is why there is always a liar, a man who goes after other men's wives, and a thief everywhere. It is because the children of the three Fetomè men were born to the three women.

[1] Lit., "land of Fe"; that is, the city of Ife, in Nigeria.
[2] Narrator: "It was the liar who had caused the war."
[3] This is an oblique reference to those who show skill in testifying at court, and special pleading.
[4] *I.e.*, control; keep from intriguing.

I I 2

Outwitting creditors: Why the *Ado* birds circle about cattle

There was a bull. The white bird Ado said to Bull. "You are clean, and you are well behaved. I want to marry one of your daughters." Bull said to him, "All right. But how are you going to marry my daughter? You who are so light? You have no strength." But then he said, "Follow me around and someday you will have my daughter."

To have a big fish, one must give something to the stream first. So Ado gave Bull many gifts. He gave cowries, he gave drinks, he gave too many things.

> *Ado, white bird, Ado,*
> *They say you always follow the cows:*
> *Ado says, when a new calf is born:*
> *"If you are really a woman I do not know;"*
> *"My child says you always follow the cows."*
> *"I always follow the cows*
> *Because long ago a promise was made,*
> *And I have gone without eating."*
> *And all the years go by,*
> *And the bird follows the cows.*
> *He is told*
> *"Tomorrow we shall settle the matter;*

Or in nine days we shall settle the matter."
Ado has worked without reward for a long time;
The calf is a woman child,
But they give it to the butcher;
When the second is born
They say she is large for Ado,
And the butcher takes her away.[1]

Now, Ado followed Bull and his family, and followed them for he had not received Bull's daughter. Ado does not want to follow Bull. "What, my Mawu, work for people without reward!" exclaimed Ado. He said to Bull, "For three years I have followed you. You promised me the first daughter would be married to me. I did everything so that the girl should be given to me. But the first you gave to the butcher. You gave the second also, and I have nothing. It is better you tell me that I cannot marry your daughter. Why do you deceive me?"

Bull answered, he said, "Be patient. Follow me always and you will see. How do you know that I deceive you? If I do not give you a daughter, I have sisters to replace my daughters."

And Ado said, "Yes, I am going to follow you."

That is why the Ado birds are always behind the herds. Bull is still promising Ado a daughter. And so it goes on until today. For this is not just a story of long ago.

[1] Record No. 127-1, 2.

113

Elephant is no riding horse: Why Hetablè cries, "Take him away"

There was a bird called Hetablè. This bird one day ate himself full of fruit and rested on a tree. He called to another bird named Amifunhè.

Hetablè said, "I am looking for a horse to ride." Amifunhè went until he reached Adja. He passed Adja and went to the Asante in the bush. He did not find a horse. He came back and told Hetablè, and Hetablè told him to go and look for one in Ayo. But he found no horse in Ayo.

Hetablè sent him to Ketu. In Ketu there was no horse. From Ketu he went to Meko. He found no horse in Meko. He went to Badã, where the Nago lived. He found no horse in Badã. He went to Abeokuta, where their king was called Ala'ake. He did not find it there. He went to see the Oni who lives near the Ayo country. He went from there to Gbomocho, a place among the people of Ayo. From there he went to Sai, also at Ayo, from there he went to Gbo-odè, near Sai. There at last he found a horse.

He asked the price of the horse. They said the horse cost three hundred cowries. He returned to see Hetablè. Amifunhè went again and spent a year journeying, and he came and said the horse cost three hundred cowries.

Now Hetablè said to Amifunhè, since he could not carry the price of the horse all at one time he should take one cowry at a time, one at a time, one at a time. . . . He spent three years journeying to Gbo-odè in order to pay for the horse.

Instead of bringing a horse, Amifunhè came away with the rope about the neck of an elephant. They started on the way, Amifunhè and the elephant. On the road, the elephant broke the rope and escaped.

Amifunhè had not seen the horse when they settled on the price, and the people deceived him. Amifunhè now came back to Hetablè without a horse, and he said to Hetablè that the horse had escaped on the way. He said, "They did not give me a horse. They gave me an elephant."

Hetablè said to him, "Now, I don't care whether I get the horse or not. I've had to wait for it four years. So, either bring me my money, or bring me my horse."

Amifunhè could not go to the people to ask them for the money, because they had given him an elephant for the money. He had no one from whom to borrow the money. So he went into the bush, and he took a heavy rope with him. Then one day having at last come on an elephant, he put the rope about its neck. He brought the elephant to Hetablè.

Now Hetablè rested on a tall tree. From the distance Amifunhè called to him, "Hetablè, here is your animal! Hetablè, here is your animal!" When the elephant came near the tree on which Hetablè was seated, he began to break the branches and shake the tree. Hetablè escaped.

Hetablè said to Amifunhè, "What kind of a horse is this?"

Amifunhè said, "This is a horse from Gbo-odè." Hetablè said he had never seen a horse like that before.

The elephant, Ajinaku, now told Amifunhè and his friends who brought him here, to play the drum for him that he might dance. While he danced, Ajinaku uprooted trees and threw them everywhere. He broke down walls, broke down everything. Hetablè said, "Take him away. Take him away. I don't want the money, and I don't want the horse. Take him back to his master."

And to this very day, the bird, Hetablè says, "Take him back to his master. Take him back to his master. I don't want him here."

114

Magic to overcome anxiety: Turtledove cannot change its nature: What Turtledove says

There was a bird called Wututu,[1] and there was Chameleon, Agama. There was Turtledove whose heart was never easy. She was afraid. Wututu said to her that as her heart was never free from anxiety, he must make a good charm for her.

"When Chameleon is on the road and sees a man, he does not worry, but goes on his way. He does not try to run away," said the Turtledove. "But I, who am larger than Chameleon, even if I see a child, I fly away."

Wututu gave Turtledove a magic preparation to eat and recommended to her that, if a man approached her, she was to remain until she saw whether the man wanted to catch her or not.

So Turtledove settled herself on the road to see if the charm was good. A man was passing by. When Turtledove saw him from afar, she flew away without letting him come near her at all. She flew to the limb of a tree, and said to herself, "The charm Wututu made for me has not done anything for me. If I do not take care, I will be caught by someone. I must try again, for I must have a charm to protect me."

She went and again settled herself on the road. There was an old woman who was on her way to look for firewood, and she had taken a stick for a cane. When Turtledove saw this, her heart began to beat, and she flew away once more. When she felt herself safe this time, as she sat on a tree, she called, "Oh, Wututu! Oh, Agama! The charm you made for me whether it gives fire or does not give fire, all the same my heart beats, beats." And it is this that Turtledove now sings,

> *Fear is killing me*
> *Little by little.*

[1] This bird is associated with the God of Thunder.

115

How Parakeet came to speak

Parakeet gave birth to a daughter. Now Hevioso, the god of Thunder, came and said he wanted to marry this girl, but Parakeet was not willing. Parakeet said, "You cannot marry my daughter, because here one gives a great deal before marrying a girl."

Hevioso said, "All right. If you do not want to give me your daughter, I'll let her go. We will see later when we meet again."

When Parakeet is to bear children, then before the children can be born, it must first rain so that the eggs can break. Parakeet laid the eggs. The time for the young to come out arrived. It was the time for rain, but the rain did not fall.

Parakeet took up the eggs and went into the bush, thinking that in the bush it would surely rain. There no rain came. She took the eggs to the Ayo kingdom, thinking there it would surely rain. There no rain fell. The instant she left Allada rain began to fall in torrents in Allada. The instant she arrived in a country, that country had no more rain.

In the village of Ayo she placed her eggs on top of a Loko tree. One day lightning came and struck the tree, and the eggs fell to the ground. Good. She gathered up the eggs, and took them to the king of Ayo, and told him what had happened. She said, "Hevioso wants to marry my daughter. Now he does all this to make me suffer."

The King of Ayo called Hevioso to come to him. Hevioso told the King of Ayo that it was because of Parakeet that there is no more rain in Ayo. "I wanted to marry her daughter, and she refused to give her to me." Now Hevioso said to the King of Ayo that he did not even want the daughter. All he wanted was her red tail. It was her tail that pleased him.

The King of Ayo said to Hevioso to make the rain come, but Hevioso said in order for the rain to fall, he must have the daughter of Parakeet. So Parakeet gave the girl to Hevioso. The day she gave her to Hevioso, it rained everywhere. He took the girl with him up to the sky. Good. After that it rained every day.

Before then, Parakeet was like all the other birds. She talked like the others. Hevioso said to the King of Ayo he would give something to Parakeet to replace her daughter, as an exchange for her daughter. The King of Ayo had Parakeet come. Now before Parakeet had a long, long tongue. Hevioso slit her tongue and said to Parakeet, "From now on, whenever you hear a man talk, you will repeat what you hear after him. I give you this right forever."

So to this day, Parakeet can repeat all that a man says. That is her gift from Hevioso.

116

Field-clearing contest: Dilemma of conflicting tasks: Why the woodpecker pecks

In olden times Dada Segbo had a daughter. This child was a bird, who was called Sofisofi. She was unmarried. All the animals came to ask for her, but Dada Segbo would not give her to any of them.

Now, among the animals, the one who was the hardest worker was Pig. When he saw trees, he would cut them down with his teeth. When he saw earth to be kneaded, he would knead it with his snout. And Pig came to see Dada Segbo, and said he wished to marry his daughter.

Now, the people of Dada Segbo's quarter had often spoken to him of an animal who was a good worker. They said he worked better than all the others, and that he was called Pig. But Dada Segbo said he did not know him. So when Pig came to ask for Dada Segbo's daughter, and they wanted to know his name, he said, "My name is Pig."

They asked him, "Is it you who live in the district of the King of Ayo?" For this was where the pigs lived. Dada Segbo said, "Yes, I want very much to give you my daughter, for I have learned that you are a good worker. But, as many other animals have asked me for her, I will now turn over a field to each of you to work."

Pig laughed to himself, but aloud he said, "I am not very strong, Master. I cannot compete with Elephant, and Lion, and Leopard and the others who are stronger than I am."

Dada Segbo said, "Do you want to try, or not?" [1]

And he replied, "I will try." [2]

And so Dada Segbo fixed the day for the test six days ahead. The field extended from here [3] to Abomey. Pig already had a wife who was called Sosi, and his mother-in-law was called Aluba. That evening Pig happened to see his mother-in-law, and she said, "My son, I have two jars full of palm nuts. Come six days from today, and crush them for me."

And so, just as Dada Segbo named the sixth day for the work in the field, so his mother-in-law fixed the same day. He had a great deal to do. So Pig was sad. He went out thinking, not saying a word. Now, both of his parents-in-law had fixed the time of beginning the task at six o'clock in the morning. Dada Segbo's field was here in Allada. That of his mother-in-law was in Ayo. It is quite far away!

The night before, Pig went and slept near Ayo so that he could be there at six o'clock. In the morning, at about six o'clock, he took his hoe and put it in his sack and went to crush the palm nuts, as his mother-in-law had told him to do. He stayed there until eleven o'clock.

The other animals had begun to work Dada Segbo's field at six o'clock. They were already on their way. One was at Atogon, another at Hwegbo, another at Akpame. His part had been left unworked. When he came, the others mocked him, "You can't do anything now."

Pig replied, "All the same, I can try." And he began his work. As he worked, he said, "Elephant has left me my part, but all the same I will overtake him." As he said these words, he left many of the animals behind him. He said again, "Lion has left me my part. But that makes no difference, for I will overtake him." As he said this, he left Lion, Horse, and Ox behind, even though they had started early in the morning. For, he worked with his snout.

Now there remained Elephant, Leopard and Monkey. They were almost up to the border of Dahomey. So he said, "Leopard, Elephant, and Monkey have left me my part. Just the same, I will overtake them." Now he had left all the other animals behind, and no sooner did he say these words, than he left even these three behind.

All the animals cried, "Isn't that Pig ahead of us? Let us hurry! Let us hurry!" Now, where the finish was, there was a bird who watched to see the one who came first, so as to tell Dada Segbo. Pig arrived in Abomey before all the other animals. He said to the others who were all angry with him, "You here? I got here sometime ago!" Nobody answered him.

The bird told Dada Segbo that Pig had come in first, and Dada Segbo was very astonished. "What! Pig who started at eleven o'clock is through first!" he exclaimed.

Dada Segbo's daughter was dressed in her fine cloths and she was seated on a mat, waiting for her husband. Pig, however, liked palm nuts, and on the way he stopped to eat some that he had come upon. He ate until he was tired. Then he fell asleep. The others who had been left behind, began to pass him.

So Elephant came to Dada Segbo and said he was first. Now, as he was so large the other animals did not dare contradict him when they were asked about it. And when they asked Lion, he said, "It is true, I was second." Then Monkey said, "I was third. The others were behind me."

At last Pig awakened. When he arrived he was the last of all. He was roused by a bird who said to him, "Get up, the others are ahead of you!"

So when Pig arrived, Dada Segbo said, "There's the animal who was ahead of all of you."

But all the others cried, "No, it was not he. No!"

When Sofisofi heard this she flew up into a tree, and she began to make holes in the tree. And today she is the woodpecker. She did not come from Mawu, but from Dada Segbo. And so she is the wife of Pig. Yet neither he nor any other animal has ever possessed her. For while they were all quarreling, she flew away. And it is she who today is called Sofisofi. And she pecks at trees.

---

[1] The narrator here dramatized majesty.
[2] This was spoken timidly.
[3] Allada; the distance is about thirty-five miles.

117

Hen goes to live among men: Why chickens and hawks are enemies

There is a bird that steals little chicks. And there is a hen. Hen said to this bird called Hawk, "We've lived here in the bush for a long time. Let us go into the village, and live in houses among men."

They fixed a day. Now when they fixed the day, they both

went to see Mawu. Mawu said, "In order to put you in houses like men, you must find seven rats called *gbedja*."

So they went home. The next day Hen brought one *gbedja* to Mawu, without letting the bird know. Day after day she did this. She brought four. Now there were three more to find. She went to tell Hawk that the day they arranged with Mawu was too close. They had best fix another day. But she was deceiving Hawk. She herself made up her mind to go on the day fixed. Now Hawk asked, "Who told you Mawu would not be there that day?"

Now, Hen had already given Mawu all the seven *gbedja*. She went to tell Mawu that she asked Hawk to come, but Hawk said, "No." She said Hawk was not to be trusted. "It is because she does not believe in you, Mawu, and she does not wish to come and live with man."

Mawu said to her, "You have done what you were to do, and now you will stay in a house, among men."

When Hen came back, she moved into a house in the village. She said nothing to anyone, but seeing straw in a house, she settled there and began to lay eggs. As no one had noticed her for several days, there were many eggs there. But one day the children of the house saw the bird and wanted to chase her away. The older ones said, "Do not chase her. Do not chase her."

The head of the family said, "When a bird comes from the bush, and stays in a man's house, that means it wants to stay among men. One must not drive it back into the bush."

So now when a chicken comes out, they throw corn to her. Otherwise she would run off into the bush to find food. So when they began to feed her corn, she got used to men. When they approached, she no longer flew away in fright. So the chicks came.

When Hawk saw that, she said, "Ah, we planned to go together and stay with man, and that one lied that she did not wish to go. Now she is among men."

Now, as the bird Hawk has claws, she rests on a tree and watches the chicks. Any chance she gets, she flies down and takes a chick.

The people said, "Ah, a bird came to stay with us, and another bird comes to take away her children." So when the hawks come, they throw stones.

That is why Hawk always takes the chickens. It is because the hen had deceived her. Otherwise, she would have been among men in villages, like the chickens.

118

Strained friendship: Friend as hostage: Why Frog is in the water and Tortoise gives fire

Good! Rabbit and Tortoise were friends. Tortoise had no fire, and when he wanted fire, he would go and get it at Rabbit's house. As Tortoise came day after day to take fire, Rabbit's fire was no longer very strong. So Rabbit forbade Tortoise to come and borrow fire any more.

So Tortoise came to get fire during the night when Rabbit was away. In this way they became enemies, each one against the other.

Elephant was their chief, and he had the two come to him. He asked Rabbit, "Why are you an enemy of Tortoise?" Rabbit answered that every day Tortoise came to look for fire at his house. And the other day, he had made a fire, and it was not strong any more. But Tortoise had come and taken the wood, and since that day Rabbit was unable to cook.

So Elephant kept the two as prisoners, and told each one that, as punishment, he would have to stay at his house for five days. Since Tortoise was an animal that escaped all the time, Elephant forbade him to escape.

Elephant summoned Lion, Buffalo, Lã, *Turo*, who is an animal like Lã and commanded all of these animals to go find Tortoise and Rabbit. The first one they caught was Tortoise and his friend, Demochi. This is an animal that never eats, but only licks its paws. It is the size of a squirrel, or of the bush-rat. They looked for Rabbit everywhere, but Rabbit had disappeared from that country.

As Rabbit and Frog were friends, they asked Frog, "Where is

Rabbit?" And they said, "Since we have not found Rabbit, we will take you in custody [1] in his place."

You have but to kill yourself,[2]
And say someone else has killed you;
A chicken that has wings to fly
Has landed on a picket fence and died.
So he did this, then said,
Someone else had killed him.

And since Elephant had no water at his house, he said to Frog, "You will have the duty of getting me water." Frog made a little hole, and there water was found.

And so, until today, if you see frog, he is found in the water. And he said to Tortoise, "You must go and find fire."

And it is for that reason that it is Tortoise who gives fire, and eats only wood that has been charred.[3]

[1] The stratagem employed by the monarchy to get a rebel who had taken refuge in some unknown parts, was to seize and torture his best friend. This was done not because the best friend was counted on to betray the whereabouts of the fugitive, but so that the fugitive would give himself up to save his friend. Cf. *Dahomey*, I, p. 393.

[2] If he died for not revealing his friend's hiding place, he could blame only himself.

[3] Cf. No. 17, above, for the same explanatory motif in a myth.

119

Why Tortoise lives in the bush

In olden days, Chicken, Pigeon, Duck, and Tortoise were friends, and they lived in the same house. They ate together.

There was a blind man who cultivated his field, and planted much corn. Good. In olden days, Duck could fly like the vulture. So one day he went to steal corn in this man's field. When he came home, they cooked the corn and the four ate together.

Good. So among these four Tortoise ate more than the others. Duck said to him, "Look here, since you ate most of the corn I brought, there is the place where I got it. Go and get some yourself now. But be careful you are not caught."

Now, Tortoise went away. He went to get the corn, and he came back home. When Tortoise came back, Duck was not there. Duck and her children had gone to the lagoon for water. So when Tortoise came home and Duck was not there, he called Partridge and Pigeon and Chicken to come and eat with him.

When they finished eating, Chicken said, "Where is Duck's part?"

Tortoise said, "I believe Duck ate already."

When Duck came back and found nothing, he went to tell the farmer that Tortoise has been stealing his corn. Now, when the animals gather at home, it is Cock who is their chief. The farmer asked Cock to call together all his birds. He said, "I have something to ask them." Cock ordered all the birds to come together, and he told the farmer to speak.[1]

The farmer said, "Tortoise took my corn without asking me for it."

Tortoise said, "No, it is not like this. I did not know your field. The duck showed me the way."

Duck said, "No, it is Cock himself who showed me, for one day he came home with a grain of corn in his mouth, and I saw it."

Cock said, "I never go into the field. I found the corn in the market. The market place is the place I frequent, but everybody knows that I am never found in the fields. The day he saw me I was coming home from market."

Everybody had his turn. Cock finished talking; Duck finished talking; Pigeon also finished talking. Cock said to the farmer, "But who was it who stole your corn?" The farmer said it was Tortoise.

Tortoise said, "I am going to take my case to Dada Segbo." [2]

So they all went to Dada Segbo. Dada Segbo asked them what they came for. Tortoise said, "The others stole the corn, and now I am being blamed."

But all the others said, "It was Tortoise alone who stole."

Good. Dada Segbo said, "Now, I cannot get to the bottom of this. Do you want to remain with these birds?" He said this to Tortoise.

Tortoise said, "No. No you must separate us."

So Dada Segbo said to Duck, "You are always to stay at home, with your friends Cock and Pigeon. Man must build your house for you. You, Tortoise, you go to the bush. To make your bed, you must make an open nest."

That is why Tortoise is now to be found in the bush. And his nest is open, just as Dada Segbo had ordered. And Dada Segbo said, "You get away far, for otherwise you will be killed." From his open nest, anyone passing can see Tortoise at once.

[1] *I.e.*, a complaint was made in the court of the chief, the court of first instance. Cf. *Dahomey*, II, pp. 16 ff.
[2] *I.e.*, he appealed to the court of the King.

120

Why animals do not talk

There was a man called Donu. He always sold okra. He knew how to grow okra better than anyone else. Now Antelope came to eat his okra every day. When he planted, the antelope ate. He planted, the antelope ate. So the man went to divine with Diviner Tortoise. The diviner said to him, "You find a trap for me." He found a trap. Now Antelope came to eat, and he fell into the trap.

The next day, the man and his wife left for work in this field. He looked for the trap, but the trap was not there. He said, "Wife, I caught the animal who eats our okra yesterday, but today the trap is no longer here."

He looked and looked until he found the trap again. Antelope said to him, "Yes, I'm the one who eats your okra." The man wanted to kill the antelope. Antelope said to him, "Do you want to kill me, Donu?"

Donu's wife stood next to Donu and she said, "Yes, he's going to kill you, because you ate all his okra." Donu killed him, and began to take him out of the trap.

As he started to take him out, Antelope said to Donu, "Are you going to take me out of the trap, Donu?"

The woman answered for him. She said, "Yes, he's going to take you out of the trap, because you ate all our okra."

Donu began to take off his skin. Antelope said, "Are you going to skin me, Donu?"

His wife answered for him. She said, "Yes, he's going to take off your skin, because you ate all our okra."

He took off the skin, and he was about to begin to cut him up. Antelope said, "Are you going to cut me up, Donu?"

His wife answered for him. She said, "Yes, he's going to cut you up, Antelope, because you ate all our okra."

Donu wanted to cut him up in pieces. Antelope asked, "Are you going to cut me up in pieces?"

His wife said, "Cut, Donu, he ate all your okra."

They brought Antelope home. She put some of it in a pot, and she wanted to put it on the fire. He said, "Are you putting me in a pot to cook me?"

The woman said, "Yes, I'm going to cook you, because you ate all our okra."

They made a stew of it. When they were ready to eat, the meat asked him, "Donu, are you going to eat?"

Donu said nothing. His wife said, "We are going to eat you. You ate all our okra. Now we will eat you. It is not only Donu who will eat you. I, too, count."

Donu finished eating and went to ease himself. The moment he bent down, Antelope came out and escaped. Donu died.

Since that day the animals no longer talk. If an animal talks, one does not eat it. If it does not talk, one eats.

Rivalry for power: Why the Gha monkey has red buttocks

There were three monkeys. The monkey Zinho, the monkey Gha, the monkey Kla. They were friends. Now each of them wanted to become chief. So they began to quarrel, and they went to the king.

The king said, "Who among you is to be chief?"

One called out, "I."

The other said, "I."

Now Kla also said he wanted to be chief. The king said Gha could not be chief because he was descended from Kla. So the king said Kla should become their chief. So they went home.

Now, sometime later the monkey, Gha, gave birth. The monkey Kla told Zinho to have the people who lived nearby fetch water for Gha. But the monkey Zinho did nothing. Good. So the monkey Gha left the new-born child, and herself went for water.

So, since Zinho did not trouble to see that Gha was supplied with water, and Gha herself had been obliged to go for it, Chief Kla himself decided to get water for Gha. He came there while Gha was still away, and put the water down in the house. Then he began to play with Gha's child. When Gha came home, she was very astonished to see the chief in her house, playing with her child. She asked him why he did this for her. The chief said he told Zinho to find water for her, but Zinho refused. So he himself had gone for water for her.

So Kla went to tell the king that he had ordered Zinho to get water for Gha, and that the monkey Zinho had refused, so that he himself had to fetch the water for Gha.

The king had the three of them come again before him. The king asked Zinho, "Why did you refuse to go for water?"

Zinho said he did not go for water, because he was angry with Gha. He said, "One day, a child of Gha's came to eat corn in a certain field. When Gha's son saw my child, and noticed that my child had more corn than he, he bound him, beat him unconscious and left him in the field. Good. So the planter came and took my child as a slave. To this very day I have not found my son."

Good. Now when this had happened, Zinho had gone to Chief Kla to tell him that that was what Gha's son had done to his son. Very well. But the chief had not called the two of them in order to judge the case. He had done nothing at all.

Now in the rainy season, there was a tree with very fine papaws on it. When the little Gha saw all the ripe papaws, he climbed the tree. No sooner did the monkey Zinho see this little Gha climb the tree, than he also climbed the tree. And when they both climbed down, the monkey Zinho beat him, and flogged him hard, and then sat him down in the fire.

That is why to this day the monkey Gha has red buttocks. It is because long ago the son of Gha had been burnt there by Zinho.

122

Unnatural mother: Why Monkey's mouth is black and her buttocks are red

There was a woman who had seven sons. The last child was called Asogbwa. She went to the spring all the time, and, because she walked slowly, she had to walk seven days to come back. If one of her children said, "Welcome, Nana Lolwè," she took him and ate him. She would let her jar fall, and take the child and eat him. It was always the oldest that spoke. She said, "No child will call my name, and not die for it." [1]

Again she went away to the spring. On her return, the second said the same thing. She took him and ate him. The third also, and the fourth, and the fifth, and the sixth.

Of all her children, the seventh had the most cunning. He was the friend of all the animals. His mother left for the spring, and he knew the day she would return. He went to see his friends and borrowed money from them. He borrowed from the animals two hundred francs. Then he bought a white horse and mounted it. He wished to go a hundred kilometers, but when the horse had done twelve, he was tired. He sold the horse in the village and borrowed more money from his friends. With this he bought a black horse. He got on it, and again wished to go a hundred kilometers to see if the horse went well.

This time the horse did two hundred kilometers without getting tired. He said, "Good, this is the horse I am looking for."

He put the horse at the side of his sleeping place and fed it. The following morning he saw his mother. A great wind was blowing. Trees were falling. Dust was flying. And his mother was in the wind. He said, "Welcome, Nana Lolwè," and jumped on his horse and dashed away. And as the horse went into a gallop, he sang.[2]

Asogbwa galloped away, and his mother ran after him. The first one Asogbwa saw was Leopard, who was a friend. Leopard asked him, "Where are you going? Stop."

Asogbwa said, "My mother wants to eat me."

Leopard said, "Good. Sit down. I will eat her, and you will be all right."

Asogbwa said, "Very well. But I have no confidence that you can do this. I will wait two kilometers away and see what happens. For she is stronger than you are."

The mother came there, and Leopard said, "Why do you want to eat my friend, Asogbwa?" The mother said, "Let me go, you good for nothing." Leopard gave her a blow with his claws. Then the mother seized Leopard, and tore him to bits. She only ate the blood.

Asogbwa said, "See, it is as I told you." And he resumed his gallop.

He met Lion. Lion asked him why he was going so fast.

He said, "My mother wants to eat me."

Lion said, "Stop. Would you like me to kill her?"

Asogbwa said, "Yes, but I have no confidence that you can do this. I will go off three kilometers and see what happens."

The mother arrived, and Lion said to her, "Stop."

She asked, "What are you going to tell me?" Then Lion attempted to seize her, but the woman strangled him with her hands.

He next met Elephant. Elephant asked Asogbwa: "My friend, what is the matter?" He replied that his mother wanted to eat him. "If that is all, stop. For, big as I am, you will see what I will do."

Asogbwa said, "I am coming, but I will wait a kilometer up the road and we will see what happens."

Elephant asked her, "What is the matter, Nana Lolwè?"

She said, "I do not want to talk now. What are you doing?" So Elephant seized her. But the woman killed him.

After this, Asogbwa resumed his flight, with the mother after him. He went to see the red monkey, who is an iron-worker. Monkey said, "What's the matter, Asogbwa?"

He said, "My mother wants to eat me."

"Stop. I'll eat her right away."[3]

Asogbwa replied, "That which Leopard, Lion, and Elephant could not do, you will do? Let me go." But he said, "All right. I'll go off four kilometers from you, and see how you come out."

The woman came, and Monkey asked her, "Why do you want to eat my friend, Asogbwa?"

She said, "I am not going to leave my child for tomorrow. I will eat him today without fail."

Monkey said, "Good. If you want to eat your child, I am going to eat you."

Nana Lolwè swallowed Monkey. Monkey came out. Monkey took Nana Lolwè and swallowed her. She came out. They did this to each other many times. Each time the one who was swallowed came out again.

But now the little animal was tired. And the mother, too. Now Monkey told his children to put two hoes in the fire. They put the hoes in the fire and they heated them well. Monkey swallowed the woman. Then he took the two hoes, and he sat down on one, and the other he put to his mouth. Nana Lolwè tried one way out, but she struck her head against one hoe. She turned, and tried to get out by way of the mouth. But she struck the other hoe.

And it is for this reason that Monkey's mouth is black, and his buttocks are all red. And that is why today one never asks Monkey, "Where is Nana Lolwè?" If you did, he would point to his chest, and you would die.

¹ This tale does not tell why her name is secret.
² This song could not be recorded.
³ Interpolation by story-teller: "He is one of the smallest animals."

123

Unnatural mother: Why Monkey has red buttocks, a large chest, and flat belly

There was once a woman. She was a monster. Her breasts were six meters long. She had forty children. The forty-first child was called Kitikli Asogbwa. The woman was called Kupa Ajasivi Nana Lolwè.

Now it was time for this woman to go to the well for water. When she came back, she called her eldest child to help her take the water jar from her head. None of her children could call her by name. In fact, no one might do this. When she called her eldest child, the child said, "Kupa, let me take a breath." When the child said this, the child ran away. Kupa followed her, and she sang,

> *Do not leave, do not leave,*
> *Wait for me,*
> *I'll catch you.*

She caught her eldest child and swallowed her alive. Now as she swallowed her eldest child, all the other forty called her name, and ran away. So the second was taken, and swallowed. And one by one, she succeeded in swallowing all forty.

The forty-first child went to Ayo, and bought a horse. He galloped on the horse from Ayo to Adja. The horse died. He went back to Ayo. He bought another horse. He galloped on this from

Ayo to Adja, from Adja to Dahomey, from Dahomey to Ayo. The horse died.

He now bought a third horse, which was all white. He galloped from Ayo to Adja; from Adja to Dahomey; from Dahomey to Ayo; from Ayo to Savè. Samezo, the horse, said, "Ah, Kitikli Asogbwa," but he did not die.

He rested the horse there for two days. On the third day, very, very early in the morning, his mother came from the well. She invited Asogbwa to come and help carry the water. Asogbwa said, "Kupa, Nana Lolwè, let me rest." The mother said, "So!" But Asogbwa ran away. Kupa followed him. Instantly, Asogbwa mounted his horse and galloped away. Nana Lolwè could not catch him. Asogbwa sang,

> *Do you hear the hoof beats of my horse?*
> *You are carrying me!*

He sang to the charm he gave his horse. When he sang this, the horse galloped faster than ever.

Asogbwa was the friend of all the animals. When he rode so, he saw Rabbit. Rabbit said, "Kitikli, what is the matter?"

Asogbwa said, "My mother wants to kill me."

Rabbit said, "Wait a few steps away. I am the king of the bush. When your mother comes here, I will burn her with my urine."

The mother sang,

> *When a child of mine calls my name,*
> *He shall die.*
> *Asogbwa called me 'Kupa,'*
> *Asogbwa shall die.*

Rabbit said to her, "Nana . . . wait!" Rabbit urinated on her face. Then he swallowed the woman alive. The woman came out, and swallowed Rabbit. When she did this, she said, "Djadja . . . You will not come out again." Rabbit did not come out.

The woman followed Asogbwa. Asogbwa found the great Lion. He said, "Kitikli, what is the matter?"

Asogbwa said, "My mother wants to kill me."

Lion said, "Wait there a short distance away. When your mother approaches, I will rend her apart." He bellowed, he growled, he jumped to show off his strength to Asogbwa. When Asogbwa saw this he was encouraged.

Kupa arrived. Instantly, Lion swallowed her alive. Kupa came out. She swallowed Lion. She repeated the words she had spoken for Rabbit, and Lion did not come out.

Asogbwa called on his charm and the horse galloped away. Now Asogbwa saw Leopard. He said, "What is wrong?" Asogbwa told him the same thing. Leopard asked him to wait. But he said he did not dare, because Lion had been swallowed. All the same, Leopard persuaded him to wait.

Kupa arrived. She was the first to swallow him. Leopard came out. He seized Kupa by the neck, and sucked all her blood. After he had done this, he swallowed Kupa. Then he climbed a tree to sleep there.

Asogbwa came to take his rest in the shadow of the tree where Leopard was sleeping. That instant Leopard's stomach burst, and Kupa came out. In all haste, Asogbwa jumped on his horse and disappeared.

Asogbwa found Mole. He said, "Kitikli, what is the matter?" Asogbwa did not wish to wait, but he waited all the same. Now Mole swallowed Kupa. Kupa came out. She swallowed Mole. Mole came out, and instantly dug a hole more than twenty meters deep. Then Mole swallowed Kupa and threw himself into the hole. He had told Asogbwa that when he threw himself into the hole, Asogbwa was to come and close the hole. When Asogbwa shut the hole, Mole came out through another hole, and Kupa remained in the hole.

Now, Mole and Asogbwa sat down to eat. When they were eating so, they heard a shaking of the earth. Kupa came out. She swallowed Mole, and Mole did not come out any more.

Now, Asogbwa left in haste. He galloped until he met Buffalo. It was the same thing. He next found Hyena. It was the same thing. He found Boa. It was the same thing.

He then found Monkey, who was a smith. "Kitikli Asogbwa, why are you in such a hurry?"

They say when the monkeys see a person, they make three gestures. They lean to one side and ask, "Do I resemble your father?" They lean to the other side, and ask, "Do I resemble your mother?" They lean back, erect, and ask, "Do I resemble you?"

Asogbwa told him his whole story. So Monkey had him hide in his room, and he shut the room with a key. Nana Lolwè arrived. She greeted Monkey, and Monkey also greeted her. Suddenly Monkey swallowed Nana Lolwè. She came out. She swallowed Monkey. Monkey came out.

When he came out, he returned to the forge. He told his assistant to work the bellows. He had no strength left to work the bellows himself. The assistant was the wasp. He said, "Hokpakala." Monkey held him so, until he became thin just like he is today. Then Monkey threw him away. Monkey had the idea of making a large hoe.

He next went to call the vultures. The vultures came. But they were not strong enough to make the bellows dance. They said, "*Gbagbawuuuu!*" Monkey said it was not enough. He took a hot iron and with it touched Vulture's head. That is why Vulture is always bald. Monkey said that was no good.

He went to call Goat, and Goat came. Goat sat down, and he said "*Futuketekete!*" Monkey saw that it was not strong enough. He pulled his testicles. That is why Goat's testicles are longer than those of any animal.

He went to get Bat. Bat came, and he said, "*Kenkenkenken!*" Now, Monkey said that was not enough. He took away Bat's two hind legs. That is why Bat has no feet to stand up.

Now, the fire was no longer hot enough to make the hoe. He sent for his eldest son who was working his field. When his son came, he said, "Fine, here you are. Hold my bellows." When he held them, he said, "May the wind come to help me hurl an iron at an enemy." When he said this, his father was pleased, and caressed his head. Instantly, the hoe became very red.

Now, Monkey swallowed Nana Lolwè again. She came out. She swallowed Monkey, and Monkey came out. So Monkey swallowed Nana Lolwè, and he ran fast toward his forge, and sat down on the red hoe. Nana Lolwè could not come out again.

That is why Monkey has red buttocks, a large chest, and a flat belly.

124

Outwitting an enemy: Goat as trickster:

Why one must have cunning

Metonofi had a large field. He called Goat to tell all the animals that he ordered them to come and cultivate the field for him. He told Goat to let them know. The day arrived and all the animals came. Lion, Leopard, Elephant, Doe, Antelope—they all came. They began to work. Each took his part of the field, and they worked until noon.

They were hungry, and they said to each other, "What are we going to eat now?"

Lion said to Antelope, "Since we have nothing to eat, come close now. As you are large, each of us will have a piece." Now, Antelope did not care to come close and be killed, so he ran away.

Lion now said to Hyena to go and catch the animal called Lã, an animal with a red skin. They began to cut him up. Goat cut off a piece of the leg, and Lion ate it without salt or pepper. He said, "It isn't sweet." Goat told him the sweet part was the thigh.

Now, when Goat came to the field, he went off to find some honey. So, when Goat cut off a bit of this meat, he put it in the honey, and when Lion took it, he said, "Ah, you are right. That part is really sweet. You must cut for me all the meat from there."

They kept on cutting until they finished the two forelegs. Lã was there, still alive.

And now Goat said, "What are even sweeter are the intestines of Lã." When Lã heard these words, he wanted to run away, but he had no more meat on his forelegs.

So Lion said to Goat, "Then take out his intestines."

Goat said, "No, tell Hyena to do it. He is stronger than I am."

At last they finished eating Lã, and he was dead. They did this until they had eaten all the animals. Only Goat and Lion remained. Lion now said to Goat, "Now it is your turn."

Goat said, "I have something that very much pleases the great

—even the king." And he shoved the honey toward Lion. Then he said, "Softly, softly into the mouth of the great," and poured it into Lion's mouth.

Lion said, "Ah, how sweet it is! You are a fine boy. That is very sweet."

Lion asked him for more, and again, he said, "Softly, softly into the mouth of the great," and poured it into the lion's mouth.

Just then another hyena came by, and Goat said, "Come here, visit with us. We are having a good time here." So Hyena came near them. Goat gave him a chair to sit down, and saying nothing as Hyena looked on, he finished pouring all the honey into Lion's mouth. He said to Lion, "Now what I need is all gone. I cannot make any more. I need something else in order to continue giving this sweet thing to you."

The Lion said, "Where can you find the thing you need?"

And Goat replied, "To make the thing, I need a piece of Hyena."

When Hyena heard this, he stood up. Lion said to him, "Take off your legs, I need them." Hyena could not escape. But as Goat started to cut off the legs, Hyena seized the knife and ran away. Lion ran after him in pursuit. Now Goat had his chance; he escaped in the other direction.

But as Goat does not run fast, he is more cunning than all the animals. That is why, in this life, one has to have cunning.

125

How the hyenas forfeited their office as burial chiefs: Why there is the Dokpwegan [1]

Man was there before there were hyenas. Dada Segbo gave the hyenas a place. They were there as burial functionaries. When a man died, they called them to take him away and bury him. Now, when they were told to bury a man, they ate him instead.

One day one of Elephant's wives died. Now, instead of burying her, they ate her. Elephant went to tell Dada Segbo that those people never buried the dead. They ate them. This time Dada Segbo said nothing. Now there was a man who died soon after. They called them to come and take the man, and bury him. They came to take away the dead. Now, Dada Segbo had one of his sons spy on them. The boy hid, so he would not be seen.

When the other hyenas saw the dead body, they began to beat the drum, to sing and dance. The dead body lay in the middle. As they danced about it, Dada Segbo's son came over and said, "May I dance, too?"

The eldest hyena said, "Yes, if you like."

Now there was also a second son of Dada Segbo there. He, too, came over, and he asked, "May I dance, too?" He, too, began to dance.

So as they danced, Hyena told the boys to go in the house for a drink. When the boys went in, the dead body was taken away, and when they returned, they saw the body was no longer there. The boys went back to tell Dada Segbo that the bodies they entrusted to these people were not buried. They were taken away.

Dada Segbo called for the hyena chief to come. He said to him, "I trusted you to bury the dead, but now I know that you do not do it. Yet I gave you all that was necessary to bury them." He said to them, "Now I command you all to change into hyenas." So they became hyenas.

Dada Segbo said, "I will call Elephant, and put him in your place." Dada Segbo told Elephant that now he would be the Dokpwegan. Elephant became Dokpwegan. He buried the dead properly. That is why to this very day, there is a Dokpwegan.

[1] Head of cooperative group.

126

Why Hyena has no friends

There was a hyena. This hyena was a friend of man, and of an animal called Lã. The three were friends. Now, Hyena had a journey to make. When he got to the village he was very, very hungry. He found a friend there. This was the village where Lã lived. There were men there who were working at the forge. As the men played the bellows, the bellows sang, "If a goat dies here, one throws it away. If a pig dies one throws it away. If a chicken dies here, one throws it away. One throws away all."

Hyena took the bellows, and his bellows began to sing, "Where is the place where the goat is? Where is the place where the pig lies? Where is the place where the chicken lies?"

So Lã led Hyena to the place. Hyena ate so many animals—he ate until he no longer knew where he was. Now, Hyena returned neither to his friend Lã, nor to his own house. He hid there, and when they threw down a dead animal, he took it. Now, when they threw down a dead man, Hyena also took him and ate him.

One day several *lã* threw down a man, and they saw how Hyena was busily eating another. They saw that he ate their dead. They threw down the dead body they carried, and Hyena snatched it up at once.

The *lã* now went to find a hunter. So Hunter came and shot Hyena.

Now, when all the other hyenas learned that Hyena was dead, they called together many, many hyenas. They said, "From this day on the friendship between us hyenas and the *lã* is broken forever. Lã killed our brother."

Formerly, Heyna and Lã were brothers. They visited each other. Man, too was their friend. If Lã did anything bad to Man, Man came to tell Hyena, and there they talked it over, and punished the one who was wrong. If Hyena did something against Lã, the three met and talked it over. The same with Lã.

After this, Lã and the hyenas became enemies. They never met in the bush without wanting to kill each other. This is so till today.

Tomorrow morning you will hear the same story told you by a bird, but you had better not listen. If you hear it told by a bird, you will die.[1]

[1] NARRATOR: "This is the end of all stories. It never changes."

127

Mock funeral: Hyena plays dead: Why Hyena lives alone

Once upon a time there were many animals, and their chief was Rabbit. Now, when Rabbit was king of all the animals, Buffalo came. He was bigger than Rabbit, and had horns. There was wild rat who was called Agbui. She is the mother of Djiso, and of Ram, too. It was said that a rat, who is good for nothing, is the mother of So and Agbo.[1] Hyena came to see the animals. He ate nothing but meat. As he ate only meat, when the animals saw him, they ran away.

One day Hyena sent word to the animals that he was dead. The animals came together to bury him. Goat and Rabbit left the animals, and Rabbit brought his children out. Mother Rabbit said, "As Hyena is dead now, one may now leave the children home. But let us all take one on our backs, and go and bury Hyena. I have my daughter on my back."

Now all the animals thought that Hyena was dead, but Hyena was only pretending to be dead. As they came nearer and nearer, Hyena opened his eyes to see what animals were there, and where the big ones were, for the little ones were in front.

An animal, *lǎ*, came close to Hyena. He is like a buffalo, but he has red skin. Hyena saw him through closed eyes. Some of the animals played the drum, and others danced. Through half-closed eyes Hyena spied and spied on the animals, but all the time the animals thought he was dead.

They danced round and round Hyena, until, all at once, Hyena threw himself at them. The others escaped.

In ancient times this Hyena used to live together with all the other animals. From that day on, he is alone. The others will not come near him.

[1] It is not explained why Agbui should be regarded as mother of these Thunder dieties, nor does this seem to have any bearing on the action of the tale.

128

The youngest is most cunning

Dada Segbo had a woman. This woman bore him two children. Dada Segbo and this woman and her children all ate out of the same calabashes, and drank from the same calabashes.[1] The four always ate together.[2]

The children said, "It is not good that we drink the same water as our father. We will go to a river from which water is never taken, and from that river we will bring water for our father."

They sang,

> *To him who has thrown*
> *The calabash in the river,*
> *I give water for the King;*
> *The sacred River Halan,*
> *Keeps within its banks;*
> *The sacred Lake Nohwe*
> *Keeps within its channel;*
> *Where water is found*
> *A monkey is there to deceive*
> *Fast, fast.*

The elder son took a jar, and they went to the river. The moment the boy put the calabash in the water, a serpent from under the water asked, "Who is it that comes here for water?"

The boy said, "I come here for water for my father, the King."

The serpent said, "Didn't you see the Halan Lagoon there? Why didn't you go there to get water for your father?" And he said, "Leave my water, and go elsewhere."

The boy returned home. He came and told his father what had happened. He said, "The serpent of the river told me not to take the water."

The second son said he would go to get water there. He took with him a cock and a chicken, and his jar. There he made two small mounds, and he killed on one the chicken, and on the other the cock.[3] Then he went and put his calabash in the water.

He sang,

> *To him who has thrown*
> *The calabash in the river,*
> *I give water for the King;*
> *The sacred River Halan,*
> *Keeps within its banks;*
> *The sacred Lake Nohwe,*
> *Keeps within its channel;*
> *Where water is found,*
> *A monkey is there to deceive*
> *Fast, fast.*

The serpent now said nothing, and the boy took the water. The father put the water in his house, and he had all his people come together.

He said to them, "Among many children, all children must not be clever. There should be clever children, and stupid children." His youngest son was the most cunning of all. He said, "Now, I have many cocks, and many chickens, but my other sons had not thought to ask me for them to offer to the river. But the youngest asked me for the cock and the chicken, and I gave them to him."

That is why when one has many children, one chooses among these children the most astute, and shares with them all confidences. And one leaves the stupid alone.

[1] Customary usage is for the man to eat out of a separate calabash.

[2] The man eats alone, or with male guests, and the woman and her children eat together.

[3] The spirit of this river was propitiated and, thereupon, allowed water to be taken without protest.

129

False friendship: The youngest is the most cunning

There was a cat who had three children. The leopard had only one. One day Leopard came to see Cat. She said, "I am alone with my child. When I am away, there is no one left to watch the house and my child." She asked Cat to lend her a child to watch over her little one.

Cat said, "Very well, I will send you one."

Now Cat called together her three children. She asked the eldest, "How many times must you be annoyed before you will be on your guard?"

The eldest said, "If I am annoyed four times, then surely, I will be on my guard."

The cat said, "Good." She asked the second one to come to her. She asked the same question.

The second said, "If I am annoyed three times, I will surely be on my guard."

Cat said, "Good."

The last said, "I think if I am annoyed once, I will be on my guard instantly."

The mother said, "Good. You will be the one to go to Leopard's house."

The child left. Now the first night, Leopard took her own child and placed it in front of her, against her belly, and young Cat against her back. And so they went to sleep.

During the night young Cat got up softly, softly, and went to sleep on the grinding stone. A little later that night, Leopard woke up, and threw herself at the sleeping Cat behind her. Her claws found nothing but the cloth.

The next morning Cat was walking about the house. Leopard said, "Where did you sleep yesterday?"

Cat said, "I slept on the grinding stone."

Leopard said, "Good. Then today you are also to sleep on the grinding stone."

That night Cat went to sleep in the cook-house. Later that night, Leopard threw herself at the stone, thinking Cat was there. Her claws struck the stone.

The next day she asked Cat, "Where did you sleep last night? I did not see you on the grinding stone."

Cat said, "I slept in the cook-house."

Leopard said, "Good. Tonight you are to sleep in the kitchen, too."

That night Cat went to sleep in the house. During the night Leopard got up, and searched for Cat in the cook-house, but he was not there.

The next day when she saw Cat, she asked, "Where did you sleep yesterday?" Leopard said, "Good. After this, we will sleep together. You wander about too much, and you are only a child."

Now, she gave Cat some beads to wear about his arm, to identify him. At night she put Cat against her belly, and her own child behind her. During the night, while Leopard was fast asleep, he moved Leopard's child to lie against his mother's belly, and himself lay down behind Leopard. Then he took off the beads and had Leopard's child wear them.

Later that night Leopard awoke. She thought Cat lay against her belly. She seized the child there, held him, and tore him to pieces.

When she tore the little leopard to bits, she believed her own son lay behind her. So she kept pushing morsels of the dead animal into the mouth behind her.

Leopard said, "I am eating Kitten." She said it in her special language.

Now Cat said, "I am eating little Leopard." He said it in Cat's special tongue.

So Leopard believed she had killed Kitten. But it was her own child. She ate all but the head. In the morning, Leopard went out to get firewood. Kitten took up the head and began to toss it up and catch it, toss it up and catch it. Now Leopard came in just then, and she saw Cat playing with her child's head. She leaped at him, but Cat climbed up the wall and escaped.

So he went home and told his mother what had happened. He said to his mother, "I told you I would not stand being annoyed even once, that I would be on my guard instantly."

To this very day, the eldest son is the most stupid. And the most cunning is always the youngest.[1]

[1] NARRATOR: "That is true!"

130

False friendship: The youngest is the most cunning: Why Leopard meets his enemy face-to-face

Leopard and Cat were friends. Leopard gave birth to one child, and Cat had three. When Leopard saw that Cat had three children, they were no longer on good terms.

Cat's three children were in the habit of going for firewood. They also brought her water, they went to market, they hunted food for her. Cat herself stayed home and did nothing.

Leopard's child was still young. She could do very little for her mother. Leopard went to see Cat. She said, "Now I get up at cockcrow and I go for wood, for water. I work all the time. Lend me one of your children to watch over my daughter, so that I may have more time to get food."

Cat promised to send her one of her children to watch over little Leopard. So Cat called her three children, and said, "Which of you can go to watch over Leopard's child, without being caught?" And the mother asked her eldest son, "How many times must you be annoyed before you are on your guard?"

The boy said, "Three times."

She called the second and asked him the same thing.

The second boy said, "Four times."

She called the youngest. She asked, "My child, how many times must you be annoyed before you are on your guard?"

The child said, "I am not sure, but I think if I am annoyed once, I will be on my guard."

When he said that, Cat said, "Good. You will go to watch over Leopard's daughter."

Cat sent her child to watch Leopard's daughter. When the boy came, they ate at night, and Leopard said to him, "Now you are to sleep on the mat over there."

When she said that, Cat went to sleep high up in the rafters. He left his cloth, however, on the mat just as though he were lying down here. But he went to sleep up there.

Towards midnight after they had gone to sleep, Leopard got up and seized the cloth on the mat.

Cat said, "Mother, what is the trouble?"

Leopard said, "Oh, nothing. I was dreaming." They went back to sleep.

So the next day she said, "Tonight you are to sleep on that stone there." That was the stone on which they crushed millet and ground nuts. Cat lay down beside the stone, but placed his cloth on the stone, just as though he were there himself.

During the night, Leopard threw herself on the stone, thinking that the cloth was Cat.

Cat said, "What is the trouble, mother?" Leopard said, "I was dreaming again. Where are you sleeping?"

The following night she said, "Now you are to sleep in my bed, because I am going to sleep away from home, and I will come back late tomorrow. You are to sleep with my child in my bed."

Leopard went out, and hid near the house. Before going out, she gave one cloth to Cat, and one to her daughter. When Cat went to sleep he exchanged his cloth for the cloth of Leopard's daughter, and he also changed places with Leopard's daughter.

At night when Leopard came back softly, softly, she saw the cloth and she thought it was Cat sleeping on the outside, as she had told him. She threw herself at her daughter and devoured her.

Cat said nothing. He had hidden himself above, and was watching Leopard. When she finished eating her daughter, Cat said, "Why did you eat your daughter? Me, I'm going home to my mother. You told me to come and watch your child. Now that you have eaten your child, I have nothing more to do in your house. I am going home."

When he came home, the mother took her children up into the Loko tree, and they took refuge there from Leopard's anger. They had a cord that reached from the ground to the top of the tree. With that cord the mother cat went down to the ground, and up again.

One day their mother went out. That day Leopard came. Whenever Cat came home, she had a gong, and she tapped it seven times, and the children knew it was their mother. Now, Leopard came and she tapped the gong, but she tapped it eight times, and Cat's children escaped.

That night before the mother came home, Leopard hid behind a tree to learn how many times to beat the gong. She heard that the mother cat gave the gong seven strokes. Leopard listened, and with her claws she made the marks on a tree, so that she would know the number, because Leopard could not count. She had it all marked.

Then the next morning, Cat went away again to find food. Leopard also went away, but later she came back, and took up the gong, and struck it seven times. The children threw down the cord, and she climbed up. She said, "I see your mother is not home. I came to visit you, what will you give me?"

The youngest one had cooked food for them, and he gave it all to Leopard. They asked Leopard, "Are you going?"

She said, "No, I will stay a while."

The youngest now said to the others, "To make her leave, you know what we'll do?"

The first said, "I know. We'll get sticks and beat her, and she will leave."

The second said, "We'll begin to insult her, and so she'll leave."

Now on this tree there was a dead branch. If one stepped on it, one got down in a hurry. The little one said they would give her a mat to rest on. "We will put the mat there, and then we will heat some water."

The children put the mat there, and they put some water on to heat. Now, they had Leopard sit so that they could throw hot water on her head, and if she wanted to hold on, she would touch the dead branch. Now, the water was hot. The little one said, "All softly, over the head of the great," and he threw the water over her. Leopard gripped the branch. The branch broke, and she fell to the ground. She fell on her left side.

Before this, when Leopard saw you, she turned her side to you. Now since she had hurt her left side, she no longer can turn. She meets her enemy face to face.

131

The corrupt seek to spread corruption:
The young are cunning

There was a man from Mahi.[1] He took the wife of his family head.[2] He took the wife of his diviner. He took the wife of his priest, who was also his best friend. This is a friend whom one trusts with everything. His wives gave birth, each to a child, a child, a child. All were sons.

Good. He said to the child of the wife he took from his family head, "My child, in the life you will live, if you come upon the wife of your family head, you can take her." He said to the one born of the wife he took from the diviner, "You can take the wife of your diviner." And he said to the other, "You can take the wife of your priest-friend."

The child of the wife of the family head said, "All right. I heard what our father said. Now, I shall wait before I do what our father advised until after his death. I want to see what his death is like."

Very well. The others said, "All right. All right. We shall wait, too, and we shall all see."

So the boys were there. The father was there, too. He had grown very old. Then he died. They sent for the funeral chief. The grave diggers came and dug the grave. They put the man in the grave. But the grave was not yet covered over.

One of his sons remained at the open grave to watch, while the others left to perform a ceremony. So the lamps were there. They were native oil lamps, made of cotton burning in oil. Now, the one who had put the body in the grave, had arranged the cloths [3] that had been given the dead man. But he did not know that one of the cloths had caught fire on a burning lamp near by.

So the cloths in the grave began to smoulder, began to take fire. As the son who was there approached, he saw smoke. He ran to tell the others, to say the cloths in the grave were on fire.

They poured water into the grave to extinguish the fire, but they had to put in so much water that the grave was filled with water. There had been many cloths in the grave. They began to dip up the water, dip up the water. They dipped until the grave was dry. In the grave they found nothing. The body, the cloths, everything had been burned.

So to represent the man, [4] they went and made a wooden figure. And they used that as a substitute for the man. They gave the image a few cloths and they buried it. Then they did all that was to be done for a dead man.

So the following day, the son who had spoken years ago counseling that they wait to see their father's end, called together all the others. He said, "Now, I want to talk to you about what our father had told us to do." He said, "Now, what I have to tell you is this: Our father died three times. First he died the soul's death. The second time he died a fiery death. The third time he died a watery death. [5] For in his life he had done three evil deeds." He said, "That is why we others must not do as our father did."

Do you not agree that he died three deaths, for the three wrongs he did?

[1] A non-Dahomean is chosen for the anti-social role assigned here to the protagonist.

[2] The oldest living male of the family.

[3] These are gifts to establish the dead man's position in the world-of-the-dead, as well as gifts given him to take to other dead of the family. Cf. *Dahomey*, I, pp. 369 ff.

[4] Cf. *Dahomey*, I, p. 397.

[5] In Fŏn: *Eku seku, eku zoku, eku toku.*

132

Sweet potato transformed into man: Origin taunted: Why one does not say what is forbidden

There was an old farm woman. Every year she planted sweet potatoes. One day she went to the field to harvest the sweet potatoes. While harvesting, she found one sweet potato which was very clean, very smooth, and resembled a person.

She said, "If this sweet potato were to change for me into a person, oh! I should be very pleased!"

When she said this, the sweet potato said to her, "No. If I change for you into a person, you will call me 'Sweet Potato.'"

She said to the sweet potato, "No. I have neither children nor husband. I live alone in my poor house. Why should I say that?"

The sweet potato said to her, "Turn your back to me." The sweet potato changed for her into a robust young man. On the way home, the sweet potato said to her, "I am to be called Bosu Agudankotin."

On the way home, Bosu Agudankotin caught two peacocks, and he took two jars and two posts of the thorny *hetin*. Then they went home. Bosu Agudankotin planted the two posts. On each post he placed a jar, and he put water in the jars. Then he put a bird on each post.

They were there. They took their meals together. Always they ate sweet potatoes. One day the villagers began to beat drums. The old woman was not at home. Then, Bosu Agudankotin took a cloth belonging to the old woman in order to attend the ceremony. Bosu Agudankotin left.

The old woman came home, and she did not find Bosu Agudankotin. She looked about the house, and she saw that a cloth was missing. She said, "There, this pig of a tuber! He took my cloth. When he was in the field he never covered his body. Then, when I bring him home, and take care of him, he wants to tear all my cloths. He will see me!"

The two peacocks flew away and sang, "Bosu Agudankotin-e . . . ," and they went close to the place where they were beating the drums. They rested on a tree and sang again. Bosu Agudankotin heard the voices of the birds, and he asked the singers to be quiet for a moment so that he might hear what the birds were saying. The birds repeated their song again. Bosu Agudankotin came closer, and the birds told him all that the old woman had said against him.

Bosu Agudankotin started on his way home. He came into the house and saw the old woman. The old woman said to him, "Why do you come now? You haven't watched the ceremony very long."

The old woman did not know that he knew all she had said at the house. Then Bosu Agudankotin took off the cloth, and fell to the ground, breaking into several pieces.

It is because of this that one does not say what is forbidden.[1]

[1] For a different version of this theme, see Nos. 46–49 above.

133

Testing loyalties: The dilemma of conflicting tasks: Why a man's best friend is first

There was a hunter who hunted. Good. This man was also a good farmer. So his best friend came and asked him to work in his field. He named the day. The diviner came and asked him to come to work in his field. He named the same day. And his father-in-law came and asked him to come to his field. And he, too, named the same day.

The day arrived. He took his gun. He hunted for a long time, *ka . . . ka . . . ka.* At last, he shot at an animal. But he did not even go to see whether he did or did not kill it. He left at once for his father-in-law's field.

He went to his father-in-law, and he said, "My diviner told me to come today to cultivate his field, and my best friend, too.

Now, when I knew this, I went hunting to kill a deer for you, my father-in-law. But when I shot, I killed a man."

The father-in-law said, "I don't want to listen. I don't want to hear anything about it. You went and killed a man belonging to the king, and now you come to hide here? I don't want to know anything about it."

Very well. He went to his diviner. "You commanded me to work your field today. My father-in-law also asked me, and so did my best friend. I wanted to kill an antelope for you, but when I shot, I killed a man."

The diviner said, "Ah, you and I have nothing to do with each other. You gave me your money, and I give you your destiny. You went and killed a man belonging to the king, and now you come here to hide? Go. You cannot hide in my house."

So he went away. He went to his friend.

He said, "My friend, your day came. But my father-in-law also asked me to work his field today, and my diviner, too, named the same day. I wanted to kill a deer for you, so that you might cook it for the people who came to work your field. But as I shot, I killed a man."

Very well. His friend said, "What? Did you tell anyone you killed a man?"

He said, "No, I told no one."

So the friend said, "All right." He took his hoe. He said, "Let us go and bury him." So they went to the bush. His friend did not even ask him the place where he had killed the man. He began to dig the grave. When he finished digging the grave, he said, "All right. I have finished the grave. Let us go where the man is."

The hunter said, "No. I don't want to go there. The place where I killed the man is over there."

So the friend went there. When he arrived, he hunted through the brush and he separated the branches of the low bush until he came on a dead deer.

The hunter said, "In the life that Mawu gave me, I wanted to know whom, among those three, one could follow until death, friend, diviner, or father-in-law." Very well. He said, "I told this to my father-in-law. I told this to the diviner.[1] When I went to my father-in-law, he would not even let me tell him what had happened. He said he did not want to hear anything about it. I must get away at once. The same thing with my diviner." [2]

In life, when deciding among diviner, father-in-law, and friend, one should always rely on the friend and leave the others to one side. It is the friend who is the first.

[1] Here the interpreter asked, "Did he also go to the *vodun* priest?" The narrator laughed and said, "No."

[2] Then, not caring to leave the impression that the *vodun* priest was not among the trusted, he said at this point, "Yes, it happens with the *vodun* priest, too."

134

Why a brother may not take a brother's wife

A man had three children. His oldest son was called Kakpo, the second Amusu, and the third Dosu. When he died, Kakpo became a farmer. Amusu was a thief, and Dosu a merchant.

Kakpo married, but he was always dirty. The thief, since he did no work, could wash often, and was always clean. The merchant was also able to wash himself whenever he needed to, and was also clean. But the thief was richest of the three, and so, when the woman who had married the first son saw this, she went to live with him.

One day the thief went away to steal. When he returned, it was time to eat. As he ate, two men came, and when he saw them, he could eat no more. His wife said to him, "Eat, eat. Why do you hesitate?" For she did not know that her husband had stolen things from the other men.

The men said, "We have come to get our property." They caught and bound the thief, and took him to their country.[1] But they left the woman where they found her.

Now, she said to her husband's brother, the merchant, "Look, two men came from somewhere and caught your brother, and bound him and took him away, but I do not know what he has done."

So he went to his other brother, the farmer, and said, "There were men who caught our brother and took him away. Let us go and find him." But the farmer refused, for the other had taken his wife.

So the merchant went away. He left the farmer in his house. When he came to the country where the men lived from whom the brother had stolen, the king of that country said, "Where is your brother the farmer?" And he told him that he had refused to come with him.

The king sent one of his sub-chiefs to bring the farmer, and when he arrived, the king said to him, "Why did you not come? He is your brother."

The farmer replied, "We do not come from the same mother, but we only have the same father. If we had had the same mother, he could not have taken my wife." But all the same they did have the same father.

The king said, "Your brother is a thief."

The farmer replied, "I have no brother who is a thief. I work for myself; I am a farmer. I have no brother who is a thief."

The king asked the other brother what he did. "I am a merchant," he answered.

So the king asked, "What do you want done with your brother?"

The two replied that they had nothing to say; that if he had done evil, he must be punished for what he had done. "Do as you do here," they said.

At the time this happened, if a person did evil, they gave him to Mingā [the Prime Minister and executioner] to be punished. And once they gave a man to Mingā, he killed him. So this is why a brother must not take a brother's wife.

¹ *I.e.,* their village.

135

A man does not take a king's wife

Throughout the ages of human life, no man has ever tried to take a wife belonging to Dada Segbo and survived. There was a man called Kakpovi who went to look for one of Dada Segbo's wives.

Now, once they do this to Dada Segbo, they kill the two of them, the man and the woman. And so, since these two had been together, they wanted to kill Kakpovi and the woman.

So they brought all the people together. And all day they held court, asking of each person what he thought should be done to the guilty. One said they should kill them, another that they should flog them. It grew dark. The man and woman found themselves among many people, and since it was dark, they went cautiously through the crowd until they were free. They hid inside a cave. But those who spoke in court thought that the man and woman were still there. For several days, they discussed the punishment for them. But during all this time, they did not see the man or woman.

For the two in hiding, it was always night. They did not see the sun. At night, the man would crawl out of the cave and go to the market to buy food. And since it was dark, no one knew it was he who had escaped. The woman now began to have children. One pregnancy followed another, until she had five children, all boys.

Now, the trial was over a long time ago. But as one of those who had attended court went to market for food one night, he met the man who had also come out of the cave to go to market. Kakpovi greeted him, not knowing that the other knew who he was. The other looked at him, and followed him. Kakpovi entered his cave, and the other watched him. When he disappeared inside the cave, the man went home and told the people of his household where Kakpovi was.

Dada Segbo gave the informer many men. They entered the cave and caught seven people, five children, father and mother. Dada Segbo said, "We had not yet finished the trial when the two left. Now instead of two, we have found seven. If you were the one who had been wronged, what would you do with them?" Each said what he thought right. Now, the king asked whether the people were through speaking.[1] Then he said, "We will kill the five children, and their father and mother. If we do not kill them, they will set a bad example for the people. They must be killed, so that everyone may see what happens to those who do this."

So, since that day when a man looks for a wife, he looks everywhere, but never among the wives of the king. If one does, it
means death.

[1] The fate of the children presented a special problem, and called for full
discussion.

136

Outwitting an enemy: The killing wheel:
Why children are never left alone

There was a woman who had several children. Good. Every day
Hyena went to take a child. Good. One day, he wanted to take a
child, and the rain began to fall. He did not know how to find
the place in the rain. And the woman was there now with her
children. She was preparing *acasa*.

Hyena came. The good woman said to him, "Sit down, my
friend." Then the woman took the wheel of a machine. It was very
heavy, and she put it in the fire. Good. She told Hyena to sit
down beside her.

In the house were six boys and two girls. As the wheel began to
heat, she said to the first child, "My child, go and get some plates
for me for the *acasa*." She told the child not to come back. She
sent the second now, she said, "Go and see why that stupid child
hasn't found the plates." The second child went out, and he, too,
was told not to come back. The third also was sent out to look
for the others. He stayed away. Now the fourth went, and he
stayed away. Fifth also.

Hyena is sitting there, yes? and he knows nothing. The sixth
also went. The seventh also went. The ninth, too.[1]

Now, there remained in the house only Hyena and the woman.
Now, the woman pretended to be very angry. "My children,
what are you doing? I sent you for plates, and what's this you are
doing, hiding?"

Hyena said, "Ah, your children are stupid. I myself will go and find your plates."

The good woman said, "No, no. Don't trouble. I will go for them."

When the wheel was very hot, the woman gave an *acasa* to Hyena to eat. As he was eating this, she took the wheel, and softly, softly, put it around Hyena's neck.

Hyena began to howl, to run. He could not take it off, and it burned him. He ran away with the wheel. The next day when they went to look for him, he was dead.

For that reason, one never leaves children alone at home. If one wants to go out, one takes the children along.

That happened long ago.

---

[1] The narrator erred in his numerical designation, but *nine* is a ceremonially important number and was substituted unconsciously.

137

Why sacrifices are made to the ancestors:
Why man should not learn animal speech

Good! There was a man. He had many children, and he was very rich. He was the owner of many cattle and slaves. Good. All these things were to be found on his plantation. He understood the language of all the animals, and he talked with the animals. He had a large dog who followed him about everywhere.

Now, he wanted to make a ceremony. This was a ceremony for the dead. He made this ceremony, but he forgot to name one woman of his family dead. She was the woman who had followed his mother,[1] and this woman was very angry.

She decided to take him away to the kingdom of the dead because she had not been asked to come and eat with the others.

She went to tell Death that she had something to ask of him. Death asked her what she wanted. She said, "In three days bring me Hunsu, with his animals, his slaves and all his possessions, because he invited all his dead to come and eat, and me he forgot."

When she spoke, Hunsu's dog was there beside the dead woman. But she did not know it. Now, the dog heard all. Good. When the dog heard this, he was sad. He kept worrying about the misfortune that awaited his master in three days.

The day arrived. In the morning, a dog from the village came to visit Hunsu's dog. The other dog said to Hunsu's dog, "Come outside and we will play." Hunsu's dog refused to go out. The other dog asked, "Why don't you want to come?"

Now, Hunsu's dog told all that was about to happen. He said, "If you had a master who would leave at mid-day, would you go away? I am not going. I will stay here and see what happens."

When Hunsu heard this, he sent a slave to the field. He told the slave to hide all the sheep and all the cattle.

At two o'clock to the minute, Death sent his guards to gather up the herd. As the slaves had been informed about it, they had already hidden the animals. The guards whom Death sent found nothing.

Death said, "You found nothing? Well, tomorrow we will burn down his houses." Now again the dog heard all this. Death said this because he had made a promise to that dead woman, and he had to keep it.

At six o'clock the next morning, another dog came to ask Hunsu's dog to come out and play with him. Hunsu's dog said, "At eight o'clock now, my master's houses will be burned. I, I am not going out. I will wait."

Hunsu heard this. He went to tell the slaves to gather all that was in the houses, his boxes, his dishes, his hats, his calabashes, everything. Good.

The guards sent by Death came again, and they put fire to the houses, burning them down. The guards went back to Death and said, "We burned the houses, but we found nothing there."

Death said, "All right. If the man knows so many tricks, we shall see. Because I am not one to be trifled with."

Later Hunsu's second mother went to see Death to find out why Hunsu had not yet been punished, as Death has promised. Death now fixed seven days. He said, "This man has too many tricks. We would have burned his houses to punish him, but because he took away all that was there, and when we came to burn the houses, we found nothing inside, we will now kill the man." When Death was talking, the dog was beside him, and heard everything, but Death did not know it was Hunsu's dog.

The day came. Six o'clock in the morning the dog was there before Hunsu's door, but he said nothing to anybody. A dog came again and asked him to come out with him to play. He refused. "If your master were to die this afternoon, would you be happy?"

As the dog talked, Hunsu was there. But he had not asked his dog anything until that last morning. Now, the dog did not know that Hunsu understood what he said. Good! Now, Hunsu's death was near. And now Hunsu called his dog, and he said to the dog, "My dog, now I am going to talk to you. I heard all you said." The dog said, "All right." He said, "Now I am going to ask you something about your talk with the other dog. What shall I do not to die? I know now that my death is approaching."

The dog said, "No. You should have asked me that before, not now. You did not ask me when I talked about your houses being burned. Then there would still have been time. You should have asked then. Now that you do not want to be taken by Death, you tell me this."

Hunsu asked again, "Is there nothing to be done now to save me from Death? Tell me, my poor dog."

"You will die today. There is nothing to stop Death."

All this was said before the door. Now the dog ran back to the house. Hunsu followed him. He had his children, his wives, his slaves, his animals come to him. It was almost mid-day. He said, "Among you children and wives, there must never be anyone to understand the talk of animals."

His eldest son asked him, "Why do you say this, father?"

He said, "I can give you no explanation. Care for my house." He divided his possessions among his children. That day he died.

Explaining to himself the death of Hunsu, his eldest son said, "I know what killed my father. It is the voice of the animals."

That is why one gives food to the ancestors. And that is also why one should not learn the language of the animals.

¹ That is, his father's second wife.

138

Strife among brothers: Firefly wins over fire: Why the improvident son does not succeed his father

Fire and Firefly are brothers by the same father and mother. One day their father died. The family came and helped with the funeral. When the burial rites were over, their relatives said to them, "Which of you is to be put in his father's place?"

Then there was a quarrel between them. The relatives said, "Good. Today it is going to rain hard. We will put you both out in the rain. He whose fire goes out will never take the place of the father."

Fire said, "All right."

The rain began to fall in great drops. There was a terrible wind. Fire said, "I am the one who will be the first to try."

The relatives said, "All right."

Fire came out into the rain with a brilliant flame. Two meters away, he was extinguished. Firefly, who had been silent for a long time, now went out into the rain, and began to sing. His fire was not extinguished. He danced in the rain, and gestured. So Firefly took his father's place.

That is why the son who is not industrious, and is disobedient never succeeds his father.

139

The relay race: Why a man without family
holds his peace

There were Horse and Frog. Frog had many children. Horse galloped fast. Frog went to see Metonofi, and he said since Horse knew how to gallop so well, he wanted to race with him.

Horse said, "You who can only hop, how can you race against me?"

Frog said, "If you and I race, you will die, and I will still be there."

The race was to begin in Paris, and was to go to Djugu, in upper Dahomey. Good. There was a man who followed them. Metonofi named a day. Now, Horse was alone. He had no children.

Before the appointed day, Frog went in the water, and he brought together all his offspring. And he ranged them along the road from Paris to Djugu, one after the other, one after the other, all the way to Djugu. Now, Horse did not know about this at all.

The day arrived. Now, Frog had told his children that when Horse called "*Gbese!*—Frog!" each was to answer "*Eh?*—What?" He also said to them, "But if he does not call you, then say nothing. When he calls you, come out so that he can see you. Otherwise stay in hiding."

Good. Now they began the race. When they took a few steps away from where people were looking on, Frog disappeared in the bush. Horse went on at a gallop. He ran till he was tired. He called out "*Gbese!*"

He heard, "*Eh?*"

Horse was surprised. "He is still following?" He ran all the faster. He went farther, and again he called, "*Gbese!*"

Again he heard "*Eh?*"

Horse was very astonished. He said, "Frog is still following?" He ran faster. He ran, and ran, and ran, till he was very tired. He said, "*Gbese!*"

He heard "*Eh?*" beside the road.

He said, "Now we'll rest a little." All was quiet. Horse rested. Now, after Horse had rested, he said nothing to Frog and began to gallop. He galloped till he was again tired. He called, "*Ghese!*"

To his amazement he heard again, "*Eh?*" There were only a few kilometers left to get to Djugu, but Horse had no more strength left. He fell down dead on the road.

Frog now went to see Metonofi, and said, "I ran a race with Horse, and here I am, the first to arrive. If you do not believe me, you can send your men, and they will find Horse lying dead on the road."

Now, Metonofi called together all the people, and he said, "No man can quarrel with another who has a large family."

That is why a man who does not have a great family cannot start quarrels against one who has. To this day when a man who has no family argues with another, he is told, "Good. But are you forgetting the story of Horse and Frog?"

140

The parakeet as master linguist: Superficiality ridiculed

As the parakeet was always traveling, he came to know all languages. Since the other birds did not know how to talk many languages, the birds of Allada invited him to come and teach them. And the birds of Abomey said to him, "You must come to teach languages to the birds of Abomey." While the birds of Kpanwiya also came to invite him to teach them languages.

So Parakeet departed. The birds of Dasa also invited him, and he left Abomey to go there. The same with those of Savalou, and of Djugu, and of Bariba, and of Savè. He was always traveling about to teach the birds.

So Parakeet taught all the birds their languages. And that is why among the birds each one speaks the language of his country. The birds of Allada speak the language of Allada, and those of Adja speak the language of Adja.

Now in Allada there was an old man. Parakeet asked to see him, because this man knew a language that the parakeet had not as yet learned to speak. Parakeet asked him, "If a person sees many things and is astonished, what is he to say?"

The old man replied, "*Ko!*"

And the Parakeet said, "I understand. It is finished," and he flew away.

He returned to Abomey. When he was in Abomey, he said to the people of Abomey that there was a man in Allada who had sent him to learn their language. An old man said to him, "*Hwa-o?*" meaning, "What?"

Parakeet said, "It is already finished," and he flew away.

The old man called "Come back, come back."

But Parakeet said, "No," and flew away to Dasa.

In Dasa he told the people that there was an Abomey man who had sent him to learn their language. The man said, "*Kileyi,*" meaning "What is that?"

Parakeet said, "I understand," and flew away.

He went to Kpanwiya, and there it was the same thing. He said that the people of Dasa had sent him to learn their language. As the old men said to him, "*Kite,*" [1] he said, "I understand," and left.

He went to live in Hweda, and he lived there for some time. Finally, he said to them, "I am a stranger here, but I have come because the people of Allada have sent me to learn your language."

They said, "*Dje-djedje,*" meaning, "What is that? What is that?"

And he said "I understand!" and flew away. He went to Savè also, and said, "Now, the people of Hweda have sent me to hear the language you speak here."

They said to him, "*Djo,*" meaning, "Wait, you will hear plenty."

And he replied "Enough!" and flew away. He now left Dahomey altogether, and went to see the birds who were related to him in other countries.

They asked him, "What language do they speak there?"

So he answered, "The people of Allada say, "*Ko!*" The people of Abomey say, *"Hwa-o?"* The Dasa people say, *"Kileyi,"* and he repeated the words he heard in each country.

So it is that people say today, "Do not give me the language of the Yoruba, the Nago." [2] We mean by this, you must know a thing before you talk about it.

[1] Informant: "This is the same word as the French "quitter."
[2] "Which is to say of the parakeet."

141

The sad turtledove learns how to have a family:
Sexual knowledge should not be exchanged

There were two birds. They were each a kind of turtledove. One says, *"Hwelè agon, hwelè agon*—too bad, too bad" and is called Agon. The other is called Kpanuhwelè, and is the white turtledove. Mawu sent these four birds into the world. Of each kind there was a man and a woman. Agon did not know what to do to make children. Now Kpanuhwelè knew what to do, and they had many children.

Agon went to see Mawu, and asked what to do to have children. Mawu said, "Go and ask Kpanuhwelè to show you." Mawu said, "If one does not know something, one asks a friend."

So Agon went to see Kpanuhwelè. He said, "What did you do to become so many?"

Kpanuhwelè said, "Very well. You and your wife come in three days, and I will tell you."

So when Kpanuhwelè wanted to show Agon what to do, he threw himself at Agon's wife. He began to have intercourse with her in the presence of Agon. Now Agon, who is stupid, kept saying while this was happening, "I understand all, I understand all." Good.

Agon's wife said to Kpanuhwelè, "Let me go, Kpanuhwelè. Let me go. It is enough."

So now Kpanuhwelè said, "There, that is what I do to make children."

Now when the two Agon came home, Agon, too, began this. Kpanuhwelè said to Agon, "Now this thing, one should never give to a friend. Never tell anyone that I showed you this. But since Mawu sent you, I'll go and tell Mawu that I told you."

So they both went to see Mawu, and Kpanuhwelè told Mawu that he showed this to his friend.

Mawu said, "Kpanuhwelè is right. Agon, you must never ask again. No one must ever ask." For, before that time men, too, used to ask, but since that day no man ever asks.

142

Appearances are deceiving

The birds had a meeting. They met on a tree that was full of fruit. When they finished eating, the fruit was finished. They finished all the trees of Dahomey.

There was a bird that came from Ashanti, and this bird told them there was a fine fruit tree there, and they could go there and eat. They all left for Ashanti. There was another bird that came from Ayo. When they had finished with the fruit of Ashanti, they went to eat the fruit of Ayo. There was among them a bird that came from Adja. They left to eat the Adja fruit. There was a bird that came from the Bariba, and this bird told them of fruit that grew in its country, and they all left to eat the fruit that grew in the Bariba country.

From Bariba they went to Djugu, from Djugu they went to Sai, from Sai they went to Savè, from Savè they came to Gwago, from Gwago they came to Kpanwiya, and from there to Dasa, from Dasa they went to Savalou, and from there they went to Gbatagba, and from there to Dona, and from there to Ungbegako. Now they were back in Agbome.

After their voyage, there was a tree here in Dahomey that still had ripe fruit. They came now and rested on this tree. When the birds finished eating, they all went to sleep. In order to sleep, these birds sleep with heads hanging down and feet in the air.

Amifunhè said to Hetablè,[1] "What kind of birds are these that hang with heads down and feet up?" He said to Hetablè, "They hang like sacks."

Hetablè said, "These are my sacks."

Amifunhè said, "If these sacks are yours, take them." The bat hangs so, head down and feet up, like an old sack.

As Amifunhè said, "Go and take," Hetablè ran and threw herself at Bat. Now, Bat awakened and threw itself at Hetablè and caught Hetablè with its teeth. Amifunhè stood at a distance. Amifunhè said to Bat, "A stick beats the dog till its back is long. If Hetablè begs you, you must leave it." For Hetablè was scream-ing, crying. Now Hetablè begged its pardon, but Bat would not let go of it. All the birds now begged Bat to let Hetablè go. Amifunhè said again, "A stick beats a dog till its back is long. Let Hetablè go."

He let Hetablè go, and Hetablè escaped. The other birds went away.

Now we say, "When you see something on the ground and it is not yours, it is better not to touch it." One never knows what acci-dent will come if you disturb something that lies very innocently.

[1] Names of the birds.

143

Revolt against pretender

When Mawu created all the birds, they had no king. Mawu ap-pointed a day when she said she would give them each a king. For each family of birds there would be a king.

Ohon, who eats nothing but meat; *aklasu*, the vulture; *gangan*, a black bird; *avunsakao*, the crow; *agbigbi*, a large bird who lives north of Dahomey; *kpeokpeo*, a bird resembling vulture; *gon*, a large, large bird, with a large beak; *ahlihan*, the crown bird, who in season calls "War! war! war!"; *ado, gbesawe, titigweti,* and many others came. All these met.

Mawu said to them that Agbigbi [Owl] would be their king. So Agbigbi became king of all the birds. But when he called the birds, the birds did not come. They were afraid if they came close, he would eat them.

Agbigbi went to see Mawu, and he complained that when there was a case to be tried, and he ordered the birds to come, the birds did not come.

Mawu said to him, "What power have you that is greater than that of the other birds, to justify your being king?"

Agbigbi showed Mawu a box of knives and said, "Here is what I have that entitles me to be king." When he showed the box, there was but a small knife inside. But the box was closed.

Now, Agbigbi had been doing this: When the birds refused to come close, he would take out this knife, and he would say, "If you do not come close, I'll take this knife and I'll kill you." So they came close.

If a bird hesitated, the others said, "Our king Agbigbi has a large knife. If we do not come, he will kill us. We had better go."

One day Agbigbi was asleep, and he let the box rest beside him. There was a bird called *hotri.* He said, "I am going to take a look at that knife our king has. I want to see if it is as long as he says it is." He approached the box of knives softly and opened it. There was inside it a very small knife, which was good for nothing.[1] He replaced it, and put the box back beside Agbigbi.

And now he began to tell all the birds, he began to say, "Our king has no great knife. He has a small, small one, which is good for nothing."

So one day, Hotri brought together all the birds, and he was telling them this. Agbigbi awoke, and began to talk. He said, "Come close. If you do not come, I will kill you with my knife."

Immediately, all the birds began to peck at him with their bills, and they said, "Take out your knife, let us see." All the birds gave him a good beating with their bills. Still Agbigbi would not show them his knife. They shouted, "You have nothing. You deceived us. You cannot rule over us."

There is an expression which the people of the country use today when they suspect deceit. They say, "Do not threaten me with Agbigbi's knife."

[1] The Creator is deceived, but not this courageous bird.

144

A challenging task to gain a wife: Ancestral gods must be propitiated

Dada Segbo had a daughter. He said he who wished to marry her must first work in his field. In that field there was a serpent called Aido-Hwedo. Now, no one had ever worked in this field. No one had ever cut down anything there.

In that district of Dada Segbo's domain there was a man called Zomadjali. Zomadjali said, "I will work in this field for you, so that I may marry your daughter." And Zomadjali named the day he would come to work in the field.

When the day arrived, Zomadjali sent his children to the field. No sooner did his son cut the first bit of brush, than the serpent began to sing,

> *Child of Zomadjali,*
> *Now you have come to the field,*
> *Throw down your hoe*
> *And dance until your neck dances,*
> *That I may see.*[1]

When the boy heard this, he threw down the hoe, and ran away. Adjali sent now another son. The serpent said the same thing, and the boy escaped. So Zomadjali sent now a third son. The same thing happened. Zomadjali said, "All right. Now I will go myself." He took his hoe with him.

As he cut down the first bit of brush, the serpent said, "Ah, so it is you yourself, Zomadjali, who come to cut down this field?"

Zomadjali, too, threw down the hoe, and he went back to tell Dada Segbo that the field he ordered him to work could not be worked.

Dada Segbo seemed very astonished to hear this. He gave an ox, a goat, chickens, palm oil, and he sent this to the field.[2] Now, there was a mound of earth there. Dada Segbo built a small house over this mound to protect it.[3] He killed the animals over this mound. He killed all. When they had done this, and began to cultivate, the serpent said nothing. So Zomadjali cultivated the whole field. Then he told Dada Segbo that the work was finished.

Dada Segbo said, "I knew that in this field there was an ancestral serpent. If the serpent had not eaten his ox, and goat, and all, no one could have worked the field." He said, "Yes, I knew before that you could not do it. But, now, as you tried so hard, I will give you my daughter."

[1] Record No. 144–2.
[2] As sacrifices.
[3] This mound would indicate an abandoned shrine. The shelter, therefore, re-establishes active worship.

IX

Miscellaneous tales

Miscellaneous tales

DRAMATIS PERSONÆ

NASIGBWEGU, a woman, who becomes
Lake Nohwè
TE AGBANLI
Woman from Calavi
DOSU, a twin
KOLO, a woman
Man of the mountain
PIG
ADAMU, a family head
RAM
BOKOFIO, who visits the world of the
dead

His captors
DOKPWEGAN, chief of cooperative
work and burial groups
AYIGBILI, an animal
ORPHAN
YEHWE-ZOGBANU
LION
SNAKE
ADJOTOGAN, chief of the thieves
JEAN, JOSEPH, two brothers
Leather worker
Two thieves

145

Origin of Lake Nohwè

There was a woman who was called Nasigbwegu. She was there, and she had no water, and Te Agbanli had given her a red silk cloth to wash. As she had no water, she took a calabash and put the silk cloth inside it. Without finding water, she began to wash the cloth.[1] Te Agbanli had told her to wash it until it was white as a piece of paper.

As the woman wept, she said, "If I truly come from Mawu, let Mawu give me water. Without it, I will be killed today."

Te Agbanli came and asked her, "Aren't you through washing this cloth yet?" As he said these words, the woman fell down and changed into Nohwè. And so this Nohwè comes from Nasigbwegu.

If you see an old person, he will tell you that in the center of the Lake Nohwè there is the calabash of Nasigbwegu. It is there now, too. The name of the lake comes from *no*, mother, *hwe*, house of, "The house of our mother." The *vodun* is called Na. The color of the cloths they wear when they dance for Na is like that of the Nesuhwe.[2]

[1] The narrator dramatized this with motions of rubbing a cloth.
[2] Cult of the royal ancestors, and those closely associated with royalty.

146

Origin of Lake Nohwè

There was a Calavi woman whose master was a bad man. He gave her a black cloth, and commanded her to wash it white; and a white cloth, and he said to her, "Wash this black."

The woman tried and tried. White remained white; black remained black. She cried for a long time, until she got angry and broke the calabash in which she was washing. Then she lay down on the ground. Beside her lay the pieces of broken calabash and the cloths.

Then little by little water began to trickle, to trickle, then to come faster, until a lake appeared. This is the Lake Nohwè.

In ancient times, where Nohwè is now, it was bush. Today if someone called this woman's name, while on the lake, he would be drowned—because the woman who is the *vodun* of this lake is an angry woman.

147

Twin becomes river-spirit: Taboo against pork

There was a man called Dosu who was a twin. He could not eat pork. Once some people of his village cooked a pork stew, and without washing the pot, cooked his stew for him. They gave this stew to Dosu to eat.

Then they said to him, "You do not eat the meat of pigs. But as you have eaten this stew that was cooked in a pot which was not washed after we cooked pork in it, you have eaten pork."

When Dosu heard this, he ran away, and went to Zado. When he reached there, he said, "I want to stay here with you. I wanted to live in Kana, but I had to leave because they fed me pork. Now I will change into water for you."

So he changed into water. Near the place where he changed, there was a shrine to a *vodun* called Agasu. Now Dosu is called Halan,[1] since he came there because of pork.

Dosu could not eat pork because Mawu had forbidden it. Mawu had forbidden him, and not others, because Dosu was born the same day as the *marabout*.[2] When he came into the world, Dosu had no water to drink. The pig took him to a stream, and Marabout also. So out of gratitude for what he had done for them, the two of them forbade their descendants to eat pork. That is why the marabout do not eat pork today. And Mawu had told him, even before he was born, that if he ate pork, he would change into a river and become a *vodun*.[3]

[1] A powerful river spirit.
[2] The name given the Moslems who come from the north to trade in Dahomey.
[3] The truncated form of this tale is obvious; at the end, the teller seems to have telescoped two different stories.

148
The origin of the Kolo Zogbanu clan

There was a woman named Kolo who lived near a mountain. The mountain was called Zo. This woman had no family. She was alone. One day the mountain opened, and a man came out of it. The man asked the woman what she was doing. She said she came here to die because she had no one to take care of her. The man told her to be patient, and he would help her.

Now, when the man spoke, fire came from his mouth. At night when he came to the good woman to clear the brush for her, he had only to open his mouth and talk for everything to light up.

Now, he came to see her, and he came to see her, until the woman became pregnant. From the mountain, the man brought Kolo everything she needed: food, drink, everything. When the man came out, the mountain closed behind him, and when he was ready to reenter, it opened.

The woman gave birth to twins, a man child and a woman child, and the man left the mountain to live beside his wife and children.

One day some hunters came by, and saw the woman and her husband living beside the mountain. The hunters asked them what they were doing there. The woman said, "This is the country of our fathers."

Now they lived there, and they cultivated. All the people from the nearby villages came to them to buy their crops. They prospered. In time there was a village there. But the man never talked. The woman alone carried on conversations. This was because the husband did not want others to see the fire coming from his mouth.

Little by little, this hard-working family had many friends, because they sold their harvest to many people. Now their children grew up; they married and bore children; and the family grew.

One day the father fell ill. The wife knew of no medicine for him. Now, there were all the neighbors, and they were all friends of the father. They came to visit him, and asked him what his sickness was. But since he must never show the fire that came from his mouth, he did not speak. People kept coming, and asking questions, but he could not answer. All this was a great trouble for him, for his wife, and his children.

Now, at night when they were alone, he said this could not go on, but that it would not be good for him to disappear and return to the mountain. People would say that she had lived with a "phenomenon," [1] and they would say it to their children. He said to be rid of the trouble of meeting people who came all day to ask him questions about his health, his wife had best bury him alive. He said, "When the neighbors come, tell them it is a law of our family that anyone who fell ill, and spoke no more, must be buried."

In the morning, the friends came. They brought medicine for the man to drink, but he could not open his mouth. They asked him what hurt him, but he could not answer. Now the woman said, "I know the taboo of my husband. Now, we must bury him. When the sick of his family do not speak they are as dead."

They buried him. That became a taboo for the family. This family has very few people today. They sell cooked foods, and make pottery. They like fire, and they like to live near mountains.

[1] The narrator, who spoke French, was quite evidently impressed with the word. He used it to describe the supernatural founders of clans—the *tohwiyo*, the abnormally born—the *tohosu*—and at times the *vodun*.

Origin of the Aganavi Mulanu clan

There was a woman. She was very poor. She had nothing. She had neither father nor mother. She withdrew into the bush to live there. There she was alone, and she raised pigs. Then an epidemic came and killed her pigs. Only one male remained, and she loved him as tenderly as a child. Now, this woman was far from all men. She had no neighbors.

So the pig grew larger and larger, and was the woman's only companion. The woman's name was Ahan. One day coming back from the field, she lay down to sleep on a mat. The pig slept with the woman. The woman awoke, and beside her lay the pig who talked like a man. He told her he had done this so that she might have children. She said, "Good." She took care of the animal as of a husband.

Now, a time came when the rain stopped falling. The harvest did not come. The woman gave birth just at this time of famine. She bore two male children, and one female. They were all half human, because their heads were like the heads of pigs.

The father, who after all was an animal, did not know what to do to feed his wife. The woman became very, very thin because of the famine. He said to her, "When there is nothing, one must make the best of it." He said, therefore, they would have to eat a child. They killed a male pig, and gave it to the woman to eat. They prepared it, and the mother ate it.

Now, when the other two children were grown up, the father and mother died. They died the same day. The children buried them, and they married each other. The woman became pregnant, and then she gave birth to three children, two male and one female.

Now, they were no longer poor like their father, but they kept the taboo of their father. That is to say, they ate one of the children, saying, "To be happy in life it is necessary that we eat."

After this, little by little, there were transformations, until the births in the family became altogether human. He who was then head of the family was called Gbochi, and he ordered that they no longer kill a child, but that all the mothers of this family, on the first day of the birth of a child were to eat pork. He also said that in order to be happy, the men of the family were to engage in killing pigs, and selling their flesh for food.

And that is why this family is destined to be sellers of pigs. But they respect the pig. For example, the family never digs the earth to make clay for building, or pottery-making, because their ancient progenitor wallowed in mud. No member of the family would tell anyone he had a large mouth. This is because a pig's snout is large. Nor may anyone of the family be struck on the nose. This is bad for a pig also. And the family eats palm nuts often, because this is the favorite food of the pig.

150

Why the Ayatovi Gamenu do not eat ram

This happened when our ancestors left their village near the Weme river. They came to establish themselves at Akpe. This is in Allada. Our family head was called .Adamu.

Now Adamu was sitting under a tree in the open.[1] He was very sleepy.[2] When he fell asleep, his head nodded from time to time. A large ram passed by close to the sleeping Adamu. He saw his head fall forward, then go back, forward and back. The ram thought he wanted to fight him. He struck the sleeping man with his horns, and struck him so many times that he killed him.

From that day on it is forbidden for any member of our family to keep, to breed, or to eat ram.

[1] *I.e.*, outside the compound walls.
[2] The family head is the oldest living man of the group. The picture evoked, therefore, is of a very old man, no longer able to do any manual work, sitting and dozing.

Visit to the world of the dead

One day, as this man, whose name was Bokofio, lay ill on his mat, he heard a whistling in his ear, and soon found himself in a large clearing where two men came forward, one carrying a long rope, the other with a whip in his hand. The first one said, "Walk in front of us. We are going to leave this place," and tied the rope about his neck. Holding the other end of it, he pulled the poor Bokofio, as he would a dog. The other walked behind him, and lashed him to make him walk faster.

The three made their way up the path. They were climbing a high mountain. They did not stop when they reached the top. They went down the other slope until they came to a river. They did not stop at the river, but walked on the water as though it were land. They had difficulty in getting up the farther bank of the stream because it was slippery, but at last they found themselves where there were great banana plantations.

As the three walked rapidly, they soon came to a clearing where there were some low thatched houses, with bamboo in front of them. There were no shrines, apparently, as Bokofio did not even see an *aizã*.[1] He could not see whether there were people in this village, but he did see smoke coming from one of the houses. Those who led him passed on quickly, and when he tried to cry out, one of them put a hand over his mouth.

A little later they were again in open country. There was nothing but earth; no trees, no water, no grass, just bare earth. Some distance ahead Bokofio saw men seated one after another in a long row, and the road which they were following led to them.

At the place where the row of stools began, his captors turned abruptly and went along a by-path which led to the slope of a second great mountain. While making his descent down the other side of this mountain, Bokofio saw another river. Again they walked on the water as though it were land. On the other side, they were met by two great dogs who barred their way, but the two who had Bokofio in charge cried out a "strong" name for the animals to step aside.

Now they faced a third mountain even steeper than the other two. The top of this mountain seemed to get farther away as they climbed, and the path grew steeper and steeper. At each step Bokofio was met by guards, who asked his name but refused to tell him their own. All this time his two captors continually urged him to go faster and faster.

When at last they reached the top, they came to an enclosure, watched over by a guard, who was seated at a door made of plaited banana leaves. The guard told them to wait, and as they waited, Bokofio heard the soft sound of many voices, and knew there were many people about. He was not allowed to look inside the enclosure.

Soon a guard came through the door, with a man dressed in raffia cloth, who held a stone in one hand. On the stone were no marks that Bokofio could see, but the man who held it seemed to be reading something from it.

Then a second man came out of the enclosure, and this one held many banana leaves in his hand, which he looked at like a notebook, each leaf like a page. This second man whispered to the first, who then answered in a language which Bokofio could not understand.

The second one, however, spoke Fõn—"the language of Abomey itself"—and asked Bokofio why he came. Poor Bokofio said that these two men brought him by force. The man who spoke Fõn then turned to them and wanted to know who had sent them. When they did not answer, the man who spoke Fõn called out "*Adjoto!* Robbers!" The man in the raffia cloth took a rock and threw it at the two who had brought Bokofio. They ran away leaving him free. The man looked at his stone again, and after studying it carefully, ordered Bokofio to raise his head. As Bokofio raised it, this man spurted water at him from his mouth, and the stream covered Bokofio's face.

At this, the guard took a great club and chased him away. Bokofio ran so fast that he had no idea how he ever got over all the obstacles he had to pass as he retraced his way home. At last he found himself at home on his mat.

Now, Bokofio's son had been far away when his "death" had occurred, and so Bokofio's corpse had been kept in the hut for four days, awaiting the first ceremony of burial. When Bokofio revived, while he knew he lay on his mat, he could not see, and he felt his mouth tied. He began to toss, and he took off the bandage that covered his eyes. Those watching him ran away. When they returned with help, they found him sitting up. The first words they heard Bokofio say were, "Water, water." Then those who had courage untied him and gave him water. He wanted no food, but lay down again, and at once fell into a deep sleep. When he awoke, he was well and hungry.[2]

[1] A shrine which symbolizes the unity of the group, and its guardianship.
[2] "A diviner was consulted. The figure in raffia who had saved Bokofio from the two captors was Legba, while the two who had enslaved him were Dã."

152

Confirmation of a chief [1]

From this day, you will no longer be called Hwegbe, you will be called Dokpwegan, and you will command all the young men of your village. But before allowing you to take your departure, let me call to your mind the ancient precepts of the King:

The King has said that in Dahomey a chief must see to it that everyone holds firmly where his hand rests. He has said that Dahomey is Aido-Hwedo, and the chief is the iron worker. If you go home and fall asleep, and Dã has cut and eaten the bar of iron which is in your custody and given to your care, you will become a lizard with a black tail.[2] But if you care for the iron, you will be a red-tailed lizard.

Dahomey is great, and must come before all else. It is because of this that the King has said, "A chief must not do as the tailor who breaks his needle, and tries to sew his cloth with his finger alone, for this is stupid."

The King has said that Dahomey is a vast land, and that everyone must confine his work to the place where he lives. That is why it is forbidden to any of the young men who cultivate the land to stop work in the fields, while the grass remains uncut.

The King has said that a country must be loved by its citizenry, and that is why he has forbidden his people to migrate from one part of the country to another, since a wanderer can never have a deep love for his land.

The King has said that Dahomey is an enemy of all the world, and that his chiefs must use as much force in killing an ant, as they would to kill an elephant, for the small things bring on the large ones.

The King has said that Dahomeans are a warrior people, and that, in consequence, it must never come to pass that a true Dahomean admit before an enemy that he is vanquished.

The King has said that the chiefs represent his authority in Dahomey, and, therefore, he commands you never to denounce a Dahomean before an enemy who provokes your country, because he does not wish another dog to bark louder than his own.

The King has said that in the region of Dahomey which you will command, there are men who are refractory, who, though they are rivers, have the will to imitate the ocean. Such small holes must be stopped up, and you must see to it that in Abomey alone the sun shines.

The King has said that those in positions like yours, who represent his authority, often do evil things. He forbids the strong to take the possessions of the weak, for this is the way of the hawk who snatches away chicks, without asking permission of the owner of the chicken yard.

The King has said that the chiefs are like the bellows that help the iron workers make the fire even redder, so that if any of you keeps for himself the air that is necessary for the fire of Dahomey, he will be used as coal to make the iron hot.

In closing, the King orders you to allow even the poorest man to come to him, and the strangers who have no protectors in the capital, so that he may help them. And here is the rule of Dahomey:

put dust on your head and rise to vow to the King your devotion, and give us your surname.

[1] An example of discursive prose. Cf. *Dahomey*, I, pp. 67–68, for the setting in which this homily is pronounced.

[2] The reference to the lizard with the black tail is a euphemism for death; just as the allusion to a lizard with a red tail symbolizes life.

153

Dangerous hospitality: Outwitting giants: Lion brought to judgment: Powerful escape vengeance: How kings profited from the law of collective responsibility

There was an animal called Ayigbili te-de-aniya-okuche-wota, that is to say, "The earth turns, and my mouth is rigid; but if I am not dead, all is not over." [1]

This animal was a friend of Orphan. Orphan was also a friend of Yehwe-Zogbanu.

Since Orphan was a friend of both, he would often bring Ayigbili to the house of Yehwe-Zogbanu to eat. Whenever they all ate there, Orphan warned Ayigbili never to eat the intestines of any animal that was killed, and served to him. But one day, they were eating there, when intestines had been put into the stew. And so Ayigbili ate the intestines that were in it, even though he knew they were there.

Orphan had told him, "If you ever eat intestines there, you will never return home. Eat only meat." And Orphan himself ate only meat there.

As they were about to leave the house of Yehwe-Zogbanu, Ayigbili put his gong and a set of paired rattles in his sack. Orphan went out, but Ayigbili could not leave, for he had eaten the intestines.

Now, there was no road to the house of Yehwe-Zogbanu. There was only a wall. If one had not eaten intestines, one could say, "Wall, open and let me go," and the wall would open. But if a person had eaten intestines, when he said this, the wall would stay closed.

In the house there were only the little Yehwe-Zogbanu just then, for the others, the large ones, had gone out. But while Ayigbili was there with the little ones, the grownups came home. When Ayigbili saw these large ones, he escaped by hiding in the manure pile.

But the Yehwe-Zogbanu said that they smelled the smell of a living being there. They began to look everywhere, and at last they spied his feet sticking out of the pile of excrement. The first Yehwe-Zogbanu said, "We will kill him."

The second said, "As we are short of money, let us sell him." The third said that they would cut him up.

The fourth said, "Let us divide him in two."

The fifth said, "Let us ask him what he came here for."

And to this the others said, "Yes! Yes! Yes!"

He said Orphan had brought him here. One of the little Yehwe-Zogbanu who was there, asked, "What have you hidden there in your sack?"

And Ayigbili said if they freed him, he would show them what he did with those things at home. So to the accompaniment of his gong and rattles, he sang,

> *Come all of you Yehwe*
> *And dance until . . .*
> *You reach the Adja fields.*

Now, in the wall nearby, a rat had made a hole, and as Ayigbili played the drum for the Yehwe-Zogbanu to dance, he came closer and closer to it. As he played, the Yehwe-Zogbanu danced from here to Atagon, and when he had got near enough, and they were a distance of from here to Atagon, he slipped through it. The Yehwe-Zogbanu returned and looked for him, but there was no one there.

Ayigbili went to see Orphan, and Orphan said to him, "Have you just come out?"

He said, "I have suffered a great deal. Never will I accompany you to that house again. If I had not the gong and rattles, I would have been lost."

While he was away, Lion came and ate all of Ayigbili's children. When he came home no one was there. The lion had even eaten his wife. He wept. Now, there was a tree there that no one ever approached. As he was weeping, he came near the tree. He saw a snake, and this snake told him that, in his absence, the lion had eaten all his children, and his wife as well.

Snake had reported this to the king of his village, and the king had called a meeting of all the animals. Lion confessed that when they had worked on the road, he passed Ayigbili's house. As he went by and saw that no one was there, he entered and ate all the children and the woman. At this, all the animals attacked Lion, for he was in the wrong. They tied him.

Everyone said that Lion ate the children, but he had not really eaten them. He had only taken them away, and had hidden them. So he gave Ayigbili's children back to him. The king forbade Ayigbili to go out any more.

Now Ayigbili had a friend, Tortoise. He told Tortoise how Lion had taken all his children while he was away, and under what circumstances he had given them back to him. And he asked Diviner Tortoise to tell him some way to kill Lion. But several days later he himself died. Once Ayigbili was dead, Tortoise did nothing more to harm Lion.

And in the olden days in Abomey, if you did anything wrong, they did not kill you outright. Instead, they brought all the people of the family of the man who had done the wrong, all their possessions, all the calabashes, plates, and water jars. They took off the doors. They took the tables, and mats and all these they brought to the king. And it was Lion who had invented this punishment. The guilty man they would put in prison and give him nothing to eat until he died. Rarely did a man survive after three days. And all his family and all his things belonged to the king.

[1] NARRATOR: "This last part is a Nago proverb."

154

Punishment by indirection: Outwitting justice by solving a riddle

In early times there was a man who did nothing but evil. So one day the king gave him some leaves of the cassava plant, a goat, and a hyena. He said to him, "Now you must put all these three in the same rowboat, and take them over to Togo, on the other side of the river."

Now, the king knew very well that if you put a hyena together with a goat, the hyena would eat the goat. And if you put the leaves with the goat, the goat would eat the leaves. The king knew this in his heart. But he said nothing about it. He just gave him the three things to take across to the other side, and said, "I command you to see that the hyena does not eat my goat. And the goat must not eat my leaves."

The man thought. He said, "Now, if I take the goat over there and come and bring the leaves there and leave them, the goat will eat the leaves. But if I take the hyena there, and come back to get the leaves, the hyena will eat the goat."

There was a man on the other side watching to see how he would bring over these three things.

He thought for a long time. Then he took the leaves and put them beside the hyena. He then took the goat over. He came back and got the leaves, and left the hyena there. But when he put down the cassava leaves, he took the goat back with him to the other side. So now he left the goat on the side from where he started, and took the hyena and brought it across and put it with the leaves. So the hyena was there with the leaves. Then he returned for the goat, and took the goat over.

Once he had taken the three things over, the man who was there observing sent a message to the king to come and see. So the king came. The man said to him, "See, the thing you have commanded me to do, I have done."

So in ancient times, when there was an evil man who did nothing but kill others, they never killed him for that reason. They arranged some difficult task for him, for which the penalty for failing to perform it successfully was death. So as the man had done the thing that had been commanded of him, the king was unable to punish him. So this evil man continued to live in his quarter, and do evil things.

155

The password: Outwitting thieves

Good! There were six thieves. They were the chiefs of all thieves. Their name was Adjotogan. Good. There was a mountain full of gold. No one knew that gold was inside it. Only these six thieves knew that this mountain was full of gold. They slept there. Good. Whatever they stole, they put inside this mountain. The mountain was their house.

There was a father who had eight sons. He called them one day and asked each of them what he wanted to become. "I am an old man. Tell me what you want to be."

The first son said he wanted to become a mason. The second said, "I want to become a carpenter." The third said he wanted to be a farmer.

The fourth said, "I want to become a great thief."

The fifth said, "I want to become a trader." The sixth said, "I want to become a liar."

The seventh said, "I am going to the forest to cut down wood, and I will sell it in the market."

The eighth said, "I will also get wood, and sell it."

The elder of the two youngest was called Jean, the second Joseph. They began to go to the forest for firewood, and they sold the firewood a franc a bundle. When Jean sold a bundle of wood, he spent the money he got for it. Joseph saved his earnings. This went on.

Once, Joseph, the richer of the two went to the forest, and

climbed up a tree. Some distance from there was a mountain. There it was all swept and clean. He could see clearly from where he was, for the mountain was only two kilometers away. Now, Joseph was curious, and he watched to see what would come out of this mountain. He no longer looked for firewood, but remained hidden in the branches of the tree and watched. He remained there all day.

This was towards two o'clock. If the thieves went out at five in the morning, they came back at two o'clock in the afternoon. At two o'clock, then, they arrived. The thieves did not know that there was someone up the tree spying on them. Now, the thieves have a charm with which to open the mountain. To open the mountain, they put the charm on the ground. It is a picket, which is hammered into the mountain with the foot, and then they say, "Open." The mountain opens.

Now, Joseph was there near the mountain, and he could look right inside. When the door opened, he saw gold, animals, everything. He said, "Oh, do such things exist!"

Now, the thieves stayed inside the mountain. They ate, and then they put away what they had brought with them—the things stolen that day.

Then, when the thieves went out, they said to the mountain, "We are coming back in two days, or three days." They always fixed the day for their return. To close the mountain, they took out the picket, and put it in at the side of the mountain for safe keeping. They went away.

And Joseph also went away. He went back home. Now, Joseph no longer wanted to bother with gathering wood. On the third day, as Joseph had a little education—he knew how to write—he went and posted himself in the same place, in order to write down what the thieves said to the mountain to have it open. Now the thieves again came back at two o'clock. The thieves put in the picket and said, "Open," and the mountain opened. Now, Joseph wrote all this down on a paper. After having eaten, they went out again towards dark.

The thieves had told the mountain that they would be away three days. Good. Now they told the mountain to close.

When the thieves were eight kilometers distant, Joseph climbed down from the tree. He approached the mountain, and took up the charm which he had seen hidden at the side of the mountain. He did just as the thieves had done. He commanded the mountain, he said, "Open." The mountain opened.

Then Joseph entered. He began to gather up the gold so that he might carry it away with him. He worked from morning till night. The next day also he kept at it from morning till night. He no longer looked for firewood. Now, during the day he slept. He no longer worked. He had other men working for him.

He put eighty sacks in the bank vault. He asked the king for land to build a great compound. The king gave him the land. They called together for him one hundred workmen. After three days, he again returned to the mountain, and again he gathered up money.

Now, all the people were very astonished to see Joseph become so rich. They said, "A man who sells only firewood cannot become so rich." The workers began to construct. They built a house of several stories, one higher than the king's house. Now all the people admired this house.

On the third day he returned again. He did once more as he had done before. He gathered up all the money he could carry away. Good. Now he was very, very rich. He went to marry a girl.

His brother Jean was very, very poor. He came to see him one day. Joseph greeted him, and gave him a good place. He told his wife to prepare a meal for him. The two ate together. He gave him money—a whole sack of it.

Jean refused. He said, "I do not want money. I ask only to know what you did to become so rich. We both gathered firewood, and you got rich. Show me the way to do it." Jean took a knife and said, "If you do not tell me, I will kill you."

Joseph said, "If I tell you now, you won't know how to act. You'll only be killed yourself."

Jean said to him, "Why do you say I will die?"

Joseph said, "If you go, you will die. You cannot read. You won't know how to manage."

Jean said, "Good. Tell me just the same."

Joseph showed him the road. He climbed up a tree. The thieves arrived. They said their words. They commanded the mountain, they said, "Open." The mountain opened.

Jean heard this. Now, towards five o'clock the thieves again went out. Jean did not want to return home, and come in the morning. He went at once to the mountain, and commanded it to open. When he entered, he forgot the words for making the mountain stay open. Instead of saying "Open" he said, "Close." Now, he had gathered up all he could carry away, and he piled up the sacks. Now he wanted to come out, but he forgot the words. Instead of asking the mountain to open, he kept repeating for the mountain to close. Now, the mountain was shut tight. He was there inside. He was there till the thieves came.

The thieves commanded the mountain to open. The mountain did not want to open, for it was tightly closed.

One of the thieves said, "Surely, we have a man inside."

They opened the mountain and saw the man seated on the sacks. They came inside. They asked him, "Where do you come from?"

"I am the brother of Joseph, who has been gathering money here. That is why he is so rich. It is he who showed me the way here."

One thief asked him, "Is it the young one who lives in the house of several stories, near the king's house?"

Jean said, "Yes."

The thieves now killed Jean. They dismembered him, limb from limb, and nailed him to the wall of the mountain. Now they went out again.

The next day, his brother Joseph came, for he had not seen Jean for three days. He was there with his notebook and a sack. He put his brother's flesh inside the sack, and put with it some money that he took up.

At the house he had all the leather workers of the village come. He said, "Among you leather workers, who is the one who knows how to sew best? For example, if I killed a goat and then I cut it up in several pieces, who could resew it?" There was a young leather worker there who said he could sew it up. So there and then they killed a goat, and they cut it up into several pieces, and then this leather worker resewed it.

At night Joseph had this leather worker come. He showed him Jean's dead body, and asked him to sew it together so that he might bury it. The shoemaker did this, and at night they buried Jean.

The next day when the thieves came back, they did not find

Jean's meat there. They said, "Joseph has courage. He came to get his brother's body, which we had cut up. It must be Jean's burial that was held yesterday. We heard the noise."

Now they began to plot how to kill Joseph. The next day, an important thief came to town to see the leather worker. He asked the leather workers of the village, "Who among you knows how to sew well?"

There was one leather worker there who said, "I know how to sew well." He said, "The other day at Joseph's house I sewed up a dead body."

"Whose dead body?"

"Jean's dead body." Thus the thief knew that it was Joseph who had taken his brother's body.

The thief went back to the mountain. Toward noon he gathered a hundred men. Good. There was one thief who came to see Joseph and said he had one hundred sacks of salt. He would bring these about midnight, and the next day he would sell them in the market. The thief went to find a hundred empty sacks.

At night, towards eight o'clock, Joseph had gone for a walk, leaving his wife behind. The thief entered Joseph's house, for he had promised to bring one hundred sacks of salt to Joseph's. He entered with one hundred men, and there Joseph's wife looked on at them through the windows, but did nothing.

The chief of these thieves told each man to get into a sack. Then he closed each sack and put it against a wall. When they had finished putting the men in the sacks, all the sacks were full, each with a man in it. The chief said, "At midnight, I shall whistle, and you are to come out of the sacks, and we will all rob the man."

As his wife had seen all this, she sent her boy to look for his master. He had prepared a charm with water, which, if but a drop of this water touched your head, you would die. When her husband arrived, she told him that these were not sacks of salt, but that there were men in them.

During the night, before midnight, they prepared the medicine, and at the hour for eating, they asked the two chief thieves to come on the second floor to eat with them. Joseph and his wife sat down on the same stool, and the two thieves sat on one stool, on the opposite side. Before they climbed the stairs, Joseph had given a revolver to his wife, and he had a loaded one, too. He had said to his wife, "Madam, when we start eating, if I put my foot on yours, it will be the signal to shoot the two thieves."

When the two brigands had climbed up, they did not want to eat with Joseph, and they said, "We will not eat with you, because we have left our sacks of salt below, and someone might steal them." Joseph told them that there were no thieves there, and gave them the chair he had placed for them. He put his foot on the foot of his wife, and they shot at the two thieves.

There were those in the sacks who said to the others, "Who is that shooting up there?"

And the others said, "Joseph is killing his pigeons."

After having killed the two thieves, Joseph came down, accompanied by his two boys, and he carried the medicine. As he came to each sack, he told the man in it, who believed that this was his master and not Joseph, "Here is some medicine, so that you will not be too tired." He gave it to the first, and the sack which stood upright fell to the ground. The second, the same thing, and the same until he had finished ninety-nine sacks. The last man escaped.

Now on top of his walls he had put in nails, so that people could not climb them, and so the one hundredth thief was stuck on one of these nails. He said, "Why have you killed my comrades?" Joseph went to sleep, leaving the bodies where they fell.

The next day he went to see the king of the country, and the king sent men to see the dead bodies. So the king of that country gave the order to make a road all the way to the mountain. And all the gold there belonged to Joseph.